Voices, Bodies, Practices:

Performing Musical Subjectivities

VOICES, BODIES, PRACTICES: PERFORMING MUSICAL SUBJECTIVITIES

Catherine Laws, William Brooks, David Gorton, Nguyễn Thanh Thủy,
Stefan Östersjö, and Jeremy J. Wells

Leuven University Press

Table of Contents

7 Figures

11 Contents of the Online Repository of Supplemental Files

13 Introduction
Catherine Laws

Chapter 1

29 Austerity Measures I: Performing the Discursive Voice
David Gorton and Stefan Östersjö

37 Part 1: Collaboration and the discursive voice
56 Part 2: Analysing the discursive voice in performance
77 Conclusions

Chapter 2

83 Being a Player: Agency and Subjectivity in *Player Piano*
Catherine Laws

83 Part 1: *Player Piano* and Saying "I"
102 Part 2: The Embodied Subject in *Player Piano*
138 Part 3: Instrument as Agent
146 Part 4: From Instrument to Ecology
158 Postlude: "Alone With My Ten Fingers"?

Chapter 3

171 Footnotes
William Brooks, Stefan Östersjö, and Jeremy J. Wells

171 Part 1
192 Part 2
212 Part 3

Chapter 4

235 Arrival Cities: Hanoi
Nguyễn Thanh Thủy and Stefan Östersjö

235 Arrival Cities: Hanoi
237 1. Introduction
239 2. Modes of collaboration
247 3. Documentary, empathy, and inter-subjectivity
257 4. The making of Arrival Cities: Hanoi
283 5. The discursive voice in intercultural collaboration

295 Conclusion
Catherine Laws

299 References

315 Notes on Contributors

319 Index

Illustrations

Figures

32 1.1. The opening twelve bars of *Austerity Measures I* (Gorton 2018a) with number annotations for a three-times performance.
33 1.2. The opening twelve bars of *Austerity Measures I*, as if played through for the third and final time.
43 1.3. Relationships that constitute the formation of a performer's "voice."
49 1.4. Relationships that constitute the formation of a composer's "voice."
52 1.5. The tuning system for *Austerity Measures I* (the tuning system sounds an octave lower than written).
53 1.6. Bars 18–22 of *Austerity Measures I*: bell-like patterns.
55 1.7. Relationships that constitute the formation of a collaborative "discursive voice."
57 1.8. The performance set-up in the Orpheus Institute Auditorium, showing microphones, Nintendo Wii remotes, the sensor surface underneath Stefan's chair, and the infrared sensors on his shoulders, right wrist, and glasses.
57 1.9. Bars 44–49 of *Austerity Measures I*: ascending arpeggio phrases.
58 1.10. Bars 53–55 of *Austerity Measures I*: broken chords.
58 1.11. Bars 59–64 of *Austerity Measures I*: final ascending line.
59 1.12. Durations of each run-through across the four performances, divided into the five sections.
61 1.13. Deviations in the duration of sections in the combined four-times performances and three-times performances.
62 1.14. Timing and phrasing at the level of the bar in section three of the four-times concert performance.
63 1.15. Illustration of the agreed perceived phrasing for bars 30 to 40 in the final run-through of the four-times concert performance.
63 1.16. Illustration of the agreed perceived phrasing for bars 45 to 56 in the final run-through of the four-times concert performance.
64 1.17. Timing and phrasing at the level of the bar in section three of the three-times concert performance.
65 1.18. Timing and phrasing at the level of the bar in section two of the four-times concert performance.
66 1.19. Bars 23 to 27 in the second section of *Austerity Measures I*.
67 1.20. Front-facing camera angle from the four-times performances used for gesture coding.
68 1.21. Timing and phrasing at the level of the bar in section three of the four-times concert performance, with selected gesture codes.
69 1.22. Movement from bars 34 to 36 in the third run-through showing "eyes closed" and "lifting head" codes in the second image.
70 1.23. Movement in bar 40 in the fourth run-through showing "expressive shoulder movement" and "freeze" codes in the second image.
71 1.24. Bars 33–37 of *Austerity Measures I*.

72 1.25. Movement in bar 30 in the fourth run-through showing "left-hand gesture" and "freeze" codes.

73 1.26. Illustration of the agreed phrasing for bars 11 to 21 in the final run-through of the four-times concert performance.

73 1.27. Movement in bar 15 in the fourth run-through showing "left-hand gesture," "lifting head," "eyes closed," "expressive shoulder movement," and "freeze" codes.

74 1.28. Iterative nodding in bar 57 in the first run-through of the four-times rehearsal performance.

75 1.29. The four run-throughs of section 5 in the four-times concert performance with phrasing information and selected gesture codes.

102 2.1. Still from performance by Catherine Laws of Roger Marsh, *Touch and Go* (with gestural choreography by Catherine Laws): this piece formed part of the large-scale performance *Player Piano*. Film by Minyung Im; sound by Lynette Quek.

103 2.2. Stage set for *Player Piano* (from premiere performance, Scenic Stage Theatre, York, 5 May 2016).

116 2.3. Performance activity, sorting through scores and LPs: still from *Player Piano*, performed by Catherine Laws, from premiere performance, Scenic Stage Theatre, York, 5 May 2016.

116 2.4. Movement piece (devised by Teresa Brayshaw and Catherine Laws) from *Player Piano*, performed by Catherine Laws: stills from premiere performance, Scenic Stage Theatre, York, 5 May 2016.

117 2.5. Stills from *Ten Bellows* by Edward Jessen, which forms part of *Player Piano*. Performed by Catherine Laws and Hannah Butterfield, Scenic Stage Theatre, York, 5 May 2016.

119 2.6. Stills of hands from the second short film, by Wendy Kirkup, that forms part of *Player Piano*.

119 2.7. Stills of hand tied with ribbons from the second short film, by Wendy Kirkup, that forms part of *Player Piano*.

120 2.8. Model pianist and doll's-house piano from *Player Piano*.

122 2.9. Stills from performance of Paul Whitty's *under and under* as part of *Player Piano*: activation of field recordings from small speakers tethering balloons, and use of portable turntable. From premiere performance, Scenic Stage Theatre, York, 5 May 2016.

124 2.10. Still from Annea Lockwood's *Ceci n'est pas un piano* performed as part of *Player Piano*. From premiere performance, Scenic Stage Theatre, York, 5 May 2016.

126 2.11. Opening of Roger Marsh, *Touch and Go* (2014).

130 2.12. Roger Marsh, *Touch and Go*, bars 61–67.

131 2.13. Still from performance of Roger Marsh, *Touch and Go*, as part of premiere performance of *Player Piano*, Scenic Stage Theatre, York, 5 May 2016.

132 2.14. Stills from live performance (Scenic Stage Theatre, York, 5 May 2016) and film, Roger Marsh, *Touch and Go* (with gestural choreography by Catherine Laws): this piece formed part of the large-scale performance *Player Piano*. Film by Minyung Im; sound by Lynette Quek. Images 1, 2, 4, and 5 from film; 2 and 6 from live performance.

135 2.15. Still from performance by Catherine Laws of Roger Marsh, *Touch and Go* (with gestural choreography by Catherine Laws): this piece formed part of the large-scale performance *Player Piano*. Film by Minyung Im; sound by Lynette Quek.

141 2.16. Annea Lockwood, "Piano Garden (1969–70, Ingatestone, Essex)" from *Piano Transplants* series. Photo by Chris Ware.

142 2.17. Stills from performance of *Player Piano*, Scenic Stage Theatre, York, 5 May 2016.

147 2.18. Excerpts from Paul Whitty's score *under and under* (2014) for piano, mp3 players, battery powered loudspeakers, and turntable.

148 2.19. Still showing process of annotating scores using transparencies, from film version of *under and under* by Paul Whitty, performed by Catherine Laws. Film by Minyung Im; sound by Lynette Quek.

159 2.20. Photo (by Edward Jessen) from workshopping of "rowing gait" movement in the process of developing *Ten Bellows*.

160 2.21. Photo (by Edward Jessen) from rehearsal of *Ten Bellows* for the first performance (given by Catherine Laws and Lucia D'Errico), Orpheus Institute, Ghent, 20 September 2015.

161 2.22. Edward Jessen, *Ten Bellows* (2015), bars 5–6: G minor cadence, with fragmented repetition then developed mechanistically, with addition of percussive prepared piano.

161 2.23. Edward Jessen, *Ten Bellows* (2015), end (bars 19–20): main cadential phrase fragmented and ornamented.

163 2.24. Still from *Ten Bellows* by Edward Jessen, performed as part of *Player Piano* by Catherine Laws and Hannah Butterfield (Scenic Stage Theatre, York, 5 May 2016): Hannah Butterfield (assistant) in her "reverie" with microphone.

172 3.1. Left to right: William Brooks, Stefan Östersjö, Jez Wells.

179 3.2. "Cage, *passim*," page C-1.

181 3.3. "Cage, *passim*," unit E.

198 3.4. "Cage," bottom of page 1.

201 3.5. "Crump," first page of score.

203 3.6. "*ibid.*," first page of score.

208 3.7. "Cotten, *loc. cit.*," score excerpt.

214 3.8. The discursive voice (adapted from chapter 1, figure 1.7).

215 3.9. Discursive voices: many instruments, many composers.

216 3.10. Discursive voices: many sets of many composers.

217 3.11. Discursive voices: many degrees of loss of many sets of many composers.

218 3.12. A graphical representation of two fundamental artistic processes identified in the qualitative analysis of the making of "Cotten, *loc. cit.*"
219 3.13. A graphical representation of two fundamental artistic processes identified in the qualitative analysis of the making of "Crump."
224 3.14. Capture of Invicta Model 30 radio with Shure SM58 and Schoeps Colette MK4.
243 4.1. Kent Olofsson, *Mirage* trio, 2009, bars 39–45.
264 4.2. Kent Olofsson, *Mirage*, 2009, duo for đàn tranh and đàn bầu, bars 9–14.
264 4.3. Kent Olofsson, *Arrival Cities: Hanoi*, 2015, trio I, bars 37–40.
268 4.4. Kent Olofsson, *Mirage I*, 2009, for trio, bars 36–39.
269 4.5. Kent Olofsson, *Arrival Cities: Hanoi*, 2015, solo for tỳ bà, bars 64–66.
270 4.6. Kent Olofsson. *Fascia*, 2002, for charango and orchestra, bars 46–49.
270 4.7. Kent Olofsson, *Arrival Cities: Hanoi*, 2015, solo for tỳ bà, bars 44–47.
271 4.8. The Ai mode with its characteristic articulation types.
271 4.9. Kent Olofsson. *Arrival Cities: Hanoi*, 2015, solo for đàn tranh, bars 1–6.
273 4.10. Kent Olofsson, *Arrival Cities: Hanoi*, 2015, solo for đàn bầu, bars 1–6.
276 4.11. *Arrival Cities: Hanoi*, 2015, the beginning of the first event score.

Contents of the Online Repository of Supplemental Files

found at
www.orpheusinstituut.be/en/voices-bodies-practices-media-repository

SF1.1 Bell-like sonorities in *Austerity Measures I*
SF1.2 Four-times rehearsal of *Austerity Measures I*
SF1.3 Four-times concert of *Austerity Measures I*
SF1.4 Three-times rehearsal of *Austerity Measures I*
SF1.5 Three-times concert of *Austerity Measures I*
SF2.1 *Player Piano* trailer film
SF2.2 *Touch and Go* (film)
SF2.3 *Ceci n'est pas un piano* (audio recording)
SF2.4 *under and under* (film)
SF2.5 *Touch and Go*, rising and falling hands
SF2.6 *Touch and Go*, plunge
SF2.7 *Touch and Go*, taking off upwards
SF2.8 *Touch and Go*, scrutiny of hands (live)
SF2.9 *Touch and Go*, scrutiny of hands (film)
SF2.10 *Player Piano*, piano entrance
SF2.11 *Player Piano*, vocalisation of piano, film (opening)
SF2.12 *Player Piano*, vocalisation of piano, film (final flip-over)
SF2.13 *Ten Bellows*, trailer film
SF2.14 *Ten Bellows*, cadential phrase and mechanistic development
SF2.15 *Ten Bellows*, example of codependency of soundworlds
SF2.16 *Ten Bellows*, example with piano preparations
SF3.1 *Footnotes*, movement 1 (excerpt)
SF3.2 *Footnotes*, movement 2 (excerpt)
SF3.3 *Footnotes*, movement 3 (excerpt)
SF3.4 *Footnotes*, movement 4 (excerpt)
SF3.5 *Footnotes*, movement 5 (excerpt)
SF3.6 *Footnotes*, movement 6 (excerpt)
SF3.7 *Footnotes*, sleeve notes
SF3.8 A True History of *Footnotes* Perhaps (Part 1)
SF3.9 A True History of *Footnotes* Perhaps (Part 2)
SF3.10 Glissentar
SF3.11 *Footnotes*, "Cotten, *loc. cit.*," Glissentar test
SF3.12 WB and SÖ in Malmö
SF3.13 *Footnotes*, "Cage, *passim*," unit C, ver1
SF.3.14 *Footnotes*, "Cage, *passim*," unit C, ver2
SF3.15 *Footnotes*, "Cage, *passim*," unit C, ver3
SF3.16 *Footnotes*, "Cage, *passim*," unit C, experiment
SF3.17 Vietnamese guitar
SF3.18 Variax guitar
SF3.19 *Footnotes*, "Cage, *passim*," unit I, ver2

SF3.20 *Footnotes*, "Cage, *passim*," unit I (score)
SF3.21 Bill's Gibson guitar
SF3.22 Bill's Gibson serial number
SF3.23 Discovering the preparations for "Cage"
SF3.24 Original preparations for "Cage"
SF3.25 *Footnotes*, "Cotton, *loc. cit.*," discussion
SF4.1 *Mirage* trio (bars 39–45)
SF4.2 *Mirage* duo (bars 9–14)
SF4.3 *Arrival Cities Hanoi* trio 1 (bars 37–40)
SF4.4 *Mirage* trio (bars 36–39)
SF4.5 *Arrival Cities Hanoi* solo for tỳ bà (bars 64–66)
SF4.6 *Fascia* (bars 46–49)
SF4.7 *Arrival Cities Hanoi* solo for tỳ bà (bars 44–47)
SF4.8 *Arrival Cities Hanoi* solo for đàn tranh (bars 1–6)
SF4.9 *Arrival Cities Hanoi* solo for đàn bầu (bars 1–6)
SF4.10 *Arrival Cities Hanoi* premiere

Introduction

Catherine Laws

Who is the "I" that performs? To ask this question in 2019 might seem strange. The self, as an autonomous, self-reflective, individuated unit, has formed the basis of Western social organisation in modern times.[1] However, this very notion of a discrete, essential self has for some decades been picked apart by social, cultural, and critical theory. And even if we ignore this theoretical critique, the everyday experience of the contemporary world, fragmented and heavily mediated, often involves a blurring of truth and fiction. As part of this, the arts of the twentieth and twenty-first centuries have pushed us relentlessly to interrogate inherited notions of the self, expression, and communication: to ask ourselves, again and again, who we think we are and how we can speak meaningfully to one another. Modernist artists characterised increasing globalisation and the development of recording and photographic technologies as prompting a crisis of identity and authenticity. At the same time, the throwaway playfulness of pop culture and digital manipulation has offered endless possibilities for self-reinvention and critique of the individuated subject as the basis of knowledge. The fluid, dynamic, and contingent qualities of subjectivity are experienced on an everyday basis. This invites us into a constant renegotiation and re-forming of the sense of self in relation to everything around us: late modern selfhood is, to use Anthony Giddens's phrase, a "reflexive project" (1991, 5).

As a result, we often now experience the sense of self not as a foundation—not as a stable, inner essence—but rather as continually produced and reproduced in and through our interactions with other people, with things, and with the structures of discourse and power within which we operate on a daily basis: through the practices of life.[2] From this perspective, subjectivity is a process rather than an inner foundation; it is constituted reflexively, every day, from our social and material interactions. As Tia DeNora puts it (1999, 45), "No longer conceptualized as a fixed or unitary entity—as something that is the expression of an inner 'essence'—identity has been recast conceptually as a product of social 'work.'"[3] There are many versions of this modern understanding of the self, from a range of disciplinary and theoretical perspectives, some more

1 "Modern times," here, refers to the period since the transformation of the public sphere from the sixteenth century onwards, through the operations of mercantile capitalism. See Habermas, *The Structural Transformation of the Public Sphere* (1989, 27), where he outlines his argument that, to quote Thompson (1995, 69) "the development of mercantile capitalism in the sixteenth century, together with the changing institutional forms of political power, created the conditions for the emergence of a new kind of public sphere in early modern Europe," a "bourgeois public sphere" conceived as "the sphere of private people come together as a public" (Habermas 1989, 27).

2 The interactional circularity of experience in constituting the self, especially in artistic practice, has been a recurrent theme in much pragmatist philosophy from the early years. See, for example, Dewey ([1934] 1980, 16).

3 DeNora here draws, in particular, on Garfinkel (1967) and Giddens (1991) in addition to her own earlier work on the social content of music (DeNora 1995).

ideological and others more pragmatic. Nevertheless, however complex and multiple and unstable the categories of subjectivity and identity, the twentieth- and twenty-first-century explosion of "identity talk", as Kwame Anthony Appiah characterises it (2018, xiii), provides evidence of an ongoing preoccupation with these matters.

In artistic practice the discourses of self and identity persist, not least in music and especially in performance training, where individuality and distinctiveness of expression are highly valued. While this book demonstrates in various ways that subjectivity is not discrete or essential, but distributed, social, contextual, and embodied, its persistence cannot be set aside.[4] The notion of the emergence of a performer's "voice" is one concern of our research for this very reason. As Paul Gilroy put it (1993, 102), music can offer "a model whereby identity can be understood neither as a fixed essence nor as a vague and utterly contingent construction to be reinvented by the will and whim of aesthetes, symbolists, and language-gamers." From this, we might conclude that in music we proceed in a state of doublethink, wherein a sense of self can persist alongside the ongoing experience and understanding of its provisionality, contingency, and multiplicity: in which a notion of selfhood structures and constitutes our experiences and what we say and do (and how we play music) but is itself structured and constituted by those same things.[5]

Theoretically, subjectivity became a key preoccupation of critical theory from the 1960s, but it was really in the "new" musicological perspectives of the 1980s onwards that these philosophical approaches started to have a significant impact in music. This engendered a deconstruction of the status of the musical work and its possible meanings. The predication of earlier musicological methods on composerly intentionality and/or apparently objective methods of musical analysis came under scrutiny. As part of that, questions of identity and subjectivity came to the fore, but often in terms of how the musical "text" might construct particular subject positions, whether normative (white, Western, male, and heterosexual) or otherwise. Chapter 3, below, traces the creation of invented composerly subjectivities from the interactions of multiple agencies. In recent years, the focus has shifted towards reception and the listener,[6] with

4 Certainly, some theorists have questioned the legitimacy of focusing on subjectivity. In arguing for a better appreciation of nonhuman agency and the "thing power" of objects, Jane Bennett suggests we should "postpone for a while the topics of subjectivity or the nature of human interiority" (2010, 120). She argues that ignoring ourselves for a while, if only temporarily, is a necessary strategy if we truly wish to understand the agency of nonhuman materials—a concern, at times, of this research, particularly with respect to instruments. Likewise, the accounts in this book of the processes of interaction between artistic collaborators, their tools and materials, and the contexts in which they operate exemplify Deleuze's assertion that "creative functions . . . proceed by intersections, crossings of lines, points of encounter in the middle" (Deleuze and Parnet 1987, 27–28), rather than by a linear process of action determined by an individual author-figure. However, as is apparent in the main text, we cannot conclude with Deleuze that there is, therefore, "no subject, but instead collective assemblages of enunciation" (28).

5 This "doublethink" has, again, been a key concern of pragmatist philosophers. See, for instance, William James's "Does Consciousness Exist" (James 1912, 1–38) and, more recently and specific to performance, Richard Shusterman's *Performing Live* (2000), especially chapters 9 and 10.

6 There are many examples here, but key relevant texts include Szendy (2008); Kassabian (2013); Clarke (2011); van Maas (2015).

considerable attention paid to the ways in which listeners "use" music to negotiate and reconstruct themselves: to enhance or change moods, to alter their bodily states (to aid exercise, or to calm themselves down to a more reflective, concentrated state, for example), and to produce a sense of social or cultural identity, a sense of belonging or of difference.[7]

In all this, the role of musical *performance* in the production of subjectivity has remained somewhat neglected. The underlying assumption often seems to be that performance is simply the means by which the music "itself" becomes manifest. Too often, still, the significance of a specific performance by an individual body in a particular time and place is ignored.[8] This is less so in the field of popular music, where performance often becomes a matter of consideration in the relationship between sound, image, and cultural identity. Moreover, here there is a strong connection to the wider field of performance studies beyond music—particularly to theatre, live art, and dance studies, both theoretically and through performance as (or artistic) research—where, as in some studies in popular music, the notion that performance constitutes and creates identity is foundational.[9] Of course, some such practice, especially in theatre and live art, explicitly deals with issues related to self and identity through race, gender, ethnicity, class, age, and so on. This happens much less often in musical performance without words, inevitably; the context of Western classical concert and experimental performance is somewhat different, but subjectivity is no less significant, for performers and audiences alike. One of the key characteristics of music is its ability to carry subjectivity without explicit characterisation: we do not need to think of a musical utterance as carrying an individual's expressive intentions for it to produce a sense of subjective identification for performers and listeners. Arguably, its relative abstraction actually facilitates this process, leaving more open the ways in which we can project ourselves into—or feel ourselves within—the music. Moreover, as Elizabeth Bell notes (2008, 19), it is not just by overtly dealing with identity "issues" that performance (of whatever kind) negotiates individuation: all performances emerge from the entanglements of self, other, bodies, and materials; all comply with or defy expectations; and as such, on one level all "performances make implicit and explicit claims about what is valued in and by the group and how members ought to act."

Nevertheless, despite important theoretical work by Nicholas Cook (2001, 2013, 2018), Philip Auslander (2006), Naomi Cumming (2000), Jerrold Levinson (1996, 2006, 2009), and many others, the discourse on subjectivity in music is still somewhat atomised. Overall, developments across arts practices

7 See, for example, DeNora (1999); Herbert (2017).

8 Mary Hunter (2005) makes a similar point, noting that even when musicology engages in some depth with questions of subjectivity there is a lack of attention to the role of performance. Hunter cites Lawrence Kramer's "The Mysteries of Animation: History, Analysis and Musical Subjectivity" as a key example: Kramer "locates the 'animation' of the music entirely in the listener's engaged response to it, and elides the performer into the listener or composer as necessary" (Hunter 2005, 361n11).

9 Terminology remains a vexed issue in our field. The preference in the UK, across the arts, is generally for variants of the phrase "practice-as-research" (with "practice research," "practice-led research," and "practice-based research" all used to signify subtly different research processes). Elsewhere in Europe the term "artistic research" prevails. The authors of this volume all work across these contexts, and we therefore use the phrases "practice-as-research" and "artistic research" interchangeably.

and the wider discourse of performance studies (beyond music) have allowed for a stronger focus on the production and experiencing of subjectivity, in the context of live events, as ephemeral, dynamic, contingent, and embodied. However, this is only just starting to be taken up in musical research. There is a range of possible reasons for this. Sometimes cited are the ephemerality of performance, or the apparently subordinate role of the performer as re-creator in composed music practices; but these also operate in forms of dance and theatre-making, and here, far from performance remaining in the shadows of artistic research, questions of liveness, performativity, mediation, authenticity, authority, and documentation have been at the forefront of the discourse. Perhaps more pertinent is Mine Doğantan-Dack's (2015a, 32) comment that, despite the substantial developments in critical musicology in recent decades and the widespread and varied ideas and manifestations of composition-as-research, in the twentieth century "classical music performance practice, as a form of art making, remained untouched by the critically reflective and socio-politically engaged stances and discourses surrounding it."

Certainly, much performance-as-research has focused on matters of style and interpretation (often in relation to matters of historicity), and much less on the tangled matters of subjectivity, agency, and identity. Composer Juliana Hodkinson (2017) notes that while in contemporary musical practices the "boundaries of agency, sociality, subjectivity and embodiment have to some extent been pushed, and conventional expectations and practices are regularly expanded and dismantled," nevertheless "the impact of the 'sonic' and 'performative' turns on contemporary instrumental music has been small and delayed." Despite recent shifts, in particular towards a stronger focus on the ways in which performance is significant in musical creativity, it still seems that we find it harder, compared with other performing arts, to consider questions of subjectivity and embodiment in and through performance. This is changing, for sure, not least with an expansion in the numbers of performers embarking upon artistic research doctorates, but many of the key questions remain underexplored.[10]

Subjectivity in musical practice, manifested through performance, is the shared concern of the contributors to this volume: not matters of self-expression or performer interpretation, but rather the ways in which the distributed processes of musical creativity produce, in performance, complex, dynamic subjectivities. For all the reasons indicated above, we recognise the problematics of these matters. How do we speak of subjectivity in performance when the notion of the subject is always already so contested, when performance is so slippery, ephemeral, and insubstantial, and when we who speak are also

10 While practice-as-research in music has for some decades been established in some areas of higher education, perhaps especially in the UK (in both university music departments and conservatoires), the recent shift of many conservatoires in mainland Europe towards a stronger focus on artistic research, at doctoral level and beyond, has been remarkable. The "white paper" on artistic research produced by the Association Européenne des Conservatoires, Académies de Musique et Musikhochschulen (AEC) in 2015 outlines the centrality of artistic research in European conservatoire education and the organisation's commitment to supporting its growth. See https://www.aec-music.eu/work--policies/artistic-research.

the subjects who "do"? On the one hand, this is inevitably a project of failure; the simple answer is that there are significant limits and dangers here. As Catherine Laws discusses in her chapter, drawing on Giorgio Agamben (2000, 117), as soon as an individual attempts to speak from a particular moment or situation—to speak subjectively of the subjective experience—she turns herself into an object. Immediately, then, she is outside: ejected from the moment, distanced from the dynamics of the subject position and no longer able to speak through it.

Moreover, in taking this perspective—using our creative work as research and reflecting on it ourselves—we risk accusations of solipsism, narrowness, extreme specificity, and, ultimately, irrelevance. Counter to this, we argue that we can only understand the broader significance of practices by attending to the *particular*, in dynamic relation with wider frameworks, practices, and theories. The specific practice and the wider practices constitute—contribute to and produce—each other, and the practitioner's perspective is important in this: the experiences and knowledge of performers are crucial to a better understanding of how embodied subjectivity is produced. Sometimes practice and reflection are synchronous, and sometimes one precedes the other; the dynamic relation between the two is important in artistic research. As Mareli Stolp puts it (2015), "accepting that there may exist a time gap between subjective experience and objective engagement with the implications of that experience allows for subjective and objective understandings to function together in the articulation of new knowledge."

All research is partial and incomplete, whatever the perspective and role of the researcher(s); explicit confrontation with and acknowledgement of those aporias is, perhaps, one of the strengths of artistic research. Doing so can expose both possibilities and limits; perhaps most importantly, it can open up better, deeper questions about aspects of activity, behaviour, and culture that are hard to grasp, that manifest through bodies and practices in ever-changing but deeply affecting, significant ways. This might relate to Henk Borgdorff's claim (2011, 61) that artistic research should be concerned not just with explicating knowledge as manifested in and through practice, but that, more crucially, "it is more directed at a not-knowing, or a not-yet-knowing. It creates room for that which is unthought, that which is unexpected—the idea that all things [in art] could be different."

Importantly, to not attempt something in this arena is, effectively, to silence the performing subject, to restrict questions of agency, subjectivity, and identity purely to musicology or music psychology, to the apparently more safely verifiable arenas of empirical experimentation, musico-textual deconstruction, or the study of performance from without: to approach the performer as a "laboratory rat," as characterised by John Rink (2004, 39). This is not to suggest any antipathy to other areas of research; indeed, in the present volume the authors are all trained in other fields in addition to working as composers and performers, and approaches from empirical and critical musicology, philosophy, and ethnography feed into the chapters. However, the fundamental concern is to pay heed to the significant experience of practitioners and the process of making and performing with respect to the constitution of subjectivity: to the ways in which, in performance, we are drawn to a particular body-subject, engaged in a process of producing meaning that will, in that very situatedness, be different each time. We both experience an "I" and relate to one; and that "I" is produced in and through the process of interaction with particular "others" (present and absent), with instruments and in a particular environment, and it is necessarily unstable, unfixed. Thirty years ago, Donna Haraway argued for a research practice of situated, embodied knowledge (and she identified this as feminist in approach, even when not explicitly concerned with gender, because it attends to elided subject positions): "I am arguing for politics and epistemologies of location, position, and situating, where partiality and not universality is the condition of being heard to make rational knowledge claims, . . . [for] the view from a body, always a complex, contradictory, structuring and structured body, versus the view from above, from nowhere, from simplicity" (Haraway 1988, 589). Perhaps we still need to pay heed to this; to do so in the context of the production of musical subjectivity is one of our concerns in this volume.

In recent artistic and musicological research there has been considerable focus on some of the issues that lie close to our topic, especially processes of collaboration, distributed agency, and the affordances and resistances of the performer–instrument relationship. It has become far more common to acknowledge—and indeed examine—the emergence of knowledge (of any kind) from social situations, rather than as individually produced. Howard Gardner's observation is crucial here: "If one wants to understand the phenomena of creativity, one cannot simply focus on the individual—his brain, her personality, their motivations" (1994, 146). Likewise, Keith Sawyer's (2008) work on group "genius" and, subsequently, on distributed creativity with Stacy DeZutter (Sawyer and DeZutter 2009), has exposed many of the ways in which artistic creativity is shaped by cultures and interactions rather than arising as an individual attribute.[11] Extended practitioner-researcher accounts of individual collaborative projects have become more common, alongside studies in which musicians work with musicologists or music psychologists to delve into the distributed processes from which performances, compositions, and improvisations emerge.[12]

Likewise, in recent years the methodologies and outputs of numerous artistic research projects have been contingent upon acknowledging both the creative agency of the performer and the significance of the individual performer's

11 The work of Lev Vygotsky (1978) on the fundamentally significant role played by social interaction in the development of the individual is very important in this field, providing a grounding for the understanding of processes of learning and creativity as social. Vygotsky's work provided a social-psychology counterpart to other, more critical, theoretical positions, especially Bakhtin's dialogism (1981), in which an apparently individual creative act is understood as always, already composed through intersubjective dialogue with others and with social structures.

12 A considerable number of such studies have been published in recent years, but those by Hayden and Windsor (2007), Fitch and Heyde (2007), and Östersjö (2008) have been particularly influential. More recently, three volumes have significantly extended the field: the special issue of *Contemporary Music Review* devoted to the topic (Taylor 2016), Clarke and Doffman's volume *Distributed Creativity* (2017), and Redhead and Glover's *Collaborative and Distributed Processes in Contemporary Music-Making* (2018).

experience as an embodied subject with a particular instrument.[13] However, this work rarely touches upon the assumptions upon which these very questions—of collaboration, interpretation, expression—are premised: the very notion of the embodied musical self, produced and differently reproduced, time and again, in and through performance. Recent work in the field of musical improvisation has taken this on; the 2016 volume *Negotiated Moments: Improvisation, Sound, and Subjectivity*, edited by Gillian Siddall and Ellen Waterman, is perhaps the closest parallel to our volume. However, the musical transactions of improvisation are quite particular and in certain ways qualitatively different to those of composed musics. Improvisation plays a significant role in some of the projects examined in this book. It is sometimes used as part of the process of generating musical material that is then "fixed," compositionally, but some of the pieces discussed also have improvised moments in performance. Either way, it operates within or alongside composition; it is not the prime or sole practice. If the nature of musical agents, their materials, and contexts are, as we argue, constitutive of subjectivity, then this difference matters. We cannot simply apply the insights across to other fields of practice without critical scrutiny.

Overall, therefore, this volume aims to address this gap in the research,[14] asking key questions about how subjectivity is instantiated and embodied in performance:

(1) How can experimentation with processes toward performance draw out, or foreground, subjectivity in action, and aid our understanding of its production?
(2) How do the dynamic relationships between performers, other artists, materials, and historical and cultural contexts contribute to the emergence of subjectivity? and
(3) How do the processes of performance reflect and produce gendered and cultural identities? How do these issues relate to understandings of creativity and identity?

These are, of course, big questions: they need to be addressed from a range of different perspectives, across practices, and over an extended period. We offer some preliminary steps. Moreover, these matters cannot be addressed abstractly or purely theoretically; they all require insights from situated practice, from specific contexts of performance.

The volume is organised in relation to the four artistic research projects that formed the research cluster "Performance, Subjectivity, and Experimentation"

13 Key examples might include Elisabeth Le Guin's study *Boccherini's Body: An Essay in Carnal Musicology* (2006) and artistic research doctorates such as Tanja Orning's "The Polyphonic Performer" (Norwegian Academy of Music, 2014), which focused on embodied performance practice as a cellist in the field of contemporary music (see https://nmh.no/en/research/projects/the-polyphonic-performer).

14 This book will be followed by a second volume, *Performance, Subjectivity, and Experimentation*, linked to the same research cluster but with additional contributions from participants in a seminar held at the Orpheus Institute, Ghent, in 2016. The two volumes complement one another; this (the first) volume offers more in-depth studies of the core research, while *Performance, Subjectivity, and Experimentation* embraces a broader field across a wider range of relevant musical research.

hosted at the Orpheus Institute, Ghent, with the projects also partnered by the University of York (UK), the Royal Academy of Music (UK), and Malmö Academy of Music, Lund University (Sweden). Each chapter comprises a substantial examination of one project within the cluster, but these projects all proceeded in dialogue with one another; although the artistic processes and outputs are quite different, and the research manifests a variety of approaches, all are concerned with the core questions and the interrelated explorations of issues of subjectivity, agency, and identity. We have developed the projects in parallel, with extensive sharing of the work (both artistic work-in-progress and theoretical perspectives) and wide-ranging discussion and argument.

As such, certain perspectives or framings of artistic research processes have been useful to us all. Some points of reference are common and pop back up now and again in different chapters, and some are specific to individual projects. There has been no attempt to maintain a regimented, univocal approach—theoretical, artistic, or methodological—in developing the research in each project, or in reflecting back upon the artistic processes and outputs, although the recurrence of certain key terms and images demonstrates the depth of interconnection. Above all, we shared two convictions: a sense that the core questions were ones that needed addressing, and an agreement that iterative, reflexive processes of artistic research—processes of making and reflection in modes of contemporary music practices—would constitute our method. In all the projects, the making of new artistic work has formed part of the research enquiry, as a means to explore the key questions.

Performance is, on one level, always a matter of emergent, enacted identity. When the authority of artistic work is shared, such as between composers and performers, agency and identity-formation are already, and always, complex. And identity is always produced through embodied interaction with materials and tools and in relation to specific spaces and contexts. Much of the creative work discussed in this volume has been developed with these issues in mind; as a result, it aims reflexively to invite the audience into the question of identity, actively examining the question of whom we are listening to as part of the thematics of the artistic work. There is, therefore, a very close relationship between the artistic work linked to this volume and the textual discourses we present. Throughout the book, therefore, we refer to related audio and video recordings, together with supplemental images and documents, all held at www.orpheusinstituut.be/en/voices-bodies-practices-media-repository: we ask readers to listen to and watch these materials, and to consider them as equal in status to this text.

Overall, there are three strands to our research, all concerned with the production of distributed subjectivities through performance:

(1) the production of "voice" through the interaction of embodied subject and instrument plus associated technological production (i.e., human⇔non-human agencies);

(2) the interaction of self and other(s): the manifestation of intersubjectivity in the context of the performer's "hosting" of multiple human agencies (performer, composer[s], past performers);
(3) the ecology of performance: the constitution of subjectivity through the interaction of embodied subject, other human agencies, and instrumental/technological mediation in the specific site of performance production.

These strands facilitate an exploration of practice–theory relations across a spectrum from the individual performing "voice" to the cultural manifestation of identity. The research cluster is situated in contemporary musical practices; the contributors work primarily in this field, though each project has specific, differentiated concerns. Such practice seems particularly appropriate for artistic research in this area. The explicit negotiation of roles, agency, and hence subjectivities, has become a more noticeable feature of contemporary musical practice in recent decades. We argue that this influences other fields of music-making, affecting the sense of creative agency that performers might carry into other contexts.

The book comprises four extended chapters, each focused around one of the artistic research projects. The strands are all present in each of the chapters, but the emphasis shifts. Broadly speaking, chapter 1, by David Gorton and Stefan Östersjö, focuses primarily on the first two strands in relation to performances of the solo guitar composition *Austerity Measures I*. In chapter 2, Catherine Laws offers theoretical perspectives on each of the three strands, linked to the reflexive engagement with these issues in her interdisciplinary performance piece, *Player Piano*. Chapter 3, by William Brooks, Stefan Östersjö, and Jez Wells, expands the frame into questions of sound production and the technological mediation of intersubjectivity in relation to the process of recording the extended composition *Footnotes*; while the final chapter, by Nguyễn Thanh Thủy and Stefan Östersjö, shifts us yet more substantially into a focus on the second and third strands, with its context of intercultural collaboration in developing performances of the music theatre piece *Arrival Cities: Hanoi*.

More specifically, the first chapter approaches the question of subjectivity in the musical practices of composers and performers through a discussion of the emergence of "voice." Gorton (a composer) and Östersjö (a guitarist) have worked together collaboratively in artistic research contexts for some years. In the research project presented here they used the process of developing a new piece, *Austerity Measures I* for ten-string guitar, as a means to explore the manifestation of a "discursive voice" within artistic practice. Detailed analysis of video recordings, using both quantitative and qualitative measures, sheds light upon the interrelations between the embodied knowledge of the performer and the musical structures in the score and, further, between the subjectivities of composer and performer unfolded through the composition and performance of *Austerity Measures I*. Gorton and Östersjö use this as the underpinning evidence (in relation to the wider field of research) for a model of how the subjectivities of performer and composer can be understood as the emergence of such a "discursive voice," defined through interactions between human agencies (composer, performer) and non-human ones (scores, compositional systems, musical instruments), all combined within a collaboration.

The second chapter, by Catherine Laws, draws on the question of "voice" as discussed by Gorton and Östersjö, but moves the discussion into a more overtly theatrical context in which the musical body-subject in performance and the relationship to both the instrument—in this case the piano—and the site of performance are more explicitly thematised. Laws's project, in collaboration with four composers, a theatre-maker, and a film-maker, involved developing a large-scale multimedia performance piece, *Player Piano*, which attempted reflexively to explore and open up to audiences the questions of agency and identity that underpin the research. As such, the chapter moves from the discussion of "voice" and performer agency—the problematics of projecting an "I" in performance—into an extended consideration of subjectivity as a product of the interactions between the performer as body-subject; the "thing power" (drawing on Bennett 2010) of the particular instrument as physical object, sound source, and cultural agent; the agency of creative collaborators; and the wider context of the situation of performance—in particular, the agential characteristics of space and acoustics. The chapter uses Judith Butler's work on performativity and embodiment, still relatively little applied to the field of musical performance, alongside Erika Fischer-Lichte's discussions of forms of performer presence, to help pick apart the dynamic interaction of agency and subjection that is brought into play in this work (Butler 1988, 1993, 2005; Fischer-Lichte 2012).

Chapter 3, by William Brooks, Stefan Östersjö, and Jez Wells, takes us more explicitly into questions of mediation, in terms of sound-recording production processes, but also into exploring questions of the self transformed across time. Evidently, between 1983 and 1985, a composer allegedly named William Brooks wrote—or, more properly, notated—a composition (a set of compositions? transcriptions? approximations?) apparently titled *Footnotes*. In 2010, that composition came to the attention of the guitarist Stefan Östersjö, who decided to record it. With the collaboration of Jez Wells, sound engineer, and William Brooks, musicologist, the result has now been released on the Innova label as a forty-five-minute LP. Early in their work it became evident to the three collaborators that the overall project required the construction of a set of different identities for six types of participant: guitar, guitarist; score, composer; hardware, engineer. This chapter—itself an intertangled multilogue of mutable voices—traces the construction of, distinction between, and eventual representation of, those identities. It considers, *inter alia*, the extent to which a single entity—a personality, an artefact, a historical event—can be regarded as an interpenetrating collection of irreconcilable differences; whether those differences can be constituted as a series of persona or fictions; and whether anything can truly be said to underlie the whole.

Finally, in Chapter 4 we move into questions of subjectivity and cultural identity. Here, Nguyễn Thanh Thủy and Stefan Östersjö outline the role of subjectivity and intersubjectivity in the creation of *Arrival Cities: Hanoi*, a piece of experimental music theatre with documentary film. The performance combines storytelling developed from memories of encounters with people in migration zones in Hanoi with personal memories of the city and of the emerging relation between the members of the project. The music was developed through an extended collaboration between the Swedish composer Kent Olofsson and The Six Tones, starting in 2009. Nguyễn and Östersjö argue that the emergence of discursive voice in this process also becomes part of the narrative of the staged performance, since this cross-cultural negotiation becomes embodied by the composed music. The authors discuss the role of empathy and engagement in intercultural collaboration from the perspective of a performative ethics in music. Further, the chapter discusses the role of embodiment and performativity in blurring the boundary between truth and fiction through the combination of documentary and staged performance in the piece.

Before proceeding, we wish to clarify the use of certain key terms in this volume. "Subjectivity" and "identity" and "agency" are all commonly used terms that can, nevertheless, have subtly different meanings in different contexts.

We understand SUBJECTIVITY simply as the condition of being a subject and the process by which we become or are perceived as such. This means having the capacity to hold beliefs, desires, and a sense of self, but it does not assume that subjectivity and selfhood are the same thing. The question of what a self "is"—whether it exists at all, whether self-awareness necessarily means having an awareness of self, and the relationship between consciousness and self-awareness (as discussed particularly usefully by Zahavi 2006)—continues to be debated in philosophy, phenomenology, and neuroscience. However, that we act *as if* we are at least partially self-determining, on the basis that our "selves" are significant in some way—behaving as if the individual subject experiences the world in particular ways and re-produces or otherwise expresses back to the world that experience—ensures that subjectivity remains significant to culture and creativity. Nevertheless, subjectivity is produced by and also feeds into discourses, structures, and systems; following Judith Butler, we understand subjectivity to be constituted as "intelligible," which means that quite how an individual can "be" or act is constituted socially and culturally, not purely individually.[15] We repeatedly perform (act out) modes of subjectivity that become naturalised and feel foundational, but that are produced in and through the constraints of our contexts. As such, the capacity to take up a subject position—and the nature of being a subject—operates within a dynamic process: subjectivity is produced in and through discourse (of any kind, and always embodied, whether linguistic, musical, or whatever), but the subject has the potential to be articulate (in whatever way) within that discourse and to articulate things *differently*, creating new meanings.

The concepts of subjectivity and IDENTITY are closely interwoven. Many writers use them interchangeably, and where a difference is apparent there is no

15 Butler's account of subjectivity is further discussed in chapter 2, but with respect to the comments in this introduction, the key texts are *Giving an Account of Oneself* (2005), Butler's Adorno Prize Lecture (2012), and *Senses of the Subject* (2015).

evident consensus as to where it lies. However, for the purposes of this book we use "identity" to refer to the more explicitly socially constituted aspects of subjectivity: subjectivity that involves a question of sameness or difference from others (Weeks 1990, 89) and that hence relates to socially constituted communities, groups, or practices. In that sense identity appears when subjectivity becomes symbolic, when an intersection forms between the sense of self and the characteristics apparent in the ways in which a group identifies itself.[16] Of course, identity is no more fixed than subjectivity; it changes, constantly. Moreover, identity can constitute subjectivity—my sense of myself as a woman can be predicated on my sense of what it is to be identified as a woman—and vice versa: the identity of "woman" can be formed from individual subjective experiences of gender. The relationship is complex and unstable, constantly evolving. Appiah (2018, 12) neatly summarises the social dynamic between subjectivity and identity: "Identities come, first, with labels and ideas about why and to whom they should be applied. Second, your identity shapes your thoughts about how you should behave; and, third, it affects the way other people treat you. Finally, all these dimensions of identity are contestable, always up for dispute: who's in, what they're like, how they should behave and be treated."

Likewise, the relationship between *agency* and subjectivity is complex. Sally Jane Norman describes agency as designating "potentially innumerable, finely differentiated capacities for action" (2013, 283), and we share that basic understanding of the term. In that sense, subjects certainly can have agency. Nevertheless, as Shaun Gallagher observes (2012, 28), agency "has multiple contributories, some of which are reflectively conscious, some of which are pre-reflectively conscious, and some of which are non-conscious," and as a result the relationship between agency and intentionality or ownership is not at all straightforward. Examples from the body, particularly with regard to motor control and processes associated with body schema (the preconscious system of motor capacities, abilities, and habits that enables movement) help demonstrate this; Gallagher notes the significant differences between deciding to move a body part in a particular way, to accomplish a defined task, and other aspects of motor control which we feel we "own" but do not consciously think of prior to (or sometimes even during) their execution: "It is possible to say that I am moving, and therefore that it is *my* movement, and thus have a sense of ownership for it, in cases where there is no sense of agency for the movement, for example in reflex or involuntary movements" (Gallagher 2007, 347).[17] This is, of course, very relevant to musical performance, in which intentionality of movement and matters of bodily agency are often very complex, due to the nature of the physical training at the instrument.

---

16 The construction of identity, both personal and artistic, has been central to the writings of the latter-day pragmatist Richard Shusterman (2000, 2002).

17 On body schema, see Gallagher and Cole (1995); on somatic agency and ownership, see also Shusterman (2008).

As Gallagher argues (2012, 17), agency is therefore phenomenologically "thin," in that it is often short-lived and tends to lie in the pre-reflective background of experience. Nevertheless, its operation across levels of awareness makes it significant to our attempts to understand the capacity to act in and hence influence the world. In its very ambiguity of intentionality, it is closely interwoven with the problematics of the sense of self: it contributes to the production of subjectivity, and manifestations of subjectivity often carry implications of agency, but the two are not interchangeable. While we might often perceive subjectivity as produced in part by the recognition of agency, subjects can, equally, lack agency. Likewise, following Bruno Latour (2005) and others, since agency is not predicated on intentionality, in a network of action any "actor"—any active entity—can potentially be agential: not just subjects but also nonhuman objects. In our context, instruments, in particular, certainly often seem to carry agency, powerfully influencing musical activity, behaviours, and meaning. Agency can also be collective, emerging from the interaction of "actors" (whether human or nonhuman). Importantly, also, as Bennett Hogg and Sally Jane Norman write (2013, 116), "agency only has significance in a world that offers resistances; not to be identified with free will, agency is directed negotiation carried out within the limits of physical reality and of the behaviour of persons and things. Agency is emergent rather than given." Again, this becomes important in terms of the ways in which musicians negotiate the affordances and resistances of instruments and the contexts of performance.

We hope that the work presented here shows that music performance has specific things to offer the field of practice-as-research, in part *because* of the very ambiguity of agency and the complex, distributed intersubjectivity that makes it a slippery and tricky subject—the qualities that have, perhaps, to date, led to its remaining somewhat in the shadows in the broader field of artistic research.

Chapter 1

Austerity Measures I

Performing the Discursive Voice

David Gorton and Stefan Östersjö

SÖ: There are some interesting moments in this version that I think might need to be changed. One of the mistakes is putting a 3 on bar 7, because what actually happens . . . I wasn't so fond of that . . . I don't know what I was thinking, but somehow it gets very simple: you have this chord, and then you have this counter thing, that goes counter to this, and then you have that again here with the same A♭, so you kind of lose the bell-like things all the way here, which is really stupid. So I think actually this should have been 3 and that should have been 2, but then this cannot be 2, so then that might have to be 1, and I know that I wanted this . . . the nicest sounding phrase is this [plays] on the whole first line . . . it's nice to have them ring together, so therefore you want . . . and I'm particularly fond of the last bar, this one [plays], so I know I wanted that to be 3.

DG: But let's hear these 3s again. I wasn't bothered by that at all, that the bell had gone.

SÖ: [Plays] The thing about making this 3, and this, is that you get the kind of [plays] . . . different . . . otherwise it's [plays] . . . but here instead you get [plays] which is kind of nice . . . so that far it's quite good.

DG: But I'm not bothered about . . . Yes, you could swap that one and that one, which would solve it. But the absence of the C, D♭s . . .

SÖ: But maybe swapping here is better actually, so 3, 1 . . . but then, no, then you get 1 here.

DG: [Laughing] no, you're not allowed to do that.

SÖ: So that would mean that this would have to be 2 and this would have to be 1, that might be ok, no? Let's try that.

DG: What's interesting is that the fact that the C and D♭ had gone in the third time around didn't bother me at all; I quite liked that sequence. And yes, it's repetitive, the E to A♭ and the A♭ repeating. But then it's sort of repetitive anyway because you've got the Cs and the Ds repeating.

SÖ: Yes. Let's just listen to it. This is quite different actually . . . [Plays] I like that better.

DG: Ok. I like it too.

SÖ: I could play the old one . . . so the previous version was this [plays].

DG: Which I also like.

SÖ: Yes. It's different. But, of course, it gives a different kind of meaning to the repeat of the A♭: it becomes very thematic.

DG: Yes. Something emerges that wasn't there before. I think these decisions are yours to take. If you want to reject that version and do a different one, that's fine; that's there as your choice.

SÖ: Yes. I remember from when I put this together that I wasn't so happy about this repeat of the A♭.

DG: It's kind of fascinating that you've become attached to certain things that you don't like being removed . . . and I think that bell, that C–D♭ tolling thing, which in the first version of

> *your 3 had gone completely, it's almost as if you're missing it a bit.*
>
> *[Laughing and agreement]*
>
> *SÖ: So, I've been thinking a little about this phrase, because there's something very likeable about what happens with it over the bar line, with this [plays].*
>
> *DG: You'll get that on 2 anyway won't you, on the second time through.*
>
> *SÖ: Yes, that's why I marked it 3–2, because I wanted it to happen at least once more.*
>
> *DG: And on 3 you get?*
>
> *SÖ: On 3 you only get this [plays] . . .*
>
> *DG: Yes, it's ok.*
>
> *SÖ: I think so too. At first, I was a bit concerned about this sonority [plays] to disappear. But actually, it's quite a nice chord.*
>
> *DG: It's nice on its own.*
>
> *SÖ: So, I think I've decided to like it.*

This transcript is taken from a rehearsal at the Royal Academy of Music in London on 13 May 2013 and represents around seven minutes from over two hours of video footage. As with any transcript, the nuance of *how* these words were said, and their accompanying physical gestures and facial expressions, are lost, as are the profusion of superfluous utterances ("yeah," "you know," "erm") that litter everyday speech. Also missing is the context of *what* is being spoken about and what the conditions and character of the rehearsal are like. Without this information it is impossible to understand not only what the frequent referencing of lower order integers in the speech refers to, but also what the basic motivations and interests of the two speakers are. On the surface level, at least, it is clear that this is a conversation between two musicians talking about a piece of music. One of the musicians *plays* and thus must have access to a musical instrument. The piece that is being spoken about appears to be incomplete, or in a condition of being edited, with decisions and their implications about possible changes to the piece being the focus of the conversation. The two musicians seem to have rather different attitudes to the discussed changes. On the one hand, the musician playing shows a particular concern about the harmonic and motivic implications of the changes that he has instigated ("it gives a different kind of meaning to the repeat of the A♭: it becomes very thematic"). In contrast, the other musician appears almost disinterested in the changes, stating that he is not concerned by the apparent problems raised by the playing musician and that he likes all the versions discussed. He clearly offloads any responsibility for the changes in musical outcome ("I think these decisions are yours to take"), although at one contradictory moment shuts down one of the suggested possibilities ("no, you're not allowed to do that"). From this a reasonable conclusion to draw would be that the musician who plays is interested in finding a specific single solution to the perceived harmonic and motivic problems identified in the piece, while the other musician is interested in the range of possibilities that the exploration of such problems affords. Yet, as shall be seen, it would be a mistake to assume that these are the *only* interests of the two musicians in the transcript, or that their identified interests might not be changeable or understood in a different way.

The piece of music being discussed in the transcript is *Austerity Measures I*[1] for microtonally-tuned ten-string guitar by composer David Gorton, written for guitarist Stefan Östersjö, and the discussion comes from around half an hour in to the first rehearsal of the piece. The rehearsal is set within the context of an ongoing, long-term collaboration between us, which by the date of the rehearsal in 2013 had already seen the collaborative development and first performance of a substantial piece for eleven-string alto guitar and optional electronics, *Forlorn Hope*.[2] From its outset in 2010, the collaboration was established as a research project that would have the following characteristics: (1) the establishment of practical collaborative sessions that would be filmed for future analysis; (2) the development of compositions that would intentionally activate *something* exploratory in the relationship between composer and performer; (3) the mixture of artistic practice with analysis and written work. By the time of the rehearsal documented above, we had already undertaken a number of extended practical collaborative sessions that had contributed to the development of both *Forlorn Hope* and *Austerity Measures I*. One such group of sessions from June 2010, referred to here as the "Malmö Sessions," saw the formation of tuning systems and prototype materials for both pieces.[3] While artistic development of the new piece is central to the discourse in the above transcript, what is being said by the two protagonists needs to be seen as coming from a context of mutual trust and ease of working that has developed over a period of years, and it should be understood as extending beyond the artistic domain into broader investigative concerns.

The score of *Austerity Measures I* consists of sixty-four bars of notated music, which in a single performance are played through three or four times, with an increasing proportion of the bars omitted and replaced with rests on each of the repetitions. The instructions printed in the score describe the parameters of this process as follows (Gorton 2018a):

> The piece should be played through three or four times.
>
> If playing four times:
>
> - Label each bar with a number "1," "2," "3," or "4." The first and last bars should be labelled "4." The numbers should frequently change order, but should be approximately equal in distribution throughout. Consecutive bars should not be labelled with the same number.
> - When playing the second time through, only bars labelled "2," "3," and "4" should be played. Bars labelled "1" should be replaced with rests.

1 *Austerity Measures I* is published by Verlag Neue Musik (Berlin, 2018), and was first performed by Stefan Östersjö at the Orpheus Institute, Ghent, 2 October 2014. It is not to be confused with *Austerity Measures II* for Howarth-Redgate oboe and string quartet.

2 *Forlorn Hope* is published by Verlag Neue Musik, Berlin (Gorton 2018b), and recorded by Stefan Östersjö in a version without electronics on *David Gorton: Variations on John Dowland* (Longbow, Sheppard-Skærved, and Östersjö 2017). The first performance was given by Stefan Östersjö (guitar) and Juan Parra Cancino (electronics) at the Orpheus Institute Research Festival, Ghent, 5 October 2012.

3 The "Malmö Sessions" are documented in Gorton and Östersjö (2016) and Clarke et al. (2017).

- When playing the third time through, only bars labelled "3" and "4" should be played. Bars labelled "1" and "2" should be replaced with rests.
- When playing the fourth time through, only bars labelled "4" should be played. Bars labelled "1," "2," and "3" should be replaced with rests.

If playing three times follow the same procedure but with only numbers "1," "2," and "3."

There is some flexibility permitted in the tempo to facilitate phrasing, and the short pauses between some bars need not always be observed. But each play-through should be approximately the same duration.

Figure 1.1 shows one of the possible distributions of numbers across the first twelve bars of the piece, if choosing to play it through three times, while figure 1.2 is a representation of the first twelve bars on the third run-through using the distribution from figure 1.1. But while figure 1.1 does look like the score as it would be seen by a guitar player, albeit with typeset rather than handwritten numbers, figure 1.2 is not something that would ever be seen in performance by a guitar player; rather, it is an image of the musical outcome of the cutting process and a reflection of the mental process undertaken by the guitar player in engaging with the system of the piece. The requirement to omit bars and replace them with rests implies rather more than the negative act of not playing at a specific moment. In performance, a strategy is needed to manage and frame the silences as they progressively increase in size and number and break up the flow of materials into isolated fragments. Derived from the array of numbers annotated into the score, this strategy comprises an imagining of where materials are cut and where they remain across the repetitions, and an identification of where musical connections between materials are lost and where new ones emerge, coupled with a live response in performance that shapes this shifting musical landscape. The conversation in the above transcript can therefore be understood as an exploration of the kinds of strategy that might be played out in a realisation of *Austerity Measures I*.

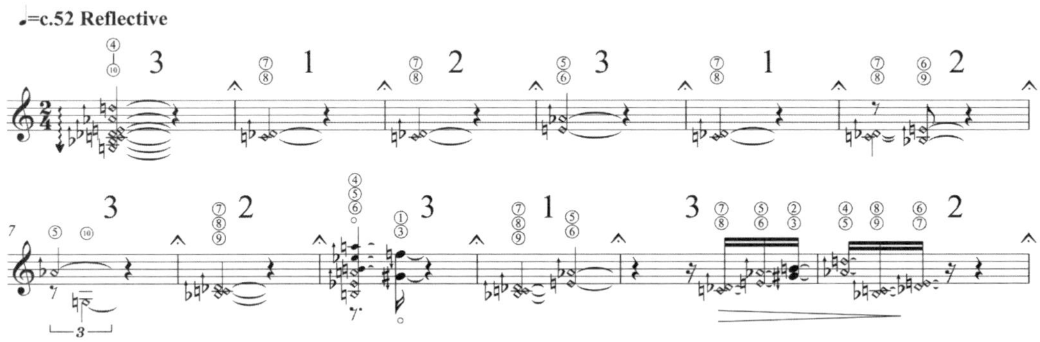

Figure 1.1.

4 The score sounds an octave lower than written.

Figure 1.1. The opening twelve bars of *Austerity Measures I* (Gorton 2018a) with number annotations for a three-times performance.[4]

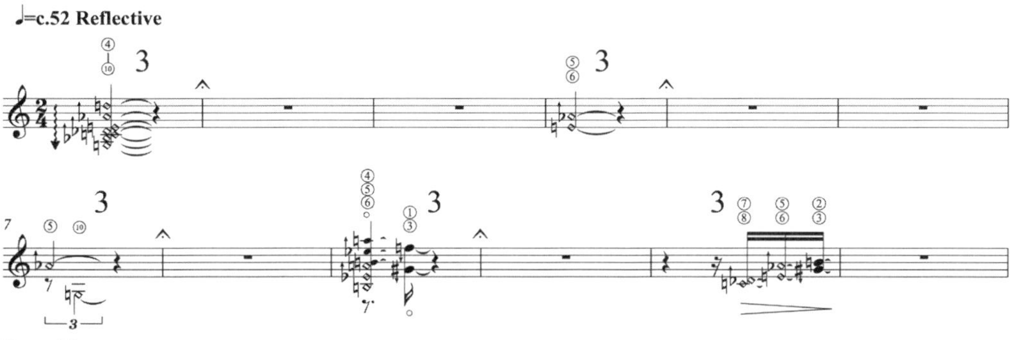

Figure 1.2.

Given that the numbers discussed in the transcript are 1, 2, and 3, it can now be seen that the conversation concerns a version of *Austerity Measures I* with three run-throughs, prepared by Stefan sometime before the start of the rehearsal, and matching the number distribution in figure 1.1. Stefan is concerned about the implications of having labelled bar 7 (and, indeed, bar 4) with the number 3, meaning that the bell-like sequence of C and D-third-tone-♭ figures in bars 2, 3, 5, 6, 8, and 10, so central to the character of the first run-through, would be omitted, resulting in a newly-exposed repetition of an A-third-tone-♭ in bar 4 and then bar 7. He identifies the sounding together of bars 8 and 9 as "the nicest sounding phrase . . . on the whole first line";[5] he is "particularly fond" of bar 9, and he has labelled this bar with a 3 so that it survives the longest. Also discussed is the two-bar phrase in bars 11 to 12, the only pair of bars in this part of the piece not separated by a short pause. Stefan is again concerned with maintaining their identity for as long as possible, thus labelling the two bars with a 3 and a 2 respectively. In the third and final run-through only the first half of this phrase is left, which initially causes him some worry, but after consideration he says that he has "decided to like it." In using the numbering system in this planned manner and attempting to alter his original numbering order in response to perceived problems with their implications, Stefan is using the cutting system of the piece as a compositional tool, identifying materials that he would like to survive the cutting process and trying to create a musical continuity across the silences and cut bars that, to him, makes harmonic and motivic sense.

As already observed, David makes it clear that he is not concerned by the absence of the bell-like dyads, or the repeating A-third-tone-♭; he is instead interested in all the possibilities that the numbering system exposes. The focus of his interest, then, is with the compositional system itself, rather than any specific outcomes from its deployment. This conclusion is supported by the repeated insistence that the decisions within the framework of the system are Stefan's to make, and the intervention when it appears that the rules of the system might be transgressed. The observation that Stefan has already become so attached to certain sonorities that he is attempting to "play the system" in

5 In the formatting of the original score the first line extends up to bar 9.

Figure 1.2. The opening twelve bars of *Austerity Measures I*, as if played through for the third and final time.

order to keep his favourite bits in the piece for as long as possible leads to further discussion later in the rehearsal when trying out a different version of the piece that comprises four run-throughs.

> *DG: There are sixty-four bars. But also, the way the rules work, is that you can . . . the 1s, I bet there are less than a quarter of 1s. How many 1s have you got? [Counting]*
>
> *SÖ: Ten*
>
> *DG: Out of sixty-four. It's really only a sixth missing.*
>
> *SÖ: Cheating a little.*
>
> *DG: Yes. Well, no, because you followed the rules. But it's interesting, the economy of it. Because you have been told to cut a quarter of your operational musical material budget, and you manage to get away with only cutting a sixth. But then you have to pay for it later . . . at some point you end up with quite a heavy cut . . . It's quite devastating by the end.*
>
> *SÖ: Yes, it is. The last round's very . . .*
>
> *DG: And you know it's coming . . .*
>
> *SÖ: I think it's quite nice also to present the material as quite full sounding and not too slow a piece. So, you let it ring, but not to die out, but more like setting big sonorities. That gives you much more space to start cutting.*

In this short section of discussion, the beginnings of the formation of two parts of the strategy for managing the cutting process can be seen. On the one hand, Stefan continues to use the system as a compositional tool kit and, by pushing the meaning of the instruction "approximately equal in distribution throughout," manages to minimise the effects of the first round of cuts in the first repetition by keeping the proportional number of 1s relatively low. As David observes, the implications of this decision will be felt later in the piece when a correspondingly large number of cuts will be implemented in a later repetition. But in addition to the pre-planned and notation-based response to the system of the piece, Stefan discusses a performative response. In keeping the tempo moving and using the resonance of the instrument to build sonority across phrases, he devises a way to approach the start of the piece that will provide a space for him to manage the cuts later on, connecting and shaping the disparate fragments of the later stages of the piece in a manner that is congruent with the earlier stages.

Towards the end of the rehearsal we attempt an experiment that removes the controlled and pre-planned approach to the numbering system by randomly assigning the numbers throughout the score. After Stefan plays this through, both observe that, like the previously planned versions, this new version is also successful. Stefan comments that there were a number of interesting moments where particular fragments had been left next to one another as a result of the cuts, which he might have instinctively avoided had he been planning the number sequence. At the end of the rehearsal this leads to a continuation of the discussion about a performative response to the cuts.

DG: For all these pieces I have wanted to have something which required you to take on some kind of problem-solving as a performer, and that problem-solving becomes a key to interpretation. With Forlorn Hope *it's the ordering of sections and then how you shape things within that, whereas in this it is a matter of how you devise performance strategies that are going to deal with these huge silences. It's a way of activating a different type of interpretation.*

SÖ: There is just one more thing that struck me, because it is kind of interesting what happens when you are presented with a new version that you haven't rehearsed, like now when we just wrote them down. That's a different kind of performance situation where you have to deal with it in real time.

DG: A kind of sight-reading, isn't it.

SÖ: Yes, in a sense, but not . . .

DG: But not so, because you know the material.

SÖ: It's a kind of sight-reading that could make sense. One could *have a computer-based version where you never know what's going to come up. You could actually just make algorithms for this.*

DG: That's true, which would mean that . . .

SÖ: . . . the bars would literally disappear, yes? It could be quite elegant.

DG: And then, live, you have to devise a shaping, nuanced strategy to make that work. I don't know, that could be quite hair-raising couldn't it? I imagine if . . . you've still got to connect the bars that are still there, and at least if you know where the gaps are going to come you can find a shape for that. Whereas, if you don't know how it's going to cut, that could be quite hair-raising. Might be fun though.

SÖ: It could be fun . . . It could be actually quite a cool kind of digital score where bars just come and go.

DG: You see them coming away. That takes the control away from you in a quite interesting way.

SÖ: Yes, it does. It would be an alternative version.

DG: Because even if you do generate these numbers randomly to make the version, you're then practising it, so you do then have a built-in control of how you are going to pace it, shape it, and so on. But if they were just dropping out in front of your eyes, then you would lose all sorts of control. It would become more of an improvisation.

SÖ: Yes, you would have to deal with it on the spot. But you still need to shape it. You might play this bar thinking that you would also be allowed to play that, but in the end it just disappears.

DG: It might disappear when you are just about to articulate the final note. That makes every difference as to exactly how you . . . what you do with it.

SÖ: In some ways it actually illustrates the whole idea of the cuts, or the real austerity measures, because then it is imposed on you. You don't make the choices yourself, but it's just someone saying, I'm sorry we can't afford this bar.

In taking the idea of a random distribution of numbers to its logical conclusion, in which a computer algorithm assigns the cuts randomly and in real time during the performance within the parameters of the instructions, Stefan appears to be changing his position from the concerns voiced at the start of the rehearsal. At the beginning, he is keen to use the cutting system as a compositional tool kit to construct his own versions of the piece; but by the end of the rehearsal he is interested in a live response to randomly generated versions. Yet looked at from a different perspective, these two approaches can be seen as part of the same objective. As David mentions at the start of the previous transcript, the idea behind the existing pieces and the collaboration as a whole is to find ways in which Stefan's "identity" as a musician, broadly conceived, can be brought into the compositions themselves through an act of interpretative problem-solving.[6] In both *Forlorn Hope* and *Austerity Measures I* this was already partly achieved through the co-development of tuning systems and prototype materials in the collaborative "Malmö Sessions" in 2010 (Gorton and Östersjö 2016; see also Clarke et al. 2017). But the varying approaches seen throughout the first rehearsal of *Austerity Measures I* in 2013 can all be seen as part of the same goal: an exploration of the ways in which aspects of the performer's musical "identity" can be brought to bear in the piece, whether through a notation-based constructionist approach, a performative response, or a combination of the two.

Up to this point the spoken voices of the performer and composer, transcribed from a video recording of a rehearsal, have been used to illustrate the evolving discourse within the collaboration. The rest of this chapter, however, will explore aspects of these voices that remain unspoken, but that nevertheless constitute important signifiers of our "identities" as musicians. Part 1 will outline a theoretical model of the subjective "voices" of performer and composer, which become manifest in the complex interrelation between artists, instruments, notation, and the contexts of traditions and practices.[7] These "voices" will be explored through the way they combine within a collaboration to form a "discursive voice" (Gorton and Östersjö 2016). Part 2 will aim to access evidence of "voice" through an analysis of four recorded performances of *Austerity Measures I*, given by Stefan Östersjö at the ORCiM Research Festival in 2014. The analysis draws on quantitative measures of timing and qualitative measures of perceived phrasing structures and performance gestures. Each of these analytical methods provides insight into the performance strategies that are discussed in the above transcripts, and then used in the performance recordings, in the shaping of phrases as materials are cut away and in the structural significance of bodily movement. But a much richer understanding can be sought

6 The ways in which a performer's identity is often already manifested "in" a composition is further discussed in the next chapter, by Catherine Laws. Also see the discussion in chapter four on the collaboration between The Six Tones and the composer Kent Olofsson.

7 The use of the word "voice" in this chapter does not refer directly to its usage in Edward Cone's *The Composer's Voice* (1974) or Carolyn Abbate's *Unsung Voices* (1991), although the metaphors therein of personas and bodies remain relevant. But rather than seeking "voices" within the scores of musical works themselves, this chapter is concerned with "voice" as a manifestation of the artistic identities of musicians, particularly collaborating musicians, which may become apparent in musical materials in written or sounding forms.

through the combination of quantitative and qualitative analytical methods; in doing so, the analysis aims to shed light on the interrelations between the embodied knowledge of the performer and the musical structures in the score and, further, between the subjectivities of composer and performer unfolded through the composition and performance of *Austerity Measures I*.

Part 1: Collaboration and the discursive voice

The argument that underpins this chapter and that is evidenced throughout this book is the claim that artistic knowledge takes shape both in the materiality of an artwork and as performative knowledge embodied by the artist. With a foundation in theories of material thinking, this entails several forms of "thinking-in-art" (Merleau-Ponty 1964) and "thinking-through-art," where the latter suggests a further communication across artistic, embodied, and discursive domains (Östersjö 2017).[8] Artistic knowledge, expressed through the materiality of an artwork, often takes shape through the singularity of its instantiation, such as is manifest in a painting or a musical score. Indeed, examples of material artwork that have multiple instantiations, such as the revisions and republications of pieces by Stravinsky and Boulez (to name just two cases from the many throughout musical history), can generate ontological confusion because of their resistance to taxonomy. Artistic practice could thus be said to emerge through a continual oscillation between such singularities and the iterative and citational practice characteristic of performance (ibid.). Barbara Bolt claims that "[although] operating against the backdrop of convention, re-iteration and citation produce repetition with difference, rather than repetition of the same" (2016, 137; see also chapter 2, below). What might be understood as a "performance practice" or "tradition" could be described as a framework of knowledge that is both formed by these processes and simultaneously establishes the prerequisite conditions within which this oscillation can take place. Artistic practice thus adds to the tradition within which it operates through the accumulation of new knowledge.

While knowledge is usually drawn from qualitative and quantitative research methods, Brad Haseman (2006) proposes an epistemology of artistic research that claims a third form: a performative paradigm. The truth claims within the performative paradigm are not related to repeatable testing, as with the other two forms of knowledge, but are instead situated within a specific context and validated through measures of force and effect (Bolt 2016). Performative knowledge belongs to the sphere of tacit knowledge (Polanyi 1967), taking shape within the context of a specific artistic event and remaining as embodied knowledge, sedimented in the artist's body.[9] This raises the fundamental ques-

8 The nature of such communication across domains of knowledge may, as suggested by Greenhalgh and Wierenga (2011), be characterised by both harmony and discord; and it entails an entire field of analogical thinking, translation, and, as phrased by Latour (2013), diplomacy between "modes of existence." A further study of the nature of such diplomacy is implicit in the project discussed in this chapter but lies beyond its present scope.

9 This understanding of artistic knowledge draws on the theory of embodied cognition, discussed further below, in which mind and body are considered as one.

tion of how such knowledge can be accessed intellectually and communicated, beyond the recognised performative and demonstrative situations of rehearsal, concert performance, and instrumental teaching, and to what extent, and with what methods, this tacit knowing can be translated into discursive knowledge. The philosopher Helena De Preester notes how "in performance, the body abruptly and explicitly comes into visibility and resists forms of objectification that may put it to rest, to clarity and obviousness" (2007, 352).[10] Any analytical engagement with performative knowledge must therefore develop methods to overcome this resistance.

The distinction between body image and body schema is helpful in understanding the multi-layered human body. The body image may be thought of as the explicit understanding that we have of our own bodies. It is an intentional state made up of several modalities: perceptual experiences of one's own body; conceptual understandings of the body in general; and emotional attitudes towards one's own body (De Preester 2007, 355). On the level of the body image, performative knowledge may be accessible through introspection and reflexive research methods, such as is common in autobiographical forms of artistic research. The body schema, on the other hand, involves "a system of motor capacities, abilities, and habits" (Gallagher and Cole 1995, 371) and is thus often unintentional or subconscious in character. An inquiry into the formation of embodied knowledge on the level of the body schema could also be approached through reflexive methods, but such an inquiry is more thoroughly conducted through combining these with observation and measurement. Hence, a discursive understanding of performative knowledge can only fully be accessed through interaction with other paradigms, employing both qualitative and quantitative research methods.

This chapter approaches the question of subjectivity in the musical practice of composer and performer through a discussion of the emergence of "voice," arguing that a musician's "voice" is continually defined through interaction with technological and psychological tools, such as scores and musical instruments or compositional and notational systems, respectively.[11] As previously described, the outcomes of artistic research can be situated in a field between the singular (represented in the materiality of the artwork) and the iterative (manifested in performance); artistic research thus offers a possibility to embrace the three knowledge paradigms. The composition *Austerity Measures I* is useful in developing an understanding of subjectivity and performative knowledge because the circumstances of its development and performances

10 Further perspectives on the multiplicity that characterises the role of the body in performance, how it is on the one hand a discursive construct and on the other an affective percept, and how it simultaneously embraces the personal and impersonal are found in chapters two and four, with reference to the work of Peggy Phelan and again to Helena De Preester.

11 Vygotsky (1978) analyses the role of technological tools, or, artefacts (like musical instruments and scores) and psychological tools, which often have a semiotic nature (like gesture, language, or compositional systems) as mediators of activity. Essentially, this builds on the observation of how tools are externally oriented, which "must lead to changes in objects" (55), while signs (or other psychological tools) are internally oriented, towards behavioural processes in oneself or in someone else. Further, both tools and signs are culturally situated, a situatedness that we will discuss further below as part of an attempt to further unpack their agencies.

both resists the notion of singular instantiation and, at the same time, necessitates iteration and citation within its compositional structure. Issues of "voice" and performative knowledge are thus reified within it, as a single performance of *Austerity Measures I* establishes a "micro-tradition" within which these issues can be seen to operate. It is therefore hoped that *Austerity Measures I* can function as a laboratory for the study of subjectivity, and that the findings from the particular circumstances of the piece may be applicable to a broader range of musical practices.

In her posthumously published book *The Sonic Self*, Naomi Cumming explores a semiological understanding of listening to music, and in so doing sheds light on the subjectivities inherent within musical performance:

> To a musician, it is hardly news that subjectivities may be attributed to music itself: tones of voice, with their emotional connotations, appearing in sound; affective states, suggested by gestural action, heard in the shaping of a melodic segment; aspects of willed direction found in the impetus of tonal harmony. The musician's work is to master these potentialities on a given instrument and to work with them in accordance with the requirements of a style, drawing out the possibilities of a composed musical moment by making his or her choices of sound, emphasis, and tempo. Something of the musician's own "character" will be heard in the choices he or she makes, in the patterns of emphasis that constitute a performance style. So it is that his or her own "subjectivity" appears. (Cumming 2000, 9)

Cumming (2000) describes the finding of her own musical character, her "voice," upon acquiring a new violin as a teenager: "When I began to play it, the sound of this new violin seemed to draw from me something I did not know I possessed. It was as if the violin had the potential to become the voice I lacked. This was quite a discovery, not made fully in a moment of time but over a couple of years" (3). Through her lessons with the leader of the second violins in the Melbourne Symphony Orchestra she begins to make sense of what this "voice" is, and how it relates to her instrument: "What he sought, somehow, was an identification of his students with the sound of the violin as a voice that could be expressive of their own passion, and yet a cultivated distance that would allow them also to draw out the best in the violin's tone, in a critical stance that recognized it as more than a projection of their subjective states" (4). For Cumming, her subjective "voice" is therefore a result of both a bodily and emotional relationship with her instrument, but also something separate, that can be listened to with critical detachment: "a relationship with the violin's sound can include the idea of projecting a 'voice' that is one's own, and also of standing apart to listen to the sound as the 'voice' of another" (5).

Accessing and analysing a musician's "voice" must consider the perspective of music perception, which has been shown to be multi-modal (Livingstone and Thompson 2006), with direct connections drawn between the visual perception of physical movement in performance and the aural perception of sonic results (Henbing and Leman 2007; Desmet et al. 2012; Thompson, Graham, and Russo 2005). Such perception is stored as motor-mimetic images of movement, action, and sounds (Godøy 2006), and thereby cognition is embedded in an environment, enacted, and put into practice through action (Varela, Thompson, and Rosch 1991; Barsalou 2008). Arguing that we project intentions to music in the same way as in other social interaction, Marc Leman states that "musical communication is based on the sharing of neural structures that pertain to movement" (2008, 161). Similarly, Livingstone and Thompson argue that musical creativity "emerges from our capacity to engage with symbolic hierarchical systems, our desire for affective social communication, and a reflexive motivation to explore our identity" (2006, 92), concluding that our musical capacities are founded in how we learn affective cues during infancy.

According to the theory of situated cognition, all types of knowledge are "inextricably a product of the activity and situations in which they are produced" (Brown, Collins, and Duguid 1989, 33) and thereby, the source for subjectivity is located in the interaction between the human body and the environment. Varela, Thompson, and Rosch, building on the results of experiments on human perception of concrete objects (Rosch et al. 1976), argue along similar lines that "the basic level of categorization, thus, appears to be the point at which cognition and environment become simultaneously enacted. The object appears to the perceiver as affording certain kinds of interactions, and the perceiver uses the objects with his body and mind in the afforded manner" (Varela, Thompson, and Rosch 1991, 177). If, as found by Rosch et al. (1976), there are basic-level objects with which we interact, "the activities performed by the perceiver/actor with basic-level objects are part of the cultural, consensually validated forms of the life of the community in which the human and the object is situated—they are basic-level activities" (Varela, Thompson, and Rosch 1991, 177). A perspective from ecological psychology is found in James Gibson's concept of affordances, which assumes a similar link between action and perception: "the affordances of the environment are what it offers the animal, what it provides or furnishes for good or ill" (Gibson 1986, 127). Following Chris Stover, musical subjectivity can be considered to be formed through performance, and is "irreducibly connected to the ecological conditions" or the affordances of musical materials through action and perception: "the ways in which their identities come to be constructed are intricately connected to the performative utterances they are making and the variable ways they are taking up those utterances and folding them into their emergent processes of becoming" (Stover 2016).

For a consideration of the agencies at play in musical creativity, two non-human agents are of central importance for the present chapter (and indeed each of the following chapters): musical instruments and scores. Alperson (2008) notes that musical instruments typically are understood as "discrete, self-subsisting material objects, intentionally crafted for the purpose of making music by performing musicians" (38). However, he moves on to suggest that this ontology is insufficient, on the one hand because of the very immediate inter-dependence between the physical object and the performer's body and, on the other, in the ways that instruments are musically, culturally, and conceptually situated. With reference to these further perspectives, a recent review chapter by Sarah-Indriyati Hardjowirogo (2017) suggests a number of parameters of the "instrumentality" of an object, which contribute to defining it as a musical instrument. Just as in Alperson's initial definition, the first parameter is an ability for sound production. She continues by noting, second, how the emergence of digital instruments has increased the complexity in this understanding, since the sound-producing device may then typically be distinct from the physical interface. This second point identifies both the maker's and the performer's intentions as necessary for defining instrumentality, with reference to McCaleb's (2014) discussion of performer intention as essentially decisive for when a turntable, or similar borderline object, is deemed to be instrumental or non-instrumental. Third, the object's learnability and possibilities for virtuosity (Jordà 2004) is a perspective that defines instrumentality through the relative impact of practising, which Jordà refers to as its efficiency. Virtuosity has been discussed as a musician's ability to transcend the physical constraints of body and instrument, either with a display of ease that can extend to an Orphic expression of the sublime or to a Promethean mastering of a perceived conflict between instrument and the performer's body (Monteiro 2007). At this point, Hardjowirogo arrives at more complex and interwoven perspectives, where effort, corporeality, and interaction come into play. Here, effort and resistance (Evens 2005; Östersjö 2008, 2013) are of particular importance, and the relation between the poles of efficiency and effort will be explored below through the notions of resonance and resistance (Östersjö 2013). These perspectives entail the relation between expressivity in musical performance and the degree of perceived effort that is projected to an audience.

However, digital instruments have come to question the role of effort in musical expression, which leads to the ways in which instrumentality is culturally situated, a concept discussed extensively by Alperson (2008). He argues that, although acoustic instruments immediately appear to be material objects, musical instruments are indeed "objects whose creation and whose musical capabilities are infused with information and conceptual structures that reflect the history and styles of musical sounds" (41). What is understood as a musical instrument is thus dependent not merely on its physical features but also on the specific cultural definitions of music and the means with which music is made.[12] Therefore, it can be argued that, in ethnographic research on musical instruments, rather than creating organological schemes for comparative study of instruments, "schemes constructed and used by the people who built and played the instruments should be used wherever possible" (Dawe 2003, 276).

All this suggests that the interaction between performer and instrument is interwoven with the specific musical culture in which they are situated, as well as with the particular embodiment of the particular performer. Alperson (2008) gives a number of examples of the latter; for example, he observes that Chet Baker's dental status laid the grounds for both his playing style and sound, as well as for his choice to shift instrument in the later end of his career (39–40), one of countless possible examples of the continuum between the instrumen-

12 Catherine Laws discusses the instrumentality of the piano in chapter 2, and further cultural and historical perspectives on such instrumentalities are added to the discussion in chapters 3 and 4.

tality of the performer's body and of an object intentionally created as a musical instrument.

This is where ecological psychology and Gibson's concept of affordances (1986) are particularly useful in unpacking the agency of musical instruments. For Gibson, affordances may have both natural and cultural origin, as De Souza (2017, 13) discusses in an example that notes how the pitches on a guitar "become higher when the vibrating portion of the string is shortened, and each string affords harmonics at the octave, at the twelfth, and so on: these are physical invariants based in the acoustic properties of oscillating strings. Fret placement and tuning involve cultural invariants, the products of musical tradition. The fretboard is designed for hands, resonating with human physiology, but it also demands learned cultural techniques."

The extent to which the concept of affordances is useful for the analysis of human perception and interaction with complex cultural objects—such as musical instruments—has been debated, and the additional concept of effectivities has been developed to better understand the ways in which, for instance, a musician's specific abilities can be developed in order to discover novel affordances in an instrument. Windsor and de Bézenac (2012) argue that "the development or application of novel effectivities can, thereby, promote the emergence of action possibilities that could not have been foreseen by the instrument's original designers and primary users" (110). Again, an instrument affords different musical possibilities to every performer, even to the degree that the instrument may even be said to be constituted only in the interaction with a performer, as in the interdependency of brass and wind instruments with the bodily constitution of the player. The affordances of an instrument are as dependent on the individual performer as on the acoustic properties of the instrument.[13] Windsor and de Bézenac provide a further reminder that musicians do not always follow the path of least resistance. Rather, they "often go to great lengths to overcome bodily and instrumental constraints in order to achieve particular aesthetic or functional goals" (ibid., 109). As also discussed by Alperson (2008), a musician's choice of a particular instrument is often related to finding the right balance between ease and resistance: an instrument's limitations may be what creates the particular "fit" that makes a musician travel with this particular instrument to every performance. Hence, a musician exploring the affordances of an instrument will learn how to play with the resistances and the affordances of this particular guitar or saxophone. This process may call for many thousands of rehearsal hours and will always be situated in a particular cultural context, like the performance practices embraced by teachers and fellow musicians.[14]

13 This is further apparent in chapter 2, where the relation between pianist and piano is discussed in depth by Catherine Laws. Chapter 3 adds to this discussion the possibility of a negotiation between several performer's voices (as represented in audio recordings) in the formation of voice in the recording studio, while chapter 4 gives extensive examples of how the affordances of instruments also are defined by cultural resistance, as embodied through a performer's habitus.

14 In a study by Ericsson, Krampe, and Tesch-Romer (1993), high-level violinists were shown to have completed more than ten thousand rehearsal hours by the age of twenty. See also Ericsson and Charness (1994).

In the argument presented in this chapter, rather than the concept of effectivities, we propose a more substantially grounded understanding of these culturally and socially embedded processes with reference to the formation of a performer's *habitus*, a concept that can be broadly understood to encompass combined prior knowledge, muscle memory, and habits that influence and shape decision-making and live response. Such embeddedness of practice within an individual is drawn as much from Bourdieu's sociological theory as from the phenomenological philosophy of Merleau-Ponty (see Coessens and Östersjö 2014). Naomi Cumming (2000) discusses these microstructures of signification and observes how a "combination of nuance and timbral characteristics produces a perception of 'voice'" (167).

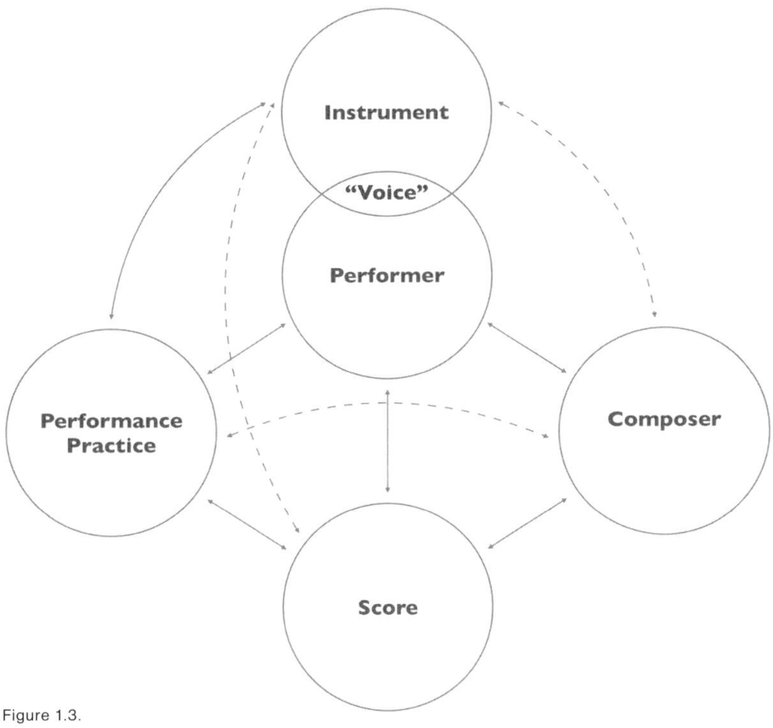

Figure 1.3.

Figure 1.3 is adapted from a previous article (Gorton and Östersjö 2016, 584) and represents the complex entanglement of interconnections that constitute a performer's "voice." Central to this model is the physical relationship between a musician and his or her instrument. Edward Cone identified the importance of this relationship in his original discussions of the "composer's voice," stating of performance that the "effect should not be that the player is improvising the music, but that the music is composing itself through the combined agency of player and instrument" (Cone 1974, 129).[15] It is her instrument, the violin,

15 See also Hunter (2005), as further discussed in chapter two.

Figure 1.3. Relationships that constitute the formation of a performer's "voice."

that Cumming identifies as the source of her artistic "voice," controlled by her physical interactions with the instrument but also something separate from her that can be listened to critically. In the rehearsal described in the introduction, Stefan's first thoughts about a performative response are concerned with the characteristics of his instrument. By keeping the tempo not too slow he is able to use the ten-string guitar's resonant properties to build sonorities and let the materials ring, and this forms the basis of a strategy for connecting and shaping phrases across the cut bars. The problem-solving character of the live response required in a performance of *Austerity Measures I* is thus derived from what the particular instrument can do (its affordances, i.e., the resonant qualities) and what it cannot do (its resistances, i.e., an inability, for example, to sustain a legato line across the gaps) but also, crucially, from Stefan's intimate knowledge and deployment of these characteristics.

Interactions between performers and their instruments are combined with other interactions in the formation of a performer's "voice": with composers, with musical scores, and with the contextual practices within which the performer operates. If the composer is alive and willing to engage with the work of the performer, then this interaction may form the basis of a dialogic collaboration of a kind represented in the previous transcripts and the "Malmö Sessions."[16] In commenting on the "Malmö Sessions" as described in Clarke et al. (2017), Nicholas Cook observes that "we might describe this as a creative assemblage on the model of Deleuze's own example: COMPOSER-PERFORMER-GUITAR" (Cook 2018, 61). While the diagram in figure 1.3 (and further diagrams below) can be seen as expansions of this assemblage, what seems immediately useful is how Cook's observation allows for an immediate negotiation of "voice" between a composer and a performer, mediated through an instrument. Otherwise, an interaction with a composer might be sought via engagement with scores, or indirectly through the performance practices associated with the composer.

In any performance of a notated piece of music the performer forms an engagement with the codified information of the score. In describing E. T. A. Hoffmann's concept of *Werktreue*, Lydia Goehr proposed that within this historical context "a musical work is held to be a composer's unique, objectified expression, a public and permanently existing artefact made up of musical elements (typically tones, dynamics, rhythms, harmonies, and timbres). A work is fixed with respect, at least, to the properties indicated in the score and it is repeatable in performances. Performances themselves are transitory sound events intended to present a work by complying as closely as possible with the given notational specifications" (Goehr 1989, 55). This has proved to be a powerful and enduring concept within both music criticism and professional practice, resulting in the former in extensive historical and philosophical discourse across decades. Within professional practice and training it is still common to hear phrases such as "composer's intentions" and "being true to the

16 Chapter 3, below, exemplifies and explores these kinds of interactions, with the additional complication that the composer in that instance is, in a sense, both alive and dead (or, at least, lost).

score" spoken in earnest and uncritically. But these concepts have also been deconstructed in ways that are useful for creating a more dynamic understanding of the agencies of composer and performer; indeed, *Austerity Measures I* can be viewed as such a deconstruction.[17]

In *Shut Up 'n' Play! Negotiating the Musical Work*, Östersjö turns to Paul Ricœur to unpack the role of interpretation in musical performance, arguing that a composer, just like the author of a verbal text, is disengaged from the work in the act of writing: "the meaning of the musical work is not equal to the intention of the composer. The construction of a score-based work consists of dialectic interplay between creation and interpretation, in which the composer—even during the act of writing—has to approach the notation by means of interpretation. This is also the reason why we encounter a surplus of meaning in scores" (Östersjö 2008, 57–58).[18] Hence, interpretation is an integral part of musical composition; it is not to be understood merely as constituting the role either of a performer of a scored work or of the act of listening. As observed by Roger Sessions ([1950] 1971, 4), "composer, performer, and listener can, without undue exaggeration, be regarded not only as three types or degrees of relationship to music, but also as three successive stages of specialization. In the beginning, no doubt, the three were one." The Western history of specialisation, and in particular the division of the musician into composer and performer has been critically discussed by Trevor Wishart, who identifies the source of this divide in the invention of musical notation and, further, in the specific limitations the Western notation system has, with its focus on pitch and duration: "The novel split which gradually emerges between composer and performer, between a score and its 'interpretation' is the concrete realisation in musical praxis of the perceptual focusing upon notatable parameters" (Wishart 1985, 21). But, following Ricœur, the observation of how interpretation is an integral part of the act of composition can be taken further into what Ricœur calls "the world of the text," which he proposes is meaning that is projected in front of the text but that is not equal to authorial intention. In "the world of the text," "reading is no longer simply listening. It is governed by *codes* comparable to the grammatical code that guides the understanding of sentences. In the case of the narrative, these codes are precisely the ones that a structural analysis brings to light under the title of narrative codes" (Ricœur 1991, 130). Analytical interpretation then appears to be a necessary tool for composers and performers in approaching "the world of the text" of a musical score. Rather than assigning interpretation to the practice of performance, and creation to the practice of composition, a more useful perspective is one that identifies the

17 A different approach to what is outlined here, which proposes a Deleuzian move from interpretation to experimentation and develops a range of artistic approaches from this philosophical starting point, is the recent European Research Council project hosted at the Orpheus Institute, MusicExperiment21. The theory and practice are discussed in several publications and through artistic outputs (Assis 2018; D'Errico 2018). In the present volume, see also chapter 3, section 1.2.

18 Of course, Ricœur's theory of narrative coincides in many respects with the broader post-structuralist critique. However, his focus on the relationship between the author and the "instrumentality" of written language is essential in Östersjö's application of Ricœur's analysis to the technology of musical notation, and thereby to musical creativity.

very fabric of these processes as they are embodied by musicians, and how they in turn are activated in the interactions with technological and psychological tools, such as compositional systems, scores, and instruments. This is where the notion of "thinking-through-music," as discussed above, allows for a more holistic understanding of how artistic knowledge takes shape through musical practice.

John Butt's discussion of intentionality in musical creativity is useful in its aim to rehabilitate an appreciation of "the latent *intentionality* in music as an art to be performed, something that can be distinguished from the more local concept of 'the composer's intentions'" (2002, 94). He guides the reader through the heated debates between analytical philosophers like Peter Kivy and musicologists like Taruskin, and introduces the inferential criticism of intention as put forth by Baxandall (1985), a critique that focuses not on a reconstruction of intention in a human agent but suggests instead that intentionality resides also in the non-human agencies at play in the creative process. Hence, Butt argues that such an understanding of intentionality would allow for a more dynamic perspective on composer's intentions, the value of which must always be critically assessed, while we "should imagine pieces as the result of an infinite sequence of decisions. This helps us to temper the view of musical works as static, timeless objects and allows us to see them as something much closer to the process of performance itself" (Butt 2002, 85).

A practical step, deriving from Wishart's comment (above), is to observe that within Goehr's list of musical elements it is tones (pitches) and their structural organisation (harmonies) that have dominated analytical engagement with musical works and that have the strongest claim to the objectified and fixed status of the work concept (although it is recognised that the relationship between the two is here oversimplified). Of the other elements listed, their exactitude within common notational practice is such that in transitory performances their repeatability is subject to significant variation: while rhythmic notation presents structures of relative values, the other characteristics pertaining to time within which these values are understood are open to flexibility; dynamic indications, where given at all, operate on a relative, but non-fixed, six- or eight-point volume scale with transitions (but no envelope information) between them; information regarding timbre, beyond specific instrument identification, is usually limited to adjectival description and technical instruction.

When a performer approaches a score, there are many personal decisions that need to be made in relation to the combination of these elements, at a moment-to-moment level, in the connection of notes and phrases to one another, and across the shaping of a whole section, movement, or piece. At times, such decisions could be said to take a compositional, or at least editorial, character in their own right. Stefan's relationship with the score of *Austerity Measures I* in the above transcripts certainly takes on a compositional character; and, indeed, the instructions for the piece demand such a level of engagement. As seen above, two types of score-based engagement form part of the discussions: the construction of a preferred version by means of the structuring opportunities the score provides and, later, a less controlled response to what is effectively random selection. Each type of engagement with the score triggers a different set of decisions at the instrument in finding ways to connect together and shape the disparate materials.

The kinds of personal decisions that performers make in their engagement with scores are not made in a vacuum. Rather, they are shaped and moderated by the socially constructed contexts within which they work: their performance practices. Such practices form a shared understanding of the style of a work or a composer's oeuvre and thereby establish guidelines within which decisions might be made. Thus, while there are no dynamic markings given at all in the opening of the Breitkopf und Härtel edition of the Beethoven Romance in F, op. 50, a shared understanding of the piece itself and the broader implications of the given performance direction *Adagio cantabile* would prohibit a very loud and strident opening and provide a range within which personal decisions might be taken. A quick listen to the opening bars of the Romance in F from a range of commercially available recordings would reveal a variety of dynamic levels, tempi, shaping of the turn, stretching of the dotted rhythms, and speed of vibrato, but all within an arguably constrained range of similarity of approaches.

Performance practices are transmitted aurally through the pedagogical work of one-to-one or group instrumental tuition found within the professional training contexts of music conservatoires and pre-tertiary-level tuition found in some schools and private practices, and they are continued through the rehearsal and performance of music. It remains a powerful concept that such transmission can be seen to claim a kind of genealogical authority—"my teacher's teacher's teacher knew Brahms"—in which an aural tradition that sits alongside a printed score is deemed to provide access to the originating composer. Through the analysis of performances in a range of early and modern recordings, Daniel Leech-Wilkinson (1984, 2012) has argued that, on the one hand, performance practices of today show significant differences to those in evidence on early recordings and, on the other hand, that contemporary recordings show very little variety in performance choices, thus critiquing the concepts of aural transmission and authenticity. In more recent publications Leech-Wilkinson has voiced particular concern about those areas of the classical music infrastructure that moderate performance practice, such as music examinations, international competitions, and music journalism, claiming that collectively these create an oppressive environment that aims to homogenise musical performance (Leech-Wilkinson 2017). Still, the complex interactions that contribute to the formation of performance practices can be seen in a rather more positive light, providing opportunity for a citational practice within which personal performance decisions can be made. In the booklet notes for his box-set recording of the thirty-two Beethoven piano sonatas, pianist Daniel-Ben Pienaar proposes just such an approach, in opposition to the idea of a homogenised Beethoven style:

> The alternative—of the player yielding to the instinct to communicate first of all (rather than to present an image of Beethoven-as-creator and himself-as-interpreter first of all)—implies manipulating pulse and tempo actively, on impulse or "as if" on impulse; of adventurously exploring sonorities to discover the colouristic and atmospheric potential of the material at hand; of harnessing details of touch and enunciation in the service of distinctive diction. In other words, to forge a whole world of human experience in all its unpredictable variety, the performer must collect a whole storehouse of pianistic and expressive tools. Gathering these devices is part of playing the canonical game because it requires, not least, an awareness of, even a confrontation with, performances and performance practices past and present—with the rich and ever-changing history of Beethoven reception and its manifestation in performance. (Pienaar 2015, 6–7)

By drawing on the characteristics of Beethoven performances by a range of different pianists, such as Emil Gilels, Wilhelm Kempff, Artur Schnabel, Annie Fischer, Samuil Feinberg, and even performers, like Vladimir Horowitz, who are "not conventionally thought of as 'natural' Beethoven players" (7), Pienaar is able to construct a framework of possibilities for materials in the sonatas that "share a family resemblance" (ibid.), such as minuets or toccata-like sections, and thus deploy a paradigmatic method of citation across the cycle as a whole. Such an approach resonates with Naomi Cumming's description of "subjects," which she states "are formed by participation in the social media of gesture, language, or music—media that provide a repertoire of possible choices—within which they achieve their personal 'style'" (Cumming 2000, 10).

In the rehearsal of *Austerity Measures I* described above, Stefan's different types of engagement with the score need to be understood within the performance practice contexts in which he works. With extensive experience in performing contemporary music, both as a soloist and as a member of a range of ensembles, and working closely with a large number of composers in collaborative capacities that include editorial work,[19] and working also as an experienced improviser in the context of "free improvisation" and in intercultural collaboration, he has a wide range of embodied approaches to music-making, within and beyond the framework of score-based music.[20] Stefan's initial responses to the cutting process of the piece are thus shaped by the "habitus" of a performer situated in a wide range of contemporary music practices: his identification of the repeating bell-like sonorities as a motivic device and his worries about replacing this device with exposed repetitions of a different pitch both derive from an intimate understanding of this context. But so too is his later interest in randomised versions of the piece and his strategies for shaping the fragmentary materials that he brings to bear in performance.

19 For example, as a part of his doctoral work on composer–performer collaborations, Stefan edited and then recorded the complete guitar works of Per Nørgård (Östersjö 2008).

20 These various capacities are evident in chapters 2 and 4, below, in addition to the present discussion.

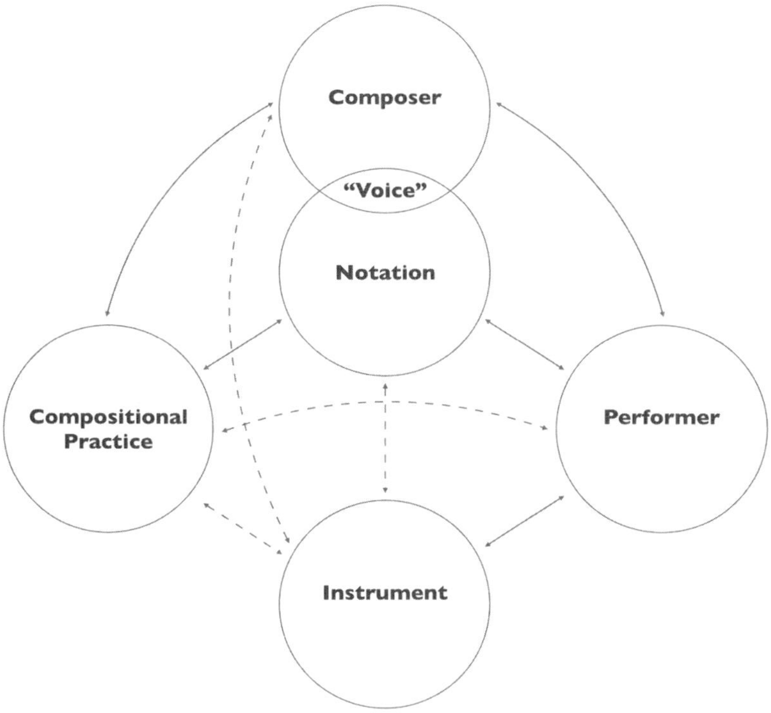

Figure 1.4.

Figure 1.4 attempts to represent the complex interactions of the previous image from the perspective of a composer (adapted from Gorton and Östersjö 2016). If performers' physical relationships with their instruments and their interactions with the affordances and resistances of those instruments can be seen as central to the formation of their "voices," so too composers' relationships with their own notations are central to the formation of their "voices." In cases where a composer's notation has a particular calligraphic or graphic quality, this relationship can similarly be intensely physical. Like a relationship with an instrument, a composer's relationship with notation involves interactions with the affordances and resistances of notational conventions. On the one hand, these conventions can provide ready solutions for how abstract musical ideas might be organised and developed and might even drive the formation of the ideas themselves. But on the other hand, some abstract musical ideas may resist being shaped into the conventions of common-practice notation; and while such notation has shown significant scope for development and evolution, new innovations have a reciprocal cost in a relative diminishing of easy comprehension. For example, any music that aims to divide the octave into a number of equal parts other than twelve or multiples of twelve, or that aims to change the number of divisions of the octave in different registers, will meet resistance from the standard forms of notating pitch.

Figure 1.4. Relationships that constitute the formation of a composer's "voice."

In considering his views on the necessary conditions for notation to adequately define a musical work, composer Brian Ferneyhough (1995) observes three characteristics. First, notation offers "a *sound-picture* of the events for which it stands"; and, second, it offers "all essential . . . instructions for a *valid reproduction*" in performance (4). Notwithstanding that the first of these characteristics seems to discount forms of notation that are *only* instructions, such as tablature or text-based notations, and that the second of these characteristics seems to discount forms of notation with *no* or few instructions, such as graphic scores, the two characteristics are similar to the two purposes of notation proposed by Charles Seeger in 1958: "one provides a blueprint for the performer, and the other records in writing what has actually occurred in sound" (Nettl 1983, 68). Ferneyhough's third characteristic is really a measure of how the first two characteristics balance against one another in any given instant, thus incorporating "in and through the conflation and mutual resonance of the two elements already mentioned, an *implied ideology of its own process of creation*" (Ferneyhough 1995, 4). It is in this balancing between the sound-image and performer-instructions qualities of notation that personal compositional decisions are made, becoming inscribed along with their ideological frameworks in the notation itself. Thus, where it might be reasonably considered that abstract musical ideas inform the musical notation that represents them, so too a composer's musical notation might be considered to inform their abstract musical ideas. It is in such interactions that a composer's "voice" might be found.

In *Austerity Measures I* the concept of cutting materials and replacing them with rests across a sequence of repetitions imposed a number of requirements upon the notation. On the one hand, it needed to allow the instructions for the cutting process to be easily applied; but, on the other hand, within this simplicity there needed to be a very large number of possible permutations. By using the single bar as the unit of cutting it was possible to organise materials into single articulations, or small groups of articulations that then undergo the cutting process as in figures 1.1 and 1.2, but also to span phrases across several bars which are then disintegrated into fragments in the cutting process, as occurs later in the piece (see below). But this notational solution in turn imposed significant restrictions upon the types of material that could be developed in the composition of *Austerity Measures I*, not only in terms of their rhythmic and metrical complexity but also by demanding a consistency of character to account for the high number of possible juxtapositions that could occur as a result of the cuts. While the notation for *Austerity Measures I* could therefore be said to be derived from the abstract idea of the piece, so too the musical materials of the piece could be said to be derived in part from the restrictions placed on them by the notation. In the transcripts of the rehearsal presented at the start of this chapter, the ways in which the cutting process interacts with the notation through the use of annotated numbers is central to the discussions. Although David is deliberately disengaged with the ways in which the cutting process is played out in the different versions, consistently stating that the decisions regarding outcomes are Stefan's to make, he is concerned that there is fidelity to the cutting process itself and to the instructions that govern it.

As in the previous model, further interactions combine in the formation of a composer's "voice." While performers may well spend their entire careers performing music by dead composers, whom they thus never interact with in person, composers can only have their music performed by performers who are living at the time, although of course they may compose music without interacting with performers, or indeed without thinking about them at all at a personal level.[21] But as with the previous model, where interactions with performers do take place, these may form the basis of a dialogic collaboration of a kind represented in the above transcripts.

For composers, access to instruments in a direct and concrete sense is often only gained through interaction with a performer, and many of the various models of composer–performer collaboration have therefore focused on testing materials at the instrument. Fitch and Heyde (2007) comment that such "collaboration is frequently a matter of the performer giving the composer access to his 'box of tricks'" (73), although it has been shown elsewhere that this kind of interaction can be exceptionally fluid in character (Clarke et al. 2017). Of course, without interaction with a performer, composers still have extremely detailed conceptions of the instruments that they are writing for, even if they are unable to play those instruments themselves. These conceptions can, at times, be highly innovative, changing and adding to the fundamental understanding of what an instrument is. In this respect, Helmut Lachenmann's comment that composing can be understood as "building an instrument" has been widely cited (1996, 77). But even at one degree removed, instruments provide affordances and resistances for the composer. By virtue of its many strings, the ten-string guitar affords possibilities for sustaining resonances and microtonal tuning. But instrumental configuration provides limitations too. Some of these are discrete limitations, such as the impossibility of playing a note lower than the lowest string, but others are more graduated: for example, it is impossible to move from one end of the fingerboard to the other instantly, but it is possible to execute that movement very fast, as long as the movement is situated within an enabling context. When a ten-string guitar is tuned to a microtonal scordatura, one of its typical affordances, of allowing many possible fingerings for each single note—what De Souza (2017) analyses as the *many-to-one* mapping in the instrument's key-class space—is shifted to a *one-to-one* mapping between pitches and their position on the fretboard. A compositional engagement with this kind of instrumental resistance can help shape and refine materials (see also Gorton and Östersjö 2016; Gorton, Shaw-Miller, and Heyde 2013).

As noted above and elsewhere, the origins of *Austerity Measures I* are to be found in the "Malmö Sessions" from 2010, in which we experimented with a number of tuning systems in four sessions across two days (Gorton and Östersjö 2016; Clarke et al. 2017). Most of this work was carried out on the eleven-string alto guitar, an instrument not dissimilar to the ten-string guitar, but pitched a minor third higher than other guitars (it is a transposing instrument) and

21 However, there is ample evidence of interactions with performers, both positive and negative, and their influence on a composer's work, across the history of Western classical music.

with extensions beyond the nut for the lowest strings. The tuning system for *Austerity Measures I*, shown in figure 1.5, is a direct appropriation of a tuning system from the Malmö sessions, but with the eleventh string pitch removed and the whole now sounding a minor third lower. Additionally, because the ten-string guitar has no extensions, the harmonic nodes are in the same positions across the strings, which was not the case when the tuning system was originally developed and tested.

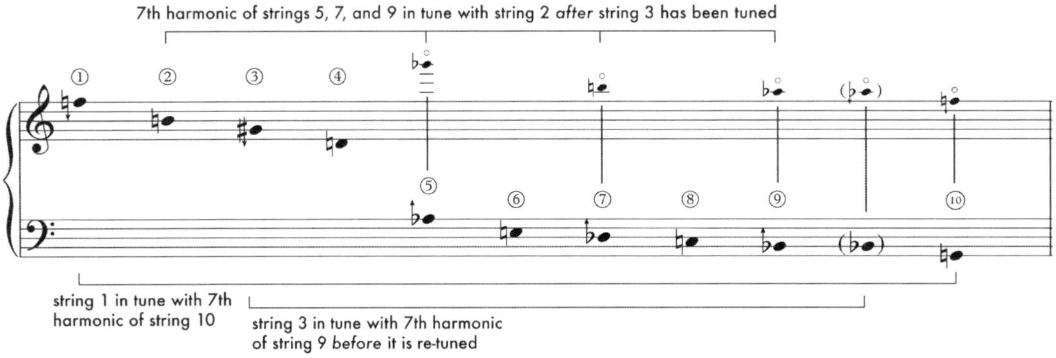

Figure 1.5.

The tuning system uses the naturally flat seventh harmonic of open strings as reference pitches. To begin with, string 1 is tuned to the seventh harmonic of the G♮ of string 10, and string 3 is tuned an octave lower than the seventh harmonic of the B♭ of string 9. Then string 9 is retuned along with strings 5 and 7 so that their seventh harmonics move from being flat to being in tune with the respective fretted pitches found on string 2. This produces an alternating pattern of strings that are at normal pitch (strings 2, 4, 6, 8, and 10), and strings that are either a sixth of a tone flat (at the top end of the instrument—strings 1 and 3) or a sixth of a tone sharp (at the bottom end of the instrument—strings 5, 7, and 9).

In the Malmö sessions it was observed that one of the properties of this tuning system was its bell-like character, particularly when playing natural harmonics across alternately-tuned strings.[22] While it could be said that guitar harmonics can often be associated with the sounds of bells, the association was particularly striking in this tuning system, more so than in the other tuning systems tested during the Malmö sessions. In a compositional engagement with the specific instrumental qualities of the ten-string guitar tuned in the manner described above, the bell-like character can be seen to be embedded into the piece, particularly in the opening materials seen in figure 1.1, which are then further developed into the motivic patterns in figure 1.6.

22 A supplemental video file "SF1.1 Bell-like sonorities in Austerity Measures I," in the online repository (www.orpheusinstituut.be/en/voices-bodies-practices-media-repository), provides an edited sequence from footage of the Malmö sessions in which we explore and discuss the bell-like character of the tuning system in relation to an alternative tuning system tested earlier; this is followed by the opening of *Austerity Measures I* in which the bell-like dyads are developed into the motivic patterns of figure 1.6.

Figure 1.5. The tuning system for *Austerity Measures I* (the tuning system sounds an octave lower than written).

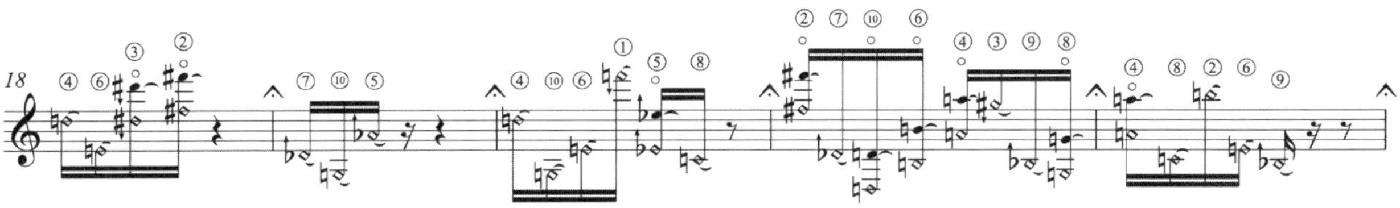

Figure 1.6.

Just as performers operate within and engage with their contextual performance practices, so also composers engage with compositional practices that include their own previous work as well as the broader practices of other composers. Despite a modernist maxim privileging originality and individuality, composers rarely work in a vacuum, and they are frequently interested in grounding their own identities within lineages of predecessors. Music criticism also has a powerful taxonomic role to play, often grouping composers together into schools or classifications of style. Yet while such influences play an important part in defining the identities of composers, compositional engagement with materials by *dissimilar* composers can be a revealing indicator of a composer's "voice." For example, the completion of Grieg's Piano Quintet in B♭ major by Michael Finnissy and his subsequent *Grieg Quintettsatz* together reveal facets of Finnissy's approach to counterpoint and large-scale shape in a new and enlightening context.

Much of David Gorton's work in recent years draws on materials from the late sixteenth and seventeenth centuries.[23] *Forlorn Hope* for eleven-string alto guitar, the other piece that has its origins in the Malmö sessions, partitions John Dowland's *Forlorn Hope Fancy* and expands the materials into a sequence of dance and fantasia sections. *Lachrymae Variations* for string ensemble similarly draws on Dowland, in this instance the lute song *Flow My Tears*, along with a selection of keyboard arrangements made of the same theme by composers William Byrd, Giles Farnaby, Thomas Morley, William Randall, Heinrich Scheidemann, and Jan Pieterszoon Sweelinck. *Concerto per flauto a becco e violino su temi Torelli* is composed using materials taken from the other end of the seventeenth century, specifically seven of the Torelli opus 6 *Concerti musicali*.[24] Writing in the booklet notes from the commercial recording of *Forlorn Hope* and *Lachrymae Variations*, Gorton explained his reasons for engaging with older materials in his recent compositional practice:

> But beyond admiration there are other reasons that I have been interested in working on the edges of transcription, arrangement and composition. It is a common practice to classify a composer's style in relation to his or her harmonic,

23 Other work discussed in the present volume also draws extensively on prior musics; see especially chapters 2 and 3, below.

24 *Lachrymae Variations* was first performed by Longbow, Peter Sheppard Skærved (director), Maison Dieu, Dover, 20 May 2016, and recorded on *David Gorton: Variations on John Dowland* (Toccata Classics, 2017). *Concerto per flauto a becco e violino su temi Torelli* was first performed by Longbow, Olwen Foulkes (recorder), Peter Sheppard Skærved (violin), St Stephen Walbrook, London, 23 November 2018. Both pieces are published by Verlag Neue Musik, Berlin.

Figure 1.6. Bars 18–22 of *Austerity Measures I*: bell-like patterns.

> rhythmic or aesthetic concerns and, where these considerations might change over a lifetime, to divide someone's output into distinct stylistic periods. Yet questions of style run much deeper than that and are influenced by the kinds of choices made by a composer on a note-by-note basis: the voicing of a chord, the pacing of materials, the dovetailing of a line between instruments, the idiosyncrasies of instrumental writing. Usually these small-scale choices become subsumed or obscured by the more obvious stylistic considerations, but when working with borrowed materials they come to the fore. The compositions on this album therefore represent a process of discovery for me, in which I have found new facets of my compositional "voice" through that of another. (Gorton 2017, 4)

In all these compositions the borrowed materials can be seen to undergo various processes of disintegration and distortion.[25] In *Forlorn Hope* fragments of the original are left in place, distorted by the microtonal tuning of the guitar and surrounded by other types of gesture derived from improvisations by Stefan in the Malmö Sessions. In *Lachrymae Variations* the various keyboard arrangements of the theme are layered on top of one another and then filleted and interspersed with new materials. At the end, a shell of the original remains, becoming progressively flatter by microtonal increments. *Concerto per flauto a becco e violino su temi Torelli* initially arranges the original materials into the kind of concerto ritornello that was emerging throughout the decade following Torelli's death. But this aim ultimately fails as sections of themes and harmonies are systematically removed from textures. While *Austerity Measures I* does not use borrowed materials, the concept of cutting that underpins the piece is similar to the compositional techniques of disintegration that occur in the previously described works, and it can thus be seen to sit within a compositional concern that is common to much of David's recent practice.

As argued elsewhere, in certain (even "typical") collaborative conditions the "voices" of performer and composer described above may join together in the formation of a "discursive voice": "the discursive voice can be conceived not simply as a combination of the composer's and performer's voices. . . . Rather, the discursive voice emerges from the process of collaboration. . . . What emerges is a negotiation; a coming together of the two voices through the exploration of a situation in the present" (Gorton and Östersjö 2016, 593). The diagram in figure 1.7 brings together the two previous diagrams in an attempt to represent the complex relationships that constitute the formation of a collaborative "discursive voice." The component parts from the previous diagrams are all still present, with the exception that "score" from figure 1.3 is now presented as "notation" in the manner found in figure 1.4.

Through figure 1.7 it is proposed that in the formation of a "discursive voice" performer and composer grant privileged access to the constituent parts of their own "voices." In a collaborative situation this could involve working jointly at an instrument to develop materials and instrumental techniques, overlapping reciprocally with jointly developing notation for such materials.

25 Experiences of similar forms of experimentation with shared voice are central to the discussion of William Brooks's *Footnotes* in chapter 3, but there the discussion is expanded to include the shared voice created when a performer adopts the "persona" of another.

Such interactions would be shaped by the respective practices of both. Over time, the composer's broader compositional practice may become influenced and shaped by the performance practices of the performer to the extent that these affect other work. Similarly, the broader practices of the performer, especially the manner in which they approach other composers' music, may become influenced and shaped by the collaborative interaction. The formation of a "discursive voice" may thus be situated within the shared contexts of practice that is common to both.

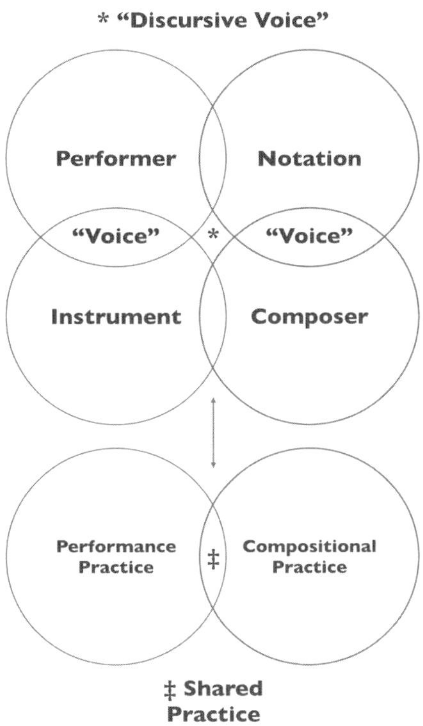

Figure 1.7.

In the case of *Austerity Measures I* it is possible to trace the co-development of materials from the testing situation of the Malmö Sessions into their codification in the score, perhaps most obviously in the tuning system itself and the use of bell-like sonorities, as discussed above. In the composition of *Austerity Measures I* (and also in that of *Forlorn Hope*), it could be said that to an extent David was composing with Stefan's "voice," as well as his own. Similarly, in applying the cutting process as detailed in the performance instructions for the piece, and thus in controlling the disintegration of materials, it could be said that in performance Stefan has also composed with David's "voice," as well as his own. This second practice is, however, less easy to trace than the first, requiring the identification of the ways in which, in live performances of *Austerity Measures I*, this "discursive voice" is continued through the interrela-

Figure 1.7. Relationships that constitute the formation of a collaborative "discursive voice."

tions between the embodied knowledge of the performer, as constituted in his "voice," and the musical structures in the score. This question is explored in the second part of this chapter: in accessing performative knowledge at the levels of both the body image and the body schema the reflexive research methods used above in the discussion of the rehearsal are supplemented with analytical observations that draw on both qualitative and quantitative data from live performances. In the study of timing, phrasing, and gesture in performance the aim is to access manifestations of "voice," embedded in the interactions between the performer's habitus and the structures of the piece, that would not be accessible through reflection alone.

Part 2: Analysing the discursive voice in performance

An analytical study of *Austerity Measures I* was undertaken with two researchers from the Institute for Systematic Musicology at Ghent University: Dirk Moelants and Esther Coorevits. Data was collected from four performances of *Austerity Measures I* given by Stefan at the ORCiM Research Festival at the Orpheus Institute on 1–3 October 2014.[26] The first recording was an open rehearsal of a four-times version that Stefan had previously prepared, played in the auditorium of the Orpheus Institute. The second was a public concert of the same four-times version, given in the auditorium with a seated audience. The third was another open rehearsal of a three-times version that Stefan had also previously prepared, played in the central ground-floor hall of the Orpheus Institute house. The fourth was a public concert of the same three-times version, given in the central hall with an audience standing around the performance space and on the central staircase.

All the performances were recorded on video, with the camera placed so that Stefan faced it directly, from the front. Two additional audio recordings were made of each performance, the first with a contact microphone on the instrument to record a dry guitar sound and the second with a condenser microphone to record the guitar with the ambience of the room. Two types of movement data were recorded in each of the four performances. First, infrared markers were placed on Stefan's shoulders, right wrist, and the side of his glasses, with movements of these body parts detected and recorded through each performance with two remote devices repurposed from a Nintendo Wii games console that streamed the data to a computer. Second, four sensors were attached underneath the surface on which Stefan was seated; these recorded the pressure and displacement of his weight throughout the performances. Figure 1.8 is a photograph of the set-up, taken prior to the first rehearsal performance in the auditorium. The following analysis concentrates on qualitative and quantitative data taken from the audio and video recordings; analysis of the movement recordings is being prepared for publication elsewhere.

26 Video recordings of the four performances are available in the online repository (www.orpheusinstituut.be/en/voices-bodies-practices-media-repository) in files "SF1.2 Four-times rehearsal of *Austerity Measures I*," "SF1.3 Four-times concert of *Austerity Measures I*," "SF1.4 Three-times rehearsal of *Austerity Measures I*," and "SF1.5 Three-times concert of *Austerity Measures I*."

In approaching *Austerity Measures I* analytically, the piece was first divided into five sections that are marked by sudden changes in the material. In performance these changes provide aural signposts for the listeners to help them perceive the cutting process and the evolving material within the repetitions. The first section consists of opening chords and dyads and ends after bar 15; the notation for much of this section can be seen in figure 1.1. The downward broken chord of harmonics in bar 1 is unique within the piece and provides an aural marker for the start of each new repetition. The second section consists of bell-like harmonic semiquavers lasting from bar 16 to bar 30, a portion of which can be seen in figure 1.6. The third section, lasting from bar 31 to bar 49, consists of a sequence of ascending arpeggios that create two- and three-bar phrases; figure 1.9 shows bars 44–49 from this section.

Figure 1.8.

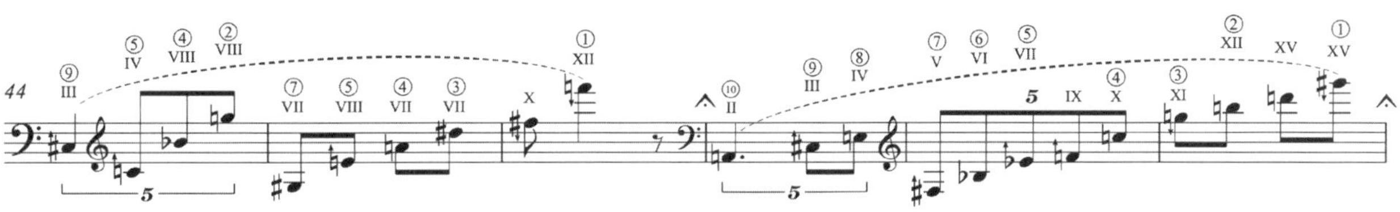

Figure 1.9.

Figure 1.8. The performance set-up in the Orpheus Institute Auditorium, showing microphones, Nintendo Wii remotes, the sensor surface underneath Stefan's chair, and the infrared sensors on his shoulders, right wrist, and glasses.

Figure 1.9. Bars 44–49 of *Austerity Measures I*: ascending arpeggio phrases.

The fourth section lasts from bar 50 to bar 58 and consists of a sequence of rapid broken chords; figure 1.10 shows bars 53–55 from this section.

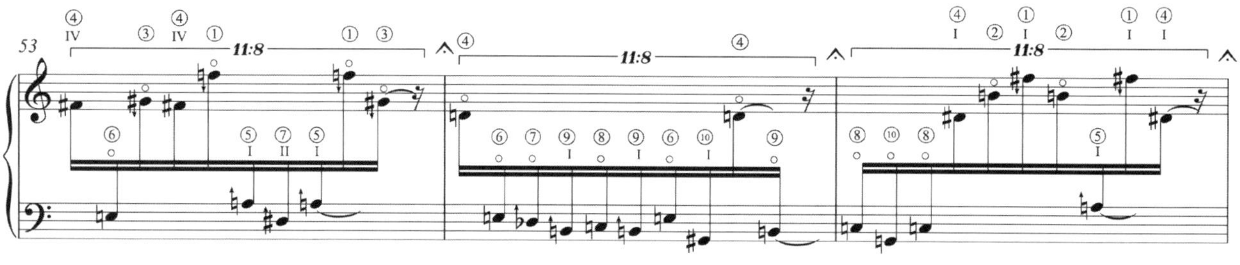

Figure 1.10.

The fifth section consists of a final ascending line, like a single extended version of the arpeggios in the third section, lasting from bar 59 to bar 64; figure 1.11 shows the whole of this section.

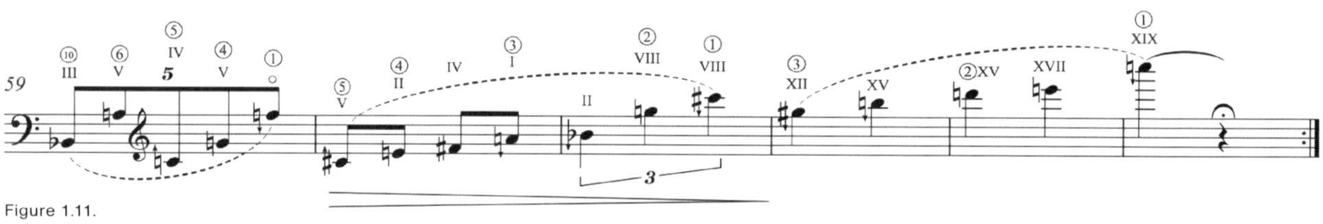

Figure 1.11.

Timing data was extracted from the audio files for each of the four performances with the beginning of each bar marked by the corresponding onset of the guitar's sound production. The exception is bar 11 (see figure 1.1), which is the only bar in the piece that begins with a rest. For the purpose of the analysis the start of this bar was marked with the onset on the second semiquaver of the second beat, making this a "short" bar, but with the timing then realigned at the start of bar 12. While the duration of the final bar could be measured during the performances in earlier run-through by the return to bar 1 and the start of the next repetition, this was not possible at the very end of each performance. For the purposes of this chapter, the final bar of each performance has therefore been assigned the duration of four seconds, which allows for the resonance of the final note but discounts for analytical purposes the extended pause at the end of a performance before the audience responds. As the performances progress and bars are removed and replaced with rests, the measurement of the duration of surviving bars is made from the start of the bar until the start of the next surviving bar, meaning that the duration of missing bars is counted in with the previous surviving bar. For example, in the four-times concert performance bar 6 is measured as 2.42 seconds in the first run-through, 2.21 seconds in the second run-through, and 2.66 seconds in the third run-through. In each of these run-throughs bar 7 also survives, with its first note marking the end of

Figure 1.10. Bars 53–55 of *Austerity Measures I*: broken chords.

Figure 1.11. Bars 59-64 of *Austerity Measures I*: final ascending line.

bar 6 with a relatively consistent duration for the bar across the three versions. But in the fourth and final run-through both bars 7 and 8 have been removed and replaced with rests; with the first note of bar 9 marking the terminus of bar 6, there results a measured duration for bar 6 of 4.43 seconds. Bar 6 has therefore been elongated as a result of the cuts. However, in the previous run-throughs the duration from the start of bar 6 to the start of bar 9 is substantially longer than in the final run-through, measuring for example 7.86 seconds in the first run-through, meaning that while bar 6 itself has been elongated as a result of the cuts, the time between bars 6 and 9 has actually been compressed significantly.

Figure 1.12 shows the durations of each of the run-throughs across the four performances, divided into the five sections previously described. The shortest of the run-throughs, by some margin, was the final run-through of the three-times open rehearsal, lasting 121.69 seconds, while the longest of the run-throughs were the second run-throughs of the four-times concert and the three-times concert, with durations of 167.76 seconds and 167.38 seconds respectively. In both the four-times performances the third run-throughs are the shortest, followed by the final run-throughs, while the second run-throughs are the longest. In both the three-times performances the final run-throughs are significantly shorter than the others.

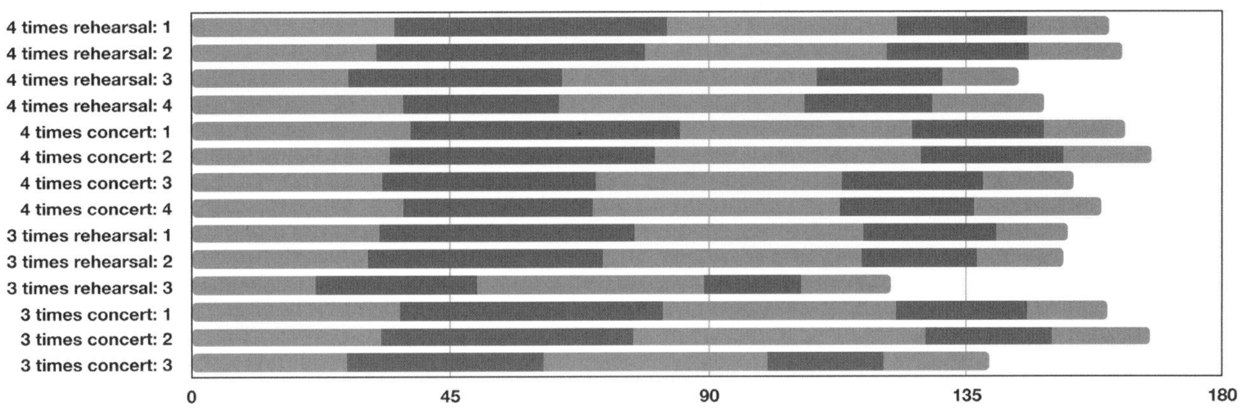

Figure 1.12.

These differences in length show how Stefan applied timing strategies in performance to manage the cutting process. It is perhaps not surprising that in the two four-times performances the first two run-throughs are of similar lengths, because by this stage of the piece the cutting of bars is relatively light. Indeed, the additional length of the second run-throughs suggest an act of preparation for the larger cuts to come, a shape that recalls what Stefan had said in the first rehearsal: "I think it's quite nice also to present the material as quite full sounding and not too slow a piece. So, you let it ring, but not to die out, but more like setting big sonorities. That gives you much more space

Figure 1.12. Durations of each run-through across the four performances, divided into the five sections.

to start cutting." As the cuts become heavier in the third run-throughs, the strategy of compression identified above assists in the management of the new silences, resulting in shorter durations. But by the final run-throughs, the aural effect of the increasing silences has been prepared, allowing Stefan to stretch the time back a little. In the three-times performances the cutting process unfolds at a different rate to that of the four-times versions: the first set of cuts in the second run-through is proportionally greater, but in the final (third) run-through the amount of surviving material is larger than in the final run-through of the four-times performances. The implication of this is that the aural effect of extended silences cannot be prepared in the same manner, resulting in the largest amounts of compression in the three-times performances occurring in the final run-throughs.

The positioning and size of the five sections in the different run-throughs in figure 1.12 show that the strategies of compression and expansion do not occur uniformly throughout the piece. The deviation in durations across the sections in the four-times and three-times performances are shown in figure 1.13, where deviation has been calculated as the difference between the longest section and the shortest section, divided by the longest section and represented as a percentage. Thus, across the four-times performances it is the second section that has the largest deviation in duration; comparing this with figure 1.12 it is possible to see that in both four-times performances the second section becomes shorter and more compressed with each repetition of the bell-like materials and that the same thing occurs in both of the three-times performances. The first section also shows a pattern of compression: in the three-times performances, this results in the largest deviation and a section that becomes shorter with each repetition; but in the four-times performances the final run-throughs reverse this trend and are instead expanded, making these run-throughs among the longest of all the first sections. In comparison, sections three and four (the ascending arpeggios and rapid broken chords) appear relatively more consistent in their durations. Yet here, too, patterns of expansion and compression can be observed. With the exception of the four-times rehearsal, section three is longest in the second run-throughs, becoming expanded in the first round of cuts, before returning to nearly its original lengths in the later rounds. A similar pattern occurs in section four in both of the four-times performances with this section being longer in the second run-through but quite consistent in duration in the other run-throughs. But in the three-times performances section four follows the same pattern as sections one and two, with each repetition becoming progressively shorter and more compressed. While section five is the shortest section and includes the final bar, which in the final repetition has been assigned a consistent yet arbitrary duration (see above), it is interesting to observe that, except for the third run-through in the four-times rehearsal, section five becomes increasingly longer and more expanded with each successive repetition.

Deviations in duration across sections

	Section 1	Section 2	Section 3	Section 4	Section 5
4 times performances	28.4%	42.9%	13.4%	13.1%	39.8%
3 times performances	40.4%	38.1%	22.8%	27.1%	31.0%

Figure 1.13.

A complex, shifting pattern of contraction and expansion can therefore be seen to operate across all the sections in all the various run-throughs of the four performances, with none of the run-throughs having all the shortest or all the longest sections within their respective performances. Indeed, in each of the two longest run-throughs—the second run-throughs in both of the concert performances—the first two sections are actually shorter than those in their respective previous run-throughs, with most slowing-down and expansion occurring in the concert performances in section three, the section that has been identified above as having some of the least deviation across durations. This can be seen at the level of the bar in figure 1.14, which shows timing data for each bar within section three of the four-times concert performance.[27]

Figure 1.14 resembles figure 1.12, with each horizontal strip representing relative durations; but rather than the whole being divided into the five identified sections, figure 1.14 divides each strip into the component bar lengths, with each surviving bar labelled numerically. In the first three run-throughs, section three is measured from the start of bar 31 until the start of bar 50. But in the final run-through it is measured from the start of bar 33 until the start of bar 51, because by this stage in the performance bars 31, 32, and 50 have been cut. Thus, from the diagram it is possible to trace vertically how bar 36, for example, survives for all four run-throughs and is played latest in the third run-through relative to the identified start of the section, or how bar 38 survives until the third run-through, but is omitted in the final repetition. Also identifiable is a "mistake" made by Östersjö in the performance, where bar 40 is cut from the third run-through, but is reinstated for the final run-through, presumably at the expense of bar 38 or 41. The processes of compression and expansion can be seen in the timing data represented by figure 1.14. For example, at the start of the third run-through bar 31 now includes the rest time from the cut bar 32 but can be seen to be considerably longer in duration than the combined bars 31 and 32 in the previous two run-throughs. Similarly, bar 33 in the final run-through, which by this stage has now subsumed bars 34 and 35, is longer in duration than bars 33, 34, and 35 in the first two run-throughs and bars 33 and 34 in the third run-through. These are both examples of expansion. In contrast, bar 41 in the third run-through is shorter than bars 41, 42, and 43 in the first run-through and bars 41 and 42 in the second run-through and is therefore an example of contraction.

27 Figure 1.14 is adapted from Coorevits et al. (2016).

Figure 1.13. Deviations in the duration of sections in the combined four-times performances and three-times performances.

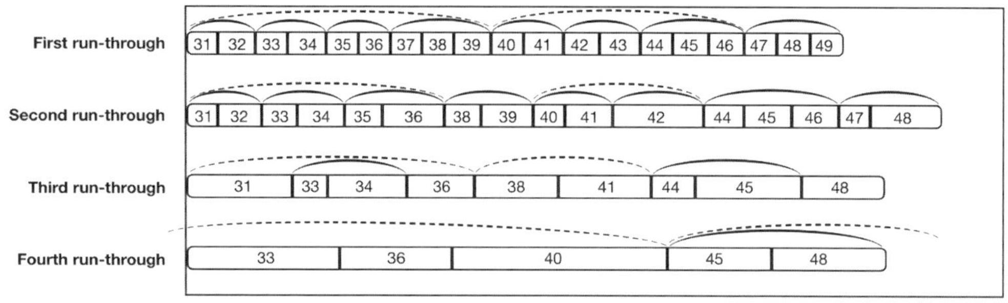

Figure 1.14.

Figure 1.14 also shows phrasing information for section three in the four-times concert performance. Rather than being derived from the quantitative data of the audio like the timing information, the qualitative phrasing information was derived from a process of stimulated recall (Bloom 1953, 161). Gorton, Östersjö, Moelants, and Coorevits listened together to the recordings of the four performances and after discussion agreed upon a joint understanding of how Stefan had joined bars together into phrases across two hierarchical levels. These phrase shapes were annotated into copies of the score that included details of which bars had been cut out in each repetition (see also Coorevits et al. 2016).

From the diagram in figure 1.14 it is possible to see that in the third section of the first run-through of the four-times concert performance Östersjö phrased bars 31–49 in groups of two and three bars, a pattern that matches the notated phrase markings in the score, as can be seen in part in figure 1.9. Additionally, these groupings were shaped into two larger-scale phrases that stretch from bar 30 to 39 and bar 40 to 46. In the second run-through, with the first round of cuts, the lower-level phrasing is retained, albeit with missing bars at the starts and ends of some phrases. This run-through has the largest amount of expansion in comparison with the first run-through, and with the cuts at this stage having little effect on the lower-level phrasing structures, the strategy of expansion can be seen to be enacted in the larger-scale phrasing. The first of these phrases is contracted, terminating at bar 36 rather than bar 39, leaving bars 38 and 39 to be articulated separately following the gap from the missing bar 37. The second large-scale phrase is similarly shortened, concluding at bar 42 rather than bar 46, leaving now two phrases to be articulated separately at the end of the section (bars 44–46 and 47–48), rather than the single lone grouping from the previous run-through. The increase in the number of separately articulated phrases thus helps create space within the expanding framework of the section. A similar pattern can be seen in the third run-through. While the lower-level phrasing has almost disappeared, because the only surviving consecutive bars are 33–34 and 44–45, the two larger-scale phrases remain. The first of these matches the phrase from the previous run-through, stretching from bars 31 through 36. But the second large-scale phrase has moved forward, starting now at bar 38 and stretching to bar 41, thus leaving intact the two separately articulated phrases from the end of the second run-through: bars 44–45, with bar 46 now removed, and bar 48 left by itself with the removal of bar 47. By the

Figure 1.14. Timing and phrasing at the level of the bar in section three of the four-times concert performance.

final run-through the cutting process has had such a devastating effect on the materials that little of the original phrasing structure remains. One lower-level phrase is identified, joining together bars 45 and 48 and thus cutting across the two original three-bar phrases at the end of the section. The two larger-scale phrases from the previous run-throughs remain, with the first phrase ending just one bar later after the end of bar 40 than in the first run-through. But their function has now changed significantly. Rather than defining larger structures within the third section, the large phrases now transgress the boundaries of the sections themselves, linking together the contrasting materials from across the sections. The first of these large phrases is identified as beginning at bar 30 with the final iteration of the bell-like material in section two, as illustrated in figure 1.15; the second large phrase begins at bar 45 and then stretches all the way to bar 56, including all the surviving material from the fourth section, as illustrated in figure 1.16. In this performance Stefan can therefore be seen to use the large-scale phrasing shapes to reorganise the structure of the materials in the final run-through as a means of coping with the large amounts of silence.

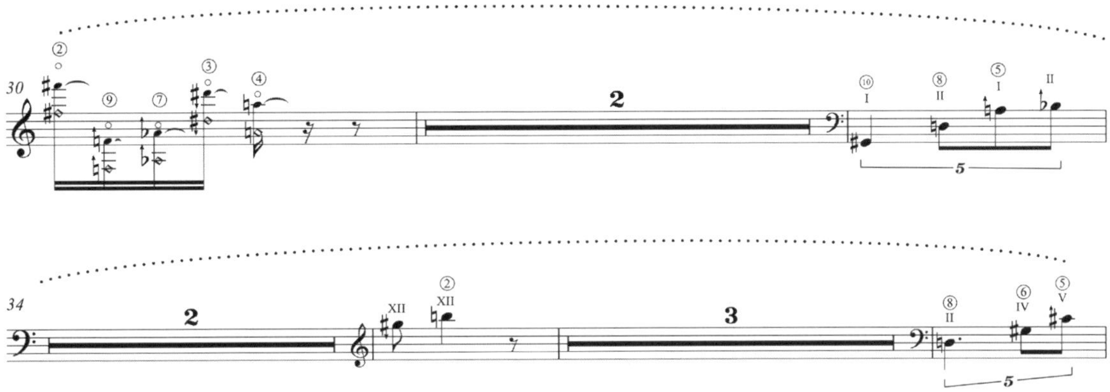

Figure 1.15.

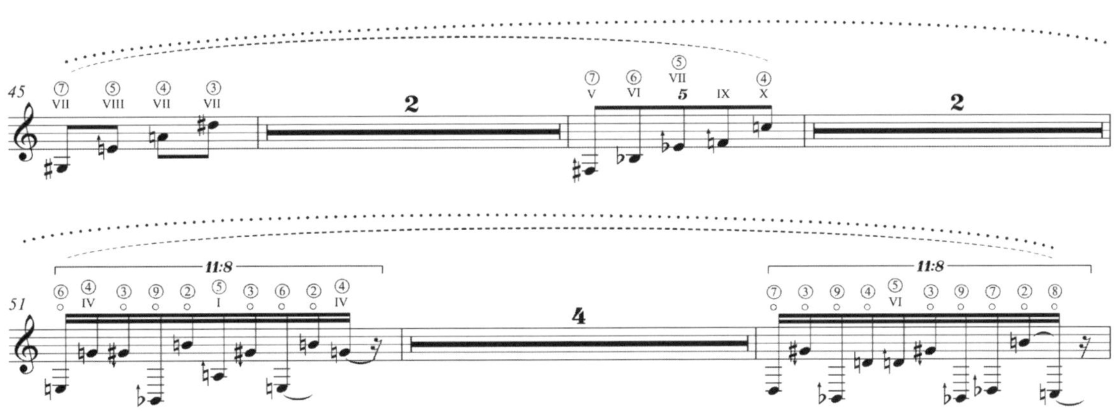

Figure 1.16.

Figure 1.15. Illustration of the agreed perceived phrasing for bars 30 to 40 in the final run-through of the four-times concert performance.

Figure 1.16. Illustration of the agreed perceived phrasing for bars 45 to 56 in the final run-through of the four-times concert performance.

A different approach can be seen in the three-times performances; figure 1.17 shows the timing and phrasing data from the three-times concert performance in a similar manner to figure 1.14. Again, we can see how the shifting pattern of bars changes across the constituent run-throughs, with bars 35 and 46 for example surviving in all three run-throughs, and bars 34 and 42 being cut out after the second run-through. It is possible to see "mistakes" in this performance, too: according to the instructions, no two consecutive bars should be labelled with the same number, meaning that in the second run-through there should not be any consecutive bars missing. Yet in the second run-through bars 36 and 37 are both missing, as are bars 39 and 40. However, these "errors" are carried through consistently into the final run-through, with none of the missing bars being mistakenly reintroduced.

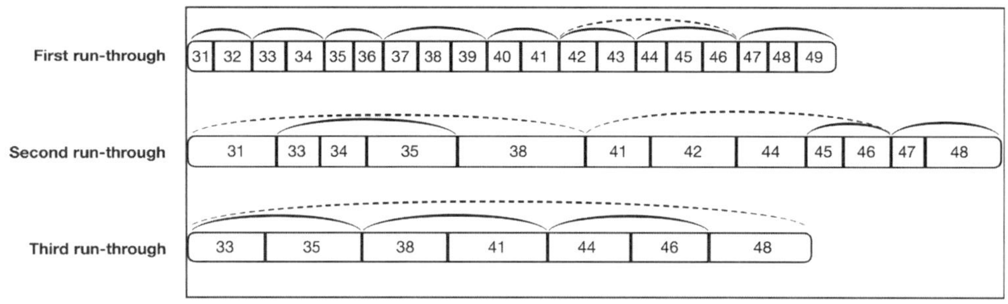

Figure 1.17.

In the first run-through the lower-level phrases are the same as in the corresponding run-through from the four-times concert, matching the phrase marks notated in the score. But, in contrast to the four-times concert performance, each of these lower-level phrases is articulated separately, with only the two groups starting at bars 42 and 44 being joined together into a larger phrase. The first run-throughs from the four-times concert and three-times concert performances are almost exactly the same length, with both lasting just over forty seconds, so the difference in larger-scale phrasing does not result from differences in tempo. Rather, the separated character of the lower-level phrases can be seen as a means for establishing a different kind of context in this performance for the different rate of cuts and amount of expansion to follow. The second run-through of the three-times concert performance has the longest of all the different versions of section three, lasting nearly fifty-one seconds; in contrast the third-run through of this performance has the shortest section three, lasting a little over thirty-nine seconds. This implies that the effect of expansion and then compression going from the first through to the third run-through in section three is the greatest in the three-times concert performance. In the four-times concert performance described above, space is created for the expanded second run-through with shifts in an established phrase pattern. But in the three-times concert performance, with a greater proportion of cuts having been made, the expansion is enacted with the introduction of new phrase

Figure 1.17. Timing and phrasing at the level of the bar in section three of the three-times concert performance.

shapes. The separate lower-level phrases of the first run-through are replaced by a more continuous delivery of two larger-scale phrases, with the second of these phrases terminating at bar 46 and leaving a single lower-level phrase at the end in a pattern similar to the first run-through of the four-times concert performance. Two additional lower-level phrases are identified within the larger pattern, and these are of interest because they transcend the previously-defined phrases: the first, running from bar 33 to 35, joins together two of the previous lower-level phrases; the second, running from bar 45 to 46, excludes bar 44, which had been present in the previous run-through even though bar 44 had not been cut. In the final run-through the two longer phrases are combined into a single continuous phrase that spans the whole of the much-compressed section. Unlike the four-times concert performance, the limits of the section in this final run-through remain defined by the phrase structures. With fewer bars having been removed by the final run-through of the three-times performances than in the four-times performances, enough material remains for the integrity of the section boundaries to remain intact. The shifting of the lower-level phrases continues in the final run-through: the phrase linking bars 33 and 35 remains; a new phrase combining two of the original phrases joins bars 38 and 41; and, finally, the previously excluded bar 44 is joined back to its original phrase.

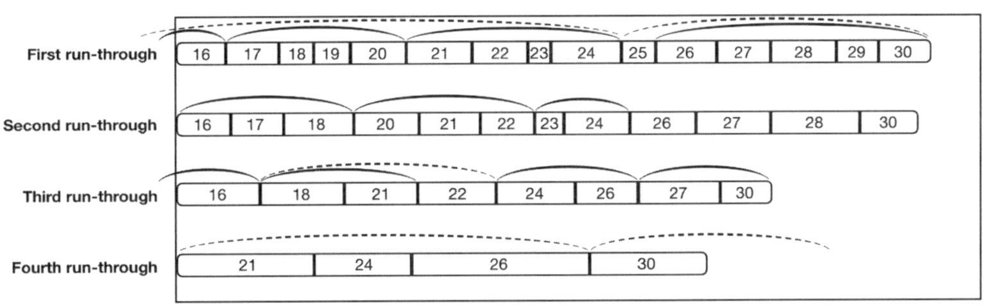

Figure 1.18.

Where the third section in the four-times performances is among the most consistent in overall duration, the second section in these performances is the least. Figure 1.18 presents the timing and phrasing information for the bell-like materials of the second section in the four-times concert performance. The compression in the overall timings from the first to the third run-throughs is immediately apparent. The fourth run-through is even shorter still, but as a result of the cuts the second section starts at bar 21 and extends to the beginning of bar 33, making its limits three bars shorter than the preceding run-throughs.

In the first run-through bars 23 and 25 are noticeably shorter than the other bars of the second section.[28] While the majority of the bell-like figures in this

28 Bars 18 and 19 are also on the short side, but both are longer than bars 23 and 25.

Figure 1.18. Timing and phrasing at the level of the bar in section two of the four-times concert performance.

section contain five or more harmonic notes per bar, bar 23 only has two notes, and bar 25 is a reprise of the (also bell-like) C and D-third-tone-♭ dyad from the opening of the piece, as can be seen in figure 1.19. Rather than hold the notated rests and the associated pauses for their full lengths, Stefan appears to push through these bars at the outset, presumably as a means of maintaining continuity and building resonance before the first round of cuts occurs. In the phrasing, bar 25 is significant, since it marks the beginning of the second large-scale phrase, being joined to the following lower-level phrase without being a part of it.

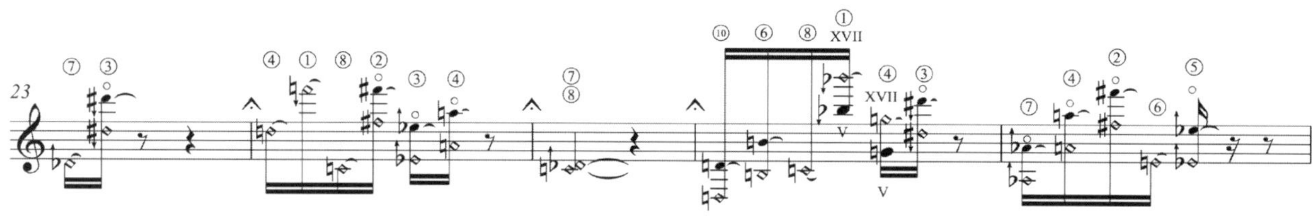

Figure 1.19.

The phrasing strategies for section two are markedly different from those described above for the third section. Since section two contains a succession of groups of semiquavers of varying length, there is no apparent structure for the lower-level phrasing like that provided by the arpeggios of the third section. Instead of the two- and three-bar phrases found in the third section, Östersjö chooses to group the semiquaver patterns in the first run-through into two four-bar phrases and a five-bar phrase. The second large-scale phrase, which includes bar 25, terminates with the lower-level five-bar phrase at the end of the section. But the start of the section is rather more ambiguous. While the first bar of section two does introduce new material in the form of the bell-like semiquavers, these can be interpreted as a development of the earlier materials from the first section, which are also bell-like in character, and which include a phrase of semiquavers in bars 11 and 12 (see figure 1.1). In the first run-through of the four-times concert performance Östersjö chooses to play the opening of section two as if it is a continuation of the previous materials, forming bar 16 into the end of a lower-level phrase that had started in bar 13 and continuing a larger phrase that had also begun at bar 13 all the way to the end of bar 24. A similar ambiguity about the beginning of the section can also be seen in the third run-through. Here, bar 16 is again joined with previous materials, this time in a lower-level phrase that had begun in bar 15, with the first full phrase of the new section starting in bar 18. In contrast, the beginning of section two is articulated in the phrase structures of the second and fourth run-throughs. The last surviving four bars of the second run-through are not shaped into phrases at all, instead being played as detached bars. At the end of the fourth run-through it is the end of the section that loses definition, with a large-scale phrase beginning on bar 31 stretching far into the third section, as described previously.

Figure 1.19. Bars 23 to 27 in the second section of *Austerity Measures I*.

Figure 1.20.

A further layer of qualitative data was extracted from the video recordings of the four performances, with a method using stimulated recall[29] and negotiation similar to that which has been used to analyse phrasing.[30] This stage of the analysis was informed by the typology of musical gesture described by Jensenius, Wanderley, Godøy, and Leman (2010), which proposes a division into four main categories: sound-producing gesture, sound-facilitating gesture, communicative gesture, and sound-accompanying gesture. First together and then separately, Gorton, Östersjö, Moelants, and Coorevits watched the video recordings of the four performances, which had been filmed with a front-facing camera angle, as can be seen in figure 1.20. Each participant identified visual cues from Stefan's body movements that they perceived as significant or "expressive" in some way but that were usually not classified as "sound-producing" gestures. These visual cues were named with a code and annotated with reference to the time code, resulting in a rich list of codes from the different perspectives of the performer, composer, and two observers. Through a process of negotiation these codes were compared; when a consensus on their expressive meaning was reached, the codes were conflated or renamed, with residual codes deleted where no consensus was reached. In a second stage, Östersjö and Coorevits individually annotated the four recordings using the new code list, resulting in two parallel annotations that were discussed and conflated in a final session involving all four participants.[31] Most of the codes used in the analysis are bodily movements that have no direct result on technical delivery

29 For a further discussion of this qualitative research method, and the specific use made of it in our study, see Coorevits et al (2016). A more extensive discussion of stimulated recall follows in chapter 3.
30 The video recordings of the four performances are available in the web repository for this publication.
31 While fourteen gesture codes were identified in the final conflated list, only half of them will be discussed in this chapter.

Figure 1.20. Front-facing camera angle from the four-times performances used for gesture coding.

and do not explicitly produce sound, such as "nodding" and "expressive shoulder movement." "Vibrato" was also included as a code even though it does have an effect on delivery, particularly in the shaping of material, and obviously it does modulate the sound even if not producing it. But what all the codes have in common is that they represent corporately perceived bodily strategies for the management and communication of the evolving musical structures.

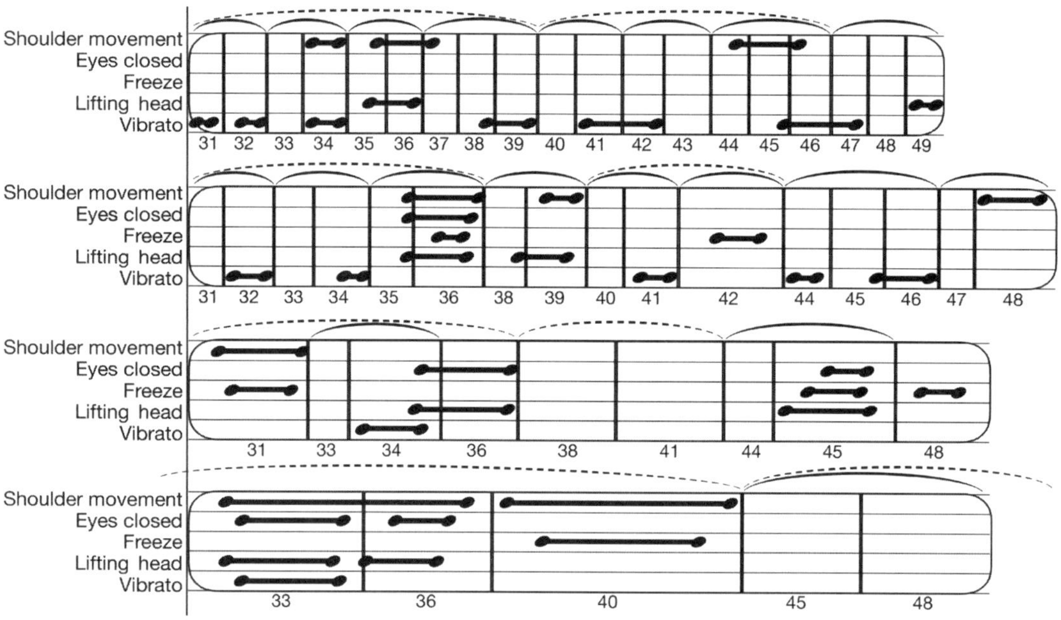

Figure 1.21.

Figure 1.21 reproduces the timing and phrasing information of section three of the four-times concert performance from figure 1.14, adding gesture coding annotation for selected codes that are characteristic of this section.[32] The four run-throughs are positioned as four horizontal strips divided into bar lengths, as before, with phrasing information for each run-through positioned above its respective horizontal strip and bar numbers notated beneath. Gesture code annotations are represented with their relative beginning and end positions in layers within each horizontal strip.

While Stefan's head moved frequently throughout the four performances, particularly when looking up and down the fingerboard and at the music, the "lifting head" code identifies specific moments where he deliberately lifts his head upwards and back beyond the usual playing position. In the first run-through this movement seems to be associated with preparing for the following phrase, occurring most notably in the last bar of the section, just before Östersjö launches energetically into the rapid broken chords from bar 50. As the piece progresses the sense of anticipation associated with the "lifting head"

32 Figure 1.21 is adapted and simplified from Coorevits et al. (2016).

Figure 1.21. Timing and phrasing at the level of the bar in section three of the four-times concert performance, with selected gesture codes.

code continues but evolves into a preparation for the encroaching rests. Often the movement is connected with a slight rallentando, becoming a means for signalling the gaps between materials; sometimes the lifting of the head occurs just before a moment of articulated rubato, and at other times it occurs just after it, in the rest from a cut bar, drawing attention to the decaying resonance. The "eyes closed" code, identifying moments where Östersjö literally closes his eyes, is closely associated with the "lifting head" code (see figure 1.22) and in the third section from the four-times concert performance does not appear independently of it. In all the places that it occurs in figure 1.21 it precedes cut bars and extended silences, heightening the sense of preparation of the "lifting head" movement.

Figure 1.22.

The code "expressive shoulder movement" (shortened to "shoulder movement" in figure 1.21) identifies a particular raising of the right shoulder and also, on occasion, the left shoulder. While there are times when the left- and right-hand positions would prohibit or restrict such a movement of the shoulders, the moments annotated with the code appear to arise not as a result of attaining other hand positions but rather from an expressive origin. In the first run-through, the shoulder movements are associated with the second parts of the continuous arpeggio lower-level phrases, where the material moves into the higher register, and appear to be connected with the shaping of the middle-to-ends of these phrases. But from the second run-through the shoulder movements change function and become associated with the playing of notes whose resonances are then held, often as a means of sustaining the idea of these resonances through the following bars of rest, even after the sound itself has died away. In this context the "expressive shoulder movement" code often appears alongside the "freeze" code (see figure 1.23). "Freeze" is applied to moments when Stefan holds his whole body rigid, as if frozen, providing a strong visual contrast to the usually fluid movements of the performance. In the example described in figure 1.21 this code first appears in the second run-through and always precedes a cut bar new to that run-through, thus signalling missing material that has been newly cut. When accompanying movement gestures, such as "expressive shoulder movement" and "lifting head," the "freeze"

Figure 1.22. Movement from bars 34 to 36 in the third run-through showing "eyes closed" and "lifting head" codes in the second image.

occurs mid-way through the movement, artificially holding the movement in a moment of stillness before returning to the usual playing position.

Figure 1.23.

The "vibrato" code identifies moments when Stefan uses left-hand vibrato in the playing. Given that all the first and second sections of the piece are composed of harmonics, and that the fourth section is made up of rapid broken chords across mostly open strings, this code only has relevance in the third and fifth sections and is particularly associated with the shaping of the arpeggio materials. In the first run-through of the example in figure 1.21 the use of vibrato matches the disposition of the arpeggio materials, with vibrato used mostly on the longer notes that occur at the beginnings and ends of the lower-level phrases. Additionally, vibrato is used when the left hand changes position, just before the shift, and is omitted at the starts and ends of phrases when the dynamic level drops. In the second run-through vibrato is used more sparingly and, apart from an appearance at the start of bar 44, is restricted to the last notes of lower-level phrases. In the third and fourth run-throughs vibrato is hardly used at all, appearing only once in each; on both occasions it is used to prolong the final note of an arpeggio across the gap of cut bars leading up to bar 36. A lack of vibrato therefore characterises the later run-throughs, with unmodulated resonances held into the gaps created by the cutting process. In the same way that vibrato is missing from the arpeggios that Stefan chooses to play at a lower dynamic level in the first run-through, the deliberate lack of vibrato in the later stages can be seen as a strategy to keep the energy levels of the surviving materials lower than in previous iterations.

The five codes discussed in relation to the third section in the four-times concert performance can be seen as directly connected to the physicality of managing the cutting process as the piece progresses, with some of the codes changing their function in the later repetitions as a means of framing the silences and continuing the idea of a held resonance after the sound itself has died away. When viewed together, as in figure 1.21, significant moments can be identified where gesture codes and phrasing align. One such moment is bar 36 in the second run-through (see figure 1.24 for bar 36 in context). From the perspective of the phrasing this bar has already been identified as significant (see

Figure 1.23. Movement in bar 40 in the fourth run-through showing "expressive shoulder movement" and "freeze" codes in the second image.

above), with the termination of the first large-scale phrase moving to the end of bar 36 as part of a broader strategy of time expansion. It is also a significant moment in relation to the cutting process, with bar 37 being the first cut bar in this section of the piece, resulting in bar 36 becoming the first lengthened bar. The coming together of the "expressive shoulder movement," "eyes closed," "freeze," and "lifting head" codes sees Stefan not only signalling the first cut bar and silence of this section but also establishing the gestural language for the framing of the future cut bars.

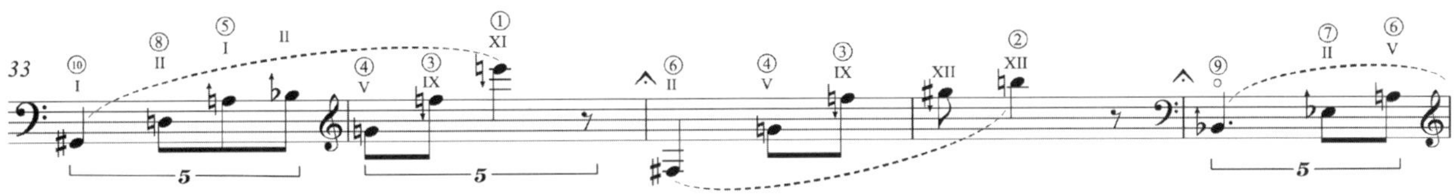

Figure 1.24.

Bar 45 in the third run-through is a similarly significant moment (see figure 1.9 for bar 45 in context). In the first two run-throughs bar 45 appeared as the central bar in the three-bar lower-level phrase. Originally, this phrase formed the final part of the second longer phrase, but in the second run-through it became a detached phrase as part of the broader expansion strategy described above. By the third run-through, with the cutting of bar 46, bar 45 has now changed function, becoming the ending of the lower-level phrase rather than the middle of it. The additional removal of bar 47 exacerbates the cutting-short effect of the arpeggio by creating an extended silence before the next articulation in bar 48. This extended silence is managed by Stefan in a similar manner to that of bar 36 in the second run-through: the "eyes closed," "freeze," and "lifting head" gestures are aligned for the second and only other time in this section of this performance. Bar 45 in the fourth run-through is also significant. At this stage of the piece, bar 45 is identified as being the beginning of a lower-level phrase linking it with bar 48, the only other surviving bar from this part of the section, and as the beginning of a large-scale phrase that continues all the way to the end of the following section, containing the rapid broken chords. None of the gesture codes associated with the sustaining of resonance and suspension of time are identified in either bar 45 or 48, meaning that a different strategy is in operation here, allowing Stefan to build a continuity that transcends the section boundaries with the long phrase across the following broken chords.

A gesture code that is identified prominently in the first and second sections is that of "left-hand gesture"; this is closely associated with the production of harmonics throughout these sections. In the playing of harmonics on the guitar the left hand must let go of the fingered strings immediately after they have been plucked. While this movement can be very discrete, it can also be extended beyond its sound-facilitating function with extraneous movement of the hand away from the instrument. In the analysis bar 9 was consistently identified with the "left-hand gesture" code (see figure 1.1 for bar 9 in context).

Figure 1.24. Bars 33–37 of *Austerity Measures I*.

Uniquely within the piece, bar 9 comprises a triad of harmonics (produced on strings 4–6) followed by the articulation of two open strings (1 and 2). The left-hand movement away from the instrument thus occurs before and during the articulation of the open strings. But while the code is consistently applied to bar 9 across the run-throughs, the qualities of the movement appear to change as the piece progresses. Building on the observation made by Rolf-Inge Godøy (2006) that musical gestures can be analysed as being either iterative, impulsive, or continuous, the four occurrences of bar 9 in the four-times concert performance were cross-referenced in relation to the recorded movement data.[33] The first two occurrences of left-hand gesture in bar 9 were analysed as continuous gestures, while in the last two run-throughs they have a more impulsive quality. An interpretation of the musical functions of these gestures is that the movement of the left hand serves to connect bar 9 with the following bar; and when this bar is cut out in the fourth run-through it instead connects bar 9 with bar 11. Additionally, in the second and third run-throughs the previous bar is cut, and in the fourth run-through bar 7 is also missing. Hence, the actions in bar 9 are increasingly shaped by the gradual cuts on either side, resulting in the more impulsive character of the left-hand gesture as the piece progresses.

Figure 1.25.

The left-hand gesture in the first two sections also aligns with other gestures and phrasing structures at significant moments. This can be seen in all four performances, but perhaps the most striking examples are in the final run-through of the four-times concert performance. As described above, bar 30 in the fourth run-through represents the final bar of the second section, but also the first bar in a large-scale phrase that stretches to bar 40 in the third section (see figures 2.14 and 2.21). Here the impulsive left-hand movement combines with the "freeze" gesture in an enhancement of its connecting quality, joining bar 30 across two cut bars to bar 33 at the start of the third section and establishing the beginning of the large-scale phrase. Figure 1.25 shows the left-hand movement in three images, first moving away perpendicular to the fingerboard, and then being held still in a position next to the body of the instrument.

33 See Coorevits et al. (2016) for details of the analytical methods applied to the recorded movement data.

Figure 1.25. Movement in bar 30 in the fourth run-through showing "left-hand gesture" and "freeze" codes.

Bar 15 in the fourth run-through provides an extreme example of the "left-hand gesture" code and represents a significant moment in the final run-through. With bars 16–20 cut by this stage, the bar precedes the longest silence in the whole piece, lasting five bars. The previous three bars, bars 12–14, have also been cut, placing the two harmonics of bar 15 in an isolated position, surrounded by silence and not connected with any preceding or subsequent phrase structures (see figure 1.26). Figure 1.27 shows the movements immediately following the second harmonic of bar 15; here the codes that are associated with the holding of silences are all present, with the lifting of the head, eyes closed, slight raising of the right shoulder, and a held position. The left hand also comes away from the instrument in an impulsive movement. But rather than being held in a position of tension as in bar 30 where a phrasing continuity is maintained, the left hand in bar 15 drops away to the side. Treating bar 15 as an isolated sound object in the musical flow, the held, "frozen" position is one of relaxation, with Östersjö listening to the decayed resonance of the harmonics and allowing the five bars to slip past before resuming with the semiquavers of bar 21.

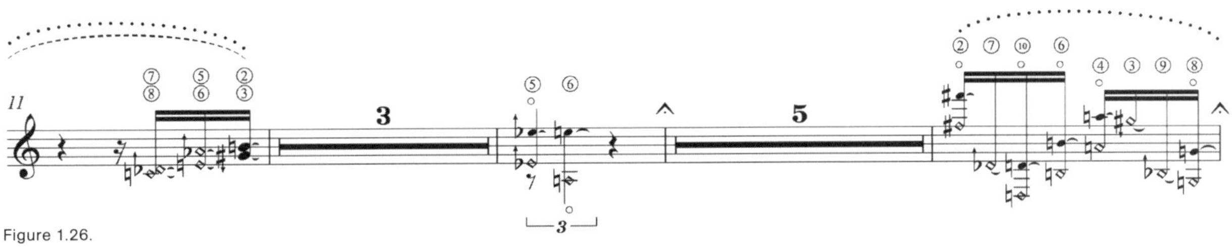

Figure 1.26.

Figure 1.27.

The gesture code "nodding" was used to identify a particular head movement that was distinct from the upward movement associated with the "lifting head" code previously discussed. Like "expressive shoulder movement," the nodding movements in the early run-throughs can be analysed as iterative gestures and seem to be associated with the shaping of materials within their respective phrase structures. Figure 1.28 shows an example of iterative nodding in the energetic broken chords from the fourth section (bar 57) in the first run-

Figure 1.26. Illustration of the agreed phrasing for bars 11 to 21 in the final run-through of the four-times concert performance.

Figure 1.27. Movement in bar 15 in the fourth run-through showing "left-hand gesture," "lifting head," "eyes closed," "expressive shoulder movement," and "freeze" codes.

through of the four-times rehearsal performance. The head is moved up and down in a rapid movement that is relatively restricted in range, emphasising accents placed within the broken chord.

Figure 1.28.

Like the other codes previously discussed, "nodding" is also aligned with the shifting phrase structures as the piece progresses. Figure 1.29 shows the last six bars, which constitute section five, from the four run-throughs of the four-times concert performance. The four run-throughs are layered on top of one another, with the negotiated phrasing information annotated onto the illustrative notation along with the positioning of selected gesture codes. "Nodding" can be seen to mark the lower-level phrase starting at bar 62 in the first three run-throughs, with a pronounced nod and lowering of the head at the start of the bar, and a continued lowering of the head with subtle iterative nodding continuing for a few beats. From this position the head is lifted with the eyes closed in preparation for the final note. In the first and third run-throughs the nodding is accompanied by "expressive shoulder movement" gestures. By the fourth run-through, the removal of bars 60, 62, and 63 has significantly changed the phrasing structure. Bar 62, which previously started a new lower-level phrase, is lost, and bar 61 has become the middle of a section-long large-scale phrase instead of the end of a lower-level phrase as it had been in the first two run-throughs. As observed elsewhere in the piece, the "lifting head" gesture is here associated with the preparation for cut bars, occurring with the last notes of bar 59 and 61 and again for the final note. But in the rests of bars 62 and 63 a pronounced nod occurs, disconnected from any actual playing, as if echoing the lost activity and placing the start of the missing arpeggio, mentally pushed a bar later now to create a "stretched" end of bar 61 (emphasised with additional "expressive shoulder movement") and an "early" final note. Across this final section this group of gestures can also be interpreted as a single compound gesture, very slowly distributed. The head movement that lifts-returns-lifts-drops-lifts can in itself be seen as a kind of very slow iterative nodding, uniting the fragments into a long single phrase.

Figure 1.28. Iterative nodding in bar 57 in the first run-through of the four-times rehearsal performance.

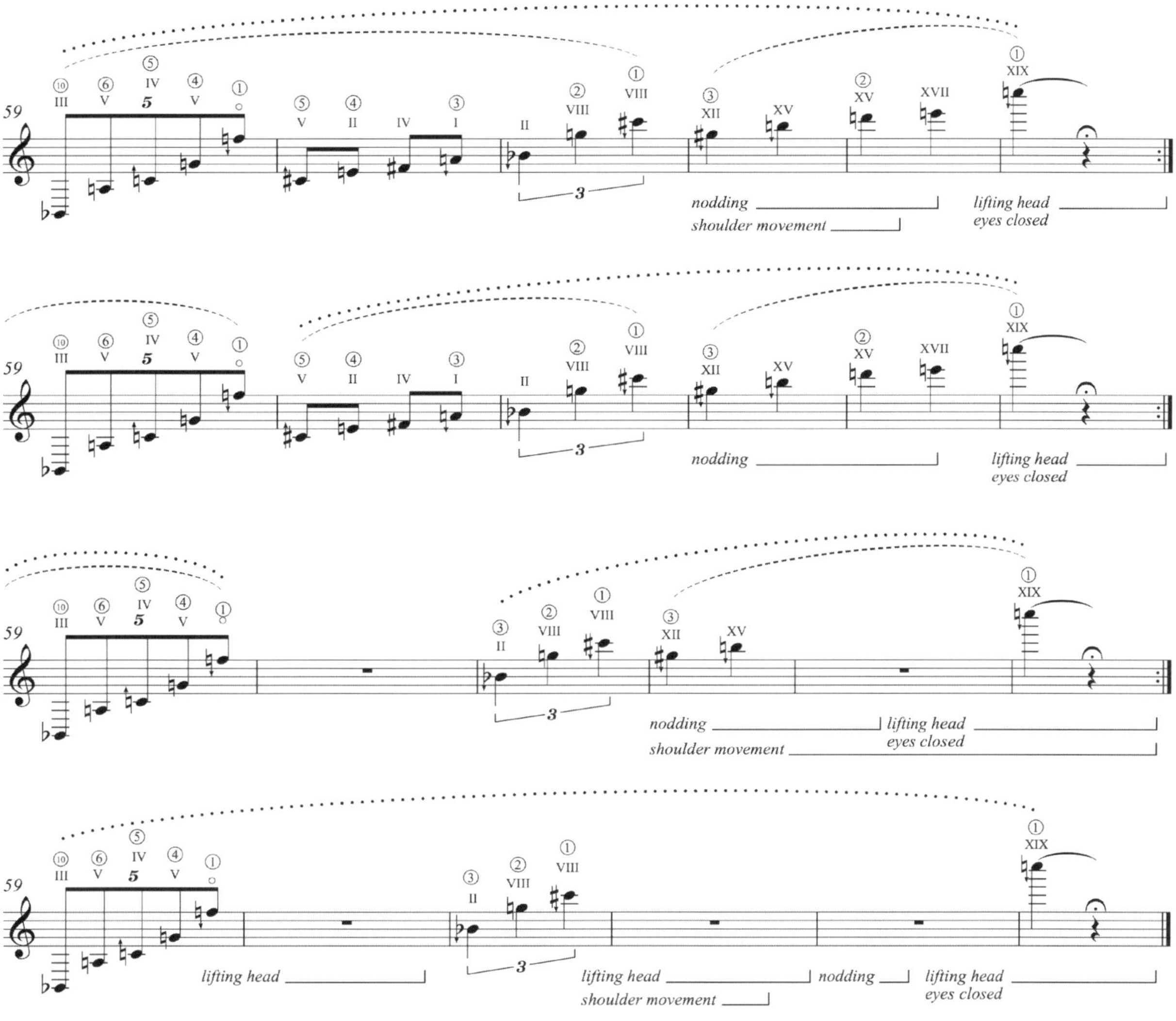

Figure 1.29.

While the "Malmö Sessions" discussed earlier could be described using Cook's Deleuzian creative assemblage of "COMPOSER-PERFORMER-GUITAR" (Cook 2018, 61), a model that is expanded in the diagrams of figures 1.3, 1.4, and 1.7, the assemblage implied by the foregoing analysis might be quite different: SCORE-PERFORMER-GUITAR. At face value such an arrangement resembles many other performing situations, with the "voice" of the performer apparent in the many personal decisions in evidence in the analysis. Yet the situation represented here goes some way further than the emergence of subjectivity described by Cumming, where "something of the musician's own 'character' will be heard in the choices he or she makes" (2000, 9). The score of *Austerity Measures I* demands a particular kind of engagement with its structures in its

Figure 1.29. The four run-throughs of section 5 in the four-times concert performance with phrasing information and selected gesture codes.

construction and then deconstruction in performance. Through this engagement the performer is granted privileged access to the compositional process and to a certain extent works as a compositional proxy in the establishment and application of the cutting mechanism. Personal decisions made in performance are thus additionally made on behalf of the composer as part of the social contract implicit in the score, resulting in the emergence of a "discursive voice." This mirrors the "discursive voice" of the compositional stage, where Stefan is absent as a person at the moment of writing but still present through the tuning system and bell-like sonorities that become embedded in the score. In live performance, David is similarly absent (or, at least, not onstage) but remains present through the compositional systems with which Östersjö is engaged.

Through the interrelations of Stefan's embodied knowledge with the musical structures in the score, the "discursive voice" can be traced in the analysis in the following ways. First, the analysis of the timing data shows how a strategy of compression and expansion is used to manage and control the effects of the cutting process. This can be seen at a global level, where cuts in future repetitions are prepared by varying the approach to tempo and resonance. But it can also be seen within individual sections, where methods of compression and expansion are applied differently to different types of material. Second, the analysis of phrasing information shows how the mechanisms of compression and expansion are controlled at the level of the bar, with the establishment of large-scale phrases and their subsequent modification used as a technique to create space and to take it away. Phrase structures are similarly used not only to reorganise the relationships between materials in response to the encroaching cuts but to both delineate and obscure the boundaries between sections. Third, the analysis of gestures shows how a repertoire of bodily movements further controls and nuances the delivery of the compression and expansion strategy. In combination the gestures create a hierarchy of significance that signals structural moments such as the beginnings and ends of large-scale phrases, newly cut materials, long silences, and even echoes of lost activity.

The agency of the score is therefore critical within the assemblage in activating the "discursive voice" within the performing situation, as is the agency of the instrument—and Stefan's relationship with it—in the composing situation. While the score does have the characteristics of a singular material artwork, its configuration is also resistant to such a classification. It enables and exemplifies the oscillation between singularity and iteration, which, as proposed in this chapter, is a mechanism through which artistic knowledge emerges. Through the combination of qualitative and quantitative methods, the analysis is able to translate the tacit and embodied knowing of the performance situation into the discursive domain. While the performance strategies identified in the analysis can be seen as being drawn from the intentionally activated level of the body image, much of the mechanisms for the realisation of such strategies, in the minutiae of timing and phrasing delivery and the surplus of meaning afforded by musical gestures, are drawn from the unintentional level of the body schema. Such performative knowledge is embedded in the "habitus" of the performer and the intimate, tactile relationship between Stefan and his instrument. Importantly, following Butt's observations above, these strategies, together with the possibilities and constraints afforded by the compositional structure, should in the final analysis be understood as expressive of the *intentionality* implicit in the entire assemblage. Hence, any of these performances of *Austerity Measures I* are not merely expressive of the intentions of its composer or of the intentions of the performer; additionally, they articulate the implicit *intentionality* which constitutes the specific expression of a "discursive voice" in each performance.

Conclusions

In the introduction to *Music as Creative Practice*, a piece of work that represents the culmination and synthesis of the five-year research programme of the Centre for Musical Performance as Creative Practice, Nicholas Cook (2018) describes his book in the following way: "This book is a study of music as creative practice: it aims to convey the sense of *people making music*. In so doing, it figures creative practice as not just based on, but made out of human actions and interaction" (1). Underlying this comment is a confession of sorts on behalf of a musicology that had for years been propping up a collection of "myths" concerning music's creation, focusing "on the individual rather than the group, . . . on composition rather than performance" (6). As Cook goes on to explain, the Kant-derived construct of artist-genius had been critiqued by creativity researchers for a period of several decades by the time that music studies caught on a few years after the turn of the millennium. Within this context, the idea that music creation is a collaborative process involving "human actions and interaction" (1), rather than a mystical process inside an individual's head, seems to be surprisingly new. But, however this change in attitude is viewed, it is certainly the case that since Cook and colleagues published a co-authored article about a performer working with a composer in 2005 (see Clarke et al. 2005) there has been a significant growth in interest in the creative act of performers collaborating with composers. Clarke and Doffman's edited volume (2017), which is also an output of the CMPCP project and which is discussed at length by Cook (2018), represents a cross section of an increasingly broad range of approaches to the demythologicalisation of collaborative practice.

In approaching a particular example of collaborative practice from the perspective of subjectivity, this chapter has had two aims. First, it has defined a model by which the subjectivities of performer and composer can be understood in terms of the emergence of "voice," which is manifest in the complex interactions between people, texts, instruments, and practices and is grounded within the concept of "habitus"; further, it argues that this model is a means by which collaboration can be understood through the joining together of these "voices" into a shared "discursive voice." Second, it has accessed evidence of the "discursive voice" in rehearsal and, more crucially, in live performance through the analysis of performative engagements with musical structures manifest in timing, phrasing, and gesture data. The explicitly iterative character of *Austerity Measures I*, which articulates a resistance to the singularity of instantiation often associated with an artwork's materiality, generates particular conditions by which performative knowledge may be accessed, thus providing the possibility to embrace the three knowledge paradigms.

The study thus provides evidence for the claims put forth by Jennifer MacRitchie that musicians' gestures in performance "carry meaning... relating to compositional structure" (MacRitchie, Buck, and Bailey 2013, 104). However, while it can be seen that several of the coded gestures are consistently related to a certain musical material or to a specific phrasing strategy, the analysis as a whole also points to inconsistencies. Roland Barthes reminds us that we may also celebrate the ways in which gesture and musical structure do not perfectly match. Musical gesture cannot be reduced to a script or to a single function: "let us distinguish the message, which seeks to produce information, and the sign, which seeks to produce an intellection, from the gesture, which produces all the rest . . . without necessarily seeking to produce anything" (Barthes 1985, 160). This is not, of course, to say that the score is equivalent to "the message" or "the sign"; the ontological status of musical compositions is far more complex than that, particularly in the case of *Austerity Measures I*. But what may be considered is how gesture is often unintentional. In his *Phenomenological Psychology* (1966), Erwin Straus made a study of expressive motions in interpersonal relationships and finds that communication does not presuppose intention: rather, he argues, more commonly intention interferes with communicative performance: "although highly communicative, they are not, or need not be, produced for the purpose of communication. This spontaneous production is paralleled by an equally spontaneous comprehension of expression" (226). Barthes may further supplement this figure of thought through his notion that gesture can be seen as linked to musical material in a pre-compositional phase. Following Barthes, this would equate these materials to "what the Alchemists called materia prima—what exists prior to the division of meaning" (Barthes 1985, 178).

The performative identity of *Austerity Measures I*, which appears to be primordially linked to the sessions in which its initial materials were developed, suggests that the function of the score is not to define the identity of the "work," but rather to instigate a negotiation of "discursive voices." In the creative process leading up to the first performances, such a "discursive voice" emerges from the collaborative process. Here, the composer has direct access to the performer's instrument, and the performer has direct access to the composer's notation (at various stages of development), with the guiding and moderating performance and compositional practices shared by both. However, although something of Stefan Östersjö remains embedded in the score of the piece, whenever another guitarist chooses to engage with *Austerity Measures I* and the structures it invites them to explore, a similar negotiation of "voice" is launched.[34]

34 In many cases, the negotiation of "voices" in the performance of scored music also involves a very active negotiation of the "voices" of several performers who are strongly associated with this music, as discussed in further detail above with regard to Pienaar's Beethoven cycle.

While the emergence of "voice" takes shape on both the unintentional level of the body schema and the intentionally activated level of the body image, in the formation of a "discursive voice" the relation between the two may be different. It may be assumed that here intentional shaping, adaptations, and negotiations are typical. However, it can also be observed that *Austerity Measures I* activates the "discursive voice" of performer and composer through musical gesture and the surplus of meaning that it affords. This enacted and embodied manifestation of the identity of the composition is then, it may be argued, also drawn from the more unintentionally driven layers of the body schema.

The philosophical conceptions articulated by J. T. Fraser have had a crucial influence on the development of David Gorton's particular approach to the structuring of musical time in scored music (Fraser 1982, 1990). David's compositional practice and approach to musical structure focuses on the phenomenological conceptions of time which Fraser finds to be expressed through a perceived temporal conflict, an "existential tension" (Fraser 1990), the perception of which in music is shaped as much through the articulation of the various temporal characteristics in performance as by their textual representation. When considered in these terms, musical structure attains a malleability in performance (see Gorton and Östersjö 2016, 586–88). Such compositions create the conditions for the "discursive voice" to be continued into performance and renewed afresh in each new performance through the nature of this malleable structure. Hence, in the analysis, *Austerity Measures I* presents an example of how the typically oscillating identity of musical compositions—between the singularity of their manifestation in the score and the multiple iterations of performance—can be further developed through the creation of malleable structures.

The study of musical gestures in performance can thus contribute to an understanding of the tacit domains of performative knowledge in musical practice. In this regard, the main contribution of the study of expressive gestures in rehearsal and performance of *Austerity Measures I* is the identification of intimate connections between musical structure and body movement. Furthermore, Stefan's performance strategies in shaping the musical material can also be traced through the co-articulation of expressive gestures in performance. The embodied knowledge of both composer and performer emerge through performance; the "sounding musical matter," the music as performed, activates multiple layers of signification, which can only be accessed through multimodal approaches to research. By way of artistic experimentation, entailing qualitative approaches to reflection and introspection and further guided by quantitative analysis, we may arrive at a better understanding of the emergence of subjectivity in musical creativity.

Chapter 2

Being a Player:

Agency and Subjectivity in *Player Piano*

Catherine Laws

Part 1: *Player Piano* and Saying "I"

Introduction

This extended chapter explores the nature and extent of performer agency, particularly as manifested through the interaction of body and instrument in the space of performance. The artistic research project used the process of developing a new, collaboratively devised performance as a lens through which to scrutinise these matters. Ultimately the aim was to explore the production of subjectivity in performance: a form of distributed or composite subjectivity, produced through the interaction of different human and non-human agents, even if it often presents as an individual performance persona.

Initially, this process involved collaboratively developing four new pieces (in one case a new version of an extant piece) with four different composers, all in response to a brief that I provided (the same brief for each composer). Subsequently, I developed a scenography to encompass these compositions within an overarching performance, along with other performance activities devised in relation to the key concerns of the research. In this way, and with the subsequent help of theatre-maker Teresa Brayshaw and later the film-maker Wendy Kirkup, I treated the compositions not as products—the final artistic work to be realised in performance—but as building blocks in devising a large scale (seventy-five-minute) piece called *Player Piano*, incorporating film, movement, and other live performance actions in addition to piano playing.[1]

As a result, the collaboratively produced compositions became material in three senses: first, in the usual manner, for creative realisation by a pianist; second, the compositions, their processes of realisation *and* the processes of reflection all fed into the further collaborative devising of *Player Piano*; and third, the materials and processes of making have been subject to reflection as part of the research—both critical reflection and reflection in and through practice. There is here a multi-layering of the iterative reflexivity that is characteristic of much artistic research.[2]

1 A trailer for the performance is available in the online repository (www.orpheusinstituut.be/en/voices-bodies-practices-media-repository) as file "SF2.1 Player Piano trailer."

2 Mareli Stolp argues for this as central to artistic research, drawing on Mary Archer's work on self-reflexivity: "once subjective experience has been reflected upon in a state of reflective consciousness,

One of my aims in developing *Player Piano* was to examine and expose some of the ways in which the particular interactions of any performance—interactions of performer with composed or improvised materials, interactions of body and instrument, of performer and environment—produce a notional performing subject. This subject is unstable, always in process, mutable and multiple, but it appears to manifest as singular, knowing, and contained: apparently a present, unified, agential self. The process involved exploring, in a playful and creative way, the instrumentalist's body as more than a vehicle for realising pre-formed, explicitly cognitised intentions; it exposed its significant agency, modified through years of practice and disciplined in relation to instruments, by the nature of a training, by other (non-musical) embodied experience, by social and cultural experience, by the specific demands of repertoire, and by the need to negotiate improvisational moments.

In this chapter I examine in some detail certain aspects of that process and their implications for questions of performer subjectivity. A discussion of the field of research identifies key critical themes that recur throughout the extended consideration of *Player Piano*, and these inform the subsequent consideration of three main forms of the performing subject:

the embodied self;

self and others: human (such as composers) and non-human (especially the piano); and

the contextual self.

In practical terms, the chapter proceeds by examining first the role of the body (in piano performance generally, then in *Player Piano*), then the instrument, then the wider performance context; the roles of composers and other creative agents are discussed along the way, because their agency is often manifested through their organisation of bodies, instruments, and contexts, sometimes explicit, sometimes more subtle and indirect. Ultimately, I argue for the emergence of performer subjectivity from an individual's interactions within an ecology constituted by all these elements, though their relative priority, and hence their significance in the production of performer subjectivity, varies.

Of course, in developing and subsequently reflecting on my own performance research, I at times recount first-person experiences; but at other times I look at the process and the performance as if from outside, taking a third-person perspective. Sometimes this shift is obvious and explicit, sometimes not, but such blurring is inevitable; my critical position is inevitably informed by my experience as the performer and instigator of the project, and the reverse is also true. Rather than this being a matter of retrospectively taking a critical position on an otherwise purely artistic project, practice and theory have infected one another at every stage (as they have, in my work, for many years). Being both the subject and the object of this enquiry is of course problematic, but it is

---

the cognition attained in that reflective state may once again 'feed into' acts of artistic engagement, performance, or practical music-making, altering or influencing the artistic practice itself as well as the potential insights gained from artistic experience. This process may be repeated indefinitely, suggesting a kind of interpretive spiral" (Stolp 2017, 5).

in part the *point*: the impossibility of disentangling the subjective and objective is central to the understanding of the embodied, contextual, and social production of subjectivity that underpins the work. In this respect the limitations of such an approach form a thematic layer in the work; the performance and the writing both reveal inside and outside positions that overlap but never purely coincide. Moreover, such an approach is no more or less problematic than the alternatives: it is *differently* problematic both to a purely experiential subject-centred account and to a critical account provided by another person from whatever perspective (critical-theoretic, ethnographic, or empirical). Overall, my aim might be summed up by the words of Estelle Barrett (2014, 3) when she describes the potential of practice-as-research to allow "new objects of thought to emerge through cycles of making and reflection; a recognition of the generative potential of the ambiguity and indeterminacy of the aesthetic object and the necessity for ongoing decoding, analysis and translation and, finally, the acknowledgement that instruments and objects of research are not passive, but emerge as co-producers in collaborative . . . approaches that may not be predetermined at the outset of the research."

To start with, it is important to set out something of the context of the performance piece itself. The programme for *Player Piano* provides the audience with these starting points:

> *Alone with my ten fingers . . .*
>
> A woman arrives with a piano.
> She plays. Plays this piano. Plays with it.
> Plays versions of herself through it.
>
> But she also has company. Other voices.
> Composers; teachers; the ghosts of other pianists.
> Memories of other pianos: big shiny grands and clapped-out old uprights.
> Other hers, with younger hands, looser shoulders, a lighter, more flexible body.
>
> *Whose hands are these anyway?*

This is followed by a lengthier background note:

> *Player Piano* started with the development of a new version of Annea Lockwood's *Ceci n'est pas un piano*, for piano, recorded speaking voice, and electronics, written in 2002 for the pianist Jennifer Hymer. I heard this piece, loved it, wanted to play it. But the original version uses a text by Hymer in which she talks about her pianistic experiences, her pianos, her sense of her body at the instrument. Lockwood was happy for me to compose and record a new text that touches on my love–hate relationship with the instrument, my hands, the sense of the piano as my "voice." This formed the starting point for the development of new compositions, each in some sense triggered by an idea of a particular kind of performing self, a particular body at the instrument. I've known the composers Edward Jessen, Roger Marsh,

> and Paul Whitty for a very long time: I've played their music over the years, they each know me well as a performer, and they all work very collaboratively. I think they all know—but in different ways—that I love piano resonance, love exploring the relationship between the performer and this strange machine, but also feel somewhat disconnected (as a performer, at least) from the traditions of the virtuoso solo piano concert. I don't even know if I'm a PIANIST, really—that word has such weight behind it, and maybe it's not one I want to carry—but I like playing.

The brief was simply to develop a new piece with me that would explore, draw out, even exploit aspects of what they think of as my characteristics as a performer, and that would bring other things into the piano scene: other sounds, objects, and activities. As composers with very different approaches and varied experiences of working with me, this would, I hoped, produce new versions of my performing self: new representations of the piano player and her instrument. From this, with the help of theatre-maker Teresa Brayshaw I started to play with what I was finding; in some cases this involved further collaborative work, further developing the compositions. Later, I invited film-maker Wendy Kirkup to join in. She made two films in response to some of the key images, sounds, and ideas.

This is, then, the simple version of the background to *Player Piano*. The "I" in that account is strong: an assertion of a performer's artistic intentions, formed around the production of selfhood through interaction with an instrument and various other artists.

Indeed, the force of the "I" in this text is quite deliberate: in the world of classical music performance, including new music, whenever a composer is involved, assumptions are made about the roles and relative agency of the participants.[3] Looking back at this text, I recognise that the insistent "I" is designed to ensure that the performer in this project cannot possibly be understood as primarily there to execute the creative ideas of others. As I reconsider the "I" constituted in that language, I recognise that it is formulated as a message—to audiences, maybe also to other performers, perhaps even to myself—in the form of a statement of agency: a claim made within and to an extent against a community of practice with certain conventions that might ordinarily elide that "I," or at the very least assume its agency and function to be rather different to what it was in that project. By this I mean that as soon as I refer to composers and a theatre-maker in the project, there might be a tendency to assume the performer's role to be interpretative and enactive, rather than creative and constitutive. *Player Piano* did not operate in quite that way, and to an extent the programme note is designed to make the audience a little more aware of the complexities of authority at work in the piece.

The text is apparently about me—it is a kind of truth—but it is also an "I" formulated in a particular way, *asserting* the subject of enunciation. It stresses—"*I*

3 I tend to agree with Clarke et al. (2017, 116), who suggest a distinction between the fluidity of roles in certain contemporary practices and their ongoing separation in related structures, institutions and markets: "In the creative economy of contemporary western musical production, the defined roles of composer and performer remain powerfully embedded, despite indications from academic writing and the statements of practitioners that this division of creative labour is increasingly regarded as highly porous."

think . . . ," "*I* will play . . . ," "*I* love . . ."—and refers to "*my* hands," "*my* voice," and so on. At the same time, the process it describes is one that is predicated on questioning—am I a pianist? what is a pianist?—and on difference and transformation: I refer to making new versions of myself and to a remediated "I," produced through the interaction of art forms.

Of course, that "I"—like any "I"—is problematic. Deixis always appears specific but requires context, situation, and location. Pronouns or grammatical shifters, as Agamben discusses, isolate the self-referentiality of language, referring to nothing beyond themselves, only to their own utterance (2006, 16–26). Following Agamben, in putting the "I" to use, in apparently bringing the subject into play, I inevitably fix it in language, refer to it as a thing, and as such desubjectify it: the "I" enacts subjectification and desubjectification at once. In the act of I-ness, I am manifested as "Not I." For Agamben, this means that it is not strictly the "I" that speaks, nor is it the living individual; rather, these are silenced and what "speaks" is language itself: "in the absolute present of the event of discourse, subjectification and desubjectification coincide at every point and both the flesh and blood individual and the subject of enunciation are perfectly silent. This can also be expressed by saying that the one who speaks is not the individual, but language" (Agamben 2000, 117).

However, underpinning Agamben's project are ethical concerns with the possibility of *testimony*, understood not simply as describing an event one has experienced, but rather the speaking of something unsayable: bearing witness to something that is impossible truly to relay. It is important to acknowledge, here, that Agamben's starting point is one of the most extreme situations: the impossibility of putting into words the experience of World War II Nazi concentration camps. This is incomparable with matters of performance. Agamben's (2000) wider project, though, is a fundamental ethics of the subject;[4] he argues that it is "precisely this impossibility of conjoining the living being and language" (130), together with the impossibility of speaking "I" revealed in this, that provides the condition of possibility of testimony: the "I" is "suspended in this disjunction" (130): "If there is no articulation between the living being and language, if the 'I' stands suspended in that disjunction, then there can be testimony. The intimacy that bears our non-coincidence with ourselves is the place of testimony" (130). In this way, he argues, "Testimony takes place in the non-place of articulation" (130). As such, "the empty place of the subject becomes the decisive question" (145).[5] The very space between the "I" and the "not I"—

4 The question of the ethical relation to the other, beyond the ethics of the individual subject and the possibility of testimony, is taken up in chapter 4, drawing in particular upon the work of Levinas.

5 Of course, Agamben is one of many philosophers who, particularly since the last decades of the twentieth century, have focused on the critique of subjectivity and its various implications. Jean-Luc Nancy (1991b, 4) notes that "The critique or deconstruction of subjectivity is to be considered one of the great motifs of contemporary philosophical work in France, taking off from . . . the teachings of Marx, Nietzsche, Freud, Husserl, Heidegger, Bataille, Wittgenstein, from the teachings of linguistics, social sciences, and so forth." We might extend this far beyond French post-structuralist thought into a broader critical field that includes other forms of deconstruction, post-Marxism, recent phenomenology, and pragmatism. I find Agamben's discussion particularly pertinent, but given the parallel I draw later in this chapter between Agamben's ethics of the subject and the position taken by Judith Butler, Butler's similar articulation of the same problematic is worth noting: "Where there is an 'I' who utters or speaks

of positing the "I" while all the time recognising its impossibility, its provisionality and contingency—is a space of potential, provisional subjecthood.

This question of the status and potential of the "I" is central to this chapter. In the above I am focused on language—on the textual production of the "I," whether spoken or written. Musical identity is always to an extent constituted in and regulated by language: in the discourse that surrounds the practice, weighs it up, critiques it; and in the language of practising, in rehearsal. As Lawrence Kramer says (2002, 42), however abstract a piece of music seems, not only is it always created in and influenced by a particular cultural context, mediated in part by language, but also it, in myriad ways, has "already, always already, been imbued with knowledge and meaning from a thousand sources outside the immediate sphere of music." Nevertheless, in the embodied, contingent and ephemeral space of performance—any kind of performance—things may operate somewhat differently; and within that space, music does not act like language, or at least not *just* like language: arguably, musical deixis is even more slippery.

I will argue that beyond text the related but different "I" embodied in performance enacts a similar, simultaneous positing and retracting of the "I." In this the multiplicity and contingency of subjectivity is more evident, due to its constitution in and through performance, with bodies, in a context and in a dynamic of presence and disappearance. Erika Fischer-Lichte's (2012) discussion of different forms of "presence"—weak, strong, and radical—becomes useful here, with respect to embodied subjectivity in *Player Piano*. As Peggy Phelan discusses (1993, 167), performance that in some sense draws attention to the status of the body in performance often operates "in the suspension between the 'real' physical matter of 'the performing body' and the psychic experience of what it is to be em-bodied." In doing so, "performance uses the performer's body to pose a question about the inability to secure the relation between subjectivity and the body *per se*" (ibid., 150–51).

In this sense, performance might be particularly relevant to Agamben's concerns, due to its complex presentation and retraction of subjecthood, constituted in part through language but substantially otherwise, through bodies and other materials, human and non-human, and appearing to manifest discrete subjects that, nevertheless, can never be fully formed. These subjects are contingent and multiple rather than autonomous and discrete: distributed and multiple, simultaneously tangible and ephemeral, present and absent. Of course, much performance pretends otherwise: naturalistic theatre requires our acquiescence, however temporarily, in believing in characters with back-stories and motivation, while music is often received as if it delivers first-person accounts

and thereby produces an effect in discourse, there is first a discourse which precedes and enables that 'I' and forms in language the constraining trajectory of its will. Thus there is no 'I' who stands *behind* discourse and executes its volition or will *through* discourse. On the contrary, the 'I' only comes into being through being called, named, interpellated. . . . it is the historically revisable possibility of a name that precedes and exceeds me, but without which I cannot speak" (Butler 1993, 225–26). As discussed later in this text, Butler's consideration of the "de-constituting possibility" inherent in the difference-in-repetition of subjective action might be considered related to Agamben's "non-place of articulation."

of apparently authentic, individual emotional experience. However, when performance self-consciously alerts us to its very performativity, the gap between subjectification and desubjectification might be productively opened up (and perhaps especially so in musical performance, with its relative absence of language, matrix, or character): this might be one situation which, in Agamben's words, "demands subjectivity as that which, in its very possibility of speech, bears witness to an impossibility of speech" (2000, 146).

In performance, then, the "I" is a useful pronomial container for the performer: a particular entity, a particular body. But that is a function, a carrier of something that is neither singular nor fixed. *Player Piano* in fact originated in the context of a research project—practice-led, artistic research—founded on questions about that very issue: it forms one output of a research cluster called "Performance, Subjectivity, and Experimentation," based at the Orpheus Institute in Ghent, with my research also taking place at the University of York in the UK.

The above provides an introduction to the concerns of this research project, but also to the practice-as-research component and the performance output that emerged: *Player Piano*. This extended chapter will consider in some detail the production of embodied subjectivity in this performance, constituted by a range of interactions: with the composed materials (in addition to improvised moments), with the piano and other sound-making objects, and with the space of performance. The first part of the discussion, however, sets the scene by considering in more detail the context of the research and matters of performer subjectivity.

Can't get you out of my . . . fingers? repetition and deviation in voice formation

First, I will take a short step backwards for a moment. To speak of subjectivity in musical performance seems to be a dangerous business. To do so is often to be understood as referring to matters of self-expression—in turn often understood, in the world of composed music, as basically a question of interpretation. However, self-expression is predicated on a discrete sense of self, and interpretation requires not just an interpreting subject but a relatively stable notion of an object of interpretation; we might legitimately question the extent to which we have these, except provisionally, in the processes of music-making.

The notion of the self as a singular, autonomous unit, subject to the pressures of society, culture, and politics, has underpinned modern Western society but has, in recent decades been thoroughly deconstructed; the critique provided by Agamben, employed above, is just one strand in a widespread critical excavation of the basis of self-determination, from a range of different philosophical and political perspectives.[6] The notion of selfhood might now be permanently in question, but the recourse to individual experience and agency persists.

6 The work of Habermas (especially 1984, 1989) is particularly influential in this context, with Foucault offering a different approach to the critique of the relationship between selfhood and the social structures of power, particularly from *The Birth of the Clinic* onwards ([1973] 1989).

Moreover, even if the "speaking" self—the self that aims, through language or otherwise, to articulate itself—does not precede (does not simply make use of) the structures and materials of discourse and expression, but is brought into being by them, this does not absolve us of responsibility for what we say or do. Following Foucault, we might then ask: who is that "we" to whom responsibility is attached? How does that agency emerge in subjective form? (Foucault 1977, 115–16). Michael Fagenblat echoes this, in his review of Jean-Luc Nancy's account of the multiple "we-ness" of subjectivity in *Being Singular Plural*: "If individualism and subjectivism are but sticky residues of our modern tradition, how is it that we continue to value the singularity of events and identities?" (Fagenblat 2002, 210). In this sense, as Amanda Dennis (2018, 6) suggests, in the twenty-first century, the challenge "to the idea of an autonomous, willing subject is to arrive at an account of agency robust enough to survive, if not the death of the subject, then at least its imbrication in complex social structures and environments."

In terms of *Player Piano* and the research of which it forms a part, this is the question of how the process of subject-making proceeds: how the subject takes its place in performance but also recedes, the "I"-ness of the "I" coming and going; how the performing "I" appears to manifest, to be there and in certain ways to assert itself as an individuated, meaningful expressive entity, but how its instability and its constitution by others becomes apparent, to different degrees and in different ways, throughout the performance. Music is certainly striking in its ability to carry subjectivity—a sense of what it is to be and feel in the world—without the specifics of character. Musical performers do not explicitly "play" a role, except in opera and music theatre, and a performer may be concerned with emotional expression but rarely pretends to be experiencing those feelings personally. Nevertheless, musical performance usually evinces a deep sense of personal engagement and identification,[7] which helps to shape the "self" projected in performance; this is the case even in contemporary experimental practices.

In chapter 1 (p. 39), Gorton and Östersjö introduced Naomi Cumming's examination of the ways in which the production of a particular musical tone through a well-balanced physical adjustment to the instrument is central to creating the impression of a musical persona; it is linked to the idea of a performer's "voice." However, the notion of a performer's "voice"—or, as Cumming termed it, a "sonic self" (2000, 23)—is a mainstay of Western musical practice (not least of processes of learning) and yet remains barely interrogated, particularly from within practice itself.

In Western music, distinctiveness of expression is highly valued as an eventual goal, often after a long process of learning that is based on the opposite: imitation and conformity to normalised expectations. As Lehmann, Sloboda, and Woody note (2007, 86), "it can become a matter of huge personal significance, even financial survival, that one way of playing a well-known repertoire

7 Nicky Losseff's work on this, with respect to processes of projective identification in classical music performance, is especially interesting (2011).

piece is unique and recognizable as quite different from another way of playing it." Research shows that performance students and instrumental teachers (especially in higher education) often regard developing an individual performing "voice" to be their main aim (Mills and Smith 2003)—whether a singing voice or a metaphorical voice projected through an instrument—and this is by no means confined to classical music; it is certainly common in jazz (Berliner 1994; Jackson 2002, 94; Haddon 2013). Likewise, popular media commentary encourages the idea of musical performance as self-realisation. Simple web searches confirm a very large number of pages devoted to providing budding musicians, across genres, with advice on how to "develop your creative voice," find a "unique artistic style," or establish your "individual artistic identity."

High-profile professional performers also frequently speak in similar terms: pianist Boris Berman (2000, 198) states that, with students, a "teacher's main role is to help them find their own musical voice," while cellist Frances-Marie Uitti (2017, 346) comments that "while teaching at Oberlin Conservatory, I was particularly proud that none of my cello students sounded either like me or like one another; each student developed his or her own sound." Jazz saxophonist Andy Sheppard discusses the emergence of musical "authenticity" in terms of the slow process from an initial focus on imitating others towards "accepting your own inner voice, and then you start becoming individual" (Haddon 2006, 199). Carlos Lopez-Real (also a saxophonist), distinguishes between his different "voices": "I have an individual artistic voice and an artistic voice embedded within a collective of musicians, a community of practice" (2017, 241).

These are just a few of many possible examples.[8] In all cases, there seems to be an assumption that we understand what an individual "voice" is—at least, when we find or hear it—and that performers all need one. While recent studies of collaborative practices emphasise the social emergence and distributed nature of creativity,[9] and while our abundant access, via the internet, to a vast range of music-making from around the world might seem to offer an implicit challenge to the notion of individual distinctiveness—singer Jane Manning suggests that this "militates against finding one's own niche" (2017, 129)[10]—little of this seems to have had an impact upon the pervasive and persistent recourse to the notion of individual authenticity. As Anahid Kassabian (2013, xxiv) argues, in her work on distributed subjectivity in listening, "individual subjectivity continues to appear to us to function, even as many of the notions on which it was based have deteriorated or disappeared (the bourgeois family, Enlightenment individuality, and so on)." Whether in classical music, contemporary experi-

8 Comments by the pianists Imogen Cooper and Ronan O'Hora, cited in Gaunt (2017, 30), similarly stress the development of "voice" in related terms.

9 The work of Sawyer and DeZutter (2009) is particularly important here, as is Vera John-Steiner's book *Creative Collaboration* (2000). Numerous more specific studies of composer–performer collaborations and group-distributed creativity have emerged in recent years, as noted in the introduction, above.

10 In contrast, Susan Tomes describes how listening to recordings of the pieces she is working on often seems to reinforce the very sense that her approach is both different and preferable (2010, 64). Of course, this is the perspective of a performer well into a long, successful career, whereas Manning's point is more focused on students. Both, although in different ways, reinforce the fundamental notion that finding a "voice" is widely considered hugely important for performers, even though little attention is paid to what it is or how it is formed.

mental forms, jazz, or pop, highly regulated notions of "good" or "great" performance—of appropriate and inappropriate sounds, actions, appearances, behaviours—lie alongside injunctions to be oneself, authentic and original.[11]

Mine Doğantan-Dack (2017) notes the potential contradictions between "the model of learning in western classical performance (and indeed in most other musical genres and cultures), dominated at least in its early stages—and arguably by necessity—by processes of *imitation* and *repetition*, neither of which seems ideally conducive to encouraging a plurality of interpretative approaches" (132), and the overarching aim of developing "a *personal artistic voice*, the most vital aspect of which is the cultivation of *expressive freedom*" (131). As Doğantan-Dack says, little attention is paid to the transition: "there has been no systemic approach to determining either the stage during the learning process when the student is supposed to move from imitating to expressing a personal artistic view, or the means by which this might be done" (132).

This is all focused on the practical training of musicians and the professional status of the distinctive voice. However, there is an equal lack of musicological or other critical attention to the "personal artistic voice" (in Doğantan-Dack's terms) or the production of subjectivity as manifested in performance. Clemens Wöllner (2013) identifies the same basic issue—that "individuality is highly valued" in music performance but poorly understood—and considers ways to deal with this empirically by quantifying the manifest acoustical differences between performances in terms of timing, timbre, pitch, and intensity. However, the equation of the culturally valued notion of authentic individuality with acoustic differences is, even within a defined cultural context, problematic.[12] Searching for more critically aware approaches, it still seems to be the case that the act of performance is neglected. Chris Stover (2016) notes that "musical scholarship tends to focus on either music's sonic materialities (the sensible; what can be heard) or the cultural resonances that locate in and through music (the political or hermeneutic: how meaning is inscribed in and for a listening subject)." As Stover says, the "embodied turn" in scholarship is increasingly connecting with work in feminist theory, queer theory, and embodied cognition, to examine the experiencing of music from the perspectives of different performers, composers, and listeners. However, from the evidence to date, I do not share Stover's sense that, for all its other qualities, very much of this has shed direct light upon the effect "that making or experiencing has on subject-formation" (ibid.). Overall, there is still relatively little work on, or through, performance that directly addresses such questions.

11 Simon Frith (1996b, 210) comments on the (mediated) doubleness of the pop-star voice in similar terms: "The star voice . . . acts as a mark of both subjectivity and objectivity, freedom and constraint, control and lack of control. And technology, electrical recording, has exaggerated this effect by making the vocal performance more intimate, more self-revealing, and more (technologically) determined. The authenticity or 'sincerity' of the voice becomes the recurring pop question: does she really *mean* it?"

12 Even within a specific cultural practice, defining individuality in terms of "deviation from a prototypical exemplar" (Wöllner 2013) is deeply problematic. Beyond the vexed question of the criteria for choosing that exemplar, the significant issue is how to correlate degrees of deviation with individual expression so as to explain why one performance might be more "highly valued" than another.

Beyond (musical) text: the social, situated performance persona

Inevitably, much of the limited research in this field turns, still, on the agency of performers relative to composers; the assumption, often, is that the subjectivity, as manifested in any individual act of performance, is substantially dependent upon the composition and hence the composer. This persists in performance despite the extensive critique of the work concept, particularly since the 1990s; even Taruskin's terse characterisation of performers as "*essentially* corruptors—deviants, in fact" (1996, 13), is predicated on that model.[13] As John Rink, Helena Gaunt, and Aaron Williamon note (2017, xxiii), despite certain exceptions (especially in jazz improvisation), even now, "from a research standpoint, the performance of western classical music seems to be viewed less in terms of the performer's creative input and more as a matter of reproduction . . . , whether of composers' intentions or the dictates of given scores and performing traditions." In certain respects, recent developments in music performance studies have led beyond this, with calls from Nicholas Cook and others to reconsider the status of musical scores—and works—in the determination of the creativity of performers. Cook's suggestion that we might think of scores less textually and more as scripts is intended to shift the focus from "reading" (textual interpretation) to embodied interaction: "Whereas to think of a Mozart quartet as a 'text' is to construe it as a half-sonic, half-ideal object reproduced in performance, to think of it as a 'script' is to see it as choreographing a series of real-time, social interactions between players: a series of mutual acts of listening and communal gestures that enact a particular vision of human society" (Cook 2001). Gorton and Östersjö, in chapter 1 (p. 45), take this a step further, drawing on the work of Paul Ricœur (1991) to argue that the very act of writing notation distances the composer from the musical material: the composer's relationship to their own notation becomes one of interpretation, alongside (though different to) that of the performer (and hence underpinning a more truly co-creative understanding of score-based musical making). Likewise, it has in the last few years become increasingly common for studies of musical performance to reference Christopher Small's term "musicking," to signal a focus on music as something we do—whether as performers of any kind, or as composers or listeners—rather than on the various reified musical objects or artefacts that are produced by that activity. However, few have taken on the challenge presented by Small's claim that "performance does not exist in order to present musical works, but rather, musical works exist in order to give performers something to perform" (1998, 8); Cook's shift from text to script does not fundamentally displace the composer's centrality to what transpires.[14]

13 This point also underpins the research by Mary Hunter and Stephen Broad into the complex ways in which performance students struggle to navigate the paradoxes of learning simultaneously to be faithful to the composer's vision and to find their own "voice." Hunter and Broad (2017, 260) conclude: "we seem to have . . . a situation where classical music practitioners, if asked, will refer to the default ideology embedded in classical music discourse, but where, in actual practice, that ideology is experienced as secondary to, or hidden behind, the more urgent and 'pan-generic' concerns of presenting a performance for a given audience in a given situation."

14 Philip Auslander's comment (2006, 101n2) amplifies this point, noting an unintended consequence of Cook's choice of terminology: "his un-marked shift from a dramatic metaphor (text) to one based on dance (choreography) is noteworthy, not least because choreography is sometimes considered to be even more determining of performance than a play script."

Philip Auslander, partly in response to Cook, seems to offer a way forward that, more substantially than Small, acknowledges the *potentially* significant role of composition in the constitution of performer subjectivity (only potentially, because in fact most performance is not of composed works); but he presents it as one factor alone in a more complex process of identity formation. Auslander (2006, 101–2) draws on David Graver's notion of the "personage": a theatre or film actor's production of a presence that is neither the "real" person nor the character portrayed, but something in between. The idea of "personage" cannot be directly imported into music performance, not least due to the absence of "character," but Auslander argues for musical performance as similarly "defined, using Graver's terms, as *a person's representation of self within a discursive domain of music*" (ibid., 102); he proposes the idea of a musical "persona" (to differentiate from the theatrical personage). In Auslander's co-option of Graver's ideas into music, then, "both the musical work and its execution serve the musician's performance of a persona" (ibid.).

Auslander's formulation is attractive because it acknowledges that in composed music the composer's agency is active in the formation of performer subjectivity:[15] the composition—of any kind, whether notated or not, and however so—of course carries some force, guiding, to some degree, the performer's activities, her use of the instrument, and her interaction with other players and other aspects of the context. But it also implicitly acknowledges the complexities of the process by which a performing self might emerge and the significant agency of other entities in the process, the other actors in the network of interaction that constitutes even solo performance. Moreover, in drawing attention to the discursive production of the persona—from the interaction of self, others, instruments, and context—Auslander's approach signals the potential similarities in its processes of emergence across composed and non-composed musics and across styles: such productions are not necessarily specific or confined to the practices of Western classical music. This is not to suggest that this approach is universally applicable; but (unlike notions of performer identity predicated on a relation to a composition) it acknowledges that the differences between the production of performer subjectivity across forms of music-making are not solely due to the presence, or not, of a composer. Ultimately, then, for Auslander, "to be a musician is to perform an identity in a social realm"; compositions sometimes constitute one part of that sociality (2006, 101).

This relates directly back to the notion of the discursive voice outlined in chapter 1. Moreover, the models produced in that chapter are directly applicable to much of the work for *Player Piano*, in terms of the emergence of "voice" through the interactions of performer, composers, instrument, notations, and the cul-

15 In *Beyond the Score*, Cook (2013, 336) responds to Auslander's critique and draws on his notion of the performance persona. However, he asserts that while Auslander's position is appropriate for popular and improvised musics, it "becomes harder to justify in contexts that are more strongly conditioned by musical works." I would argue that Auslander pays more heed to composers and their pieces than he is given credit for, here: he frequently acknowledges their agency in certain musical contexts, but (productively, in my view) questions their conventional primacy, in favour of a more dynamic model in which musical signficance is produced discursively and constituted in the persona.

tural contexts of the related practices. Given the nature of *Player Piano*, however, the question becomes focused on the ways in which subjectivity is discursively constructed in a context that incorporates theatrical practices, elements of improvisation, and film, in addition to collaboration with four composers.

One consequence of thinking of performer subjectivity as produced in this way—negotiated in context, through interaction with materials, instruments, time, and space—is to acknowledge that the "sonic self," "voice," or "persona" is created differentially each time. In this sense, we do not simply perform a "self"; rather, the event is performative of selfhood: selfhood emerges as a process, not merely as something that becomes reflected in or somehow expressed through performance. Likewise, the performance might not always be "about" a self or explicitly expressive of personal emotion, but a musical persona is nevertheless produced: musicians often engage in sophisticated self-reinvention through performance. In a study of how a range of women use music, as listeners, in their personal and social lives—to regulate emotions, change energy levels, create and negotiate memories and narratives of the self, form social bonds, develop a sense of personal and social identity, and so on—Tia DeNora argues for music as a "technology of the self" (1999, 31).[16] Examining her respondents' consumption of music, she focuses on the "musical reflexive practices they employ to constitute and reconstitute themselves as specific types of agents" (31). However, if, for listeners, music is "a material that actors use to elaborate, to fill out and fill in, to themselves and to others, modes of aesthetic agency and with it subjective stances and identities" (54), then surely the creative work of musical performers is, on one level, a similar project of emergent self-determination, albeit with different materials, interactions, and contexts. As DeNora says, "it is curious, then, that music . . . has been little explored in relation to the constitution of the self" (32); and while DeNora addresses that gap in terms of music "consumption," the performance gap remains.[17]

Importantly, performer subjectivity is differently and more overtly embodied than listening,[18] and in more than one sense: the complexities of physical activity determine the nuances of sound quality, but also the gestural content of a performance contributes to the perceived expression, and hence to the process of subject formation. In particular, musicians work in gradations of tone, and for the performer there is, as Doğantan-Dack puts it, an "experiential continu-

16 The article referenced here and elsewhere in this chapter was subsequently republished with minor modifications in DeNora's book *Music in Everyday Life* (2000, chapter 3).

17 Mareli Stolp (2017, 2) notes that "while studies of performer consciousness and music cognition have already received much focused attention, explorations of consciousness, self-awareness and subjectivity as these apply specifically to issues of artistic research have perhaps not received comparable attention and such studies may yield much that could enrich the field."

18 Listening is most certainly an embodied activity, as has been explored by many recent studies in musicology, sound studies, and psychology (this is touched upon below, drawing on Peters 2012). However, the extent to which a listener is explicitly aware of this varies considerably, according to both the listening subject's perception of the bodily "work" they hear in a performance, and also according to their awareness of their own embodiedness in the listening process. This variation has implications for the reflexive constitution of the self that, DeNora argues, emerges from music consumption. In contrast, for a performer there is no getting away from the active involvement of the body in the production of musical sound.

ity" between tone colour and gesture (2011, 250). Certainly, for me, sound production is at the heart of piano playing; my sense of myself as a performer with, perhaps, "something to say" is deeply bound to this embodied experience, to tone, timbre, resonance, and touch.

Moreover, as noted in chapter 1, performers' apparently personal performance decisions (of all kinds) are mediated and moderated by the social and cultural contexts in which they operate. The individuated sonic self is, in part through its very embodiment, social: it is multiple, dynamic, and contingent. What comes to feel my own—*my* sound, *my* sense of *my* body at the instrument, *my* something to say—is developed through processes of teaching, cultural practice, and listening based on mimicry, repetition, comparison, and deviation. It is developed and received socially: collaboratively and differentially.[19] I would argue that this is central to the "gap" that Doğantan-Dack identifies between the imitative basis of instrumental pedagogy and the notion of the development of an individual voice. To address this requires, first, a reconsideration of the function of repetition and mimicry, acknowledging its differential potential: the repetitive practice that is fundamental for musicians does not just facilitate technical dexterity but sometimes also other forms of insight, manifesting fragments of music as objects of embodied attention. Bruce Brubaker notes that "replaying is our practice, a structuring of time, and, for the player, a structuring of life" (2016). Second, however, we need better to understand the production of the apparently individual voice as formed socially and contingently, through the taking into oneself of the practices and ideas of others, embodying them, repeating aspects of them in new contexts, with one's own body, so that they in certain respects transform—whether substantively, with new content, or more subtly, with new articulations of old content—perhaps revealing something new, particular, and different.

Me and my piano face: constructing the performer

The historical emergence of the notion of the performer's voice in Western music is significant. In her article, "To Play as If from the Soul of the Composer" (2005), Mary Hunter scrutinises the shift from Enlightenment to early Romantic notions of the performer—a shift towards performance as the place where a number of musical dualisms would be resolved: those of composer and performer, performer and listener, the performer and the music "itself," and of technique and expression (371–72). Hunter describes the Romantic idea of performance as "imaginative reconstruction" (372);[20] the nuance a performer applied in realising a score was no longer, as in Enlightenment aesthetics, conceived as a continuation of the process of composition, but increasingly as a matter of *re-creation*, re-enactment, uniting composer and performer (375). "To play as if

19 Linson and Clarke (2017, 55) make a similar point, stressing "the socially constructed nature of musical materials and performance practices," "since what appears to an individual as an immediate, local environment includes practices developed over generations and shared across social groups. . . . an individual's knowledge is fundamentally interconnected with the knowledge of others."

20 Hunter takes this phrase from Bonds (1997, 393–94).

from the soul of the composer" was for the performer to act *as if* a kind of real-time composer, but simultaneously guided by the spirit of *the* composer. The gap between composition and realisation, absence and presence (or "the I and not-I of performer and music," as Hunter puts it [371]), was thereby—apparently—resolved. Importantly, Hunter argues that with the imperative for the performer "to transform oneself in the direction of a pre-ordainedly greater spirit" (392), subjectivity becomes woven into the idea of performance. In the very moment of possession by the composer's spirit, the performer is, it seems, more than ever "himself" (almost exclusively male, of course, in this historical context), ever more unique, individual and authentic in his expression.

One of Hunter's key points is that this same Romantic aesthetic of performance, summarised as "honor the composer; express yourself; don't think of this as a contradiction" (2005, 393) remains prevalent in classical performance practices and pedagogy today. In further research with Stephen Broad, Hunter evidences the ways in which high-level music students struggle to negotiate the paradox of simultaneously finding a (differentiated) voice while directing all efforts to honouring the composer's higher ideas (Hunter and Broad 2017). There are many further examples from professional practice. Pianist Susan Tomes describes a coaching session with violinist Zoltán Székely in which the players struggled with the different possibilities for the dynamics in a particular passage by Beethoven, discussing alternatives, trying them, and finding that Székely agreed that one approach was convincing but continued to worry away at whether it was "right." Tomes writes: "That is the question. Do we have the right to get louder, or must we resist, for Beethoven's sake?" (2010, 36).

Hunter is concerned to show why this aesthetic—persistent in performance practice, despite extensive musicological critique of the work concept and substantial study of the co-creative basis of most music-making—is anachronistic with respect to understandings of earlier music, particularly of the late eighteenth century. However, from this, Hunter continues: "In modern times, we have, I think, translated what early Romantic writers would have figured as a psychological or spiritual capacity to identify with the genius or intentions of the composer into the catchall adjective 'musical'" (2005, 393). Post-Romantic performance carries many of the same obligations; we have naturalised into much of our pedagogy and performance expectations these very same notions of what it is to be expressive and musical. I would argue that this underpins ideas not just of how a performer should respond to a score, through choices of sound quality, timbre, phrase shape, and articulation, but also how they should look, move, and behave. The notion of a "musical" performance is mostly a nineteenth-century notion of how to manifest an idea of subjective engagement with certain kinds of musical materials. "Musicianship" here involves negotiating nuance, which is understood as signifying the personal, within a highly regulated notion of what is stylistically appropriate, so that it's not *too* personal: "Too much invention and you're out of bounds, but too literal an understanding of historical obligation and you're equally wrong" (Hunter and Broad 2017, 268). A particular, recognisable, culturally sanctioned *idea* of subjectivity is not only what we expect to hear produced in performance but also what we expect to see, physically embodied in expressive gestures.

Arguably, this is especially true for the piano and the pianist. Of course, the development of the grand piano is key to the evolution of the concept of absolute music and the *Werktreue* aesthetic throughout the nineteenth century. It was primarily through the development of the solo piano concert (initially thanks to Liszt) that Schopenhauer's notion of music as the highest art form, the unique manifestation of the will in itself, came into practice. The lone, pioneering virtuoso, using his—mostly "his," historically—extensive pianistic prowess and harnessing the formidable beast of an instrument, personifies this. The piano in this sense becomes the symbol of Western individualist humanism: the pianist often, still, acts within this mode, reproducing an idea of subjectivity, sonically and physically, that derives from nineteenth-century ideals of expression, truth, authenticity, and transcendence.

We see this not just in the reproduction of normalising of modes of musical expression and shaping—ideas of a "good" sound, of appropriate nuances of timing, and so on—but also in the vocabularies of expressive hand and arm gestures, the action of the upper body, and intensities of facial expression. Arguably, this is the case not just in extensions of the classical tradition, but also in many performances of avant-garde music, in jazz, in some performances of experimental music, and in many singer-songwriters at the piano. Auslander points out that the phenomenon of the rock "guitar face," identified by Isaac Guzman and catalogued into a range of forms, including "suffering, satanic possession, surprise at the guitarist's own virtuosity, swagger, sex god status, spirituality, and stoicism" (Auslander 2006, 112), manifests across Western styles as a signifier of authentic emotional engagement. The acceptable forms vary according to the conventions of style and context, but they are pervasive and notable: Auslander argues, for example, that Julian Bream's classical guitar face (discussed by Godlovitch 1998, 141) or Pavarotti's "tenor face" perform the same basic function (as do vocabularies of gesture beyond facial expression): "an idealized image of the musician as emotionally expressive is conveyed through dramatizations of the process of music-making that purport to expose the musician's internal state while performing" (Auslander 2006, 112).

The same is certainly true of the sound-accompanying gestures of pianists,[21] whether the frown and nodding head that so often accompanies the placing of a particularly sonorous and resonant chord (used by many classical, jazz, and singer-songwriter pianists), to the raised eyebrows and open-mouthed delight at playful, decorative runs (especially in jazz and more light-hearted classical

21 Of course, these gestures might sometimes be classed as communicative—communicating expressive content to the audience—depending on the intentions of the performer and the perceptions of the audience. However, the point here is that pianists often make such gestures without any apparent communicative intention, but rather as part of the process of physically "following" the music, tracing with the body certain features of its manifestation (Jensenius et al. 2010, 23–28).

pieces).[22] "What is my piano face?" I started to wonder—and this formed part of my scrutiny of my performing gestures for developing a choreography for Roger Marsh's piece *Touch and Go*, as part of *Player Piano*, as discussed below. We look for the performance persona—for signs of authentic subjective engagement—in many of the same ways: the ideas of having found a voice, of having made the music our own, of being at one with it, are all traces of this. Often, its manifestation, sonically and visually, is encoded in modes of musical expression and behaviour that are all too recognisable and repeatable: we follow the signs that point to that *idea* of self-expression.

The discourse of performer subjectivity thereby produces the expectation that certain patterns of behaviour signify authentic, individual expression: the individual act is constituted through that discourse but also contributes to it, helps constitute it. For myself as performer, then, the key question, for each situation, is: *do I produce myself in performance or does the situation—do the structures of performing—produce me*? Here I am very obviously echoing the ways in which Judith Butler theorises the performativity of gender (1988), as is briefly discussed below. However, the implications of these critical points, extensively discussed in other fields—especially gender studies, philosophy, and critical theory, and performance studies outside music—are still little considered in music performance studies, where agency and subjectivity remain primarily focused in relation to composers and works or, in non-classical forms, almost exclusively towards socio-cultural matters.[23] Should we, then, consider subjectivity as an *effect* of performance, rather than the subject as the prime agent in producing an individuated performance?

The "deconstituting possibility" of performance: doing and undoing the performing self

Even Auslander's assertion that "to be a musician is to perform an identity in a social realm" might imply that identity precedes performance, rather than that, following Judith Butler (1988), identity is performative. Butler's primary focus has, of course, been gender, but her argument that gender is not a seamless

22 This becomes particularly evident when viewing compilations of piano performances on film, including historical footage, such as the DVD *The Art of the Piano: Great Pianists of the Twentieth Century* (Philips 1999). The YouTube video "Top 10 facial expressions of famous piano artists" provides additional (and amusing) substantiation (RubyCell Entertainment 2017). Of course, there are also examples of pianists (especially earlier in the twentieth century) who restrict their playing gestures as far as possible to those necessary for sound production and rarely allow their faces to betray any form of emotional engagement. However, in its extreme opposition to the characteristically animated pianistic face and body, we might understand this as a different manifestation of the same situation: such a reaction against demonstratively expressive physicality, in favour of restraint and containment, is produced in a context where certain modes of behaviour become normative as signifiers of authentic expression. Either way—if the alternatives on offer are a normalised vocabulary of physical behaviours or the shackling of the body to constrain its possibly excessive behaviour—this suggests a lack, in practice, of a more nuanced approach to the true (potential) role and significance of the musical body in musical experience.

23 Simon Frith (1996a) notes that "The academic study of popular music has been limited by the assumption that the sounds must somehow 'reflect' or 'represent' the people" (108), neglecting the ways in which identity is constituted through musical activity and is, therefore, "*mobile*, a process not a thing," with "our experience of music . . . best understood as an experience of . . . self-in-process" (109).

identity but rather emerges from "the stylized repetition of acts through time" and can as such be transformed through "a different sort of repeating, in the breaking or subversive repetition of that style" (ibid., 520) is one that has been applied in various ways in the context of performance studies beyond music, and to an extent in musicology, but surprisingly little in music performance. Naomi Cumming (2000, 7) herself might have been referencing Butler when she asked: "does the self form the sound, or the sound the self?" Likewise, Simon Frith (1996a, 108–11) seems to parallel Butler's ideas of performative identity but without referencing them when he critiques the academic study of popular music for its failure to consider identity as a process formed (and continually reformed) through performance, rather than solely reflected in it.

However, recently, Butler's work has been explicitly put to interesting use in the context of improvisation studies in music. Chris Stover's account of musical performing bodies as emergent subjectivities (referenced in the previous chapter) draws directly on Butler: he notes that "Like gender, musical identity is performed—we inscribe upon ourselves an emergent subjectivity through acts of performance and perception" (Stover 2016). More extensively, in the 2016 book *Negotiated Moments*, which examines the production of subjectivity and the negotiation of identity through improvisational practices, Tracey McMullen uses an interview with Butler to explore whether an improviser responds with individually determined freedom to the musical context of the moment or reproduces the possibilities of the musical system their training has engrained in them. McMullen (2016, 23) uses Butler's formulation to ask, "Does the subject *do* improvisation? Or is the subject *done* by improvisation, much like it is *done* by gender? Or is it something in between?" This loop—of enaction and constitution—is exactly that which underlies Cumming's question above; it lies at the heart of Butler's project, and it turns on the simultaneity of conformity and potential subversion, repetition and possible deviation, reinscription and transformation. Moreover, this points to something more crucial: the potential politics and ethics of the subject, posited in different terms but comparable to Agamben's articulation of simultaneous subjectification and desubjectification.

Central to this is the question of agency and constraint. Butler argues that an individual operates in relation to the "law" (the "rules," whether of gender, of improvisational or other musical practice, or in any context, and whether explicit or implicit). However, the law requires its repeated performance: one can choose to reproduce it through what one does, or to modify, differ, or even violate it: "The subject embodies and repeats the law—but this repetition is not mechanical or completely predictable. . . . In this sense, paradox is the subject's condition of possibility" (McMullen 2016, 23). Butler contends that we are not free agents: the subject is disciplined for exceeding norms or sometimes chooses to perpetuate norms "in order to be intelligible within the social field" (ibid., 23). This is exactly what Hunter and Broad discuss—though not in these terms—in considering the limits of performer "deviation" (or the dangerous manifestations of ego) in music performance practices.[24] But the agential condition of possibility is there: Butler calls it a "deconstituting possibility" (1993, 10).

This central preoccupation resurfaces with slightly different emphases across Butler's writings. In *Giving an Account of Oneself*, she asks "how a theory of subject formation that acknowledges the limits of self-knowledge can serve a conception of ethics" (2005, 19), while in *Senses of the Subject* she notes that "norms, conventions, institutional forms of power, are already acting prior to any action I may undertake" (2015, 6). In her Adorno Prize Lecture, Butler articulates this similarly: "it may well be true that the only terms by which this 'I' grasps itself are those that belong to a discourse that precedes and informs thought without any of us being able fully to grasp its working and its effect" (2012, 11). However, through all this there runs a thread of resistance; the sense that the impossibility of total self-knowledge and the force of the established "law" should not mean that we abandon responsibility. The Adorno Lecture continues: "And since values are defined and distributed through modes of power whose authority must be questioned, I am in a certain bind. Do I establish myself in the terms that would make my life valuable, or do I offer a critique of the reigning order of values?" (ibid., 11).

This is in one sense the bind of the musical performer: the contradictions between repetition of and deviation from the conventions of practice, and hence between the manifestations of subjectivity that are constituted therein. However, the conditions of performance, as discussed above, offer the possibility to reflect this back, to self-consciously mark the "unmarkedness" of performance (in Phelan's terms [1993]), exposing the simultaneous "now"-ness of the self in performance—apparently present, unique, and authentic—with the "not-now"-ness of its obvious repeatedness; its "reiterated corporeal behaviors," as Diana Taylor puts it (2016, 26), or "twice-behaved behaviour," in Richard Schechner's characterisation (1985, 36).

I would argue that these negotiations of identity and the performative constitution of subjectivity are just as central to music as other forms of discourse, and also (noting the uses to which Butler's work has been put in musical contexts) just as relevant to composed music as improvisation. In *Player Piano* I attempt to explore these questions through practice itself, reflexively and by means of iteration: that is, through modes of practice that expose some of these issues and try to make them evident. To explain this, I first examine the role of the body in some detail, thereafter exploring the dynamic emergence of embodied subjectivity through interaction with the instrument and the broader ecology of the site of performance.

24 On the basis of their ethnographic and other research, Hunter and Broad note that "concern about the propriety of the overt intrusion of 'ego' in performance and interpretation is especially acute in classical music" (2017, 256).

Part 2: The Embodied Subject in Player Piano

Piano body

Figure 2.1.

In *Player Piano*, the pianist's body is, at times, brought to the fore, presented as more than a means of making sound. I work around, in, and through the piano, but also away from it, with some activities elsewhere in the space, though always in some sense in relation to the instrument. Due to the key concerns of the project, in designing the scenography of *Player Piano* I wanted to think about the arena of performance as a whole, beyond the localised, intense focus on an individual player seated at her instrument that is characteristic of the piano recital. (The basic set-up of the stage can be seen in figure 2.2.) The intention was to induce a certain reflexivity into the performance, whereby pianist, instrument, and performance—and their relationships—were not just the prime media but also the subject matter. On one level the piece was to be, at least in part, "about" the embodied site of performance-making as itself a kind of technology of the (performing) self (to echo the words of Tia DeNora quoted earlier); it should be revealing of the "musical reflexive practices [we] employ to constitute [our] selves as specific types of agents" (1999, 31).

Figure 2.1. Still from performance by Catherine Laws of Roger Marsh, *Touch and Go* (with gestural choreography by Catherine Laws): this piece formed part of the large-scale performance *Player Piano*. Film by Minyung Im; sound by Lynette Quek. (The film is available in the online repository [www.orpheusinstituut.be/en/voices-bodies-practices-media-repository], file "SF2.2 Touch and Go.")

In this sense the emergence of a subject, however unstable, in and through the act of performance was thematised through its interactions with instrument, compositions (and by extension composers), objects, and the performance environment: the performer was both subject in a process and an object of scrutiny. I would argue that this could not have been achieved by presenting the conventional situation of a piano recital, whatever the musical material; it was important that the audience should not simply receive this event as a piano concert, even if some of the performance reverted to that mode or at the very least referenced its conditions. The performance needed to be marked, self-consciously, as something other: not simply *as* piano performance, but in some sense as asking us to think about the situation of piano performance.

Moreover, it was important to signal the emergence of performer identity as a function of the interaction of the various agencies of performer, composer, and the instrumental and environmental contexts. That performer agency should in some way be overtly significant here was vital. It is hardly unusual for performers of contemporary music to be asked by composers to do more than "simply" play their instruments; the various notions of the "expanded performer," increasingly common in Western new music practices since the 1960s, whether couched as instrumental theatre, music theatre, composed theatre, or Jennifer Walshe's recent conceptualisation of the "new discipline," all involve a willingness to, as Walshe puts it, "accept that the bodies playing the music are part of the music, that they're present, they're valid and they inform our listening whether subconsciously or consciously" (2016). For Walshe, this pushes beyond the specific notion of music placed in a theatrical context or performers "acting" into a broader sense of music as an embodied practice: "these compositional techniques—they are not 'music theatre', they *are* music. Or from a different perspective, maybe what is at stake is the idea that all music is music theatre" (ibid.).

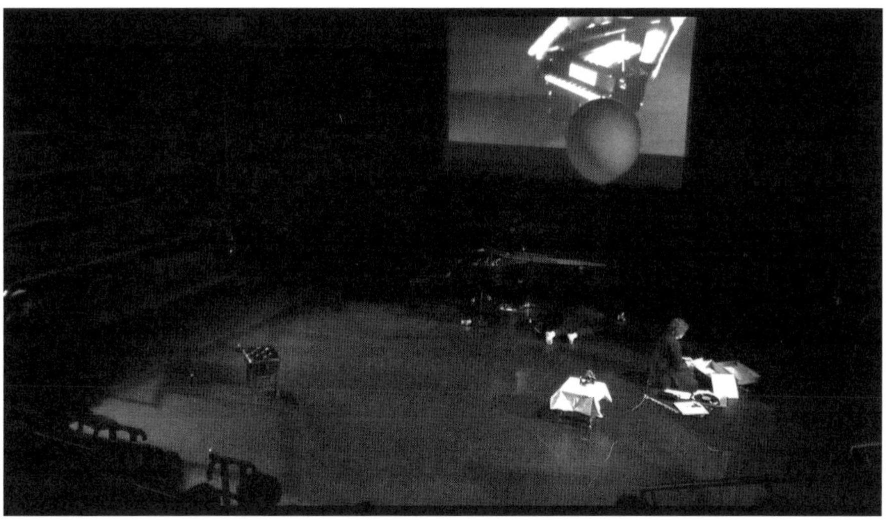

Figure 2.2.

Figure 2.2. Stage set for *Player Piano* (from premiere performance, Scenic Stage Theatre, York, 5 May 2016).

Certain forms of notation—tablature and forms of action notation—have, historically, directed performer attention towards what to do, physically, to produce sound, but with some composers, recently, the conventional priorities of sound and movement are fully reversed.[25] For example, in Simon Steen-Andersen's first *Study for String Instrument* (2007), which can be played by one or more players of any string instrument, only the players' movements in time (not the resultant sounds) are notated, with the bow and string hands represented on separate, parallel staves. Broadly, certain sounding results are inevitable, as a result of the determined actions—the trajectory of the hand movements with various forms of glissandi, up and down in different durations—but the pitch range and details of sound quality will vary considerably, determined entirely by the movement on the particular instrument. What is the material, the "Movement of the sound or sound of the movement?" Steen-Andersen asks in the preface to the score (2007).[26] Some composers further disentangle the parameters of sound-producing actions in multi-layered scores. In Aaron Cassidy's *The Crutch of Memory* (for unspecified string instrument), hand position, finger spacing, and fingerings are each notated on separate staves. Cassidy (2004) regards "physicality and gestural choreography as a primary determinant for material" (47), arguing that "the primary morphological unit—not only in my music but also in music in general—is not merely the aural gesture, but far more importantly, the physical gesture" (34).

In her discussion of the body in performance art, Helena De Preester (2007, 351) notes: "In recent history of art, the body is no longer solely the content or subject of a work of art, but also functions as canvas, brush, frame, or platform. As a brush, for example, the body has become a tool for painting, and leaves traces of itself and its activities in the work of art." The effect of this is to foreground what previously had remained implicit: the active agency of the body. In music, a parallel process has taken place, but from the opposite starting point: historically, in most musical performance, the body has been more comparable to the brush; the body produces the content, but disappears into sound, serves it. The body is usually, in Erika Fischer-Lichte's terms, a "weak presence": phenomenally there, before the gaze, but primarily semiotic (2012, 106–8).[27] In such cases the body is not, itself, the subject. However, in the range of recent practice identified above, the action of the body comes to the fore: to different extents, and in different ways, it becomes overtly significant, becomes content.

25 It is notable that a whole chapter of Jennie Gottschalk's recent book *Experimental Music Since 1970* is given over to "Physicalities," including a section on the physicality of performance (2016, 77–106).

26 A further example is the piece *Disjointed*, written by William Brooks for me and percussionist Damien Harron. Here, a little similar to in Steen-Andersen's piece (though to very different effect), it is gesture that comprises the basic compositional material and precise movements that are notated (trajectories of the hands, related to the keyboard and percussion instruments). For a film of the piece, see Laws, Harron, and Brooks (2013).

27 Victor Ramirez Ladrón de Guevara characterises this as the "imagined body": "one that inhabits a performance act, usually associated with the creation of characters" (2011, 30); this seems to be the theatrical equivalent of the conventional "disappearance" of the musical performer's phenomenal body into the service of the musical work. Phillip Zarrilli's notion of the "aesthetic body" is also comparable (2009, 58).

Moreover, recent research in embodied cognition, and specifically in the relationship between music and movement, has changed our understanding of the intimate connection between bodily art-making activity and the apparently reified content. Gesture research proves the multimodal nature of perception not just on the surface—in terms, especially in music, of the impact of what we see a body do upon what we hear (and vice versa)—but more integrally: neuroscientific research has proved that even without seeing a performer in action, with no visual stimulus, the motor areas of our brains are active when we hear musical sound. That we understand music at least partly *as* movement is now clear. Specialists in embodied cognition in music now confidently assert that "experiences of music are intimately linked with experiences of movements: Musicians make music with movements, and people very often make, or imagine, movements when listening to music. We would go so far as to claim that music is basically a combination of sound and movement, and that music means something to us because of this combination" (Godøy and Leman 2010, ix). In this sense, even the most apparently abstracted musical content is "about" the body. Considered this way, the new music practices that place the body in the foreground are not just creating a new context for the thematisation of the body but are drawing out, making more explicit, what is already "in" our perceptions.

In most of this work, though, the composer is still the prime creative agent, instigating performer action and hence shaping and forming the performer's body. Indeed, Walshe suggests that one question for the "New Discipline" is "how to dissolve the concept of the single author and work collectively" (2016), but her focus elsewhere seems to be on the extension of the composer's authority: "in the rehearsal room the composer functions as director or choreographer, perhaps most completely as an auteur." While the compositions produced for *Player Piano* all to some extent involve a composerly organisation of the performing body, the point here was that this should be only part of the story. The ways in which performer subjectivity is, indeed, often produced in part by undertaking embodied activities dictated by composers, forms one strand of the performance. However, for a performer this process is always one of bodily negotiation, experiencing what it is like to enact these activities, some of which feel "natural," some more "alien"; as Elo Masing (2014, 4) says, choreographic notation such as Cassidy's "forces the performer to completely rethink his [*sic*] way of approaching the instrument." Part of that implicit negotiation is always resistant: it involves experiencing the limits of the body in relation to the composer's demands and finding ways to accommodate or adapt—to re-form the body so as to perform the required actions, or sometimes to adjust the actions to make them manageable by the body.

Performer agency is significant in this process, but often not explicitly so for an audience (and for some performers, for sure, Masing's use of the word "forces" is significant; the extent of bodily sublimation to the composer's wishes can be extreme). In *Player Piano*, though, as I describe below, the aim was to explore and reveal the dynamics of the body as being always, already, in some sense, composed—by training and past experience, as well by the specific requirements of a composition—but simultaneously situated and agential. As Donna Haraway writes (1988, 592), in her argument for a feminist epistemology of situated embodiment: "Situated knowledges require that the object of knowledge be pictured as an actor and agent, not as a screen or a ground or a resource, never finally as slave to the master that closes off the dialectic in his unique agency and his authorship of 'objective' knowledge."

As such, the enaction of composed musical activities was placed in dialogue with other aspects of the performance in which the performer's embodied agency might emerge as more complex. Overall, then, bearing in mind the context of recent contemporary practices, I wanted to avoid the possibility that audiences might resolve the performer-subject of *Player Piano* as compositionally produced—that is, as an effect of the intentions of one or more composers (and/or a theatre director). Compositions therefore formed one part of an overall dynamic in which various agencies were active—performer, composers, other artists, and, as discussed below, non-human actants in the form of instruments, other sound sources, and the environment of the performing space. Through enactive engagement in that space of interaction, a performing subject might emerge. As De Preester (2007, 352) says, "To render the body explicit within the context of performance . . . very often conflicts and discords with what is subjectively and/or socially expected from the body and its embodied subject." At times, *Player Piano* deliberately produces such a "discord," in order to pose the body in performance as a question, to invite reflection upon its significance in the production of performer identity.

The intention, on one level, was to encourage reflection on the relationship between player and instrument, understood at one and the same time as separate entities, each with their own significant histories and agency, but also, in the situation of musical performance, as intertwined and co-dependent. For this reason, the piano needed to be presented in certain respects as independent of the player: as a cultural object with a particular historical weight, a certain material identity even. Similarly, in this respect, the performer needed to be doing things beyond the piano—to be seen to have an embodied identity constituted by pianism, by an extended involvement with the piano and piano-related activity, but also by other things: a lived, embodied experience away from the piano, but perhaps never entirely disentangled from it. She might, in this way, be considered multiple, rather than singular: "performing versions of herself," as I put it in the text for the performance flyer. Overall, the complexities of the performer-instrument dyad offered possibilities for artistic exploration, with implications for the research questions about the constitution and production of the performing subject.

Piano as physical context

These hands of mine: I sometimes wonder where they come from, how they got this way. They're not much like my mother's: hers are thinner, whiter, more elegant; the fingers look long and slender where mine are stubby and chunky. And I haven't looked after mine: the skin is tougher and darker, from sun and wind, and you can see that I used to chew my nails all the time.
I'm not sure they're pianist's hands, really.[28]

In her article on the role of the instrument in artistic research, Mine Doğantan-Dack (2015b, 173) notes that "the expressive and communicative meanings that emerge as a result of particular kinds of embodied interaction with different instruments constitute a largely unexplored research territory. Consequently, we do not have a clear understanding of how the experiences of performing music on, say, an oboe and a concert grand piano differ." This is certainly true, though current research, in many cases by performers, is pushing further in this direction.[29] I would argue that the piano occupies a particular place in the consideration of the interaction between performer and instrument.

In much of the literature on this relationship, with respect to different instruments, there is a blurring between ideas of bodily extension and incorporation, or even prosthesis. Helena De Preester and Manos Tsakiris (2009) consider this distinction in some detail, examining the ways in which prosthetic limbs replace or substitute, their incorporation into the body schema resulting in a feeling of bodily completion: the process of incorporation involves an internal reorganisation of the individual's body-model, leading in many cases to a full sense of ownership. They contrast this with tools—and musical instruments would be included here—which extend the body into the world, their use changing our motor and perceptual capacities but without changing our sense of body ownership.

De Preester and Tsakiris articulate the significant limits of tools with respect to incorporation. Nevertheless, in many accounts of the relationship to musical instruments, the ideal is for any player to feel "as one" with their instrument (eventually, after many years of practice). Nijs, Lesaffre, and Leman (2013, 468), for example, discuss the "shared and intuitively apprehended" experience of musicians that "the musical instrument has become part of the body. . . . Such integration leads to the transparency of the musical instrument that just like 'natural' body parts disappears from consciousness." While some musicians certainly do experience their instruments in this way at times, this blanket characterisation seems to ignore the complexity of interaction across instruments of very different sizes and modes of operation relative to the body. Moreover, this "transparency" is often characterised as necessary for high quality perform-

28 This epigraph and those that preface subsequent sections are all taken from the text I wrote and recorded for Lockwood's *Ceci n'est pas un piano*, to be played back through the piano, as part of the performance (as described above).

29 There are many examples, but in the field of contemporary practices recent and current doctoral research by cellist Tanja Orning (2014), flautist Kathryn Williams (2017), and percussionist Jennifer Torrence (2019) are all good examples, focused upon the specific embodied interaction of performer and instrument. The work of guitarist Stefan Östersjö is particularly significant (Östersjö 2008, 2013; Clarke et al. 2017, 116–35; with David Gorton in this volume).

ance—"a necessary condition for a fine-grained expressive communication of musical meaning" (ibid.)[30]—and some researchers have even suggested a link to overall psychological wellbeing (Simoens and Tervaniemi 2013).[31]

Likewise, the development of gestural interfaces for controlling sound, or of new musical instruments, is often predicated on models of incorporation, perhaps more than extension; this is especially so as technologies develop to allow for smaller, lighter, and often wearable instruments: the evolution of various electronic musical gloves is a good example, from Michel Waisvisz's "Hands," developed in the 1980s with Johann den Biggelaar and Bert Bongers, with a range of sensors attached to wooden frames worn on the hands, to Laetitia Sonami's much sleeker (and ironically named) "Lady's Gloves," with various sensors sewn into thin lycra (first used in 1991),[32] or the complex fusion of various textiles and sensors in the MI.MU gloves pioneered by Imogen Heap and her team, starting in 2010.[33] The most recent stage of this lies with bio-musical instruments that "turn the human body into an instrument," as Atau Tanaka puts it (2019, 150), such as by taking electromyogram (EMG) biosignals generated by the nervous system to cause muscle contraction and mapping them into audioparameters: Tanaka's "Myo" armbands, with which he performs, using muscle contraction and arm movements to generate and control sound, are a key example.[34]

As a result of all this, theoretical discussions of instrumentality by Philip Alperson and others (introduced in chapter 1, pp. 40–42, and recurring in subsequent chapters), often focus on the difficulty of determining exactly where the body ends and the instrument begins. Alperson notes that "vocalists frequently speak of their bodies, or parts of their bodies, as their 'instruments'" (2008, 39), and that even with instruments similar ambiguities are apparent; he invokes the example of a guitarist's fingernails, grown and sometimes artificially strengthened so as to facilitate picking, or a wind player's breath, which is as much a determinant of the sound produced as the mechanics of the external instrument. In these cases the distinction between body and instrument starts to become less clear; Alperson argues that we should "keep in mind the continuity, often the seamless continuity, between the physical instrument and the player's bodily connection with the instrument" (ibid., 40). In the empirical

30 This idea seems predicated on the assumption that musical meaning consists of linear transmission of a musical message and that therefore the complex messiness of the relationship between body and instrument should be minimised. In this view, full integration of body and instrument allows for a smooth and direct process of musical communication. To my mind this is a simplistic representation of the process of musical meaning, fundamentally different from a more ecological understanding in which musical meaning arises out of the interaction of a range of agents that might include some or all of composer, performer(s), instrument(s), context (physical, historical and/or cultural), and audience. Within this, the notion of the "resistance" of the instrument (Östersjö 2013, 203), discussed below, allows for a more nuanced understanding of the embodied relationship to the instrument, which may sometimes be "transparent" but also sometimes productively opaque.

31 In contrast, Charles Rosen is enjoyably dismissive of this idea with respect to piano playing: "The sense of physically becoming one with the instrument is the origin of the various delusions about the production of a beautiful sonority" ([2002] 2004, 23).

32 See http://www.sonami.net/lady_glove2.htm.

33 See https://mimugloves.com/tech/.

34 See Di Donato, Bullock, and Tanaka (2018).

study of expressive gesture in musical performance, this can also be a recurrent theme.[35] Nevertheless, that performers sometimes *feel* as if they temporarily achieve an ideal unity of body and instrument, and might regard this as an optimum state is, as confirmed by the studies cited by De Preester and Tsakiris, by no means the same as a prosthetic quality of full integration and ownership. Nor do these theoretical discussions pay adequate attention to the ways in which such a phenomenological experience of "oneness" with the instrument comes to be achieved—the years of learning to play the instrument, adapting the body to accommodate it and to refine the movements necessary for its subtler operation.

Moreover, little attention is paid to the significant differences between the ways in which instruments variously extend or feel co-extensive with—*feel* incorporated into—the body. With any one instrument, this is complex: Alperson's "seamless continuity" might be more easily experienced with respect to a wind player's breathing than their fingering, given that no sound can be produced without breath (except when circular breathing is employed) and there is no additional, separate process of inhalation and exhalation occurring concurrent to the sound production. The fine control of fingering possibilities and key operation are not similarly co-extensive (though this is not to suggest that the nuances of finger action are greater, in themselves, than those of breath control, and of course the interaction of the two is crucial). The point here is that the body is itself rarely experienced as a singular, seamless entity in performance; in practice it is often fragmented, with practice necessarily focused on separating its different functions. Even if this occurs prior to a subsequent integration, the instrumentalist's body is only occasionally experienced holistically. As Merleau-Ponty argued ([1962] 2002, 114), the totality of the body does not simply override its parts: the subject operates on the basis of the "active integration of these latter [the parts of the body] only in proportion to their value to the organism's projects."

Importantly for my context, in discussions of these aspects of instrumentality the piano is mentioned only rarely, which is hardly surprising considering its size and mechanics. Pianists cannot wrap their arms around the instrument like a cellist or guitarist. We don't put any of it in our mouths or feel a transference of breath through us into it. As De Preester and Tsakiris note, there is

35 An interesting contradiction, here, is that in studies of musical gesture the perception of effort is often central to the identification of expression and meaning, even though the focus on the body schematic incorporation of instruments is predicted on the performer's ability, after practise, to play without apparent effort, no longer having to think about how to play a melody (for example), since "the melodic pattern is just something that appears to come out of the body" (Leman and Godøy 2010, 8). I do not dispute that there are many times when practised musicians experience their instruments as if incorporated, nor that there is very often a relationship between perception of effort and musical expression. However, neither are prerequisites for meaningful musical performance. Quality or degree of expression is not always related to effort, and hence there needs to be critical consideration of the object of the effort in relation to its perception. Additionally, the overt negotiation of the instrument's affordances and resistances, in relation to specific musical materials, can often feed into the perception of expressivity. Overall, the relationship between these two ideas is under-explored. For a detailed discussion of instrumentality that considers a wide range of perspectives and attempts an "inventory" of its properties, see Hardjowirogo (2017, especially 17–21).

plenty of evidence to show that "our body schema . . . can expand and morph to encompass inanimate objects that we touch and control" (Linden 2016, 205), and musical instruments are often cited as key examples. But not the piano. Instead it is played *at*, or *on*. Luc Nijs (2017, 52) describes the experience of "merging" with a musical instrument, through the experience of transparency and incorporation, as not only necessary for musical "flow" but leading to a situation in which "the instrument is unconsciously considered as an aspect of the self." However, a deep connection to the instrument and the experience of "merging," or of an indistinction between self and piano, is troublingly simplistic.

Ironically, pianists feature significantly—significantly more than other instruments, in fact—in the studies of instrumentalist's bodies and gestural expression that have emerged in recent years.[36] This perhaps results in part from the ease with which motion data is captured when there is a clearer physical distinction between body and instrument, in contrast to instruments that are held and therefore move with the performer's body, or those that are operated in part by breath. Moreover, however significant the size of the instrument and the relative physical separation, this does not prevent pianists from feeling a strong corporeal connection to the body of the instrument, a sense of touching sound, bringing it to life and shaping it with the hands and by extension the rest of the body. There are many examples of pianists writing about this, but John Tilbury's evocation of the erotics of piano touch in certain performances is particularly striking: "When David Tudor or Cardew played Feldman what you heard and experienced with great intensity was the limb as it performed, the fingerpad—that most erotic part of a pianist's body—and the resulting sound was raw and thrilling" (Tilbury 1993). Susan Tomes (2010, 128–29) describes her willing complicity, when she plays, in the illusion that she is direct contact with the sound: "I was watching my own hands on the keyboard this afternoon, and I suddenly realised that I had completely lost sight of the fact that the sound does not come out of the keys. When I touch the keys I imagine sound is created directly under my fingers, . . . that you can stroke a singing tone out of the keys themselves, and have them sing back at you."[37] Pianists know that on one level, as Charles Rosen (2004, 24) says, "there is nothing one can do with a piano except play louder and softer, faster and slower. A single note cannot be played more or less beautifully, only more or less *forte* or *piano* and longer or shorter." Nevertheless, we work endlessly to refine these characteristics relatively, so that differentiations of weight and touch become sonically, structurally, and expressively meaningful and also come to *feel* significant: we refine touch experientially but also comparatively, in relation to others, through talk about it, demonstrating, experimenting, listening, and feeling.

---

36 See, for example, Davidson (1994, 2007); Dalla Bella and Palmer (2004); Furuya and Altenmüller (2013); Goebl (2017).

37 David Sudnow expresses this even more directly, in his phenomenological account of his development as a jazz pianist: "I sing with my fingers, so to speak, and only so to speak, for there's a new being, *my body*, and it is this being (here too, so to speak) that sings" (2001, 130).

Importantly, in further considering the extensive properties of tools, De Preester and Tsakiris (2009) note that while incorporation is constrained by the constancy of the body-model—prosthetics, for example, have to conform to the body model to be fully incorporated; only internal reorganisation is possible—the relationship between body and tool has "more degrees of freedom"; "This means that the feeling of embodiment can be extended with tools, and that the body-model is not a normative constraint for *extending* the body with tools" (ibid.). This speaks to the complexities and instabilities that are surely part of most instrumentalists' relationships with their instruments—the continually changing dynamic whereby the instrument can from one moment to another feel absolutely part of oneself and then impossibly other, extraneous, awkward, and disjunct. These are perhaps especially apparent with the piano, and this experience formed one strand in the devising of aspects of *Player Piano*, particularly in the performance of *Touch and Go*, by Roger Marsh, as described below.

Finally, the bodily relationship to the instrument affects and is affected by the performer's corporeal experience of the world more broadly. I have played the piano for over forty years. I am who I am in part because of the piano. My body is shaped and formed, trained and refined, but also strained and deformed by the time spent at the instrument. What I hear in music is in part conditioned by the forms of pianism I've engaged with—the music I've played, the ways I've attended to details of contrapuntal thought, to resonance, tone, and timbre. Beyond this, everything I do is in part related to this—affecting it and affected by it: how I swim or play football, how I listen to people talk, how I argue, how I think through situations, how I type on my laptop; particularly how I touch. We know, now, how important a part touch plays in brain formation (Linden 2016); the relationship between touch development and sense of self is significant, particularly the social constitution of the self. As neuroscientist David Linden comments, we use touch socially "to soothe, reconcile, form alliances, reward cooperative actions, and reinforce bonds of kinship and friendship" (2016, 19). The differential and discursive formation of a personal sense of piano touch, described above, is perhaps one aspect of this. As Erin Manning writes, "the surface of the body is a thinking, feeling surface" (2007, 9). Moreover, Deniz Peters argues, from the perspective of embodied cognition, that even as a listener the experience of "hearing" touch is embodied, social and empathic. In hearing performances that involve touch, he proposes, "what we hear is, by physical necessity, the sound of contact and excitation; and we have embodied knowledge of the making of such contact to effect such sounds. Even without knowing how these sounds and sound sequences were made in terms of instrumental playing technique, we may hear them *as* touch. . . . [This] is given to all listeners as part of their bodily experience, and, if sufficiently so, it can enable mutual empathy. It can amount to an invisible yet palpable bodily presence in the music which, given the awareness, may be anticipated, arranged, and apprehended" (Peters 2012,

20).[38] In this way, my own experience of touch, in itself and as musical expression—in life and at the piano—is formed not just from touching and being touched, but by seeing and *listening to* touch, not least of other pianists. From this perspective too, then, the manifestation of the musical self through pianistic touch is at once individuated and multiple.

Again, this continuity between the body-instrument relationship and felt experience of the world is experienced by all performers, but with each instrument the specifics of bodily engagement are different. Moreover, the piano perhaps functions somewhat differently in the domestic environment of the home. Smaller instruments can easily be packed away in their cases and kept safe, particularly from children. They then need to be taken out and, in some cases, pieced back together, or otherwise set up in order to be played. Pianos are sometimes closed up or locked away, but in my experience this is rare; more often they simply sit there, accessible to anyone in the house. For me, the piano is part of my domestic as well as professional environment, used for serious musical activity but also for messing about—sometimes both at once. When I first encountered a recording of Lockwood's *Ceci n'est pas un piano* (the only composition in *Player Piano* extant before the project began, and in many respects the instigation for it), one of the things that I liked about it was the ways in which the pianist, Jennifer Hymer, spoke in the recorded text about the domestic context of her piano, both in terms of her own use of it and her children's play. She talks about practising pieces that require her to use the insides of the instrument, commenting: "Things that I've needed for those pieces have fallen through the strings and I can't get them out: pieces of a broken guitar pick, a dime, a 50 cent piece used for preparing, a piece of wire. . ." (Hymer 2007). She continues: "Even the kids, they'll just climb up on the bench and start fooling about with the superball mallet." Of course, not all pianos are treated this way, but the sense of the instrument as part of the furniture—as simply "there," available for playing or even for climbing on or under—is perhaps quite common but also somewhat different to most other instruments. If the piano is, as noted earlier, the facilitator of some of the grandest, high-art notions of absolute musical prowess, it is, at the same time, perhaps the most domestic of instruments in the Western world. Both of these narratives inform the pianist's embodiment.

Overall, then, we might say that the piano provides a very particular context for exploration of the body–instrument relationship, neither divorced from the considerations at play with other instruments nor fully comparable.

38 The complex case for this is more fully argued by Peters in the referenced chapter (2012). Chapter 4 in this volume makes more extended use of Peters's argument in the discussion of the role of empathy in the constitution of subjectivity.

The social body in *Player Piano*

The tendons in my hands are becoming more pronounced. I quite like this; it reminds me of my first piano teacher, and maybe for me hers are always going to be what I'll think of as real pianist's hands.

The foregoing section has introduced the complexities of the embodied relationship between performer and piano in order to provide a context for explaining the dynamics and significance of the body in *Player Piano*. For me, in developing the performance in relation to the research questions about the performing subject, the process of exploration was iterative, with cycles of playing, reflection, generation of new ideas and new materials that were then played over and over, reflected on, and so on. Within this, my body was both subject and object, at times unreflective, immediate, and responsive, at other times subjected to scrutiny, reshaped, and directed (by myself and others). As with all practice, sometimes there was no distinction between these two modes, and sometimes the shift of focus was so sudden and so fleeting that distinguishing between them seemed either impossible or pointless.

Now, with some critical distance on the process of performance-making, I am able to examine the different ways in which the performance explored and exposed the significance of the body. Broadly speaking, there are three modes of embodiment here: the social body, the represented body or body image, and the schematic body. Within this, I also draw out ways in which the body is sometimes "textual"—whether literally, when we hear a voice speak of the body, or figuratively, in its representation as an object of attention to be scrutinised or "read"—and note the significance of the remediated body image in *Player Piano*, when the performer's body is explicitly reproduced in the different media of film and in a clay model. However, these modes rarely operate entirely separately, as is apparent in the discussion that follows, and there are times when one mode of embodiment shifts to another (particularly from body schema to body image).

In the context of recent live art, De Preester (2007, 351) considers the different "layers" of the body in performance, asking "*in what way the body becomes explicit* in these situations. First, are we able to trace and understand the operations by which the body becomes explicit? Second—and since the body is no monolithic given—*which* bodily level or layer is exhibited, *which* bodily functions . . .?" De Preester's approach provides a useful frame for my discussion of the body in *Player Piano*, partly due to her application of the distinction between body image and body schema (Gallagher and Cole 1995) to art and artists. Both layers are active in the production and representation of subjectivity: "these concepts enable us to consider, on a theoretical level, the body as represented object, as subject, as motor means for being-in-the-world, as origin of subjectivity and emotions, as hidden but most intimate place of impersonal life processes, as possibly distant image, as sensitive, fragile and plastic entity, as something we owe and are owned by, as our most personal and yet extremely strange body" (De Preester 2007, 380–81). These words connect directly to the various manifestations and layers of the (singular) performer's body in *Player Piano*; the approach helps to explain not only the different but interacting modes of bodily activity and representation at play in the performance but also their roles in the production of performer subjectivity.

The action of the body at and around the instrument was important in *Player Piano*; but, as should be clear from the above, I was concerned to present the performer away from the instrument, too, even if always in some sense connected to it. This forms one layer of bodily significance in the piece, in particular signalling the social formation of the performing body: "social," here, in the sense of its relationship to the world beyond the particular situation of sitting (or standing) at the piano and playing. Later, in drawing on the work of Deniz Peters on the empathic significance of touch (2012), this is complemented by an additional social dimension, operating at the level of the body schema. At different times the piece invokes the relationship between piano playing and other physical activity, activities beyond the piano that feed into piano playing, and the piano as a context not just for performance but also for play: not just practice but also playful activity.

This is *enacted* by means of various activities, but the significance of the piano to the performer, both inside and outside the context of performing, is also overtly *spoken of* in my version of *Ceci n'est pas un piano*.[39] Taking Jennifer Hymer's text as a prompt, I wrote and recorded my own text. A recorded voice—mine, though not everyone in the audience might realise this—is heard, relayed through the body of the piano such that it takes on additional piano resonances. The text explicitly invokes the player's relationship to the instrument: we hear about the body at the instrument, the effects of years of practice, and so on. Additionally, at times, the commentary speaks of the relationship between piano performing and everyday life: there are references to the piano as a domestic object in the home ("dropped and bashed when we've moved house"), used for serious work but also for amusement, for play with (and "thumped by") children. The text is also suggestive of the interplay between everyday physical activity, piano practice, and the ways in which these manifest in physical changes, over time: "Arthritis runs in my family, and I do worry what that might mean for me. So far I've been lucky, but with every little twinge I imagine the worst. Paranoid pianist." Many of these consciously echo Hymer's original text, but the experiences described are mine; the similarities were striking.

Ceci therefore provides the audience with a textual body, in the literal sense of its mediation via spoken language, that connects to but does not coincide with the live, performing body. The text speaks of the body at the piano, and it speaks through the piano, with piano resonances, but even if the speaker of the

39 The complexities of subjectivity and identity in the performance of this piece are discussed separately and more fully in my forthcoming chapter, "This Is Not a Pianist: Embodiment, Gender and Subjectivity in Performing Annea Lockwood's *Ceci n'est pas un piano*," in *Performance, Subjectivity, and Experimentation*, edited by Catherine Laws (Leuven: Leuven University Press, 2020).

text is understood to be the pianist the audience watches and listens to, and even if the content of the speech refers to the embodied experience of live performance, there is an apparent disjunction between the discursive mediation of the body through composed and recorded text—produced in another time and place—and the "now" of the body active in the moment of performance.[40] The body can never operate beyond textuality (to echo Kramer's comment, cited earlier), and yet its presentness and layeredness in performance resists reduction to a text. Victor Ramirez Ladrón de Guevara (2011, 24) articulates this paradox: on one level the body always "acquires a semantic value that is inscribed within a semiotic system. The body is yet another text that needs to be interpreted and is open to be *read*," but simultaneously "we just need to think of our own body and those concrete and specific bodies that surround us to realize that the body is *not* a text. Although it can transmit signs and meanings, the body resists signification and meaning. Certain aspects of the body can be selected and then interpreted in certain ways. But the human body . . . is formed of a series of elements that make it impossible to reduce that body to a single aspect, resisting a single definition and unitary, simple and definite significations" (ibid., 24–25).[41]

At other moments in the performance I spend time in other areas of the stage, away from the instrument. At one point, for example, while a short film is played back on the screen, I sort through piles of scores and vinyl LPs of piano recordings, choosing items for use a little later, in the piece by Paul Whitty (discussed below and shown in figure 2.3).

40 This piece feeds productively on the paradox of presenting autobiographical text, which purports to provide "authentic" insight into subjective experience but which is repeated, mediated by recording or re-enactment in performance. This creative strategy, which opens up the questions of narratorial reliability, memory, and the performativity of the subject as constituted and expressed through language, has become common in contemporary theatre and performance practices in recent years (not least in the subgenre "verbatim theatre"). This specific theme is taken up more overtly in the discussion of biographical narratives in *Arrival Cities: Hanoi* in chapter 4. Chapter 3 is substantially concerned with matters of authenticity from a different perspective, in the construction and reconstruction of identity through compositional, performance, and recording practices.

41 This is very close to the quotation from Helena De Preester given in chapter 1: "in performance, the body abruptly and explicitly comes into visibility and resists forms of objectification that may put it to rest, to clarity and obviousness" (2007, 352). There, Gorton and Östersjö use De Preester's observation to support their discussion of the significant (but "resistant") relation between bodily practices and knowledge. My discussion of the layered significance of the body in *Player Piano*, as manifested both in the practice processes and the instantiation of the body in performance (and on film), parallels this.

Figure 2.3.

This gives a sense of the pianist's physical relationship to the personal archive of piano-related experience—playing, listening, and the handling of scores and recordings—that feeds into a performing life. In another section, I perform movements on and around a piano stool placed some distance from the piano (see figure 2.4)—an abstracted but highly patterned sequence that would be entirely incongruous in the context of a piano recital but that does, in fact, derive from the piano playing gestures of the composition that forms the next section of the performance, *Touch and Go*, by Roger Marsh.

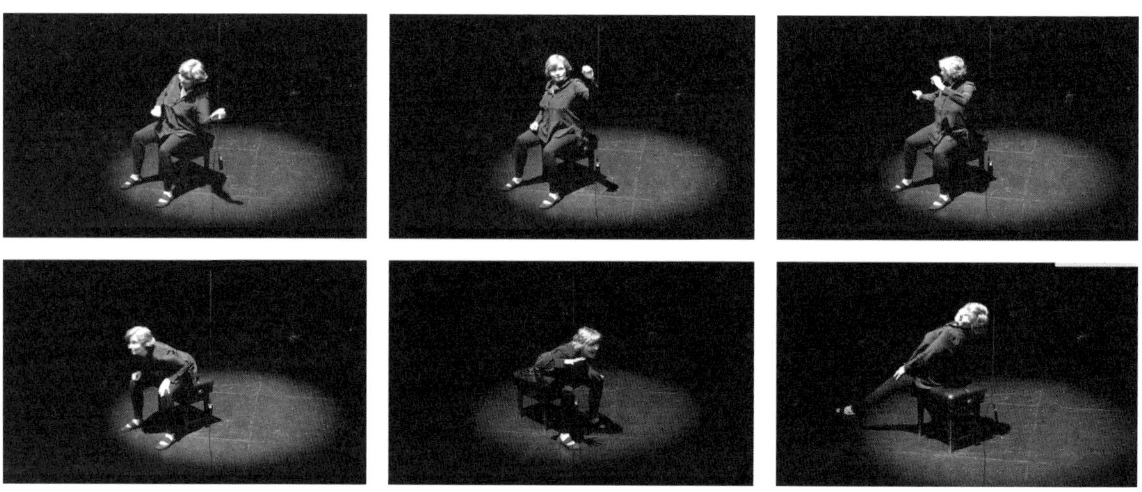

Figure 2.4.

Figure 2.3. Performance activity, sorting through scores and LPs: still from *Player Piano*, performed by Catherine Laws, from premiere performance, Scenic Stage Theatre, York, 5 May 2016.

Figure 2.4. Movement piece (devised by Teresa Brayshaw and Catherine Laws) from *Player Piano*, performed by Catherine Laws: stills from premiere performance, Scenic Stage Theatre, York, 5 May 2016.

In *Ten Bellows* by Edward Jessen, I perform rituals of fetching and carrying, aided by a co-performer; these repetitive routines of habitual behaviour take place away from the piano (or, mostly, on journeys to and from the instrument). However, there is a strange continuity between the qualities of focused repetition manifested in both these routines and the recurrent, gradually transforming motives of the piano playing; both are simultaneously intensely focused and somewhat obsessive, as if deeply meaningful but inscrutably so (see figure 2.5). Moreover, the movements produce sounds that, we might gradually realise, form part of the fabric of the piece.

Figure 2.5.

As suggested by these examples, throughout *Piano Player* the performer's activities are predominantly task-based: there is no "acting" of a character and I do not speak to the audience (other than via the recorded text in *Ceci*, about which, as noted above, there is some ambiguity with regard to its status). The whole is quite diverse; the activity seen or evoked in one section of the piece is often quite different to that of another. Some of it is clearly composed—by someone, whether a "composer" or theatre director. But some of it is just "stuff" that needs to be done. Through these and other similar little moments of activity around the performance space, something is suggested of the physical and mental activity of life in and around piano performance, of a body trained and constrained by years of piano playing but also by other activities—by the objects, activities, and routines that constitute a performer's embodied identity, their memories, their life. Throughout *Player Piano* as a whole, the audience is invited to experience not only the particularities of piano performance but also a certain contiguity with life beyond the space of performance.

Player Piano therefore stages the body as more than "instrumental," more than a means of producing piano sound. Georgina Born, in welcoming recent interest in the corporeality and materiality of arts practices, comments critically on the lack of attention to the social "valences" of such practices: "The body in these accounts is then, invariably, *de-socialised*—as though the boundary between individual and (social) environment was absolute, and as though the operations of the body can be understood without reference to that environment" (Born 2012, 165). The *social* body in *Player Piano*, its behaviours suggest, are formed and transformed over time through its work at and away from the piano. What it has to do is both serious and playful. It follows instructions, patterns, rituals dictated by others; but it also acts spontaneously, improvisationally, apparently in and for itself; and it is spoken of in these terms, too. In

Figure 2.5. Stills from *Ten Bellows* by Edward Jessen, which forms part of *Player Piano*. Performed by Catherine Laws and Hannah Butterfield, Scenic Stage Theatre, York, 5 May 2016.

this sense it is contextualised, located—not in the sense that the piano playing body is usually positioned, at the piano, but in a wider context of action, situation, and activity. This perhaps connects to Donna Haraway's suggestion that we need the view from the "structuring, and structured body, versus the view from above, from nowhere, from simplicity" (1988, 589).

The explicitly (re)mediated body

Sometimes in performance . . . there's an agility, an assuredness I don't recognise.
I'm performing being a pianist.

The "beyond" of the embodied relationship to the instrument is therefore an important part of *Player Piano*. This extends to its explicit representation in other aspects of the performance through the use of film and other imagery. By now it should be apparent that *Player Piano* is in part concerned with the ways in which the musical performing body is mediated—particularly by the instrument and composers—and the significance of that to the production of a notional performing self. This is further dissected below with reference to the approach to the live performing body. However, in addition to the textual body that appears in *Ceci n'est pas un piano*, in dialogue with my performing, sound-producing body, the body is also explicitly re-mediated—put into different media—in other ways.

The opening line of the spoken text of *Ceci* is "These hands of mine: I sometimes wonder where they come from, how they got this way," and this leads into further discussion of both the appearance and feel of my hands, at and away from the piano. Later in *Player Piano*, the second short film, by Wendy Kirkup, includes close-ups of hands in various positions: stretched open and clenched shut, arched and twisted, still and moving, from different angles and with fingers sometimes prominent, sometimes hidden (see figure 2.6). With no body, these hands are scrutinised in and for themselves: they become strange, dismembered, almost abstract forms, positioned this way and that; objects often with no apparent function, unlike in their actions in live performance, where they are always busy but always in service. Again, this seems visually to echo some of the words heard in *Ceci*, where I describe occasions in performance when I experience my hands as if they are moving automatically and I find myself watching them as if they belong to someone else: "Sometimes in performance it's as if I become detached from my hands: they're outside me, dancing for me. Watching films of my playing has the same effect: there's an agility, an assuredness I don't recognise."[42]

42 Somewhat similarly, pianist Susan Tomes (2010, 212) writes of this temporary estrangement from her hands, this time in terms of assessing their performance as if from outside: "Often . . . I follow my own hands as I play, with a coldly judgemental eye, or worse: with a kind of out-of-body sceptical observation which paradoxically makes it much more likely that I will make mistakes." David Sudnow (2001, 76), in his account of learning to play jazz piano, often refers to his hands as if they are related to but not quite "of" him: "Looking down at these hands of mine, . . . seeking practically useful terms for conceiving my relationship to their ways . . ."

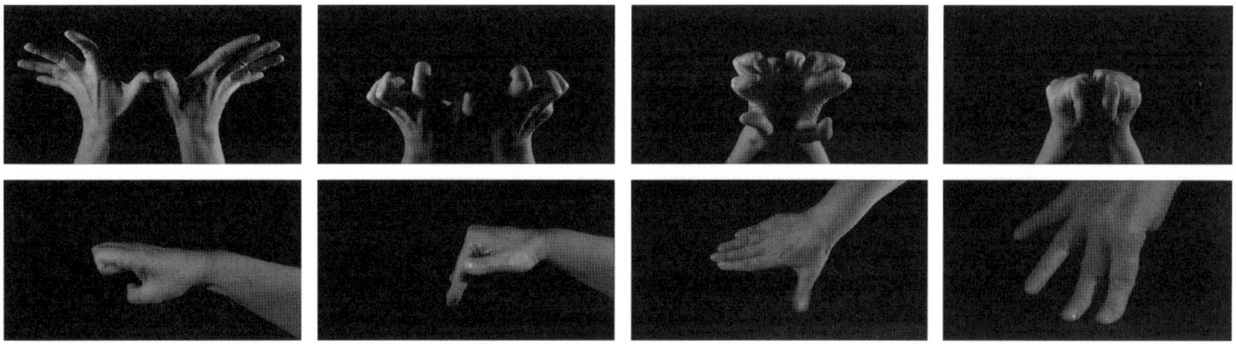

Figure 2.6.

In the film we often see nothing but these hands, but occasionally the fingers have red, green, or yellow ribbons tied around them. The hand here is vertical, fingers pointing downwards, and the ribbons are tied with bows, as if to suggest that the fingers are parcels, for presentation and unwrapping, perhaps. Subsequently, the ribbons are pulled, gradually but strongly, to one side, though we can't see by whom (see figure 2.7). With the fingertips still rooted to a surface, the pulling of the ribbons strains the hand sideways; someone offscreen is trying to pull the fingers away. The coloured ribbons form a visual echo, since they match those we have seen used to bow piano strings in the performance of *Ceci n'est pas un piano* (see figure 2.10, below, linked to the discussion of the physical effect of this). Rather than the fingers pulling ribbons, though, here the ribbons pull the fingers. The fingers are in the power of someone or something beyond the frame of the screen.

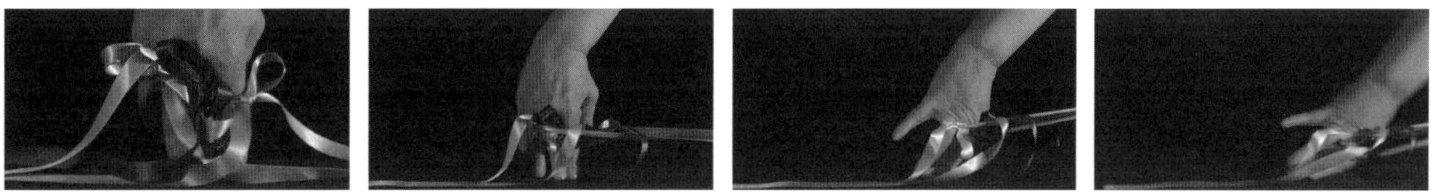

Figure 2.7.

In contrast to the giant hands foregrounded on the screen in this film, throughout *Player Piano* a miniature model pianist sits at a doll's-house piano, positioned on a small table to one side of the stage (see figure 2.8). The little pianist looks a little like me—we are both dressed in black, and she has shortish brown hair—but there is no attempt to model her identically.

Figure 2.6. Stills of hands from the second short film, by Wendy Kirkup, that forms part of *Player Piano*.

Figure 2.7. Stills of hand tied with ribbons from the second short film, by Wendy Kirkup, that forms part of *Player Piano*.

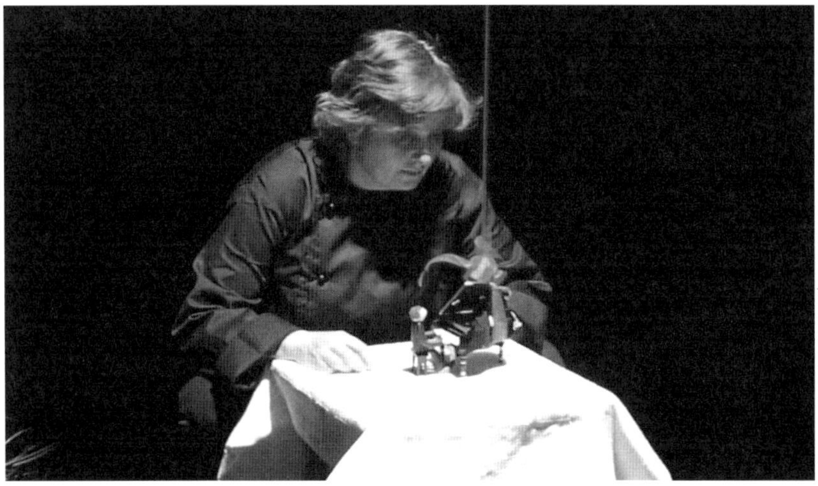

Figure 2.8.

A large helium balloon is tethered to the back leg of the little piano; the balloon is big enough, relative to the piano, to be capable of lifting it into the air. At the end of the performance this is exactly what happens: weights are removed from inside the body of the little piano, so that it can float into the air, with very quiet piano music—Satie's *Vexations*—playing from it (via a tiny soundcard hidden in the piano) as it floats up; this is a version of another piece by Annea Lockwood, entitled *Gone* (2007), though Lockwood does not specify the music. Overall, though, the little pianist perhaps serves to reinforce the idea, manifested differently throughout the performance, that the piano-player duo is an object of attention; that it is, in De Preester's terms, the subject as much as the brush. Additionally, the performance in different ways plays with themes of size and weight; as is discussed below, the size and weight (both physical and metaphorical) of the grand piano becomes significant, as does the performer's struggle with these different forms of weight. In contrast, at times we see film of tiny pianos that can be manipulated by giant fingers or huge ribbons, and the helium balloons in various places onstage and tied to the doll's-house piano form an extension of this reversal of the dynamic of size (and perhaps of power) between performer and instrument.

In these ways, the performer's body, in itself and in relation to the piano, is remediated for the audience: the constructedness of the performer's body, through practice, and its objectification, through endless scrutiny—by the performer herself, teachers, adjudicators and examiners, audiences, composers, and so on—is represented and reconfigured. This, then, is a textual body in the wider sense—not, as with the spoken narrative in *Ceci n'est pas un piano*, transformed into language, but nevertheless very much represented. It is cut into parts or explicitly reformed for representation and, as such, it demands "reading," interpreting. This (re)mediated body therefore forms a layer that connects with but operates separately to the live body-subject. Unlike the live

Figure 2.8. Model pianist and doll's-house piano from *Player Piano*.

body, which may, at times, be "itself"—at least *might* be acting in and for the moment, might be an embodied subject in action—someone must be behind these plastic representations. The name of a film-maker on the programme signals an "other" with some authority here, but this is complicated by the direct connection to images and actions seen variously elsewhere, live, in the performance, in composed pieces but also in various other, unattributed activities. Do the films use the performer's body or not? Did the images from the film come first, feeding the thematics of the performance (and hence the composers', performer's, and theatre-maker's agential contributions), or vice versa? Likewise, who is responsible for the re-presentation of the pianist in model form? The answer, in each case, is something in between: there was a back and forth in the sharing of ideas, and images, from the starting point of wanting to perform *Ceci n'est pas un piano*. However, this is not really important: the answer serves only to underline that what matters here is the ambiguity produced due to the overlapping agencies that feed into the re-mediation process, both demanding and resisting a "reading" of the represented body, an ambiguity that is then reflected in the manifestation of the live body in performance.

The situational body

> *. . . what I do love is getting right inside the instrument, head under the lid of a big resonant grand, with the overtones bouncing around, the blooming buzzing confusion, where you can't tell what's in your head and what's outside it. . . . There's still so much to discover in there, and sometimes it starts to feel like I'm burrowing into the instrument's own space, not just knocking on it, asking to be let in.*

Notwithstanding the different manifestations of the performing body discussed above, in *Player Piano* it is vitally significant just how the performer interacts, physically, with the instrument. Two of the compositions, *Ceci n'est pas un piano* and Paul Whitty's *under and under*, demand physical engagement with the whole instrument, beyond the keyboard: snippets of the live performance of both pieces are incorporated into the trailer, but an audio recording of *Ceci n'est pas un piano* and a film version of *under and under* (relocated into a domestic environment, as noted below), are available.[43] Both use recordings which might (in *under and under*) or should (in *Ceci*) be played back through the body of the instrument, but there are significant differences; unlike the written, recorded, and produced text in *Ceci*, the playback in *under and under* is of environmental field recordings made by the performer in locations of her choice and played on mp3 players; it is up to the performer whether to relay some or all of this material through the piano or simply through speakers elsewhere in the space. In addition, *under and under* includes the playback of a vinyl recording of piano music via a turntable; this, too, can be placed inside the piano, if the performer wishes.

43 Both the audio recording and the film are available in the online repository (www.orpheusinstituut.be/en/voices-bodies-practices-media-repository); see files "SF2.3 *Ceci n'est pas un piano* (audio recording)" and "SF2.4 *under and under* (film)."

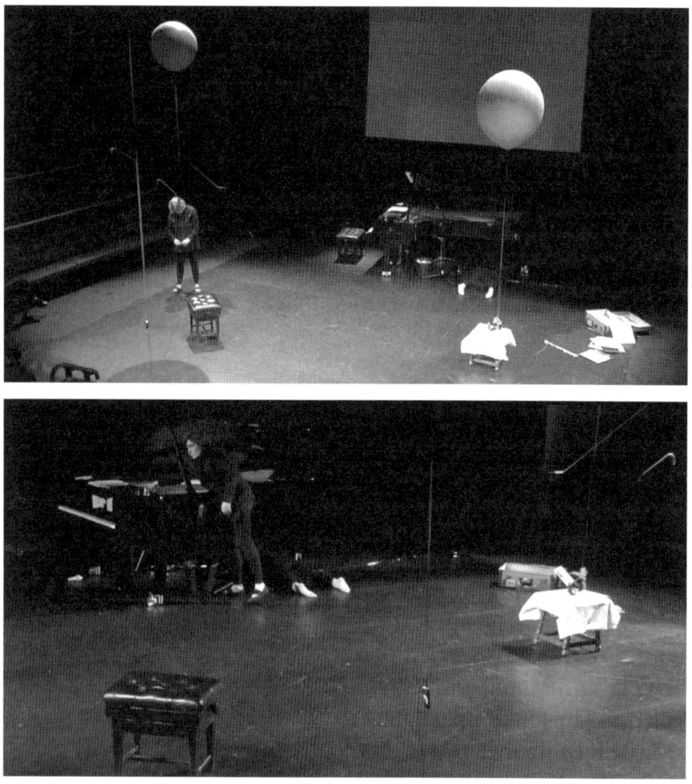

Figure 2.9.

In playing this piece, the performer therefore moves around the instrument, perhaps shifting recording devices in and out of its body, activating and deactivating them (see figure 2.9). Both pieces also involve the full use of the sounding resources of the piano—the keyboard, the strings, and the frame—and incorporate various objects for use on the strings and metal struts: again, in *under and under* the choice of objects is entirely open, while Lockwood designates the tools—E-bows, superball mallets, rubber balls, chime balls, ribbons, and stones—but does not always specify when, where, or how they should be used; indeed, sometimes the performer is invited to improvise with the range of objects.

For most of *under and under* the performer has the freedom to choose how and when to play the instrument. Quite how she engages with the insides of the piano is undetermined by the composer, but that she will do so is clear. The score instructs the performer to listen to the field recordings during the performance, through headphones or speakers, and to "use the field recording as an audio score using the piano as a means of filtering the audio data in the recording. This can be done using a strategy of your choice." With the vinyl recording of piano music, the performer again, as part of the performance, listens and responds by playing: "Listen to the recording of piano music. Identify an event and try to re-create it using the piano. You can stop the recording if you choose to and repeat the event several times or alternate the recorded

Figure 2.9. Stills from performance of Paul Whitty's *under and under* as part of *Player Piano*: activation of field recordings from small speakers tethering balloons, and use of portable turntable. From premiere performance, Scenic Stage Theatre, York, 5 May 2016.

event with your re-creation of the event or you can leave the recording running and when you are happy with your re-creation of the selected event you can select another one and continue the process." What is clear is that the piano is not just an instrument but an environment in which creative action takes place. Moreover, with these instructions we see the performer actively listening and responding; actively making creative decisions in the moment, in reaction to what she finds interesting in what she hears. The audience does not know the score or the ways in which the roles of composer and performer are here delineated, but the performance explicitly stages a process of engaging in the moment with the various sound objects: the action-perception loop of the performer as simultaneously an embodied listener and creator of sound is apparent both visibly and audibly. Physically, the performer operates the recordings in and around the piano and reaches and stretches to position and reposition them inside the instrument or to play the strings, struts, and frame with various objects, responding to the recordings as they evolve and interact with the piano resonance. The body of the piano becomes a space for creative work, in which the pianist is fully engaged.

In Lockwood's *Ceci n'est pas un piano* some of the actions are comparable, with the composer similarly requiring the use of the inside of the piano, activated with both fingers and objects, and the keyboard. However, there are important differences. I have written briefly elsewhere (Laws 2018) about how, in playing *Ceci*, the performer enacts a kind of choreography in and around the piano as necessary to realise some of Lockwood's instructions, reaching and stretching to pluck, bow, and flick the strings, roll rubber and metallic balls on them, stroke or strike them with superball mallets, and so on. None of these techniques are new, but some of Lockwood's choices demand a particular kind of physical engagement. In particular, using four brightly coloured metallic ribbons to bow the strings both looks and sounds very different to the more commonly used fishing wire or horsehair, and the gesture required to make the strings ring properly is more expansive, even flamboyant—particularly so for someone who is not very tall: in order to pull the ribbons far and hard enough to produce the required sound, I have to stretch onto my tiptoes and extend the pulling gesture as high as possible and some way sidewards (see figure 2.10). To some extent, then, Lockwood composes a certain physical engagement with the piano, drawing attention to the performer's specific embodied relation to the instrument. This is underlined by the ways in which the text speaks, in part, about exactly this (as can be seen in some of the extracts used as epigraphs in this section of the chapter), overtly drawing attention to the embodied performative identity.

The contrasts between the ways in which the body is engaged in and around the piano in realising Whitty's *under and under* and Lockwood's *Ceci n'est pas un piano* are important. Some of the activities are similar, and in both pieces the composers' instructions are such that the physicality of sound production is apparent. Lockwood's piece composes the body more directly than Whitty's, but some of her choices in themselves are such that the specifics of the individual performing body become significant and noticeable in the process of realising the instructions, and the explicit thematisation of the performing body in my text emphasises this. With Whitty's *under and under* there is no specific composition of the body at the instrument—all decisions as to what and how to play are made by the performer—but the instructions foreground the idea that the piano becomes a space in which the performer engages physically, playing with sound production.

Figure 2.10.

De Preester discusses bodily space as situational rather than positional: "the body's spatiality is a subjective spatiality of *situation*, not an objectified spatiality of *position*" (2007, 353). Of course, for an audience, the performing body in *Player Piano* is positioned, framed by the stage, the relationship to the piano, and the film screen, and this reflects the intentional bodily representations developed through the process of devising. However, this framing itself allows for a focusing in on bodily activity that involves orientation—and constant reorientation—in relation to the situation of sound production: the activities in *under and under* and the nuances of enaction in *Ceci* are not choreographic—not purely positional, so as to render them objectively meaningful in visual terms—but are dependent upon the embodied negotiation of the space of the instrument so as to produce the particular sound required *by the performer* in the moment. The moving body is here constitutive of both space and sound. Merleau-Ponty writes ([1962] 2002, 116–17), "as soon as I try to posit bodily space or bring out its meaning, I find nothing in it but intelligible space. But at the same time this intelligible space is not extracted from oriented space, it is merely its explicit expression, and, when separated from that root has no meaning whatsoever." From this, De Preester (2007, 354) suggests that "we should not look for explications that transform oriented, bodily space into homogeneous, positional, Cartesian space, but rather should render the oriented bodily, situational space itself explicit. But how should we do this?" This interplay between phenomenal body, experiencing space, and its objective framing is, in part, what is attempted in *Player Piano*.

Figure 2.10. Still from Annea Lockwood's *Ceci n'est pas un piano* performed as part of *Player Piano*. From premiere performance, Scenic Stage Theatre, York, 5 May 2016.

Body image and the schematic body

The piano has such a weight of musical history hanging over it. All those piano heroes conquering great works: flailing arms, flashing fingers, gurning faces. I'm supposed to have mastered, definitely mastered, *this beast of an instrument, but my body has been trained, modified, disciplined by it, too.*

So far, I have identified ways in which *Player Piano* reveals the body as textual, remediated, and socially constituted (and sometimes a combination of these). Much of this is concerned with examining performer body image as a representation of self—body image, that is, as defined by Gallagher and Cole: "a conscious idea or mental representation that one has of one's own body" (1995, 369). As suggested above, there is plenty of ambiguity as to who is constructing these body images for the audience—me, the composers, the film-maker, the theatre-maker, or some combination thereof. Certainly, though, there is what Gallagher and Cole call a "reflective intentionality" (ibid., 371), a self-conscious producing and reproducing of the body by the performer and others intended to draw attention to its habits, its normative (re)production and playing with those, re-shaping and re-framing from both within (by the performer) and without (by others). As Helena De Preester says, in working this way "the intentional subject takes her own body in an act of reflective intentionality as the object of her act: she bends over, in an act of representation, belief or attitude, to her own body" (2007, 355–56).

The moments of task-based physical activity to an extent contrast with this reflexive mode: in these, I am seen to be doing things, musically and non-musically, that may sometimes be in response to composed directives but in which the choices are spontaneous and there is no self-conscious performance of body image beyond the fact that it is there, in front of the audience, as an object of perception. In one sense these moments might be constituted more in terms of body *schema* rather than body image: "In contrast to the reflective intentionality of the body image, a body schema involves a system of motor capacities, abilities, and habits that enable movement and the maintenance of posture" (Gallagher and Cole 1995, 371); "The body schema does not have the status of a conscious representation or a belief. It is a preconscious, sub-personal system that enables and supports intentional motor activity" (De Preester 2007, 356). However, all performance (as part of all motor activity) relies upon body schemata; I cannot really argue that the social, situational body-subject constituted in these less self-conscious moments of performance brings the schematic body into play in any notable way. More significant to this distinction, then, is the contrast between the reflexive interference with body image apparent in certain aspects of *Player Piano* (an approach which, as De Preester says, is abundant these days, across forms of performance [2007, 365]) and the avoidance of any such self-consciousness elsewhere.

However, there are also sections in *Player Piano* when the playing gestures become scrutinised more intensely and during which, I would argue, the interplay between body schema and body image is directly invoked as part of the process by which a performing self is produced. This happens in various places, but especially in the piece *Touch and Go*, composed by Roger Marsh.[44] In many respects the score that Marsh gave me is the most conventional, in Western classical terms, of all the pieces produced for *Player Piano*: it is the only piece for piano alone, without additional sounds, recorded or otherwise, and it is through-composed, the notes and rhythms fully determined, with no extended techniques or playing inside the piano. Much but not all of Marsh's work is in the field of music theatre, and on the face of it this might almost be a purely musical composition. Beyond the notation of pitches, rhythms, plus a few dynamics and indications of articulation, there are only two hints in the score of something more than this. First, the brief preface suggests that in this piece the performer undertakes a process of discovering the instrument,[45] and the very beginning is characterised as follows: "Magic . . . sense of wonder . . . bringing the piano to life" (the ellipses are Marsh's). Second, Marsh gives physical instructions for the first two musical gestures of the piece, instructing the hands to "float" between the two loud chords, high then low, which open the piece;[46] then, after a long pause, a sustained, quiet, trill should be played "intently, face close to fingers, watching the sound" (see figure 2.11). Except for at the very end, there are no further instructions of this kind throughout the twelve-minute piece: the rest of the score comprises musical notation only, until the final chord is played, when the pianist should "keep hands in place (on the keyboard) and stare ahead as light fades."

Figure 2.11.

44 An extract from the live performance of this piece is included in the *Player Piano* trailer, but a full film version is also available in the online repository (www.orpheusinstituut.be/en/voices-bodies-practi-ces-media-repository); see file "SF2.2 *Touch and Go*."

45 The piece is prefaced as follows: "An impossible idea. The performer has never seen a piano before. She sits down at the instrument without fear but with a degree of curiosity. She explores the instrument with thoughtful curiosity. Amazingly, she seems to be able to play it quite well. The long pauses are thoughtful pauses (but visually motionless)" (Marsh 2014, 2).

46 The passage can be seen in the online repository, file "SF2.5 *Touch and Go*, rising and falling hands."

Figure 2.11. Opening of Roger Marsh, *Touch and Go* (2014).

Superficially, the process of making *Touch and Go* was perhaps the least obviously collaborative aspect of an otherwise very collaborative project. Ordinarily, much of my work with composers takes place in the rehearsal room, workshopping ideas, improvising and devising materials, often with a score generated much later in the process and sometimes only after the first performance, as a consolidation of what happened rather than the starting point for a realisation. In contrast, with this piece, I initiated the brief, but Marsh then composed independently, handing over a score. However, I have worked with Marsh for over twenty years. I have played many of his pieces, including, for a long time, in Black Hair, the music-theatre ensemble that he founded. As a result, my hands recognise many of the shapes and patterns from playing other pieces of his over the years; the audible characteristics of his music are for me embodied. More than this, the more I have *handled* this music over so many years, the more my hands have become shaped and formed by its demands. Not just this music, of course—I am a pianist who plays all kinds of music but who has, for over twenty years, played more new music, of many different kinds, than anything else. However, with much of the other music I have performed over the years, I already knew it, as a listener, prior to playing it. With premieres that is never the case, of course; but while I have given many premieres, either as a soloist or in ensembles, the difference here is that there are only a few composers for whom I have played a number of pieces, whether new or old, and without recordings being available, with repeat performances, sometimes over a period of years. As a result, in learning *Touch and Go* the feeling of embodied recognition in encountering what was actually an entirely new piece, nobody else had played before, was *tangible*.

That pianists might develop an embodied form of musical syntax in their hands that influences the anticipatory capacities of their motor systems has been the topic of recent research in neuropsychology; recent experiments have suggested a build-up of motor action expectations in relation to long-term experience of certain musical patterns (Sammler et al., 2013).[47] Comparably, the ways in which Marsh's music is both similar to and different from that of other late-twentieth-century and twenty-first-century composition is, for me, manifested in my body—especially my fingers—as much as in sound. Singer Loré Lixenberg (2017, 295), also a specialist in performing new music of various kinds, makes a similar comment: "It's often occurred to me that every composed tone I have ever produced is etched into my throat. So the relationship to every new piece you learn, and by implication to every composer, is peculiarly intimate." Mandy-Suzanne Wong and Nina Sun Eidsheim (2016, 217) broaden this, noting that to play music: "is in part to bring oneself under the influence of other bodies from the past. We perform memories, our own and those of others. My body and my bodily practices are partly molded by memories personal and cultural—which means that my body, my practices, are not wholly

47 This research is concerned with diatonic chordal sequences, but it would seem logical that the embodied experience of repeated patterns of any kind might well have the same effect, providing that the music employs a coherent harmonic language.

mine." As I ask in my text for *Ceci n'est pas un piano*, "Whose hands are these, anyway? They're so much mine, they know so much of what I know, maybe more than I do. They can find notes, feel distance, decide on musical emphasis. But other people, teachers and composers, have moulded them too, pushed them into peculiar shapes over and over, until I can no longer say what's truly natural to them." Erin Manning suggests that "Touch connects bodies, human bodies, bodies of thought, intermittently" (2007, 9).

With *Touch and Go*, specifically, learning the piece, touching the piano keys, feeling the shapes, recognising certain gestures (physical as well as sonic) and certain kinds of attack, put me *back in touch* with previous experiences of practice and performance, with earlier manifestations of my pianistic self, as well as with the notation and sound of other pieces. This observation is bolstered by recalling Deniz Peters's comments on the empathic and social constitution of tactility, even in listening. He argues that in hearing—hearing touch in—music, we do not just hear mental states (as many philosophers argue, though in different ways), but "feel" them; the process of "*hearing in* . . . amounts to *feeling in*. . . . We may experience sonic gestures haptically, feeling their tactile qualities as arising from *our* bodily knowledge" (Peters 2012, 21). If hearing music is in some senses tactile—and for the pianist, hearing piano music is, especially, an embodied hearing and consequently *feeling in* of piano touch—and if the qualities of the touch of others can, through listening, be "understood" (felt meaningfully) through my own experience of touch, then playing the piano is always a manifestation of the felt experience not just of my own sense of touch but of my embodied, empathic sense of the touch of others. In bringing this to the surface in the experience of learning this piece, this particularly connective form of tactility is exposed; the social layer of the body, articulated earlier in terms of the contiguity with lived experience and embodied experience beyond piano playing, is therefore in part constituted at this deeper, schematic level.

This idea of the composer being "in" my hands of course works both ways. Marsh may have written the piece independently, producing a conventional score, but he did so with substantial practical knowledge of my work as a performer, with years of direct experience of what it might mean to give me something to do. At the time of writing he had little idea of the context for which the piece was being produced—*Player Piano*—but he knew it was to form part of a somewhat theatrical performance. He knew, on the basis of our past association and my current interests, that I would do more than simply play the notes: afterwards, he commented that despite not knowing where the project was heading, "I had expectations that you would do *something* for it. . . . I know you would bring a theatricality to it, and that I could rely on that" (Marsh 2019). However, with the exceptions described above, none of that was specified in the score: it operated at a different, more tacit level of interaction.[48]

48 Martin Iddon comments similarly with regard to David Tudor's work on John Cage's pieces, especially in the late 1950s, noticing the ways in which apparently independent choices by the performer in response to indeterminate scores were often, actually, strongly conditioned by practices engrained in the extended musical relationship between composer and performer. Iddon (2013, 55) concludes: "Though Cage might have been controlling the sounds he had left undetermined only from a distance, and with-

In his essay on instrumentality, Philip Alperson (2008, 47) notes that the relationship between people and instruments is both recalcitrant and intimate: recalcitrant "insofar as it [the instrument] must be 'mastered' so that the instrument can be utilized in the service of the production of musical works—and intimate—insofar as musical instruments are inevitably connected with the bodies and bodily actions of the performer." Aden Evens (2005, 161) takes this rather further, developing the idea that the relationship between instrument and performer is one of resistance: "the instrument does not just yield passively to the desire of the musician. It is not a blank slate waiting for an inscription. Likewise, the musician does not just turn the instrument to his [*sic*] own ends, bending it to his will against whatever resistance it offers. Rather, musician and instrument meet, each drawing the other out of native territory." Picking this up, Stefan Östersjö (2013, 203) notes the musical significance of the complexities of this resistance, beyond more simplistic notions of mastery or virtuosity: "Virtuosity emerges in the interplay between a performer and a musical instrument, but the significance of the more subtle levels of a performer's interaction with musical materials reaches into the finest components of the performance: the significance of different fingerings, the movements of the hands, the pressing of keys, all the physical properties of balance between a performer's technique and the 'resistance' of the instrument." As a result, Östersjö proposes a reconfiguration of instrumental mastery into a focus on the meaningful negotiation of instrumental resistance: "the way in which a performer responds to the instrument is not simply a development of strategies to overcome this resistance, but rather a continual learning of how to 'play' the dynamics of its resistances" (ibid.).

In learning *Touch and Go*, there was a strange combination of recognition, in the familiarity of many of the shapes and patterns with respect to some of Marsh's other music, as discussed above, and also estrangement, in moments when the piece seems to actively disengage from those patterns in order to produce a contrived awkwardness, extravagantly difficult or even impossible for the hands. This was not a simple contrast, because the familiarity in this context was in part experienced in relation to technical difficulty; it is the very awkwardness, in pianistic terms, of some of Marsh's musical language, that leads to it being tangibly memorable, because it is this that marks its gestural characteristics as different to those of other post-tonal composers, even where certain harmonic characteristics are shared. For the music to be familiar to the hands, it has to be marked as different in some way, and awkward enough to require a process of practice focused on negotiating the idiosyncrasies of the shapes and patterns under my (not terribly big) hands. Examples of this, experienced in playing a number of Marsh's pieces and therefore recognisable in *Touch and Go*, include very fast runs, in one direction, up or down the piano, sometimes with

out necessarily meaning to, the specific route that he and Tudor had taken to reach these realizations meant that Cage's control over the language available to Tudor was still near enough absolute." The nature of the scores and associated musical practice is very different to my own situation with Marsh's *Touch and Go*, but the point about the processes by which a composerly influence might extend beyond the individual piece is comparable (and rarely acknowledged).

composed-in accelerations to create the effect of plunging down or taking off, and usually with some scalic repetition across the octaves but occasional chromatic changes, making it impossible simply to learn one pattern or hand shape and simply repeat it across the keyboard.[49] Likewise, certain recurrent chordal shapes and ringing, accented attacks for sustained notes provoked a particular sense of embodied recollection.

These, then, were all features of passages that were tricky to learn and yet familiar in particular ways. Certain other passages, though, were different, even more awkward—to my hands, at least—and used techniques not especially prevalent in the other pieces by Marsh that I had played. This was particularly the case with the use of quiet tremolo chords spread across widely spaced intervals, in both hands at once, with individual pitches gradually shifting so that the chords slowly moved down the piano over an extended period (figure 2.12 contains an excerpt from this section).

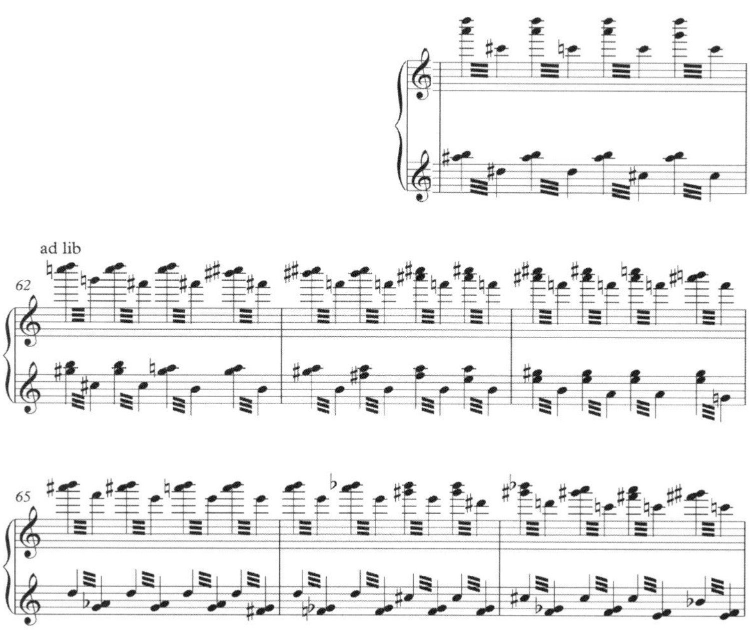

Figure 2.12.

49 Two clips in the online repository (www.orpheusinstituut.be/en/voices-bodies-practices-media-repository) illustrate these scalic actions; see the files "SF2.6 *Touch and Go*, plunge" and "SF2.7 *Touch and Go*, taking off upwards."

Figure 2.12. Roger Marsh, *Touch and Go*, bars 61–67.

These passages demanded a particular kind of physical engagement in order to be realised, not least due to the pain resulting from the combination of holding these stretched hand positions in this region of the piano and maintaining a quiet tremolo over time; they were intensely awkward passages which I could only play with an unusual body position, with very low shoulders and arms, facilitated by stretching my back away from the piano but rounding the upper body inwards (see figure 2.13).

Figure 2.13.

Overall, the piece in this way seemed intended thematically to produce a drama that would contrast moments in which the piano seems a strange, unfamiliar object, requiring a distorting and contorting of the body, with others when the body and instrument seem reconciled and united, when the notes flow. Marsh has commented that this piece was one of a few composed around this time in which he was able to draw virtuosic elements he had previously tended to reserve for concert music into what he knew was to be a theatrical context:

> I was interested in writing lots of notes—lots of runs, lots of big chords, which has always been stuff that I've done in instrumental music, but generally in theatrical music I've taken a slightly different approach, and I've kept things rather simple and I've concentrated on theatricality rather than on . . . the complexity of the music. But in this piece, there was also an aspect of virtuosity that I wanted to exploit because you are a virtuosic contemporary music pianist. . . . So in a way this piece brings together purely instrumental thinking with theatrical thinking more completely. (Marsh 2019)

Figure 2.13. Still from performance of Roger Marsh, *Touch and Go*, as part of premiere performance of *Player Piano*, Scenic Stage Theatre, York, 5 May 2016.

In this sense, beyond the explicit theatrical instructions for the first gestures and the very last, Marsh was indirectly composing the body in quite particular ways, writing music that would sometimes require me to reconsider my habitual body and hand positions. On one level this is simply an extension of what a performer does with any challenging musical material, but the *extension* is significant; it imposes a more extreme and more noticeable—to both pianist and audience—repositioning of the classical pianist's body than most virtuoso classical music. It constitutes an interference with the pianistic body image that is somewhat similar to the remediations elsewhere in the performance; but this time it is live, with an agency that is obviously distributed between the composer who demands certain sounds and the performer who finds ways physically to produce them.

The experience of performing this piece in this sense relates to Östersjö's characterisation of resistance; the process of practice became a continual learning not just to play but also to play *with* the resistances of body and instrument, negotiating their interaction. More significantly, though, this process became generative; the more I focused on it, both reflectively, thinking about my realisation of the score, but also reflexively, considering in and through playing why and how I was practising it quite as I was, what I was doing with my body in relation to the instrument, with my pianistic technique, with my understanding of this piece, and how that derived from bigger questions outside this piece—of bodies, pianos, the authority of composers and agency of performers—the more the process afforded a different response. In his discussion of the significance of acts of repetition in the practice of Western classical music, Bruce Brubaker suggests, "As hand and fingers find increasingly efficient ways through a piece of music, the performer may also find artistic insight" (2016). Here, in repeating the phrases over and over, partly simply to be able to play them better, I started to focus on my playing gestures, to interrupt and freeze them, then to exaggerate and extend them (see figure 2.14).

Figure 2.14.

Figure 2.14. Stills from live performance (Scenic Stage Theatre, York, 5 May 2016) and film, Roger Marsh, *Touch and Go* (with gestural choreography by Catherine Laws): this piece formed part of the large-scale performance *Player Piano*. Film by Minyung Im; sound by Lynette Quek. Images 1, 2, 4, and 5 from film; 2 and 6 from live performance.

For example, a lot of the fast descending or ascending runs in the piece break out abruptly from sustained tremolo chords, racing up or down the piano in a brief flourish that ends with a staccato note. The tremolos have the effect of building a moment of tension, with the subsequent fast run acting as a sudden release, like the action of a coiled spring. Practising these phrases, I realised I was manifesting this physically, feeling as if the hands were somehow locked in position with growing tension while playing the tremolo, until they exploded out, escaping away up or down the keyboard, with an exaggerated physical sweep of the hands facilitated by an accompanying lateral upper body movement. Suddenly freezing my position at the end of each of these, I would find my hands in extreme positions: high in the air above the keys or flung low off the bass end of the piano. This produced a series of "how did my hands get there?" moments, with the freezing process revealing fragments of gestures that would ordinarily have passed me by in the continuity of playing. Noting these positions then allowed for their extension and exaggeration, drawing attention to this aspect of the performance. In addition, I incorporated into the performance the occasional possibility of freezing a gesture, as in my practice process. Sometimes this might be accompanied by a sudden staring at the hands, perhaps holding them in place while moving the head to view them from different angles, as if they had become an object of scrutiny outside or strange to myself. Finally, in making a film of the piece, the film-maker Minyung Im suggested adding somewhat self-conscious editing techniques to further emphasise these moments: occasional freeze-frames, slow motion, or blurring of images.[50]

Gradually, then, through the process of practice, I generated an additional, semi-choreographed, semi-improvised layer of gestural enaction which foregrounded the kinds of bodily engagement already in process. Barbara Bolt argues that, in research through practice, "originary knowledge or the new is revealed through handling, rather [than] through conscious acts of transgression" (2016). Likewise, in chapter 1 (p. 37) Gorton and Östersjö argued that artistic practices develop through a dynamic "oscillation" between the singular instances of material manifestation and the cycles of repetition and difference that constitute the processes of practice. My iterative process of repetitive, scrutinised practice in *Touch and Go* exemplifies that "handling," not just because it was literally focused on the hands (and gradually, by extension, on more and more of the rest of the body), but because of its use of the everyday practice of the piano performer as a means to produce both new self-awareness of the body at the instrument and also new ways to creatively engage with that as material for performance. This subsequently took on an additional form, with the same gestures further developed collaboratively with theatre-maker Teresa Brayshaw into an abstract movement piece performed away from the piano, prior to *Touch and Go*, as an additional means of "looking again" at the pianistic body, this time out of the context of the instrument.

50 Two examples can be seen in the online repository (www.orpheusinstituut.be/en/voices-bodies-practices-media-repository); file "SF2.8 *Touch and Go*, scrutiny of hands (live)" is taken from a live performance, while file "SF2.9 *Touch and Go*, scrutiny of hands (film)" is the same passage excerpted from the film and incorporates a freeze-frame.

As De Preester (2007, 368) says, performances that operate on the basis of body schema are far less common than those interrogating body image, but where they do occur they often proceed "via a 'denaturalization' of bodily actions and activities," by in some sense exposing "the complexity and non-obviousness of daily and 'simple' motor actions and activities painfully clear to a spectator."[51] Playing the resistances in the context of this generative process towards the performance of *Touch and Go* meant not just learning how to play the music in this context, but also how to play with the sound-gesture relationships and, perhaps, to playfully work in and through the precariousness of performance hinted at in the title: when we consider that something might possibly work but might not, when we might succeed but might fail, even when someone very ill might or might not recover, we say the situation is "touch and go." That is how I feel about performance in general, and particularly about the process of realising particularly demanding music. However, at some point in the process of working to expose and sometimes exaggerate the body's role in playing the notes for this piece, my aim became one of creating a space in which embodied agency becomes more apparent: where the specifics of this bodily engagement with—rather than a body's mastery of—the challenges of the piece would become more prominent.

As noted above, this in part involved a reflexive foregrounding of the performer's body image. However, that was founded in a process that involved an attempt to intercept my body schema. The iterative practice process, with its stop-motion interruptions, was itself a practical researching of what goes into the gestures constituted by my bodily engagement with the notation. The "how did my hand get there" approach was, inexplicitly, an attempt at "making body schematic activities explicit and visible, such that the body-schematic activity is no longer unconscious and residing at the side of the subject (as a source of motor activity), but becomes conscious and object like" (De Preester 2007, 369). The notion of the body as an always evolving archive, constituted in the history of its behaviours and actions, apparently personal but in fact formed as much by others and by the modifications of cultural practices, is manifested in this performance.[52] Of course, there are two important points here. The first is that it is impossible for me fully to "reach inside" the embodied processes that have formed the pianistic "me": the paradox of embodied self-presence is, as discussed early in this chapter, one of the issues underpinning the whole project. As De Preester says, in performance dealing with body schema, "the task . . . is not to regain an originary presence of and to its body, but to produce and re-produce its body time and again" (ibid., 371). Second, although the process here was concerned primarily with "catching" the action of body schema, the issue for performance is that repeating and representing that process cannot avoid a transition into the realm of body image: even in the moment of freezing my gesture and scrutinising it, the schematic becomes image—initially

51 As Victor Ramirez Ladrón de Guevara notes, notwithstanding the cultural constructedness of the idea of the "natural" body, there is in "an undeniable tension between the ideological inscriptions of the body and the body as a lived entity" (2011, 31).

52 This topic will return as a principal theme of chapter 4.

for me, and subsequently, in incorporating this into the performance, for the audience.

In this sense, we might simply conclude that all this becomes performance of, or even about, body image: body as object of representation. However, I would argue that in the performance of *Touch and Go* the body schematic aspects of my embodiment are invoked by the continuity between necessary performance action and the sudden framing of the body in extensions of some of the strange positions that the schematic functions lead me to. I think (but cannot know, other than from audience reaction, which after each performance has seemed, anecdotally, to confirm my impression) that the apparently organic continuity and fluidity between the various gestural types in the performance—the gestures necessary for sound production and to facilitate sound production, the additional, unconscious gestures that tend to accompany my playing, and the more explicitly theatrical gestures that these sometimes resolve into, frozen for scrutiny—itself suggests this very transition back and forth from schema into image and from body-subject into object. This is emphasised by the fact that I mostly behave as a conventional performer, fully engaged, physically, in the process of playing the piece, with no apparent distinction between mind and body, but then suddenly, on occasion, respond directly to my hands in the positions in which they finish at the end of a phrase, looking up and down at them, or peering round at them from one side and then the other (see figure 2.15).

Figure 2.15.

Moreover, playing with the "touch and go" situation of the piece in this way opened up a space in which performer agency emerged. This happened for me, in practice, through my process; this may seem personal, but it is important to note the significance of a reflexive attention to practice as (sometimes) sig-

Figure 2.15. Still from performance by Catherine Laws of Roger Marsh, *Touch and Go* (with gestural choreography by Catherine Laws): this piece formed part of the large-scale performance *Player Piano*. Film by Minyung Im; sound by Lynette Quek.

nificant in generating forms of understanding or awareness that can feed into research. Additionally, this awareness, and my agency in subsequently transforming these actions into gestural objects, becomes evident in the performance itself, with its overt interference in bodily schematic and body image processes. The approach therefore brought into focus the complexity of agency in the shaping of my hands and what they can do over time, including the role of composers in that process. It also, however, opened up the possibilities for a performer who intercepts that process and attempts to expose it, becoming more than a semiotic body (in Fischer-Lichte's terms) and proposing instead the interaction of composer and performer agencies in the production of this strange, self-conscious body-subject.

In *Agency and Embodiment*, Carrie Noland (2009, 175) argues that "gestural routines are particularly vulnerable to processes of de-skilling and re-skilling; these processes undermine the culturally regulated body discourse relation and produce intense kinesthetic and affective experiences of dissonance. . . . In short, the moving, trained, and trainable body is always a potential source of resistance to the meanings it is required to bear." The self-conscious scrutiny, repetition, and subversion of the pianistic gestural vocabulary in the performance of *Touch and Go* is intended this way: as a means to expose embodiment as "the process whereby collective behaviors and beliefs, acquired through acculturation, are rendered individual and 'lived' at the level of the body" (ibid., 9). In this context, agency is "the power to alter those acquired behaviors and beliefs for purposes that may be reactive (resistant) or collaborative (innovative) in kind" (ibid.). The gestures stem from those my body made "naturally"—as a result of the encultured training—in playing the piece. However, this additional process draws attention not only to their oddities but also to their significance: it encourages us to look and look again, to consider the instrumentalist's body as more than a vehicle for realising pre-formed, cognitised intentions. The body re-enacts the "laws" of piano performance, but this kind of repetition exposes its strangeness and constructedness and then focuses in on that: it offers a deconstituting possibility (in Butler's terms) in which agency is suddenly apparent.

As Peggy Phelan says, in performance bodies are never just bodies, but become "metonymic of self, of character, of voice, of 'presence'" (1993, 150). On one level, *Player Piano* attempts to disrupt that; to work with what Phelan calls "the anxiety raised by the gap between the discursive construct 'the body' and the affective experience of embodiment" (ibid., 171),[53] with the tensions within a pianistic body that is both expressed and expressive, simultaneously feels natural(ised) while knowing it is shaped and formed from both within and without, by self and others. In doing so it attempts to stage the explicit interaction of body-instrument-sound. At times, most especially in the performance of *Touch and Go*, it also works to stage the performer's embodied interception

53 Phelan's discussion is somewhat similar to some of the comments by Helena De Preester (2007, 352) cited in chapter 1, particularly with regard to the ways in which the body in performance is never "just" itself, nor clearly representative of something "other": it resists stable objectification.

and interrogation of the composer's meaning-making, though not by simply asserting pure bodily presence: the performing body is never fully there, fully self-present, any more than it ever fully disappears into whatever it "means." It is always active in the process by which subjectivity is produced in performance, but it is also objectified at the moment it seems to concretise performer subjectivity. In this respect we might agree with Elizabeth Grosz that "corporeality can be seen as the material condition of subjectivity" (1995, 103), but also acknowledge that the body is already, always disciplined, shaped by discourse.

These layers of the body—the body image and body schemata, the remediated and textual body, the situated, contextual, and social body—overlap and coincide. At different times, one layer might temporarily become foregrounded or recede into the background, but each is active in constituting the versions of the performing subject that emerge and transform in the performance.

Part 3: Instrument as Agent

The piano as habitus

My own piano is nothing special. It's an old English upright, a Windover. My parents bought it when I'd been learning for a year or two, when it was clear I was making some progress and our brash, pretty much untunable upright would no longer do. Maybe I like this one because I'm so used to it. The sound is relatively even and the keys are weighted quite well. It's been fairly badly treated, dropped and bashed when we've moved house, stored for long periods in a freezing garage, thumped by children, but it still stands my inconsistent use. It can't do lots of things I really care about though: there's no deep, rich tone, and I can't mess about inside it; I have to go elsewhere for that. So I put up with it and it puts up with me.

Thus far, in much of the discussion it sounds as though the body—or rather the body-subject—simply acts on the piano, employing it as a tool. I have, however, argued that the piano might occupy a particular place in the consideration of the relationship between performer and instrument, due not only to its size and mechanics and to the particular ways in which we interact physically with it but also to the weight of its cultural history. I also noted the ways in which the piano is significant in my domestic as well as my professional environment (and the ways in which the texts written for *Ceci n'est pas un piano*—both mine and Jennifer Hymer's—make that explicit in the context of performance). Finally, it is clear from some of the discussion that what and how I play is strongly conditioned by my particular experience of pianism as a social and cultural construct related to the physical properties and historical uses of the instrument. This is mediated through the composers whose music I have played and the performers and teachers I have watched and listened to. Bodily behaviour *constitutes* the performance (and hence the subject-in-process), but it is also *constituted by* the norms, conventions, prior practices, training, cultural forces. Stover (2016) draws attention to this doubleness: "Performative acts, therefore, are not simply enacted by bodies; if identity is performed, then the acts themselves are what define the very bodies performing them."

Following Kathleen Coessens and Stefan Östersjö (2014), the contemporary piano, considered this way, is not just my instrument but my *habitus*. Östersjö and Coessens take this concept from Aristotle, Mauss, and Bourdieu—as a dialectical system that both determines the behaviours of its participants and is shaped by them—and explore the ways in which an *artistic* habitus both "enriches the expertise and potential of the artists" and also "implicates a space of resistance, be it between the musician's acts and the encountered materials or between the musician's acts and the cultural space with which he or she interacts" (Coessens and Östersjö 2014, 333). Above, I discussed the resistant relationship between body and instrument. The notion of the piano as habitus takes this a little further: the piano's history and repertoires, its cultural status and contexts of performance, as much as its design, manufacture, and physical operation, form but are also in part formed by my set of embodied patterns for action and behaviour—physical, cognitive, cultural. In this sense, its resistances and affordances are deeply bound up with my embodied sense of self.

Following from this, in this section I consider the piano more substantially—as more than a tool for production and expression—examining how it exceeds its purely instrumental function, acting as a significant agent in itself.

As is clear above, the piano offers a particular context for understanding instrumentality, artistic imaginings of selfhood, and the interactions and divergences between embodied and aesthetically focused attention. This involves thinking of the performer-instrument relationship as one of interaction—a two-way, rather than unidirectional, process—and the title of *Player Piano* is suggestive in this respect, invoking something of this dynamic. I play the piano, certainly, but to be a "player" can mean something more; it connotes agency, sometimes even domination or exploitation: to play someone means to use them for one's own ends. I am certainly a player of the piano in this sense, and the insistent "I" in my framing of the performance as a whole, discussed in the introduction to this chapter, also is an attempt to position "me" as a significant creative "player," alongside the composers, film-maker, and theatre-maker. However, the subject of the title *Player Piano* is deliberately ambiguous: perhaps the piano is equally a "player," with influence over the performer, composers, and audience? Moreover, a player piano—the instrument—is a piano that does not need complex human operation. Unlike a standard piano, nuances of expressive gesture are pointless and hands are redundant: this instrument does not need truly playing, just *operating* via the pedal power of the feet. There is no player piano as such in the performance, but the title evokes this kind of instrumental agency. In various ways there is an ambiguity as to who or what is the player. Drawing on Butler again, in many ways it comes down to: do I play the piano or does the piano, in all it might be, play me?

I often wish I didn't play the piano. It can seem such a beast of an instrument, barely of our times: monolithic, immovable, and inflexible in an age of speed, lightness, portability, and ephemerality. Some of the lines in my text for *Ceci n'est pas un piano* express this ambivalence: "I'm never sure what I think about the piano anymore. It's like a part of myself that can't be detached and considered objectively. It seems such an anachronistic monster, so massive and unwieldy when everything else is ever neater, faster, more mobile. But the sound can be so wonderful. . . ." On a bad day, I would argue that the piano's centrality to the grand, virtuosic, and primarily masculine tradition of nineteenth-century mastery, extended into extreme complexity and interventionist preparations in the twentieth century, serves only to emphasise its status as a relic. This, I recognise, is a somewhat personal perspective. Moreover, it lies alongside an ongoing love of much of the music and a huge admiration for its star performers. Nevertheless, a sense of alienation from the weight of that tradition—from my own instrument, and to an extent my own training—persists, and I am certainly not alone in this.[54]

---

54 Anecdotally, I have found that whenever I express this ambivalence, in talks or presentations, other pianists often approach me afterwards to share their similar views. This includes many highly accomplished pianists. Some composers have also expressed their reluctance to write for the piano in similar terms.

It is perhaps not surprising, then, that many other artists, not all musicians, have wanted to scrutinise the instrument, deconstructing (sometimes literally) all that it seems to carry with it. There are many examples of this, from Fluxus performances of the 1960s that require the nailing down of keys or the stretching of the highest strings until they "burst" (in George Maciunas's compositions for Nam June Paik),[55] the pushing of a piano through a wall or offering it hay to eat (in pieces by La Monte Young),[56] through to Joseph Beuys's *Homogeneous Infiltration for Piano* (1966), in which a grand piano is completely covered in grey felt with a red cross on the side. Wrapped like this, the piano can no longer play; we might want to infiltrate the skin, but the felt seems to insulate the instrument from the world (or perhaps the world from it). The piano, perhaps a symbol of European high culture, seems, from the red cross, to be sick, in need of healing and recuperation, perhaps quarantined from people, not least musicians. In Rebecca Horn's more recent mechanised sculpture, *Concert for Anarchy* (1990),[57] a grand piano is suspended, upside down, from the ceiling, and every few minutes a mechanism causes the lid to fall open and the keys to fan outwards from the keyboard, clanging noisily, then retracting back into position. The piano here seems to have acquired its own ability to perform, independent of human operation. It seems almost to vomit its innards towards the audience, spitting forth its keys with a clatter and jangle, and its position is also somewhat threatening to the viewer standing beneath.[58]

Annea Lockwood, composer of *Ceci n'est pas un piano*, explores similar territory: her *Piano Transplants*, from the 1970s, seem to want to free the piano of some of this weighty backdrop, to find it a new home in different environments.[59] Most dramatically, Lockwood's piano burnings suggest an antipathy to what the piano represents—a desire to destroy or renew it. However, the transplants have a tenderness, too. Sinking into the sand, on a beach, or in a pond, or with the tendrils of plants growing around them (see figure 2.16), the pianos look ridiculously out of place; and yet there seems to be the suggestion that, with time, the instruments might be accommodated in these environments, might find their place.

55 See https://www.moma.org/collection/works/127428.
56 See https://www.moma.org/collection/works/127638.
57 See https://www.tate.org.uk/art/artworks/horn-concert-for-anarchy-t07517.
58 This piano previously appeared in Horn's film *Buster's Bedroom* (1990), where it lived in a psychiatric clinic: "Having freed itself from the psychiatric clinic, it now hangs upside down from the ceiling, composing its own music, developing a new tonality" (Horn 1998, 250).
59 See http://www.annealockwood.com/compositions/piano-transplants/.

Figure 2.16.

Lockwood's transplants, like the other artistic and performative examples discussed, are all predicated on the very particular cultural status of the piano, historically but also physically, due to its unusual size and peculiar mechanics. All these seem to ask us to look again at this instrument, to consider what it has come to stand for, how it has been used but also, perhaps, how it might *be*, if allowed. Importantly, despite transplanting and burning it, Lockwood has continued to compose for the piano. Likewise, I still want to play it, even if I often wonder quite why, especially when it comes to solo performance.

Overall, then, the cultural and physical specificity of the piano—the apparent expectation not just to play the piano but to be a "pianist"—is something I struggle with in certain respects. Nevertheless, as a pianist who primarily plays new music in its many different forms, both composed and improvised, and often in collaborative and interdisciplinary contexts, this is my world: the piano is the primary site of my creativity, its limitations and possibilities deeply bound up with my sense of self. As Sally Jane Norman notes (2013, 276), in artistic practice, "while materials may be configured and constrained to assume convention loaded, prescriptive roles (e.g., those of tools or instruments), the creative querying of these roles and their underlying assumptions can itself

Figure 2.16. Annea Lockwood, "Piano Garden (1969–70, Ingatestone, Essex)" from *Piano Transplants* series. Photo by Chris Ware.

specifically be a source of artistic value." This became something I wanted to explore in *Player Piano*, partly in terms of the agency that resides in the instrument's history and mechanics.

Piano as player in *Player Piano*

> *. . .it's nothing more than a machine: all you can do is push the keys harder or softer, faster or slower, but the tiny nuances within that make me think I'm interacting with a living being.*

In *Player Piano*, the instrument sometimes appears as we might expect: for much of the performance it sits there, centre stage, commanding our attention. It is grand and expensive, black and shiny. Its weight and status is impressive, as usual in a piano recital. It is often played in the standard manner, too, with a certain virtuosity (particularly in *Touch and Go*) and moments of more conventionally expressive pianism (in passages towards the end of *Ceci n'est pas un piano*, for example). However, it is also in some respects presented quite differently. Importantly, at the start of the performance it is noticeably absent from the stage. There is a piano stool, and also the piano double: the doll's-house piano, with mini model pianist, on a small table, with a helium balloon attached to one leg of the piano, as described earlier. But no piano. When the time comes, a little way into the performance, after other events have taken place, the piano enters, edging onto the stage, apparently of its own accord.

It needs help, though: it doesn't seem to know quite where to go, so the pianist has to get involved, with considerable effort. There is something of a struggle, pianist and piano apparently trying to get to the right position, but the piano has the upper hand: it moves pretty much when it wants to, in the direction it prefers. It can be coaxed—I can push it—but sometimes it seems to resist or, like a supermarket trolley, to suddenly have a life of its own and start rolling in the wrong direction (see figure 2.17).[60]

Figure 2.17.

60 The online repository (www.orpheusinstituut.be/en/voices-bodies-practices-media-repository) illustrates the full sequence of the piano's entrance, taken from the premiere performance; see file "SF2.10 *Player Piano*, piano entrance."

Figure 2.17. Stills from performance of *Player Piano*, Scenic Stage Theatre, York, 5 May 2016.

By this point in the performance, we've already seen something of this relationship, but mediated by film. In the earlier entrance, the piano is tiny, fragile, and again has trouble getting to its position: it has to be dragged in, pulled by ribbons. Also, this time it lies on its side and struggles to get to its feet—or perhaps it is the piano that resists the action. After a short while it is helped by a giant human hand that descends into the frame, from above: suddenly the power lies elsewhere. Finally, the piano stands in position, but then is immediately, flippantly knocked back over by the hand, discarded. All this is vocalised by the live performer: straining, croaking, creaking and groaning accompanies the struggle and resistance of the instrument, half comically, half surreally.[61]

The point of all of this was to playfully consider the piano as at once my tool, or a part of me—of my sense of myself and my creative potential—but also a thing with its own power, history, culture, weight, and status: an entity that carries agency in the process of making the work and in the moment of performance, perhaps in ways we might not immediately recognise. Matthew Sergeant suggests that we should consider alternatives to the "normative body-over-instrument orientation" (2017, 4); in *Player Piano* it is not simply that a human subject puts to work an inhuman object, but rather that the piano, in this context, is a "player" of a kind: it has what Jane Bennett, in her advocacy of "the active role of *nonhuman* materials in public life," calls "thing power" (2010, 2). There is a dynamic of cooperation and resistance in these moments, just as there is in the embodied experience of playing the instrument. The piano becomes more than an object or even a tool, and this corresponds to the way that I experience the power of the instrument when trying to play it. In her book *Vibrant Matter*, Bennett cites W. J. T. Mitchell's distinction between objects and things: "'objects are the way things appear to a subject—that is, with a name, an identity, a gestalt or stereotypical template. . . . Things, on the other hand, . . . [signal] the moment when the object becomes the Other, when the sardine looks back, when the mute idol speaks, when the subject experiences the object as uncanny'" (Bennett, 2010, 2).

Bennett's concern, building from Latour's actor–network theory, is to make us acknowledge the shared materiality of people and things, considering the ways in which we are affected by the things around us, so as better to understand the interactions and distributions of agency.[62] While every performer experiences a sense of resistance or recalcitrance from an instrument, the nature and status of the piano marks this quite peculiarly. When Adorno writes that a pianist is defined by producing "a certain sense of hewing the sound out of the piano, or playing corporeally, as it were inside the piano" (2006, 113) (adding that this

61 Two excerpts in the online repository illustrate this sequence; see files "SF2.11 *Player Piano*, vocalisation of piano, film (opening)" and "SF2.12 *Player Piano*, vocalisation of piano, film (final flip-over)."

62 In certain respects this position (and my discussion of the interaction of human and non-human agency as a whole) relates to John Butt's specifically musicological argument for the latent intentionality carried by music (2002, 94), introduced in chapter 1 (and subsequently used in chapter 3). My focus in this chapter on "agency" (in preference to "intentionality," even when reconfigured) is to avoid the possible confusion or even conflation of human intention and wider agency (as discussed in the introduction).

is exactly what his own playing lacks), his use of the word "hewing" carries the idea of the piano as itself *being* the material that simply needs excavating and shaping. The piano (like the sardine) looks back at Adorno: "The piano does not do what I would like it to, but at the same time it is always saying: this is how it can be, this is how it should be" (ibid., 130).[63] Bennett notes that ascribing such agency to the non-human risks a "touch of anthropocentrism" (2010, 99); I certainly do that with the piano, in contriving its entrance in *Player Piano* in quite this way. However, Bennett argues that this can be part of the attempt to expose non-humans—animals and things—as not just "behaving" but truly "acting" (ibid., 108); this is the attempt in *Player Piano*.

Significantly, Bennett (2010, 120) argues that one way to "cultivate this new discernment might be to elide the question of the human. Postpone for a while the topics of subjectivity or the nature of human interiority, or the question of what really distinguishes the human from the animal, plant, and thing," because sooner or later we always "insinuate a hierarchy of subjects over objects, and obstruct free thinking about what agency really entails." Despite drawing on Bennett's ideas to help think through the agency of the piano, there is of course a disjunction between Bennett's method and my concerns in this chapter, with its excavation of matters of subjectivity. Bennett's position is in many respects persuasive, but in the context of performance—as both process and product—it does not seem viable to elide or even postpone the human. There are plenty of examples of non-human performance, of course. However, my concern is to expose some of the complexities in the production of apparently discrete, human subjectivity, inviting reconsideration of some of the assumptions upon which the persistent discourse of individuality and authenticity in music performance is based. In this context, it seems more productive not simply to present non-human agency (as Rebecca Horn's *Concert for Anarchy* does so effectively), but rather to explore the co-constitution of subjectivity from the very interaction of different ideas, bodies, and things. As Rosi Braidotti (2018, 3) puts it, "Subjectivity is not restricted to bound individuals, but is rather a co-operative, trans-species effort . . . that takes place transversally, in-between nature/technology; male/female; black/white; local/global; present/past." Likewise, the piano is not one thing in *Player Piano*, any more than "I" am; it transforms, both by appearing and sounding somewhat differently from one piece to another, but also through its mediated form in the two films and as the doll's-house model. Sometimes it seems more tool-like, played and used; sometimes (as I discuss more fully below) its agency is more explicitly apparent.

Fundamental to this is the attempt to show how, as Karen Barad (2003, 822) says, "materiality is discursive (i.e., material phenomena are inseparable from the apparatuses of bodily production . . .), just as discursive practises are always already material (i.e., they are ongoing material (re)configurations of the world)." This seems deeply relevant to the context of musical performance, which is (still) too often considered a linear process of transferring a

63 I am grateful to Stacey Sewell for pointing me to Adorno's comments.

message from one human entity to another, rather than an ecology in which subjectivities are produced and meaning is afforded from complex material interactions.[64]

In the final minutes of *Player Piano*, the mini doll's-house piano takes off into the air, in a realisation of Lockwood's instruction score, *Gone* (2007). Small weights are removed from the body of the piano, allowing the helium balloon to slowly lift it up and away; in this context, it seems significant that it floats away from *both* pianists: the live one and her tiny, clay double. The thematic and symbolic presentation of the weight and size of the piano is recast here; the piano is perhaps free, light... and it keeps playing, without the performer, who retreats under the grand piano, curling up under a blanket.

64 Murphy McCaleb provides an important critique of the persistent tendency to formulate musical performance in terms of linear communication (2014, 22–46).

Part 4: From Instrument to Ecology

Sometimes in *Player Piano* this piano agency is manifested more subtly, produced and experienced through musical interaction rather than by thematising (or even theatricalising) the performer–instrument relationship. One instance is the section in which I perform the piece *under and under*, composed for me by Paul Whitty. Here the piano takes its place alongside other materials—scores, recordings, other sound-making objects and devices for playback—all of which carry a particular kind of agency in the performance. The very *materiality* of these things, including the piano, is evident in the emergence of a performance system, or ecology, in which performer and composer play a part but are not always fully in control.

The score for *under and under* is a set of instructions (see figure 2.18): a verbal score that brings together certain kinds of materials: field recordings, plus other recordings of piano music, selected by the performer and played back through the piano, via small speakers and transducers placed inside the piano or elsewhere in the space; live, semi-improvised playing in relation to those recordings; and live performance of operations on scores chosen from the performer's personal collection.

This way of working is on the one hand classically "experimental"[65] in its interest in process (as much, if not more, than in the performance as a "product") and in that it seems to forsake a composerly role for a facilitative one that leaves many decisions about content to the performer. The composer instructs the performer to undertake certain processes prior to the performance; but within that, the performer is the one who chooses the material, selecting scores and recordings to be played and also thinking about the tools that might be used for playing inside the instrument. Quite what then transpires in performance is also very much up to the performer, in the moment. Structurally, *when* the performer chooses to do things is completely up to her, and the piece has no fixed duration; in the context of *Player Piano*, it usually lasts about 17 minutes.

Nevertheless, as with many verbal scores, the instructions are strongly characterised: the tone of the writing has a particular kind of neutrality and objectivity, but this is meticulously constructed. A particular voice emerges in the very concrete—dry, even—instructions, and in the attention to certain details and the complete but purposeful disregard of other aspects of the creative decisions. In general, Whitty seems more interested in what should be done than in the content (the exact choice of objects, scores, recordings, or the playing in response to those). I recognise this voice personally, having worked with Whitty for many years. However, even if I did not know him, the deliberate tone and the care with which he has carefully constructed a particular kind of instructional voice would, I think, still be apparent: the subtle negotiation of suggestion, obligation, and necessity is an aspect of verbal scores that is carefully considered in John Lely's study of the grammar they employ (2012). Moreover, the

65 As set out in Nyman (1999, 1–30).

Preparation

1.
This piece can be performed using either an upright or grand piano. You will require:
Mp3 players (4)
Battery powered speakers (4)
Turntable(s)
FM Radios
Headphones
Any number of object with which to interact with the piano both inside and outside including e-bows, rulers, paper, magnets, cellophone, tea-cups, hand-held cappuccino frothers etc...

2.
Gather any number of piano scores you have previously performed. These should have performance annotations on them made by the performer. Using tracing paper isolate these annotations from the piano score. Print or photocopy these sheets of annotations onto acetate so that they can be placed over other piano scores - you will need a selection of these.

3.
Make four field recordings. These could be recordings of the ambient situations in which you have previously played piano, or they could be recordings made in rural or urban environments. They can be of any length. Transfer these recordings to the four mp3 players - one recording per player.

4.
Look in your attic, on your bookshelves, in skips and charity shops for records of piano music to be played on the turntable. Procure as many of these as you can.
[...]

Performance Activities

The performance consists of any combination of the following activities. The activities can be carried out one at a time or can overlap in any viable combination:

1.
Place one or more of the acetates over one or more of the piano scores. Use the annotations as a filter to select which materials you perform from the piano score. Treat each series of activities instigated by the annotations as a separate event.
[...]

2.
a. Put the headphones on and plug them into the headphone socket of one of the mp3 players. The four players should be playing throughout the piece whether or not they are connected to a speaker or headphones.

b. Listen to the field recording.

c. Use the field recording as an audio score using the piano as a means of filtering the audio data in the recording. This can be done using a strategy of your choice.
[...]

3.
a. Attach a number of the mp3 players to the battery-powered loudspeakers. Experiment with the volume of the recordings. Experiment with the positioning of the loudspeakers.
[...]

b. When you have positioned the loudspeakers use the strategies outlined in 2 to interact with the piano.
[...]

4.
a. Place the turntable in a suitable location. This could be inside the piano, on a table, or somewhere else in the performance space. It is important that you can hear the sound it is making.

b. If you have FM radios you may then wish to place these in different locations around the space or in a pile inside the piano or elsewhere. Tune them to the output frequency of the turntable or tune them to any other frequency.

c. Listen to the recording of piano music. Identify an event and try to re-create it using the piano. You can stop the recording if you choose to and repeat the event several times or alternate the recorded event with your re-creation of the event or you can leave the recording running and when you are happy with your re-creation of the selected event you can select another one and continue the process.

Figure 2.18.

Figure 2.18. Excerpts from Paul Whitty's score *under and under* (2014) for piano, mp3 players, battery powered loudspeakers, and turntable.

idea of performing certain kinds of operations on found materials, from scores and recordings, such that they are at one and the same time vaguely recognisable and made strange, filtered and distant, is something that has, through a sequence of compositions, become an aspect of Whitty's composerly identity; he sometimes refers to this as a form of sonic or auditory archaeology.[66] The composer's "voice" in that sense retains presence even in a context where it seems to cede agency. This is not to imply a duplicitous authoritarianism on Whitty's part; I simply want to note the intricacies of what or who is "in" the performance actions and resultant sounds.

Figure 2.19.

There is, then, a trace of composerly identity mapped across processes in which a performer makes substantive material choices. Additionally, though, the process towards the piece was quite a personal one. This piece was requested for *Player Piano*; like the other compositions, it can be performed separately, but the initial context was performer-led: an invitation to respond to my specific interests as a performer. With Whitty, the process in part involved excavating the ways in which my piano playing self, or selves, have developed. There were many initial discussions about how I came to play the piano, what I have played, the piano music and performers I have listened to and where and how, memories of particular pianos I have practised on, memories of specific

66 See, for example, Whitty (2012).

Figure 2.19. Still showing process of annotating scores using transparencies, from film version of *under and under* by Paul Whitty, performed by Catherine Laws. Film by Minyung Im; sound by Lynette Quek.

performances, of piano notes that did not work properly, of different performance contexts and acoustics, and so on. This was, then, all very personal. The instruction score that emerged is at once abstracted from that mining process but specifically requires the inclusion of sonic materials related to a personal history; this will be the case whoever is performing, since each performer works through the same process afresh, producing and selecting their own materials. In particular, the player is asked to trace (onto transparent acetate sheets) markings she has in the past written into scores she has played, and to place these over pages of other scores, also from her playing history (see figure 2.19). The superimposition is random, such that the personal is significant but defamiliarised. The process disrupts embodied habits of playing, making it somewhat awkward to play otherwise familiar music. Certain characteristics of the sound are retained, while others change; there is a "making strange" of something held as familiar in both the cognitive and embodied memory.

Looked at another way, this "making strange" is also a process, for the performer, of tracing connections across an individual performance history. Sonically, the result of imposing the markings from one score onto another is one of simultaneous recollection and defamiliarisation. Sometimes the changes result in what sound like mistakes, whether of pitch or rhythm—for example, where I have marked into the original piece an accidental (a sharpened or flattened pitch) that needs to carry through a bar, and subsequently transferring this to another piece results in a wrong note. Other times, the additional markings change the musical shape or emphasis; they might, for example, introduce a stress, accent, or additional dynamic marking that alters the balance of a phrase or its articulation, and this can result in a sudden moment of stylistically inappropriate playing. However, at times the change brings the physical articulation of one piece into the sonic context of another (or vice versa); whenever the marking refers to fingering, phrasing or articulation, it carries an embodied memory that is superimposed in the new context. Sometimes this change in how to play a phrase is easily accommodated; sometimes it jars (aurally, physically, or both). Sometimes the memory might be carried in the oddity of a particular fingering—the twist of the wrist or the particular reach of the thumb—and sometimes simply in hearing once more a piece practised a long time ago, on a particular piano in a particular house. As Tia DeNora says (1999, 44), accounts of musical meaning pay close attention to matters of style and history, but "equally important to the matter of music's social 'effects' is the question of how musical materials relate to extra-musical matters such as occasions and circumstances of use, personal associations, and so forth, where the relevant semiotic unit is more likely to be a fragment or a phrase or some specific aspect of music such as its orchestration or tempo."

The found scores are not, then, simply the focus of performer interpretation. Rather, the traces of past performer action become materially significant. The marked scores therefore act as an archive in which historical compositional practices collide with individual, but culturally contingent, performance practices. The re-enactment simultaneously brings the past performing self into the present and displaces it from that present. I don't just hear music that carries memories; I feel recognition in my fingers. In the phrases with no additional markings this is simply the recognition one experiences in playing again a piece last played years ago; but where there are additional annotations this causes an explicit moment of introjection: I am brought hard up against myself, against the simultaneous repetition and difference of the self. [67] Traces of myself, marked by piano playing and in relation to the history of piano performance, are suddenly material *for* myself, for performance.

In addition to the scores, the performer has to find an old recording of piano music to play back on a portable turntable. Whatever disc the performer chooses—I often use a recording of Schubert's Sonata in B♭ Major (D960), played by Artur Schnabel—and whether or not the audience recognises the piece, its historical status as an old recording and the particular sound of vinyl playback are significant, in addition to any personal associations. The record, like the scores, acts as a remnant of a history that is both cultural and personal, but this does not remain purely evocative, untarnished: the recording is transformed through interaction with other, non-pianistic recordings and other sounds introduced with and through the instrument. Writing about another of Whitty's instruction pieces, Jennie Gottschalk comments that "musical tradition and indeterminacy overlap at every turn in this piece" (2016, 261). That is the case here, too. The piece both uses and makes strange the traditions and conventions of practice, drawing on and resituating the materiality of scores and recordings in and through performance, producing a situation in which the constraints and possibilities of performance—and of agency and identity—are very obviously at work in and through the event.

The field recordings, too, are materially significant, despite their lack of historical associations. They are produced by the performer and therefore carry personally significant sonic traces of being in a particular time and place, of individual experience that can be brought back into play, as material, but never fully recovered. Even for an audience that has no knowledge of any personal significance to the performer, the very fact of hearing such recordings played back marks the entry into the sonic present of something from elsewhere and another time, but marked by its recorded status, its repeatability; this topic is explored more fully in chapter 3.

67 Pianist Susan Tomes likewise describes this simultaneous recognition and strangeness in her own experience of returning to a score used in the past and finding old markings written in many years ago. Some of her markings stand the test of time, coinciding with her present sense of how she wants to play the piece, but some are too much "the product of that particular time": "My written remarks are a bit like the passages I used to mark in novels as being especially memorable. Sometimes I look back at a book, see my own pencil marking from teenage years, and can't imagine why I found that passage so scintillating" (Tomes 2010, 114).

Paul Stapleton (2013, 169) considers the relationship between musical improvisation and autobiography in terms of the improviser's "real-time manipulation of sonic memories, or the restructuring and honing of past materials and interactions." In most "free" improvisatory contexts, the performer works explicitly in and through memories of what has transpired in the preceding minutes of the performance but also, implicitly, with (often tacit) memories of musical materials heard or played in the past. This happens in *under and under*, but within a context composed explicitly out of memories, personal and cultural, and in which memories have in part become traced within an archive—of scores, objects, recordings, past performance actions—but without the composer in any way determining that content or its specific use. Memory becomes material, here: the materials carry personal weight, but not only that: in the context of performance, they also carry their own histories (and additional, different histories for the listener) and their own materialities, as scores, in vinyl form, as mp3 recordings, as additional objects. Stapleton suggests that improvisation shares with autobiography "the opportunity to inventively iterate on one's own identity" (2013, 169). Again this is made more explicit in the context of *under and under*, where the choice of materials on one level tells some kind of story, offers the performer a particular opportunity to include content with personal significance. It should be noted, here, that in making a film version of this piece,[68] we decided to relocate everything to my domestic environment, explicitly remediating the idea of the performer drawing on and working within her own, everyday environment. The film shows me making the performance preparations, finding materials around the house for incorporation into the piece, and annotating scores, and the location also allowed for the incorporation of live environmental sound from the house and especially the garden (with the windows open) alongside the recorded materials and piano playing.

As Stapleton suggests (2013, 169), the enaction of these processes in the event of performance, in front of an audience, exposes the contingency of self-making: "improvisational identities are neither stable nor self-contained." Nevertheless, in this and other accounts of improvisation as a negotiation of selfhood, there is a lack of attention to the extent to which the materials of music, of whatever kind, are not just *used* by the performer but are actively agential, partially constituting, not just supporting, the musical discourse and the musical subject produced through performance.[69] DeNora, in her study of music listeners, considers how "musical materials are active ingredients in identity work, how respondents literally 'find themselves' in musical

68 The film is available in the online repository (www.orpheusinstituut.be/en/voices-bodies-practices-media-repository); see file "SF2.4 *under and under* (film)."

69 Karen Barad's comments on materiality as discursive are useful here: "Material conditions matter, not because they support particular discourses that are the generative factors in the formation of bodies but rather because *matter comes to matter* through the iterative intra-activity of the world in its becoming" (2003, 823).

structures" (1999, 49),[70] and this certainly happens in performance too, including in *under and under* (and in much of *Player Piano*). However, as suggested above, in finding my way through this—even in the very act of making versions of myself through performance—I also *lose* myself; I sometimes lose the sense of myself as a discrete entity, even while still *acting*. "I" get lost in the dynamic interaction of the multiple agencies at play, even while a musical subjectivity—the impression of an individual musical persona of some kind, apparently in control of the nuances of content and expression—is being produced. I encounter the ways in which any sense of "myself" produced in and through this performance is a "myself" constituted and produced by others, human and non-human: composers, other performers, instruments, objects, devices, and materials.

In observing this, it is important to note that the process involves the real-time configuring of the subjective musical response in relation to the sonic environment. With the recordings played back in various ways through speakers or transducers near or inside the piano and with the pedal down, extensive sympathetic overtonal resonances are produced. There is no external amplification: all sound runs through the piano, all activating extra sound, with the recorded sounds and those I make intermingling to produce additional overtones. Things can take off in unpredictable ways, and there are times when the piano-resonance system seems to have agency of its own, or when the situation feels more dynamic and dialogic than one would normally expect in a fixed media context.

The same thing happens in the performance of *Ceci n'est pas un piano*, which similarly runs recordings—though in this case of recorded speech—through the piano. This system has fewer components but is perhaps even more unstable. The recorded text is sometimes relayed through a transducer placed inside the piano, sometimes over a speaker directly underneath the piano in whatever position will provoke most overtones, and sometimes both. Compared to the field recordings in *under and under*, the volume of playback is quite loud, generating considerable additional piano resonances in response to the vocal frequencies: my (literal, speaking) voice, my instrumental "voice" (articulated in the nuances of my piano playing), and the piano's "voice" (its particular resonances, according to its size, design, physical configuration, tuning and so on) all combine.[71] Moreover, there is an additional microphone in this system, ostensibly to amplify some of the tinier sounds produced inside the piano (with a small stone or fingers, for example), and this picks up everything played: all sound is relayed back through the speaker under the piano. While the systems

70 DeNora's listeners were nearly all "explicit about music's role as an ordering device at the 'personal' level, as a means for creating, enhancing, sustaining and changing subjective, cognitive, bodily and self-conceptual states" (1999, 34–35). This is, though, very much a user-oriented perspective: the focus is on how a subject configures herself in and through her listening choices and how these are "used" in the self-reflexive project of self-making. The counterpart to this would involve a change of perspective, considering the material agency of the music in terms of how an encounter with its specific properties affects or brings about change in the human subject.

71 This can be heard in the audio recording in the online repository, file "SF2.3 *Ceci n'est pas un piano* (audio recording)."

of interaction of *under and under* and *Ceci* are both dynamic and unpredictable, the amplification and the generally louder soundworld of much of *Ceci* produce a more volatile situation: frequencies can very quickly generate multiple additional frequencies, the sound texture building very much more suddenly.

Additionally, though, in *under and under* I have the space, within the more open improvisational context, to draw out in my playing aspects of what I hear in the recordings—quite literally so when I choose to echo or reproduce a particular tone or texture heard in one of the field recordings, in that the resonant body of the instrument, with the pedal down, blends the recorded and live sounds, reinforcing certain frequencies and producing additional tones out of their interaction. Here, I am the visible, active agent, but the resultant texture is partly constituted by the recording(s), is partly mine, and is partly the piano's. Disentangling this is sometimes impossible.

In both *under and under* and *Ceci n'est pas un piano*, I seem to feel the force of the piano, the additional sound technologies and objects, and the spatial context as having their own powers, powers that shape the performance—and the performer—as much as my own creative decisions. Latour attributes agential capacity to the *event*, undermining the distinction between subject and object in certain contexts, and signals the ways in which this destabilises the sense of overarching human determination in a manner that resonates closely with this experience: "There are events. I never *act*; I am always slightly surprised by what I do. That which acts through me is also surprised by what I do, by the chance to mutate, to change, and to bifurcate" (Latour 1999, 281). The "slightly" is important here, signalling the ambivalence of agency as I experience it in this context—the feeling of acting with intention and creative self-determination comes and goes, ebbs and flows, in counterpoint with that sense of surprise.

Matthias Haenisch describes something similar taking place in Andrea Neumann's *Inside Piano*, which also involves the use of additional musical tools and everyday objects in the context of the piano body, with results that similarly move in and out of control of the various agents: "The artifacts involved enable or hinder certain actions, demanding physical and technological adaptation to their material nature and resistance. ... The materiality of body and artifacts enter into reciprocal coupling" (Haenisch 2013, 156–57). For Haenisch, this "offers instruments and artifacts recognition as material actors in the improvisation" (ibid., 169). However, Neumann's *Inside Piano* is an instrument in itself, made up of a piano frame with strings but no keys or piano action, fitted with various pick-ups linked to a mixer, with a set of objects used for playing and preparing the strings.[72] This system therefore has a similar dynamic to that of *under and under*; but whereas Neumann more radically deconstructs the piano, *under and under*—like *Player Piano* as a whole—is in part predicated on the cultural, embodied, performative, and material significance of the piano as *piano*.

Overall, in *under and under*, the materiality of instruments, scores, recordings, and objects becomes significant in the various ways described above. Their inclusion in a temporally open-ended, improvisatory context provokes a

72 For details, see Neumann (2011).

particular dynamic between their agency, that of the composer as architect of the situation, the past performer as an archive of and for herself, and the performer who is active in the space, choosing which materials to use and when, and playing interactively with them. As Haenisch says, we need "to integrate the influential presence and meaning of artifacts and objects into our notion of artistic ingenuity" (2013, 169). In *Player Piano* as a whole, the classical pianistic tradition becomes part of the experimental context, its conventions reframed. Sally Jane Norman (2013, 282) writes that "defiance of normative affordances and patterns of use, generating friction and resistance, is integral to creative endeavour. . . . Defiance and resistance may be manifest as the disruption or hijacking of instruments and/or their familiar uses, in contexts where human and non-human actors are equal contributors." *Player Piano* pushes in this direction; yet at the same time, by including Whitty's piece, the conventions of experimentalism, with their historical aims of detachment from tradition, of nonrelation and objectivity, are also put into play: composer, embodied performer, instrumental identity, performing context are all constituted and deconstituted, quite explicitly. Memory, relations, resistances; again, these become subject, object, and process, performatively.

Radical presence and emergent subjectivity

Peggy Phelan asserts that the life of performance is always in the present—that it lessens its own ontology when it enters an economy of reproduction (1993, 146)—all the while acknowledging that the fully present is impossible, that the presentness of performance is only discernible in its impossibility, its disappearance. The more we scrutinise the subject produced in and through performance—the performing self—the more it, too, disappears, revealing its instability, and multiplicity, its distributed and relational contingency: its "not I"-ness. This happens, I think, in performing *Player Piano*, and in each of the pieces within it. A space of performative agency is articulated: what I do matters, but, simultaneously, the more self-consciously evident my performing self seems to be, the more its contingency is exposed. I *almost* disappear into everything that constitutes "me" in this context: I retain a sense of myself as an active, creative, expressive agent, doing things, but with a heightened sense of that subject as constituted by others—by the dynamics and resistances between people, traditions, practices, discourses, instruments, contexts—and as produced from the interaction of a number of agencies, human and non-human. In these ways, *Player Piano* attempts a reflexive opening up of the "becoming material" of piano performance and, indeed, of the piano subject.

Likewise, the more directly we seem to encounter the performing body, the more we lose a grip on it: this takes us back to Phelan's comment (1993, 150), cited earlier, that performing bodies are always more than "just" bodies: "in the plenitude of its apparent visibility and availability, the performer actually disappears and represents something else—dance, movement, sound, character, 'art.'" The condition of performance is one of indeterminacy in its very determinacy, but this is often hidden under the surface of presence and the desire to communicate, the need to determine: we are not always called to attend to it, and anyway we are very good at looking elsewhere, at apparently more concrete objects, more graspable concepts, more reliable authorities than performers, and especially at texts of various kinds.

At the same time, this ontology of performance as disappearance—or, in Herbert Blau's terms, "at the vanishing point" (1982), beyond representation—is not without its problems (as many have noted).[73] If performance is distinct from object-based artistic forms in the ways that Phelan and others suggest, that is central to its difference, its significance, and its politics of subjectivity: its refusal of fixity, stability, and hence of commodity, is fundamental. Nevertheless, this is not absolute: live performance often includes or otherwise embraces—or is even dependent upon—overtly mediatised materials (whether film, recorded sound, and so on), and there are many ways in which performance "remains": in documentation, scores, notebooks, archives, reviews, memories, and so on, none of which substitute for the performance, but all of which, in different ways, provide traces of it, carry it forward, and mark something of its significance. Ben Spatz (2015, 58), drawing on the work of Susan Melrose and Stefanie Sachsenmaier, notes that for the performer, in particular, the process of making a performance is far from ephemeral, taking place over time, through the kinds of repetitions and transformations of embodied practice described above.

Rebecca Schneider (2012, 66) asks: "in privileging an understanding of performance as a refusal to remain, do we ignore other ways of knowing, other modes of remembering, that might be situated precisely in the ways in which performance remains, but remains differently?" In *Player Piano*, remains of these kinds are variously called into play: the archives of the performing body, of the history of the piano and its pianists and composers, of repertoire, its mediated reproduction in film and words. This happened as part of the iterative process of making and reflecting, but they remain at play, still, as traces in the performance, forming a layer in its thematics and effects: the piece is in part about the ways in which, following Schneider (2012, 75–76), performance, in its very disappearance, both is formed from remains and continues to remain, but in our bodies, our ears, our touching and feeling, as much as in our minds. *Player Piano* in this sense attempts to capture something of the "becoming material" of piano performance, to open the question of how performance and the performer come to be perceived as something or someone, with effect and yet without stable identity.

All this involves explicit repetitions—of processes of piano performance, of piano repertoire, sounds and materials, of the bodily actions of practising and performing—but in particular ways, self-consciously and with modifications, with different configurations or even violations of the traditional context of classical performance. Returning to Butler, this relates to her notion

73 Philip Auslander's critique, in *Liveness*, is perhaps the most notable (1999, especially 39–43). Diana Taylor also warns of the dangers of romanticising the ephemerality of performance (2003, 5) and Ben Spatz concurs (2015, 58–9).

of the deconstituting possibility of repetition, where recognisable acts are reinscribed but neither mechanically or predictably, opening up a space of agency and opportunity.

Erika Fischer-Lichte (2012, 106–8) distinguishes between three forms of presence in performance. As noted above, she defines "weak" presence as requiring the bodily co-presence of both performer and spectator, with the performer "here," before the gaze of the other, but where her prime function is to refer to something beyond her corporeally present body. In Western theatre since the second half of the eighteenth century, this referent is the dramatic character the actor pretends to "be." I have suggested that musical performance, other than vocal performance involving characterisation, is one manifestation of "weak presence": the performer's body is, conventionally, subsumed into sonic signification, primarily there as a means to produce sound and reinforce the expressive characteristics of its nuances.

"Strong" presence, in Fischer-Lichte's account, is characterised by "the actor's ability to occupy and command space and to attract the spectators' undivided attention" (2012, 108) such that the "spectators sense that the actor is present in an unusually intense way, granting them, in turn, the intense sensation of themselves as present." Fischer-Lichte draws on Martin Wuttke's performance of Arturo Ui in Heiner Müller's production of Brecht's *The Resistable Rise of Arturo Ui* with the Berliner Ensemble to exemplify this (ibid., 103–6). In this sense, and contrasted with "weak" presence, "presence occurs as an intense experience of presentness" (ibid., 109). A musical version of this is perhaps apparent when an instrumentalist's body becomes more than a vehicle for sonic signification, such as when a performer's physical gestures seem to exceed or differ from those conventional to the common practices of the music and yet add to the intensity of the performance. In such cases we become aware of the body as powerful and idiosyncratically expressive, dynamically charged with a peculiarly physical intensity that partly serves the individual musical expression but also has a corporeal presence that engages the audience more explicitly, producing a more overtly embodied response. For me, a good example of this would be Keith Jarrett, whose jazz piano performances often involve an intense physicality and extremity of movement way beyond what is *apparently* necessary for sound production or even expressive communication and yet that is deeply bound up with the forceful "presentness" of the experience.

However, Fischer-Lichte defines a third kind of presence, "radical" presence (2012, 112–6), which relates to both strong and weak forms but is marked by the problematics and limits of both. There are times when the construction of weak presence breaks down: when the tension between the phenomenal and semiotic body erupts, and the performer's body is suddenly perceived as present beyond the signifying construct. Simultaneously, however intense "strong" presence might be, it is impossible that the body can ever simply "be"—that is, be simply present in and as itself—for more than a few moments at a time before it is pulled towards signifying something. In contrast, Fischer-Lichte argues that "radical" presence is experienced when the body is in a dynamic process of being both intensely physically present as a living organism and drawn into meaning something beyond that, even while it resists. For Fischer-Lichte, the performer then "appears and is perceived as embodied mind" (2012, 115); this "radical" presence is predicated on the intensity of the phenomenal body but experienced within the dynamic of its presentation at any particular moment, in its attempt to both "be" and to "represent," and in its self-conscious acceptance of the failure of both as the condition of embodiment.

In such performance, Fischer-Lichte argues, the performer "exemplifies that body and mind cannot be separated from each other"; "Through the performer's presence, the spectator experiences the performer and himself [*sic*] as embodied mind in a constant process of becoming. . . . This I call the radical concept of presence, written as PRESENCE: PRESENCE means appearing and being perceived as embodied mind" (Fischer-Lichte 2012, 115). "Radical" in this sense is not, of course, a value judgement: radical presence makes for no "better" or "worse" a performance. However, Fischer-Lichte's terms simply capture what I experienced as the performer of *Player Piano*—what emerged from the process of making and reflecting. Her notion of radical presence encompasses the layering of the body in *Player Piano*, with its (inevitably failed) attempt to both "be" itself onstage, beyond its learned pianism, alongside its self-conscious capturing of the moments in the process of practice when it almost "was" itself—frozen, in the process of forming an idiosyncratic expressive gesture—but immediately "became" something else in the moment of its scrutiny. This notion of radical presence also seems to encompass the dynamics of disappearance (Phelan) and remains (Schneider) discussed above: in *Player Piano*, the presentness of the live and lived body in the act of performance, and hence its non-repeatability beyond that, is crucial. The performance is constructed such that the embodied interactions of the moment are evident, emerging from the ecology of agency described above, but manifesting differently each time. At the same time, that very presentness is constituted self-consciously by the subjective relation to the past: past repertoire, past performances, training and practice, remediated ideas of piano bodies, and so on. Any "strong" presence in this sense is marked by traces of this working through of the body, of the body brought forth as an embodied mind.

The radical presence articulated by Fischer-Lichte is, I would argue, closely related to Butler's deconstituting possibility, with its predication of a dynamic of repeatability and legibility in terms of the "law" of performance—of the performer as apparently semiotically "readable"—but which, through its very repetition of that law, with a particular body in a specific dynamic context, insistently opens up a space where difference is always emerging, where the particular, agential embodied presence starts to act. This can produce an embodied subject that is always in the process of becoming; a presence at once "there," as if evidence of "I," and yet always in the process of becoming object, or "not I": simultaneously subjectified and desubjectified.

Postlude: "Alone With My Ten Fingers"?

At various points in this chapter I have noted the significance of composers in the formation of performer subjectivity. This has been discussed broadly, with regard to all performance of composed music, drawing on Mary Hunter's argument that the historically specific identification with the composer has become (problematically) naturalised within the Western classical conception of musicality. More specifically, the role of the composer has been noted in the discussions of the embodied, instrumental, and contextual aspects of subjectivity. However, this chapter perhaps has less to say about composers than one might expect. This is for three reasons. First, the composer–performer relationship forms a substantial part of the discussion in chapter 1. Second, while that chapter focuses on a single piece by an individual composer, the context of *Player Piano* was intentionally very different, with a number of composers involved alongside other creative artists and also with the compositions serving a particular role within a larger-scale musical and scenographic framework developed by myself as performer, with the subsequent, invaluable input of theatre-maker Teresa Brayshaw. Third, and as a result of that very different context, the agency of the individual composer within *Player Piano* as a whole is certainly significant, but not more so than other constituents of the overall performance ecology.

Underlying all this lies a questioning of the distinction of these roles. Like David Gorton and Stefan Östersjö in the previous chapter, I argue that the composer's "voice" feeds into a discursive production of subjectivity in performance. At the same time, my discussion also attempts to articulate the difficulties of disentangling composers and performers as discrete identities, not just in the individual act of performance but even prior to that, in related processes and practices. Considering how the body-subject is shaped and formed in and through the relationship to the instrument, the performance situation, and the personal archive of past musical experience, all of which might be configured *in part* by composers, involves acknowledging the specific ways in which these composers (and other agents) are "in" me: "me" as a performing subject. At the same time, "I"—and other performers—are "in" them. The composers are always already working in and through a sense of the specific performing body-subject: the characteristics of the performer for whom they are writing the piece. But those specifics are already constituted by the wider cultural, compositional practice, itself formed from the congregation of individual voices, of which that composer is one. The performance practice in turn modifies (as much as it is modified by) that compositional practice, both individual and cultural. As such, the distinction between self and other, composer and performer, individual and community of practice, is problematic, even while difference and distinction persist: even while the "individual subjectivity continues to appear to us to function," to echo Anahid Kassabian's point from early in this chapter (2013, xxiv). It also draws out the roles of other "others," suggesting that an apparently exclusive composer–performer relationship is actually, always and already, multiple: other musicians, instruments, contexts are always "in" there, too, though often without acknowledgement. This is not a collective subjectivity (such as the plural or "we" subjectivity of an ensemble),[74] nor quite intersubjectivity as usually theorised, because within that dynamic the self is structured as an apparently individual entity. Rather, it is a constitution of the singular by the others. Jean-Luc Nancy's notion of the "first-person plural" (2000, 5) or "being singular plural" (28) is perhaps useful: "There is no 'meaning' except by virtue of a 'self,' of some form or another. . . . But there is no 'self' except by virtue of a 'with,' which in fact structures it" (94).

In this coda to the chapter, I return to this topic as part of a discussion of the relationship between self and other in *Player Piano*. The piece *Ten Bellows*, composed for me by Edward Jessen for inclusion in *Player Piano*, through a collaborative process of workshopping, is particularly useful to consider in this regard, due to the multiple couples at work in the piece and its making. Beyond the composer-performer couple, *Ten Bellows* is the only piece in *Player Piano* that includes another performer: the pianist is coupled with an assistant, who "services" the physical and musical routines enacted by the performer, providing her with the props she needs, and fetching and carrying for her (as can be seen in figure 2.5). However, there are also material couplings: of sound and movement; of language (speaking voices, in recorded form) and music (or other sounds); of acoustic and recorded sound; and of snatches of a romantic musical language—moments of almost sentimental musical melancholy—set against somewhat mechanical processes of repetition and accumulation. All these contribute to a dramatic scenario that is somewhat inscrutable, without apparent explanation for the action, or motivation for the "characters," but which has its own logic, based upon the interactions of different kinds of repetitive behaviours and the interdependencies of the actors and materials.

In *Ten Bellows*, a performer makes repeated halting journeys across the stage, aided by a stick, moving with a strange, "purpose-filled rowing gait" (as Jessen describes it in the score, though it is important to note that the score was produced only at the end of the process of workshopping, during which this movement style emerged). On each journey she carries a tray of little glass bowls filled with marbles that clink and chink as she moves (see figure 2.20).[75]

Figure 2.20.

74 As discussed by Hagberg (2017), for example.

75 A full film version of the piece is currently in production, but a film trailer produced by Edward Jessen from live performance footage is available in the online repository (www.orpheusinstituut.be/en/voices-bodies-practices-media-repository) in file "SF2.13 *Ten Bellows* trailer film."

Figure 2.20. Photo (by Edward Jessen) from workshopping of "rowing gait" movement in the process of developing *Ten Bellows*.

The repetitive action is both bizarre and apparently purposeless and yet, in its intensity and reiteration, it becomes somehow significant. The assistant aids her, handing her the trays of marbles, taking them from her when she reaches the piano so that she can play, and carrying them back to the starting position so that the performer is never without her props. The assistant attends to the performer in other ways, too, sometimes following her closely with a microphone, bending and stretching with her, so as to keep the microphone close to the tray, apparently recording the sounds of the marbles (see figure 2.21). The performer needs the assistant but the assistant also, it emerges, has her own eventual purpose: at the end she appears, carrying a loudspeaker that plays back the marble sounds: she has made something from these journeys. The performer and assistant form a kind of co-dependent unit, but they do not speak to or even acknowledge one another. Their repetitive routines are interwoven: the score suggests "the two women form a connected pairing, recognisable though hard to explain. . . . The action is airtight. Minor doings without comment" (Jessen 2015, 5).

Figure 2.21.

The fabric of the musical sound couples live and recorded elements. Recordings of found sounds—the tapping and knocking of the marbles against one another, electronic whines and stutters, blues guitar riffs, birdsong—occur repetitiously across the piece, sometimes literally and mechanically, with exactly the same phrase repeated over, and sometimes incrementally, with a phrase gradually evolving from a brief initial motif. Likewise, the piano music includes phrases of a Romantic, tonal musical language; somewhat grand, G minor cadential phrases, underpinned by widely spaced resonant tonic and dominant chords (see figure 2.22), but often with suspensions (especially minor sixths) and, towards the end, increasing ornamentation, as the phrase develops (see figure 2.23).[76]

76 The online repository includes "SF2.14 *Ten Bellows*, cadential phrase and mechanistic development," a film clip that illustrates these Romantic phrases.

Figure 2.21. Photo (by Edward Jessen) from rehearsal of *Ten Bellows* for the first performance (given by Catherine Laws and Lucia D'Errico), Orpheus Institute, Ghent, 20 September 2015.

Figure 2.22.

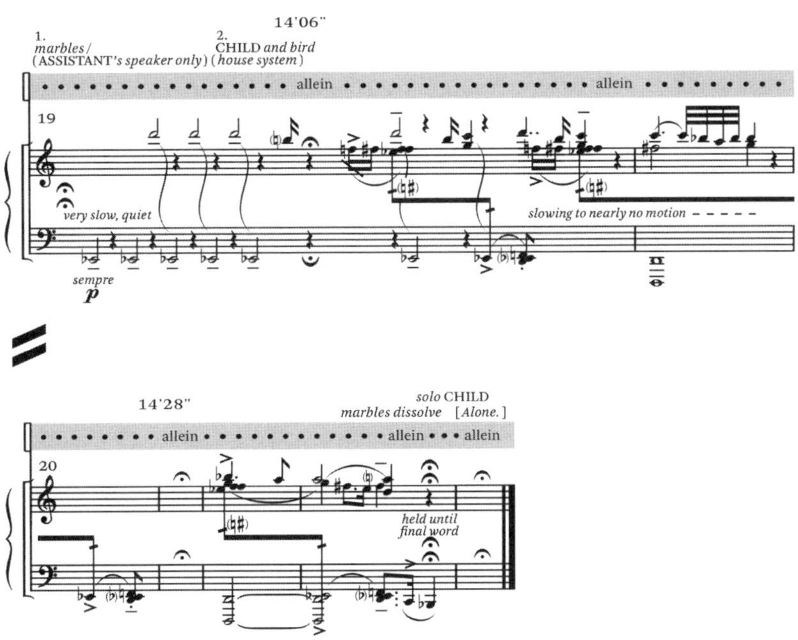

Figure 2.23.

Figure 2.22. Edward Jessen, *Ten Bellows* (2015), bars 5–6: G minor cadence, with fragmented repetition then developed mechanistically, with addition of percussive prepared piano.

Figure 2.23. Edward Jessen, *Ten Bellows* (2015), end (bars 19–20): main cadential phrase fragmented and ornamented.

These phrases momentarily have the majestic, ornamental feel of the climax of a Baroque keyboard prelude, or the coda to a long and complicated fugue, but with their exploitation of the resonance of the modern piano, use of pedal, and wide dynamic range, the melancholic grandeur is perhaps more reminiscent of a late Romantic transcription of earlier music, for example by Busoni. Transcriptions such as Busoni's already self-consciously draw on the cultural memory of a particular music, nodding to past great work but repurposing it, employing it within a new composerly vision. Known music, with an established affect, is reworked, the grandeur of the Baroque peroration becoming exaggerated and self-consciously Romantic, with the use of additional octave doublings, additional harmonies and development into more extended structural forms. In imitating something of this style, in short fragments, Jessen adds a second set of quotation marks, drawing on the Romantic sensibility of that romanticising of the past. He invokes the expressive power of that music, but its positioning in this theatrical context and in this eclectic soundworld also reflects it back to us: it draws attention to its very echoing of Romantic clichés, as if pointing out to us the ways in which we use music for sentimental succour, to recall the affective qualities of particular ideas or memories. In this respect the music is both sentimental and not; the sentiment is directly invoked but offered up as an object for reflection, reworking.

This music is often presented in repetitious fragments: sometimes individual motifs are simply played over and over, reduced to empty mechanistic repetition; and even when longer passages are managed, near the end of the piece, they are emitted fragment by fragment, interspersed with pauses. Often, the repetition of these snippets of material involves the gradual, incremental transformation of a phrase or accumulation of notes: this effects a self-conscious building of phrases, as something tiny is heard, then again with very slightly more substance, and again, and again. As a result, the more expressive and extended lines seem to emerge from the mechanistic, repeated fragments, and yet those fragments themselves derive from the expressive phrases: each is identifiably characterised, but they are inextricably co-dependent, as can be seen in figure 2.22. Likewise, while the live and mediated soundworlds are distinct, sonically and spatially, the contrast is undermined by the presence in the recorded sound of fragments of some of the same sounds we hear produced through performance: the sounds of the marbles and fragments of the piano phrases are all present in the recording, but electronically manipulated to sound thinner, more brittle and tinny, less resonant; perhaps distanced. These things are all evident in a video clip taken from a live performance of *Ten Bellows* as part of *Player Piano*. At the same time, there are moments when the live piano music echoes sounds from the recording, with repeated, gradually accelerating and decelerating iterations of harsh percussive tones produced through the use of piano preparations, seen in a second video clip.[77] All these couplings

77 The two clips can be found in the online repository (www.orpheusinstituut.be/en/voices-bodies-practices-media-repository), files "SF2.15 *Ten Bellows*, example of co-dependency of soundworlds" and "SF2.16 *Ten Bellows*, example with piano preparations."

of material types, live and recorded, expressive and repetitious, are simultaneously distinct and interrelated, echoing one another.

The performer, then, is caught in reiteration and routine, as well as in the reproduction of apparently expressive materials; and yet somehow, in the very repetitions of these processes, in trying things out again and again, something individual and nuanced starts to build, something of meaning starts to emerge. Similarly, the assistant is generally "absorbed by logistics," preparing the trays of marbles and carrying them to their positions, but at odd moments she is not needed. This is usually during the more extended piano phases: as I build these, working in and around the phrases, absorbed, apparently, in more expressive, creative activity, the assistant is seen entering a kind of reverie. On the spot, she sways back and forth, playing with the microphone and cable she holds ready for use, watching them closely as her arms twist and turn them around in what the score describes as "her customary diversion from her tasks" (see figure 2.24). Just like the pianist, for a moment the assistant is in her own world, playing, without purpose, but with exactly the same tools and similar movements used when she follows the performer with her microphone.

Figure 2.24.

The coupling of language and music works analogously. At the start, an absent authority in the form of a recorded, authoritative male voice commands the scene into action, his voice relayed through the PA system—"And away. . . . And again. . . ."—and then continues to issue repetitive directions, interspersed with gaps for sound and action: "Wait"; "And again"; "Move" "To the left"; "Go back"; "A little more like that." The instructions seem related to, yet at one remove from, the action; the voice sets things off, and we see movement and pauses, but not really quite as described: "wait" does not cause the action to cease, and my movement is along one continuous line, not adjusting to the instruction "more to the left." Instead, as it goes on the voice seems to have

Figure 2.24. Still from *Ten Bellows* by Edward Jessen, performed as part of *Player Piano* by Catherine Laws and Hannah Butterfield (Scenic Stage Theatre, York, 5 May 2016): Hannah Butterfield (assistant) in her "reverie" with microphone.

its own logic, interspersing movement directions with other words: "Alone" "As a stone," "Solitary," "With my ten fingers," "Solitary as a stone." Just as the instruction words seem *almost* to relate to, but do not quite fit with, what we see and hear, so might "alone" and "solitary" relate to the performer who enters the stage as the voice speaks, towards a piano to be played "with my ten fingers," but the "stone" reference seems more obscure, and then the assistant emerges: again, there seems to be a relationship between parts, but not quite an integration. We might hear this voice as that of the absent composer (or director, perhaps); this is the only place in *Player Piano* where that absent creative "voice" materialises more concretely, dramatised. However, while the performers' movements might be in response to these instructions, they do not really seem quite to conform; if anything, they seem more absorbed in reproducing their routines in and for themselves. If this is the composer, he seems to have limited authority.

A little way in, the authoritative voice disappears, replaced by that of a young boy, who whispers phrases in misheard Yiddish, taken from Saul Bellow's novel *Herzog* ([1964] 1976, 135):

> Alein, alein, alein, alein
> Elend vie a shtein,
> Mit die tzen finger—alein

The phrases are from a scene in which a small boy listens to his father translate lines sung by a drunken, melancholic shopkeeper, huddled in a freezing stairwell; it is a small scene of overhearing and translating. In *Ten Bellows* we do not have this context—we simply hear the words, juxtaposed with the music and action—and inevitably, therefore, some of these phrases seem to refer back to the performance situation: "alone with my ten fingers" starts to mean something different in a piano performance. Only the title of the piece (with "Bellows") hints at the origin of the piece in this tiny novelistic scene, and even here "ten" refers us back to the "ten fingers," perhaps, now, imagined as little pumping machines: bellows. Overall, these voices, while asserting the state of aloneness, in their very presence form another counterpart to—or become company for—the pianist: a different form of company to the silently attentive assistant.

As such, these interrelated layers of voices, movement, music, and additional sound are abstract and even somewhat bizarre, in terms of the forms of movement and the repetitious circularity of their processes, and yet everything seems to make a kind of sense, in its determined, repetitious enaction. The ritualistic journeys are apparently purposeless, but their intensity of focus implies significance. On each level, the bits and scraps of movement, their traces in sound, plus the additional music, all gradually evolve *something*; a mark is made, a sound heard, a gesture enacted; and then again, with something added; and then again but adjusted: the activity is generative. The performance gradually seems to take on meaning, expressive weight, even while remaining unexplained, but it is also *about* the evolving of that something.

In certain ways this seems strongly reminiscent of the work of Samuel Beckett. Beckett's work is full of couples who depend upon one another, using each other for company, whether antagonistically or sympathetically, in the face of isolation. Perhaps the most famous example is the pairing of Vladimir and Estragon in *Waiting for Godot*, but there are many more. Beckett's work is also famously spare and stripped back, lacking conventional narrative explanations of character, location, and action, and is both fragmented and repetitious. Patterns of words and actions recur, on both the stage and the page, with minor transformations. We look again and again at a scene, or read versions of the same words, as if zooming in and out (literally, the case of the television plays), scrutinising bodies, movements, words—"what is the word?", Beckett repeatedly asks (Beckett 2012, 226)—in an ultimately hopeless attempt to pin something down, to find a satisfactory form of meaning or expression—to find a form that can "accommodate the mess," as Beckett himself put it (Driver 1961, 24). Beckett's work, self-consciously and reflexively, increasingly becomes *about* the processes of speaking, listening, writing, reading, making: about the act of being heard, being seen, being credible. Moreover, Beckett's fragmented, schizoid selves bear little relation to the Romantic ideal of self-presence and self-expression, but they often draw on it, feed from its persistent re-imagining. In some of Beckett's plays, this happens through music. In the television plays *Ghost Trio* and *Nacht und Träume*, for example, and the radio play *All That Fall*, snippets of the music of Beethoven and Schubert are heard, and this forms part of his scrutiny of subjectivity; he seems interested in how we attempt (but fail) to latch onto or recapture a coherent sense of self by revisiting much-loved musical performances, unlocking the affective memories stored in them. Beckett draws on the Romantic sensibility of the music, threading it into the fabric of his work, using its expressive power but also reflecting back to us the ways in which we use music for sentimental succour, to recall the affective qualities of particular ideas or memories. In this respect his plays are both sentimental and not; the sentiment is directly invoked but offered up as an object for reflection, reworking. There is, here, an exploration of selfhood as a process of prosthetic imagination, through the "company" of other, imagined sensibilities: Beckett traces a Romantic subjectivity, imagines self-presence, while exposing its impossibility, its constitution through others, and the fragmented, unstable condition of the self. Ultimately, we are all "devised devisers, devising it all for company" (Beckett 1980, 46).

Jessen's compositions often exhibit this kind of reflexivity: he has described this (and specifically linked it to Beckett) as "some sort of writing mechanism where the situation provides the clues. Something where what is happening is also the thing being described. . . . like a voiceover provided by an often lost/neutral performer" (email, Edward Jessen to Catherine Laws, 18 March 2015). His pieces often home in on the detail of a situation without explanatory context: a tendency "to focus upon something but to learn very little about it; a location, a person, an object, a saying" (ibid.).[78] This is always specific and individuated, derived in some sense from external components—perhaps a snippet of an idea, an image snatched from a film or, as here, a phrase book—but also from a sense of the characteristics of the performers concerned.

This strange combination of specificity and vagueness is in part produced through the particular approach to repetition—or near repetition, with gradual changes—and fragmentation. Jessen describes his interest in the ways in which repetition, or inexact repetition, can "drain away the meaning of something. Hearing something, in my own case, both reinforces the thing, the phrase and then also reinforces the sound of it, to where it becomes 'the sound' sometimes over 'the meaning'" (email, Edward Jessen to Catherine Laws, 18 March 2015). Although we often think of repetition as a means of reinforcing an utterance, the opposite is perhaps more often true. The piece at times seems to ask what happens when a Romantic piano phrase, which initially seems imbued with a certain melancholic expressivity, is revolved and dissected: does its affective power remain or drain away, or is it transformed? For me, as the performer of this piece, these expressive piano phrases are deeply familiar and recognisable in their idiom from my past experience of playing older keyboard music (particularly, here, Baroque and late Romantic repertoire). They represent the normalised mode of musical subjectivity that Mary Hunter critiques; they revisit that sound world and evince certain musical behaviours, in musical and gestural expression. I again perform being *that* kind of pianist. However, the process here seems to open up the question of what happens to that subjectivity as the phrases are directly reiterated, retaining the musical content but in a structural form that is not at all part of the Romantic idiom. What happens to that expressive quality as the phrases disintegrate into jolts and sputters, as the contrast between the rich, Romantic acoustic piano phrases and the clicks and whines of the electronic sound break down, as I hear my "sonic self" reflected back to me through speakers?

Revolving the same and similar phrases perhaps suggests a redundancy of meaning, a draining out of this expressive content: it can't be uniquely poignant this time, and this time, and then again this time. I can play the phrases with expression each time—repeating the gesture of expressive musical subjectification that is expected in piano performance—but the very act of reiteration undermines it. I have to find something else. But at the same time the repetitions and links between sounds produce a fluidity, a tissue of connectivity that starts to map a credible process of making some kind of sense, evolving something meaningful, but through a web of interactions rather than in a Romantic, individualised mode. A different kind of subjective complex evolves, multiple agencies all active, never subsumed into an overall performing presence. The others—composer, assistant, material, instrument—

78 These characteristics are apparent in two other pieces by Jessen that I have performed: *Companion* (2008) and *Chambre 119* (2009). *Companion*, for four performers (two vocalists doubling toy piano, plus violin and cello) was written for the music theatre ensemble Black Hair: I performed one of the voice and toy piano parts. Films of these can be viewed at http://www.vimeo.com/7520730 (*Companion*) and https://vimeo.com/7452393 (*Chambre 119*).

all are there, evident in the interactions of sound and activity. In this sense the performative response enacts the complexity of subject formation: drawing on the individualised Romantic subjectivity of the lone pianist but prodding away at it until it becomes something else.

Here, then, in the last part of *Player Piano* a range of interdependencies is exposed within which each component is individuated and characterised but simultaneously produced in and through an "other"; this operates at the level of composer, performer, and assistant, but also the constitution of materials. While I am often, in *Player Piano*, apparently "alone with my ten fingers," in fact this citational, iterative approach attempts to reveal the problematics of that lone, pioneering, pianistic subject. A performing subject emerges, but co-constituted by other selves, materials, and contexts.

Chapter 3

Footnotes

William Brooks, Stefan Östersjö, and Jeremy J. Wells

Part 1

1.1. Prehistory

In my email I find a message I wrote to Stefan Östersjö on 3 July 2010: "I finally remembered! Here are PDFs of the score to *Footnotes*." Thus this project began.[1]

1.1.1. "I finally remembered!"

In a narrow sense, that implied only that Stefan had requested a score, some weeks or months earlier, and that I'd just then recalled his request. But in a larger sense, it was the exclamation that animated the next nine years. *Footnotes* became an investigation of *memory*, of *truth*, of *fiction*, of *authenticity*; and what is ultimately "remembered" is compounded from all these, in varying measures, to uncertain ends, and with almost no assurance. Nor did its creative potential arise from well-defined contributions from three individuals (who might be called "composer," "performer," or "sound engineer"); rather, it is precisely the confusion of roles, the muddle of tasks, the interpenetration of ideas, that sustained and enhanced the exclamation point in that opening three-word phrase.

We write this chapter as three voices—three persons, if you will—and we manifest our identity in three type fonts:

William Brooks appears in <Times New Roman>.
Stefan Östersjö appears in <Calibri Light>.
Jez Wells appears in ‹Nueva Std›.

You, the reader, are invited to commingle our words—or, if desired, to disentangle them. Our voices are distinct only in the sense that our hair is (figure 3.1): they offer you an opportunity to recognise each of us—to *remember* us—and to construct your own map of the interactions and confusions that constitute your experience of *Footnotes*.

1 The most tangible result of the entire *Footnotes* project is not this chapter but rather the recording itself, and readers are strongly recommended to listen to that and to read the sleeve notes before continuing with this chapter. Excerpts from all six movements are provided in the online repository (www.orpheusinstituut.be/en/voices-bodies-practices-media-repository); see files "SF3.1 *Footnotes*, movement 1 (excerpt)" through "SF3.6 *Footnotes*, movement 6 (excerpt)." The sleeve notes are also provided there: "SF3.7 *Footnotes*, sleeve notes." To obtain the full recording, visit the Orpheus publications page (http://orpheusinstituut.be/en/publications/footnotes) or Innova Records (http://www.innova.mu/albums/stefan-östersjö/footnotes).

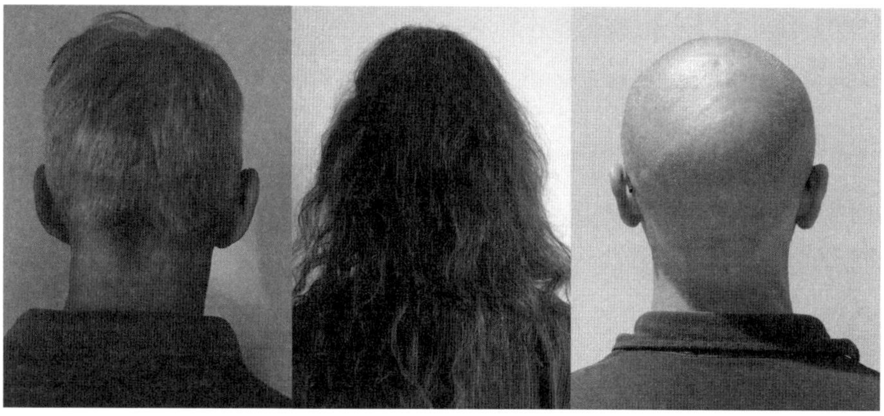

Figure 3.1.

1.1.2. Notes on *Footnotes* before *Footnotes*

When I wrote "I finally remembered!" I remembered only that I had a score scanned, and that I should send it to Stefan. I had at best a very dim recollection of how that score came into being—indeed, of who the person was that had written it. But I was aware that the score had a history, and I felt obliged to discover that. William Brooks, musicologist (hereafter BillyMus), wished to know what he could learn about William Brooks, composer (BillyCom).

After eight years of trawling through files and messages, BillyMus can report as follows.[2] By early 1980 BillyCom had been introduced to guitarist Michael Cedric Smith (hereafter MCS) by a mutual acquaintance, musicologist Katherine Preston. MCS was then planning a London debut, which eventually took place in the Purcell Room, Southbank Centre, on 30 November 1981. BillyCom had a slight presence in London at that time; he'd lived in England for two years (1977–79), and his *Madrigals* had become a kind of party piece for the London group Electric Phoenix since they were premiered in January 1979. MCS wanted to include an American world premiere, and BillyCom was a logical choice. For the Purcell Room concert BillyCom wrote the first three movements of *Footnotes*: "Cotten," "Cage," and "Crump," in that order. Composition began at the end of April 1981 and was completed on 6 October.

Early in the conversations, however, BillyCom planned the full set of six movements, writing the other three later, between December 1981 and February 1984. From letters and the score itself BillyMus concludes that BillyCom was animated by three principal concerns: a pluralistic view of the instrument ("guitar") and the styles and players with which it was associated; a deliberate pedanticism, manifested not only in abundant explanatory footnotes scattered through the score but in unnecessarily severe structures and methods (the entire set is based

2 The online repository (www.orpheusinstituut.be/en/voices-bodies-practices-media-repository) contains a full account of these sources in the document "SF3.8 A True History of *Footnotes* Perhaps (Part 1)."

Figure 3.1. Left to right: William Brooks, Stefan Östersjö, Jez Wells.

on the proportions 3:4:5, which add up to 12);[3] and an overarching homage to John Cage,[4] most evident in the first and last movements but also, throughout, in details of structure and materials.

The premiere took place as planned, and Barry Millington (1980) offered a brief assessment in the London *Times*: "Michael Cedric Smith's task in giving ['Cage'] its premiere was to convince that [the preparation] was all worthwhile. That he was unsuccessful probably was not his fault, and he produced some effective 'bottlenecking' in 'Crump' and some catchy rhythms in 'Cotton.'"[5] Thereafter MCS gave nearly twenty performances of the three London movements, in various combinations and circumstances, between 1982 and 1984, including one at Carnegie Hall, and he made a studio recording at Brooklyn College in March 1982. But he never performed the other three movements, though the paper trail indicates that he offered advice for "Cotten, *loc cit.*" That movement was performed by guitarist James Marron at least twice in the 1990s. The other two movements had never been played when I sent Stefan the score in July 2010.

While BillyMus was probing this history, the ghost of BillyCom was whispering in his mind. Memories gradually surfaced: a childhood experience of hearing guitar music drifting in and out of focus on an AM radio; the practicalities of designing the preparations for "Cage" and finding suitable materials; John Cage's *Sonatas and Interludes* as recorded by Maro Ajemian in the 1950s; the sound of David Behrman's "Music of Our Time" LPs . . . Were these "true"? Were they "authentic"? Were they necessary to perform the music "correctly"? BillyMus couldn't decide, but it was clear that BillyCom would not go away: his memories, filtered through BillyMus's analysis and scholarship, would become central to the music Stefan Östersjö would create and Jez Wells would record.

1.2.3. Cousins and ghosts

Conversations between BillyMus and Stefan really commenced after January 2009, when BillyMus joined the community of researchers at the Orpheus Institute, where Stefan was already a fellow. But the web had begun to be woven before then, when Stefan undertook the performance of Michael Edward Edgerton's massive *Tempo Mental Rap*.[6] In the late 1980s, Edgerton had studied with BillyCom, who was then teaching at the University of Illinois, and *Tempo Mental Rap* was thus a kind of second-cousin-once-removed to *Footnotes*. BillyMus first heard part of Edgerton's piece in a recording that Edgerton played at the University of York on 23 October 2007, and it quickly became evident that the two pieces (by BillyCom and by Edgerton) shared a fair amount of DNA: the *Rap* is a set of six distinct variations, *Footnotes* has six distinct movements; both reference specific performances in American popular music; both are structurally and notationally rigorous;

3 The proportions are those of the smallest right triangle with integer values; they also usefully divide various twelve-element sets: of pitches, of pulses, of bars.
4 BillyMus has written extensively about John Cage: see, e.g., Brooks (2002, 2009, 2012).
5 "Cotten," intended to be the surname of Elizabeth Cotten, was misspelled as "Cotton" in the first copy of the score and in related early documents. In this chapter, the misspelling has been allowed to stand in any quotations from these.
6 For more on this composition see Edgerton (2008).

both are dauntingly difficult, requiring that the performer exercise considerable invention as well as conventional virtuosity. But more profoundly, both pieces call into question the composer's *subjectivity*; in each, a conventionally constructed "author" is concealed behind an adopted mask, an alternate persona: Frank Zappa for Edgerton, John Cage for Brooks. More than that: each of the variations in the *Rap* and each of the movements in *Footnotes* problematise even the masks that are worn, albeit in different ways. In the *Rap* the source material is constant, and always Zappa, but it displays different aspects, suggests additional persona as the work develops: the Xenakis turn, the Ferneyhough turn, the Braxton turn. In *Footnotes* the aspect is constant, and always Cage, but the material is captured from additional persona: from Elizabeth Cotten, from Francisco Tárrega, from John Lee Hooker. The Cage mask is an operator; the Zappa is operated upon.

After the July 2010 message there was a hiatus in formal communications. But BillyMus and Stefan met several times a year, usually at Orpheus Institute events, and they recall that in many of these encounters *Footnotes* was mentioned. Stefan made occasional forays into the score, but much of his time was devoted to other projects, including collaborations with David Gorton (see chapter 1, above) and perfecting the later variations in *Tempo Mental Rap*. At the beginning of 2013 a flurry of emails among Stefan, Michael Edgerton, and BillyMus focused very much on the kinship between the pieces and the compositional genealogy; scant attention was paid to the multiple subjectivities or even the stylistic range of the two works. The notion then was that a single, conventional CD that contained both works in full would be economically viable if marketing was concentrated in the United States. With Edgerton taking the lead, a range of labels were considered, and preliminary contacts were made. By April Edgerton had drafted a formal proposal that was duly conveyed to the labels, and by July Jez Wells had been brought on board to engineer the recording of both pieces.

In the meantime BillyCom had continued murmuring in BillyMus's ear. Between 2010 and 2013, BillyMus began gradually to construct a narrative around *Footnotes*—part historical account, part reminiscence. Old documents supplemented BillyCom's recollections: the first two movements to be written were "Cotten" and "Cage"; "Crump" followed somewhat later, with almost two years intervening before the other three movements were composed. Other, less verifiable memories began to surface: the student, not yet BillyCom, who had learned rudimentary folk guitar, as 1960s youth culture required, and who had attempted to play Elizabeth Cotten's repertoire; and before that, the epiphany an aspiring, ambitious pianist had experienced when he first encountered John Cage's *Sonatas and Interludes*; and even earlier, the clandestine nights a young teenager spent listening to classical station WQXR on an old radio on which reception teetered on the edge of static, music emerging and fading with the wind and the weather.

The ghost of John Cage murmured as well, especially the late Cage who opened *Composition in Retrospect* with "My memory of what happened is not what happened" (Cage 1993, 5). BillyMus had imagined himself to be a writer of *history*—but as wisps of BillyCom took ectoplasmic form around him, it became clear that in this instance (and maybe always), he was writing only a *story*. The irritating but comforting mutterings by BillyCom compelled BillyMus to reconceive who he was and what he was doing: another subjectivity brought into question. And as more wisps took shape, more identities, more persona, were discovered. The boy that heard the radio was not, after all, the pianist who encountered Cage's prepared piano; and neither of those was the BillyCom who made *Footnotes* in the 1980s. It became clear that *Footnotes* was about multiplicity—it inhabited a pluralist universe[7]—with multiple authors (conveniently clustered under the umbrella "William Brooks"), multiple instruments (clustered under "guitar"), and multiple moments (clustered under "a life").

By July 2013, as a recording seemed more and more practical, it suddenly became evident that the recording, too, could inhabit a pluralist universe—that "one" recording could be fractured into many authors, many performers, many times, many engineers. Each movement—and each unit of "Cage, *passim*"—could be characterised differently: one might be a field recording from about 1950; one might be the site-specific documentation of a church service; one could be an immaculately produced avant-garde track from a 1970s LP. If BillyMus was condemned to storytelling, he might as well embrace that whole-heartedly.

The history of the recording is not the story of the recording.

And so *Footnotes*—the vinyl artefact, entirely different from *Footnotes* the score or *Footnotes* the music—began.

1.2. Protagonists

The story of the making of *Footnotes*, the recording, can only be understood by acknowledging the agencies of the score and the instruments used. What follows is a first-person account from the perspective of a guitarist; but equally influential in shaping the result were the presences of a composer and a sound engineer. But so also were the guitars, the recording technology, and the tools for signal processing and other post-production. Indeed, although we will refer repeatedly to our joint attempts at recreating the intentions of the composer (first, as noted above, by the composer trying to bring these intentions correctly back in mind), equally central are the intentionalities[8] inherent in the score and the instruments.

My first encounter with the score to *Footnotes* was in 2010. Although Bill had mentioned that he had an early piece for guitar, which had only been partially premiered, it was only when he sent copies of the score that I realized the scope of the composition. And, even then, some movements were omitted from the version he sent. My immediate response was that it looked like a great recording project, and this idea grew even stronger as I came to realize how each movement

7 Much later, BillyMus would become deeply engaged with William James; note the links between the phrase "a pluralist universe," James (1909), and Brooks (2009b).

8 John Butt (2002) proposes that intentionality should not merely be attributed to the agency of a composer, but rather, as discussed in chapter 1, as a quality that characterises both human and non-human agents in musical creativity. Our discussion of the agency of instruments (broadly understood) should also be read in the light of Catherine Laws's exploration of the "thing power" (Bennett 2010) of the piano in chapter 2 (p. 143).

of the piece more or less specifically requested a particular sound and the choice of a specific instrument. Since my entire professional career had been devoted to the exploration of how novel sonorities can be drawn out of different plucked string instruments (with or without the additional use of signal processing), this in itself seemed like a viable and attractive approach. While this made sense musically, looking at the substantially postmodern nature of the composition, it also posed questions regarding the feasibility of touring the entire work. In the back of my mind, therefore, the piece was framed as an idea for a future recording project; and three years later, we got started, looking into programming ideas for a release of a studio recording of the entire piece. The composer suggested, in conversations at the Orpheus Institute,[9] that perhaps we should create a research project to embrace this recording project. To this I responded that we might "consider, in effect, 'HIRP': Historically Informed Recording Practice." And Bill continued by observing that "this makes perfect sense for *Footnotes*, because the score itself is historically and stylistically eclectic. So one could, as an extreme instance, record the 'Cotton' movement on a wire recorder and with the mics that would have been in use in 1930s field work. 'Crump,' which is a bizarre reworking of electric bluesmen, could be done with 1960s technology; 'Cage' is notionally from the late 1940s, and so forth."[10]

On July 23, Bill contacted the audio engineer Jez Wells, who was immediately keen about the project and its implications for recording, both technological and processual. A week later, Brooks reported on their conversations; they had concluded that

> it would be nice to preserve as much analogue technology as is appropriate. Jez's thought was that we would use vintage equipment to record, informed by what we can find out about standard mic placement, etc. But the storage medium would be digital, so that we have a reliable copy to which we can return. We would then record the digital file on analogue equipment (r-r tape, acetate, whatever is appropriate) and edit and process using that medium. At the end the final version is converted to digital form (with NO "improvements"!). The idea is that the digital medium is simply a "black box" that is inserted between the mic output and the tape input; it does nothing except provide a backup. (Email, WB to SÖ, 30 August 2013)

Thus we set off with dedicated attention to authenticity-as-sound, grounded also in an interest in authenticity-as-practice.[11]

Ideas for how to record, post-produce, and release *Footnotes* continued to be negotiated not only among composer, performer, and sound engineer but also, importantly, among materials, institutions, and geographies, a process in which many compromises were made and many creative solutions eventually found.

---

9 The conversations took place during sessions at the Orpheus Institute on 9 and 10 July and were recapitulated by Brooks in an email to Mike Edgerton on 23 July, which can be accessed in the online repository in file "A True History of *Footnotes* Perhaps (Part 2)."

10 This exchange is quoted, in part retrospectively, from an email from Brooks to Östersjö, 28 July 2013. For more details, see the file "SF3.9 A True History of *Footnotes* Perhaps (Part 2)" in the online repository (www.orpheusinstituut.be/en/voices-bodies-practices-media-repository).

11 "Authenticity-as-sound" and "authenticity-as-practice" are phrases taken from Peter Kivy's influential typology of authenticity (1995), which is discussed in more detail in section 2.1, below.

It was agreed that the recording sessions were to be made in a studio at the University of York on 19–21 September, with rehearsals taking place at the Inter Arts Center in Malmö on 13–14 September. As it turned out, some recordings for "Cage, *passim*" were actually made in Malmö on 14 September; but even before then, I had made some recordings at home, with various electric guitars recorded straight onto my digital workstation.

In August 2014, I worked more or less simultaneously on all the materials in the score. Personal authenticity raised some initial concerns, particularly with one of the movements, "Cotten, *loc. cit.*" While I could relate my voice as a performer to virtually every part of the entire compilation, despite the extreme stylistic diversity, it was difficult for me to embrace this piece, which evoked a type of classical guitar music of the kind associated with Andrés Segovia. It is a tremolo étude, and the first footnote captures the identity and the basic structure of the music quite succinctly: "The sense of 'Cotten, *loc. cit.*' is sentimental and nostalgic: a serenade, or rather a memory of a serenade, heard at a distance and many years ago. The serenade (tremolando) fades in and out, frequently interrupted by a kind of static (arpeggiate)—like an old man's memories, sometimes clear, sometimes confused" (Brooks [1986] 2019). My professional career up to this point had been devoted to the performance of all kinds of music outside the standard classical repertory, and this piece, with its outspoken reference to the more sentimental and nostalgic side of this music, was certainly a rather difficult exception from this rule; in effect, it was asking me to become other than what I thought I was. In attempting to resolve this internal aesthetic conflict, I turned to my co-partner in producing "voice": the instrument.[12] I brought out my fretless guitar, an instrument that I often use when improvising and which had been part of several important works I had commissioned over the past years. This instrument, I hoped, could provide a personally authentic opening for a rendering of this piece, and as a test I recorded one of the three sections of the piece and sent it to Bill, saying that "I wonder if the fretless Glissentar[13] could create the right kind of nostalgia in Cotton *loc. cit.*" (Email, SÖ to WB, 28 August 2014).[14] Bill's response was polite but not too enthusiastic, and he turned his initial sentence over into the suggestion that we might "factor the process into the overall 'historically informed recording' agenda"—which seemed like an elegant way of postponing the decision, hoping that a different option would then be on the table. I wrote back to say I also thought the obvious solution of

12 See the discussion in Chapter 1 and especially figure 1.3.

13 The Glissentar is a fretless string instrument created by Robert Godin. All its basic physical features—scale length, body size, depth, fingerboard radius, and string height—are standard guitar dimensions. In a similar vein to an oud, it has eleven strings, comprising a single bass string and five courses of nylon strings tuned in unison. The instrument is sometimes used also by oud players when looking for a more powerful amplified sound but also it appears to frequently be used with different open tunings in various folk music contexts (see for instance http://www.unfretted.com/reviews/gear-reviews/glissentar-vs-multiac/). Östersjö first used it in a project with the Swedish composer Kent Olofsson, ultimately aiming to include it in the array of instruments used in Olofsson's prize-winning concerto for guitarist and orchestra titled *Corde* (2008). For a photograph, see file "SF3.10 Glissentar" in the online repository (www.orpheusinstituut.be/en/voices-bodies-practices-media-repository).

14 This recording can be heard in the online repository; see file "SF3.11 *Footnotes*, "Cotten, *loc. cit.*," Glissentar test.

recording on a classical guitar was fully possible, and that we could see what to do with it in the post-production. The next day, he responded to this comment with the following idea (as it turned out, immediately related to the first footnote on the score, quoted above), which completely shifted my view of the composition: "Post-production I imagine an (old fashioned, analogue) radio station that drifts into and out of range. So some (very gentle!) white noise comes and goes . . . as do we all!" (Email, WB to SÖ, 29 August 2014).[15]

This for me was a total game-changer. It was exciting to think of creating a version in which there were actual shifts from the tremolo étude to radio static (represented in the score by the loss of focus in the arpeggiated passages), and it immediately implied an entirely different aesthetic, in which classical guitar playing would only be one component.[16] I wrote back enthusiastically saying, "I really like this drifting radio signal idea. Beautiful! So if we produce the recording like an old Segovia 1920s recording and then process it like you describe below I think we have something very poetic" (Email, SÖ to WB, 29 August 2014). While writing, I realised that what we were now discussing was no longer merely a recording "of" the piece, but rather an idea for a little electronic composition, to become part of a new version of the piece. This eventually provided a conceptual foundation for the making of the entire album.

It also implied that the performed "voice" would in this case be, very explicitly, comprising person plus instrument, and that the partnership between them would continue but vary over the course of the movements. It further suggested that the eventual negotiation of a "discursive voice" (see chapter 1) would also involve voices from the history of audio recording, and indeed also the means of production from a specific time. When we met in Malmö to work at the Inter Arts Center a little more than two weeks later, we rehearsed "Cotten, *loc. cit.*"; ideas for how to shape the performance as well as the recording took more concrete shape:

> Stefan: There are many moments that bring you back to what Segovia would have done, . . . It has some moments of Manuel Ponce . . . [*Bill laughs*]. . . . but it's also, it's somewhere between that and a more Spanish idiom like Moreno Torroba. If you bring those two together and they kind of, you know, a late night—they make a kind of . . .
>
> Bill: . . . duet!
>
> Stefan: . . . a tremolo étude together. It's a little bit like that. So, if we could make it sound like an old Segovia recording—when he started getting a little tired, he played really slowly but still had this really beautiful tone, I think that might be . . .

15 The complete exchange, and those discussed below, can be found in the repository document "SF3.9 A True History of *Footnotes* Perhaps (Part 2)."

16 The solution (or resolution) of this aesthetic dilemma is interestingly similar to the resolution of what Coessens and Östersjö (2014) call "resistance of culture" in the production of *IDIOMS*, a music theatre project that brought together actors from traditional Vietnamese theatre and American and European contemporary theatre. They illustrate the negotiation of conflicting cultural capital, here related to the instrumentality of traditional costume, through observations of the development of the performance of Nguyễn Đức Mạnh, an actor from traditional Tuồng theatre. Coessens and Östersjö analyse this resistance of habit, as it takes shape in Mạnh's performance, as an expression of "hexis," an approach that stretches beyond habit and, here, also beyond a particularly articulated resistance of culture. The *IDIOMS* project is also related to *Arrival Cities: Hanoi*, which is discussed in chapter 4, below.

> Bill: I think that's just right.
>
> Stefan: I had some of those, some of the last LPs.
>
> Bill: I had, yeah, I had one of those late ones, I don't remember which one it was.
>
> (Conversation, WB and SÖ, 14 September 2014)[17]

Around the same time in August, I had started working on unit C of "Cage, *passim*," and this piece also became an important pointer towards the design of the entire recording project.[18] Here, again, I drew Bill into an email conversation about the interpretation and the realisation I had made of the score. In unit C, the performer is invited to "prepare a transcription" rather than to read from the notation, which presents three systems in which the compass, indicated by horizontal lines, can "equal any pitch range desired," and within which patterns of dots are situated (see figure 3.2).

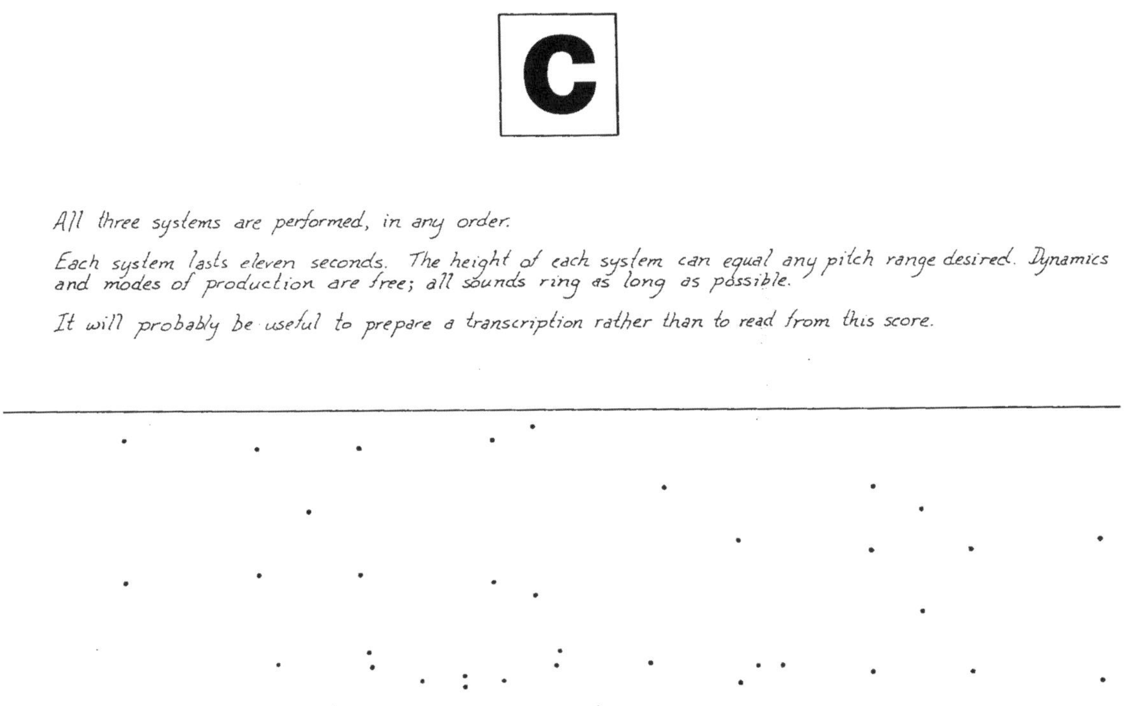

Figure 3.2.

17 A video of this conversation is included in the online repository (www.orpheusinstituut.be/en/voices-bodies-practices-media-repository); see file "SF3.12 WB and SÖ in Malmö," beginning at 3:05.

18 "Cage, *passim*" contains twelve units of material: nine labelled A–H and three others labelled P, Q, and R. The units are extremely diverse sonically and notationally, and the score permits them to be arranged in a very large number of possible orders.

Figure 3.2. "Cage, *passim*," page C-1.

Rather than creating just another Cage pastiche,[19] the openness of the score became for me an invitation to relate this unit to other parts of *Footnotes*, and it occurred to me to make this "transcription" into a jazz guitar solo, thus linking it with other evocations of vernacular traditions in, for example, "Cotten" and "Crump." A pitch system was then created, which I applied by means of a scordatura that I realised on a semi-acoustic electric guitar, which would give a rather authentic 1940s jazz sound. Each system should last eleven seconds, but in the first version, the third system was dragging a bit, and Bill was keen to get it all a bit tighter. With another day's work, practising the material, I made what became the final recording, sent to Bill on 5 September. He wrote back enthusiastically the next day, and we agreed to use this little piece as a trial balloon for the post-production methods. The clean line signal recording was sent to Jez with the suggestion that he process the track to resemble a Wes Montgomery live recording.[20] A week later, and just a few days before the recording sessions were to start, Jez sent back a first edit, with the following remarks:

> Here, as a very quick experiment just to see if I'm thinking in the right area, is an "analogue tape recording of Wes Montgomery in [a] small club" attempt. I've used materials that are to hand and I'd expect to be more choosy about everything: the noise (need to add some 60 Hz mains hum), the amp sound (doesn't yet seem quite warm enough, although I'm listening on quite bright speakers), the audience noise (a bit too polite, and I'm not even sure you want applause), the tape distortion (a bit too harsh) etc. etc. It's in stereo (which I think is OK for fifties and spatial presentation will be one very clear way of making the jump from 30s to 50s). (Email, JW to WB and SÖ, 15 September 2014)[21]

Both Bill and I responded with enthusiasm, and for a good while this version was the only model we had for how the entire recording project would eventually deal with each movement. Through the making of this little pilot study, we not only had begun to establish a working method but also, very importantly, had launched a collaboration that included all three parties. The project was truly started.

I was travelling during the week of 8 September, and since the recording sessions were nearing, I brought the full score with me, including the pencilled realisations that I had made from instructions in "Cage, *passim*," units C and F (the former of which I had already recorded, as described above). On 11 September, alas, I had to send the following message to Bill: "When boarding a flight at Kastrup I was on the phone and a bit distracted (poor excuse, I know). I realized only when about to disembark that I had left the plastic bag with the full score for footnotes by the gate. I have made every possible attempt to secure its current status but still without success" (Email, SÖ to WB, 11 September 2014). I asked

---

19 Pastiches appear explicitly and unavoidably in the movement "Cage" and in units A, P, Q, and R in "Cage, *passim*."

20 The three successive versions can be heard in the online repository: see files "SF3.13 *Footnotes*, 'Cage, *passim*,' unit C, ver1"; "SF.3.14 *Footnotes*, 'Cage, *passim*,' unit C, ver2"; "SF3.15 *Footnotes*, 'Cage, *passim*,' unit C, ver3." For the email correspondence, see the document "SF3.9 A True History of *Footnotes* Perhaps (Part 2)."

21 This recording is available in the online repository; see file "SF3.16 *Footnotes*, 'Cage, *passim*,' unit C, experiment."

whether Bill could bring a new full score along when travelling to our rehearsals in Sweden, since we were arriving in Copenhagen on the same day and my time for printing the score again would be limited.[22]

Hence, the "transcription" of C discussed above was lost at Kastrup airport on 11 September. I have still not made any attempt to reconstruct it, and I will probably decide just to make a new version when I wish to play the piece again. Ironically, even the post-production version made by Jez eventually also caused us trouble, since the original session was lost. When later we returned to this unit, Jez had to devise technical work-arounds to reconstruct a version that would allow him to integrate it successfully into the whole.[23]

E

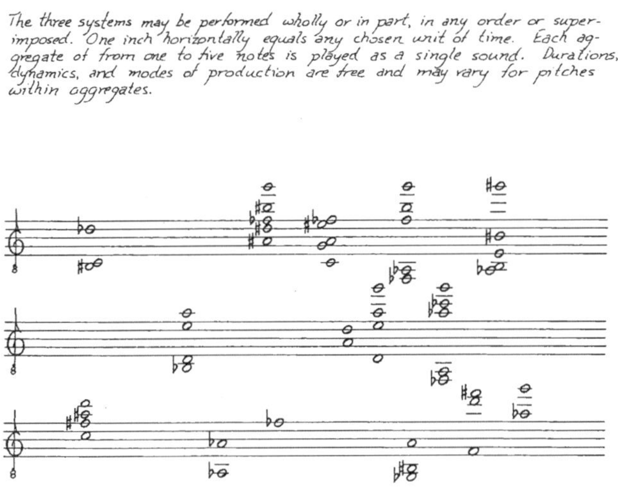

Figure 3.3.

22 Needless to say, this didn't go too well. Bill was already travelling and was not able to print a new score. Once in Malmö we comically spent half a day trying to get the printers at the Inter Arts Center and in the Academy of Music to work. Only in the evening were the issues with the IAC-printer resolved, at which time we were so exhausted with the many attempts that we entered the access code in the window for the number of copies. After the first full printout we panicked and turned the printer off, leaving the unfinished job of printing the other four thousand copies to the person who would start the copy machine on the coming Monday.

23 As put by Jez in an email in June 2019: "When we got together in September 2017 to finish off items from Passim, C that was one of the very first things I mocked up to see what might be possible in 2014 was inaccessible because the Reaper project file was corrupted (I've just checked the file again, and it is definitely un-openable). We had the audio render, and the different elements used (mains hum, tape noise, etc.) but we did not have the project, which we had to have because we wanted to make a number of changes. So it had to be reconstructed using the original render as a guide" (email, JW to SÖ, 9 June 2019).

Figure 3.3. "Cage, *passim*," unit E.

During the Malmö sessions, after some negotiation and discussion, we also recorded two other sections of "Cage, *passim*": units E and F. The instructions for unit E explain that "the three systems may be performed wholly or in part, in any order or superimposed. One inch horizontally equals any chosen unit of time. Each aggregate of from one to five notes is played as a single sound. Durations, dynamics, and modes of production are free and may vary for pitches within aggregates" (see figure 3.3).

Looking at the chordal structures and considering the possibility of choosing a temporal grid that would provide a slowly proceeding set of harmonic textures, it occurred to me that using multi-tracked E-bows could be a good option. Turning the guitar into a somewhat psychedelic (and rather simplistic) organ, this E-bow choir would provide the movement with a contrasting and very slow layer of sustained sound. I also imagined recording some of the chords (those that could be played without multi-tracking) on the same semi-acoustic guitar, so as to create a structure of very long sustained chords, sometimes interrupted by a plucked chord or emerging out of one.

Unit F was recorded in another multi-tracked session on the same day. In this I used a Vietnamese electric guitar[24] and the above-mentioned fretless guitar, the Glissentar. This track was imagined as the most contemporary—that is, contemporary with the imagined composer, or the actual composer at the time of composition in the 1980s—of all the tracks on the album, and it aimed to capture the sound one could have heard in a radio broadcast of contemporary jazz at the time.

In summary, working through documentary evidence in email and in video and audio recordings, it becomes evident in retrospect that the formation of a set of compound subjectivities was embedded in the entire project from a very early stage, was explicitly acknowledged in preliminary discussions through 2014, and became a focal point of our work during the preparation for the recording sessions in September of that year. And it becomes evident also that the three human agents—Jez, Bill, and me—were already assuming multiple subjectivities, multiple personae, as part of negotiating the multiple authenticities and intentionalites at play. *Footnotes*, as a recording project, became a celebration of multiple manifestations of non-human agents—instruments, notations, technologies—through which the entire project became both fractured into uncounted, fleeting, stipulated, or fictional identities and unified by an underlying inquiry into the nature of subjectivity and its construction in performance, composition, and recording. When the three of us met in York on 19 September, all this was tacitly understood.

24 The Vietnamese guitar is an instrument that exists both as a steel string acoustic and as an electric guitar. (A photograph appears in the online repository in file "SF3.17 Vietnamese guitar.") It was adapted for the performance of traditional music—mainly within the instrumental music of tài tử (for further information, see chapter 4) and also in a closely related form of music theatre called Cai Luong—and therefore has very deeply scalloped frets and is typically tuned very low, in order to allow performing the bending ornaments typical of this music. Thus the Vietnamese guitar is a central example of how "the development of many types of Vietnamese music [can be] labelled as both a reaction to French colonization and enabled by it" (Cannon 2016, 154). I play traditional Vietnamese music on this instrument but have also used it extensively in free improvisation and in a number of compositions for the group The Six Tones; one of these projects is discussed in chapter 4.

1.3. Records

> This points in turn to the predominance of a *realist* sonic discourse in both classical and many popular music recordings, one in which the goal has been a finished recording that appears simply to capture, and to be faithful to, a prior musical event. Thus music recording, with the aesthetic and rhetorical traditions and practices that it has engendered historically, has at its core an antimony in which illusionism and realism are emphatically not in contradiction. (Born 2009, 294)

At the start of the September sessions, final decisions about the ultimate form in which the audio would be presented had not yet been made. In fact, aside from some brief conversations with BillyMus and Stefan, there was little prior planning other than to make the usual preparations for the capture of performances in a modern recording studio. One of the many profound changes in the technology, and therefore affordance, of the studio that has occurred over the last thirty years is the capacity of the recording media. In 1990 a reel of two-inch analogue tape for 24-track recording would have cost somewhere in the region of £100, and it offered 30 minutes of recording time at a tape speed of 15 inches per second or 15 minutes at twice that speed. If we assume that the audio quality possible with that tape was equivalent to that possible when making a digital recording for CD release (not an unreasonable assumption, if one uses a very high quality tape machine with Dolby SR noise reduction), then such a reel of tape offered a storage capacity of approximately 3.6 gigabytes. This was way beyond the storage capacity of a single disk drive at that time, and assembling such capacity from multiple drives would have cost in the region of £20,000 (Komorowski 2009). The situation in 2014, when the recording sessions for this project took place, was the complete reverse, and the cost of storage media was so low that we could essentially consider it limitless: the low price of terabyte drives enabled 3.6 gigabytes of storage to be available, on one device, for about 15 pence.

Ironically, in one sense, we have embraced this new storage technology and the contemporary digital equipment to which it is attached in order to create impressions of eras when analogue was the only economically, and often technologically, viable recording, storage, and playback medium. There are a number of reasons for this apparently paradoxical approach. First, it was not yet precisely planned at the time when we began recording. It was very likely that inter-contingencies would exist: future production decisions would depend on outcomes of the performing and recording processes. One way of keeping options open for dealing with contingencies was to capture performances many times and with many microphones, enabling a particular performance to be constructed with a chosen perspective, in some instances many months *after* the (recording) event. Fact does not need to be designed, but fiction does; real life does not require rehearsal and post-production, but films of real (or fictional) lives do.

Second, the entropy of an audio signal typically increases as it travels through the programme chain, from origination in the studio to final destination on media for domestic playback. Reverberation entangles the signal with itself via the process of convolution (from the Latin *convolutus*, "to roll together"); mixing takes multiple independent streams and merges them together; dynamic range control of mixed signals causes complex intermodulations. All these are impossible, or at least profoundly difficult, to unpick, since the entropy has moved in the wrong direction. Moreover, the term *fidelity* does not have a universally agreed meaning; but if we are careful to avoid the trap that Sterne (2012) warns of in equating "definition" with verisimilitude, we can still observe that—afforded by, among other things, increasing storage capacity and greater transfer bandwidth—it has quantitively increased. By all possible relevant objective measures, levels of distortion and noise and inconsistencies of frequency response have all fallen over time. While Ray Dolby's statement (1998, 2472), made over twenty years ago, that "microphones, loudspeakers, amplifiers, recorders and transmission channels are all solved problems; all the tests and ordinary experience confirm this," may be controversial outside the engineering community, it is not contentious to say that unwanted interferences, contaminations, and inconsistencies have all been reduced in signal transduction, transmission, storage, and replay. Therefore, it is easier to distress recordings than it is to restore distressed recordings to their original condition.

Third, spatially and temporally dislocated collaboration is more straightforward with contemporary audio production technology. In creating artefacts imagined from different times and places with a trio of individuals residing in different places in the northern hemisphere and engaged in different activities, there are also geographic and economic pressures that are not representative of the imagined scenarios and working relationships behind the artefacts that have been created. As already noted, capacity and bandwidth for audio production has increased significantly and monotonically. Capacity enables the retention of audio signals; bandwidth enables them to be moved more quickly from one place to another. Sometimes these distances are small (e.g., from one end of a single universal serial bus—USB—to another); sometimes they are long (e.g., from one continent to another via the internet). Digital encoding of signals enables far greater flexibility in storage and transfer. High-quality recording, transfer, and processing of analogue audio signals almost always requires the use of bespoke hardware; and this can be expensive (since its design and manufacture does not benefit from economies of scale), unreliable (particularly as a result of age—although it does not exhibit the "buggy" behaviour of computer software), and quite possibly unavailable, either completely (consider the current dearth of high quality analogue tape machines available either first- or second-hand) or partially (the lack of spare parts with which to service such machines). Digital audio signals, on the other hand, since they are a code constructed from combinations of the same two binary states that can also characterise digital text, digital images, digital spreadsheets, and so on, can avail themselves of more generalised hardware for storage and transmission. The analogue audio signals require bespoke hardware for conversion to and from their digital codes; but, otherwise, the memory and the disks in and on which they reside, the screens on which their shape can be displayed, and the interfaces with which they can be scrolled and controlled are the same hardware that can be used for a myriad of tasks in the modern personal computer: word processing, accounting, image manipulation, web browsing, and all the rest. And the humble telephone wire can pass audio signals of great definition (albeit not necessarily in real time) right across the world's general-purpose network of networks: the internet.

For this project, then, we have used modern tools, first, to give us the flexibility to make decisions late in the production process by creating and maintaining a large archive of high-definition recordings over a number of years and, second, to enable a geographically and temporally dislocated workflow. The alternative would have been to adopt authentic, historically informed production practices and equipment. This would have dramatically constrained workflow and reduced flexibility; indeed, it would likely have been economically unviable, even if the appropriate equipment could have been sourced. It would also have inhibited the expression of production technique, since there would have been a lack of familiarity with the "period instruments" being employed in the production. Leech-Wilkinson (1984, 13) proposes that a flautist playing a Bach sonata suffers under "the illusion that he has . . . been involved in an 18th-century experience"; much the same might be said for the participants in a twentieth-century recording studio attempting to capture a performance of "Mr. Crump's Blues."

Of course, this all begs another question: if you eschew period instruments, then how can you expect the results of your production processes to plausibly sound as if they came from those devices? Analogue representations of sound, which are at the core of the earliest sound recording and reproduction instruments and the vast majority of those introduced through the hundred or so years afterwards, enable sound to escape its acoustic shackles. Whereas acoustic signals are transitory and localised to their original generating object (since as sound propagates outwards and interacts with materials, its intensity continuously reduces), analogue signals, since they exist in different media, can transcend these limitations. All that is required to create an analogue signal is a medium that exhibits a characteristic parameter that can vary in an *analogous* way, over either time or space, to the variation of air pressure over time that characterises an acoustic signal. The flow of time can be represented as position along the length of a spiral groove and the amplitude of the pressure at a point in time can be the lateral or vertical excursion in that groove. Another analogy is the magnetic flux density at a particular point along the length of a strip of tape. In both these examples the representations are permanent and no longer fleeting. Fleeting analogies, such as modulations in radio waves, do not offer permanence but they do enable signals to survive travel over far greater distances than the acoustic signals that they represent.

However, analogue signals are limited by the ability of the materials in which they are stored (or through which they pass) to exactly mimic the variations in air pressure that they are intended to represent. Because the signal is represented by direct analogy, any imperfections in the medium are heard as distortions, noises, or inconsistencies across the audible spectrum. Because these exist in the medium, they are inseparable from the wanted signal. Therefore, the sound of the medium is heard together with the signal. Tape hiss and the surface noise of vinyl disks become the texture on which, or through which, the signal is heard. Analogue recordings sound, to a greater or lesser extent, of the materials on which they have been made. The state of the medium *is* the signal. To place recordings in a particular temporal and economic context from the analogue era it is necessary to include these material interferences and distortions.

Digital signals, on the other hand, are distanced from the materiality of their containing media by being a numerical code that represents the amplitude of the pressure variations, sampled at particular instants in time. Noise caused by inconsistencies in the medium is not encoded and so does not become entwined with the signal. Noise, distortion, and frequency response irregularities do hamper the retrieval of the code, but the binary digits that it is constructed from have only two states, 0 or 1, and there is no ambiguity. Check codes can be placed within the actual audio data to detect all errors and perfectly correct them, provided the contaminations and interferences are not overwhelming. Therefore, digital recordings do not sound like their media, they sound like their code and the processes that convert the signal into, and back out of, that code. With the ever-increasing storage capacities and bandwidths of computer hardware, it becomes possible to capture high-definition audio signals and to reduce noise, distortion, and frequency response irregularities to inaudible levels. In this sense digital recordings can be regarded as transparent.

Digital, then, is the ideal storage container and conduit for our signals: it preserves them in their current state at every stage of the process in which we dress them for the historical drama we have created. That shifts attention to the dressing processes themselves, and these are described in detail in what follows. Many of these combine analogue imperfections (which appear with the signal but do not interact with it) with digital simulations or analogue enactments of those that interact with the signal in some way (for instance, harmonic or intermodulation distortion or spectral variation). Here the term "enactments" means recreations of the analogue processes that impart such imperfections. For example, a digital signal of a recording session can be recorded onto, and immediately reproduced from, analogue tape and then stored, in its new state, as a new digital signal (retaining the previous digital version, in case we wish to retrace our steps in order to take a different route). "Simulations" are created when a computer is made to behave like an analogue process when a digital signal is passed through it. In the same way that enactments are only as good as the equipment and media that the signal passes through, so simulations are only as good as the instructions to the computer (and the understanding of the analogue processes on which they are based). Both offer solutions and both present challenges.

This is the pragmatic, flexible, and collaborative approach that we have taken for these productions. In retrospect it is not so different from the reconciliation of realism with illusionism that Born postulates in the quotation that opened this section.

1.4. Method

1.4.1. Allegory

In the beginning Composer created *Footnotes* and nothingness. And *Footnotes* was formless, and void; and it stirred in the void, and it had no substance. So Composer created sound, and separated sound from appearance, and called sound Music and appearance Score. And Composer saw that it was good. And that was the first Time.

Then Composer made Form; and Form separated *Footnotes* in two parts. And Composer called one part Material and the other Structure; and it was so. And that was the second Time.

Then Composer divided Material by means of Structure; and there were six Movements, divided by silences that Structure had made. And from Material, Composer called forth notation for each Movement: notes, and rests, and colours, and intensities; and these together were fruitful and multiplied, to make Scores of every kind, each movement separate from the next. And that was the third Time.

And Composer called upon a new power that stood apart from *Footnotes*, to transform Score into Music. And this power was called Performer. And Performer brought instruments to bear upon Score, so that appearance became sound; and Performer and instruments transformed Score to make performance; and when the transformation ended, there was not performance; and thus a series of performances came one after another, each distinct but like the preceding. And each instrument transformed Score differently, so that each created its own succession of performances; and each succession was different for each instrument and also for each Movement. And *Footnotes* became an abundance, and passed from Composer's hands. And that was the fourth Time.

And Composer and Performer together called upon one who stood outside time itself and was called Producer. And Producer captured each performance in a circle of time, and grouped these circles by kind; and each kind moved differently, across time and space; and the shapes of each were changed. So the abundance that was *Footnotes* became scattered, and the circles multiplied and drifted and fractured, and they became as dust, without form, and void. And that was the fifth Time.

Then Composer and Performer and Producer gathered up the circles and the dust, and together they shaped those into a new *Footnotes*, which was not the same as the old *Footnotes* but was made in the image of what had been before. They made six Movements, and they breathed into each a part of themselves; and each contained the notes, and rests, and colours the Composer had made, and an instrument the Performer had brought, and the circles and the successions and the times. And they gave each of the six Movements a new name, and they gave them dominion over time, and memory, and loss. And they commanded them to go forth but never to multiply; each Movement was commanded to be itself alone. And that was the sixth Time.

And now their work was done, and the seventh Time had begun. So they all went to the seaside for a little R and R.

1.4.2. Account

Footnotes (the score, the performance, the recording) was made by a process of differentiation and aggregation. The making of *Footnotes* (the score) proceeded from a single concept to distinct and differentiated movements, to an abundance of devised materials, to a diversity of notations. *Footnotes* was composed, BillyCom recalls, on guitar—specifically, on the battered but responsive Gibson he had bought back in 1972—but that unitary instrument quickly became multiple and differentiated through a series of experiments with preparations and playing techniques. Most movements contained structural units that were themselves differentiated, ranging from the entirely obvious twelve units in "Cage, *passim*" to the subtle but precise parametric characterisation of each twelve-bar subsection in "Cotten." In short, the creation of a score from a central idea required assigning to external entities, from physical objects to abstract principles, a kind of agency that would break unities into ever-smaller components. And this fragmentation called into question the unity of the composer; as early as 1982, BillyCom recalls wondering: Just who is *making* this score? Where is "my voice" in all this? He remembered (but couldn't really embrace) John Cage's delight when Cage discovered that he couldn't recognise recordings of his own music; and he clung to various abstractions (the strict adherence to certain number schemes, for instance) as comforting representations of his singular selfhood.

A similar kind of diversification characterised the second phase of the project: *Footnotes* (the performance), which Stefan created. On the title page for the entire set, BillyCom wrote, "Different instruments . . . may be used for different movements," modestly suggesting using steel strings for "Cage," a twelve-string instrument for "Crump," and an electric guitar for "Cage, *passim*." But BillyCom is quite certain this page was written at the very end, after the ink master copies were complete for all the movements. The first three movements were all conceived for BillyCom's Gibson, which has a mellow sound (for "Cotten"), steel strings ("for Crump"), and the sturdiness required for some of the preparations ("Cage"). It was only when BillyCom heard "Crump" on Michael Cedric Smith's very refined, nylon-stringed instrument that he began to consider using different instruments, rather than merely different techniques and preparations. In making the other three movements—especially "Cage, *passim*"—that option came to the fore, with the resulting latitude suggested on the eventual title page. But it was BillyMus who encouraged Stefan to explore his multitude of instruments; and both Billys were astonished at the pluralist variety that resulted. From 1981 to 2014, a single guitar had first accumulated physical and performative transducers to produce multiple sonic results, then (when that proved insufficient) divided itself into three closely related instruments, and ultimately distributed itself over at least a dozen physically differentiated agents performed with even more differentiated techniques and transducers.

The third phase of the project—*Footnotes* (the recording)—extended from September 2014, when Jez, Stefan, and BillyMus entered the studio, to 2017, when editing was complete. In the studio, another process of disintegration occurred, as it usually does: the six movements were broken into 391 takes that ranged from single sounds to continuities of several minutes. These were further partitioned during editing (again, as is conventional), as takes were trimmed or chopped into an estimated 800 fragments. Yet, at the same time, a process of aggregation had already begun: each of these fragments melded diverse agencies—composition, performer, instrument, technology—into a single, irreducible alloy. Each occupied a single point in the matrix of possibilities, and each would *always* occupy that point: each could only be itself, a single gene with unchanging properties. These elemental fragments were then edited together, combined into longer and longer continuities that in turn became fixed and immutable. In effect, the genes were sequenced into longer strings of musical DNA that were themselves conjoined; and when these reached certain requisite lengths, they were cut loose: the six movements of *Footnotes* (the recording) were given life as distinct individuals. In each, all the fluidity and diversity in the composition and performance phases was frozen into an unchanging form; as individuals, they were irredeemably blessed or cursed by the specific values their creators had given them.

In the fourth phase of the project these individuals were clothed, coiffed, and situated, given a home both temporal and geographical. Each was assigned a name, a history, and memories, and these were designed to convey each movement's ostensible nature to anyone who might encounter it. This, the final phase, overlapped the earliest studio work and extended to October 2018. It drew on new, alternate pluralisms: post-production processing that ranged from the mundane (equalisation, reverberation) through the eclectic (noise, found recordings, outré transformations) to the extraordinary (mediated acoustic reproduction and re-recording). These were chosen, ordered, and applied in a series of experiments, much as one might select, sort, and try on items of apparel. Once made, however, each choice established a new, fixed aggregate on which the next set of alternatives was tested: with this equalisation, which compression? with this hat, what scarf? More than once a later choice required disaggregating or transforming earlier fixed entities: equalisation was readjusted *after* materials had been equalised, processed, and bound together; the underwear was changed *after* the hat was selected. At the end, in their final forms and fully clothed, the six individuals were given life stories and sent out into the world. The stories drew on familiar tropes—the solitary artist, the unrecognised folk artist, the amateur experimentalist—with sufficient detail added, we hoped, to allow the six created individuals to pass as found musical discoveries. Their creators watched carefully as they entered society, and when the mask slipped (think of Eliza Doolittle at the races), they were brought back into the studio for further adjustment.[25]

On the surface, this history is fully consistent with conventional composition-performance-recording projects. A score is created; it has ambiguities that require the performer to choose from a field of possibilities; once chosen, the sound is captured in digital form in a series of takes or excerpts; these are fragmented and then recombined into longer artefacts; these artefacts are transformed in various

25 "Passing" is the subject of countless narratives, both fictional and historical: women passing for men, black passing for white, age passing for youth. For one of thousands of examples, see Martha A. Sandweiss, *Passing Strange* (2009). But the identities in *Footnotes* resemble more closely narratives about aliens or robots passing for human: Asimov's *I, Robot*; Ridley Scott's *Blade Runner*, or even Robert Louis Stevenson's *Dr. Jekyll and Mr. Hyde*.

ways; and the result is disseminated. But *Footnotes* differs in two significant ways. First, at every stage of the process the fields of possibilities are far more vast than is conventional. Indeed, in some cases there are fields of fields, multiple possibilities for the domain itself; thus, in choosing where an individual is situated, the first selection is from a large field of domains (church, home, club, concert hall . . .), each of which calls up different particulars—and all this is subject to change. ("Crump" was first placed in a nightclub, then moved to an outdoor festival.) Second, selection from these fields of possibilities is based on entirely different criteria than usual. Conventional recordings seek to recombine genetic fragments in such a way that the DNA, in essence, clones a stipulated or real musical performance, which itself seeks to give life to an organism whose makeup, it is assumed, is inherent in the score. *Fidelity* to *reality* is the overriding criterion, even if definitions of those concepts vary; the perfect recording cannot be differentiated from a live performance by a blindfolded listener. In *Footnotes*, however, the criteria explicitly disavow such fidelity; on no account is the listener to hear a concert performance by Stefan Östersjö of a score by William Brooks. Rather, the perfect recording is one that convinces the listener of a wholly fictional narrative: this or that movement was recorded in the field or at a festival, in 1950 or in 1971, by a guitarist or a composer; and the narratives for different movements must not intersect in any way whatsoever. Conventional recordings purport to be history but are really stories; *Footnotes* is a collection of stories that actually share a single history.

1.4.3. Analogy

In her seminal text *The Imaginary Museum of Musical Works* (1992), Lydia Goehr draws on an eighteenth- and nineteenth-century metaphor to situate the concept of "the work" historically and culturally. The metaphor—a "museum" in which musical works are stored for posterity, as artefacts and artworks are stored—makes a historian neither a scholar nor a storyteller, but rather a curator whose task is primarily to sort, label, and order. The model that emerges is a Copernican universe, in which objects orbit around more powerful objects, and those around still more powerful ones, until the musical universe appears in regular, unchanging glory. The composer is the Creator, the maker of many works, many worlds. Each work is a sun; around it orbits planetary bodies—manuscripts, versions, editions—and surrounding the whole is a kind of Oort cloud of performances, some of which approach the planets or even, occasionally, impact them. The regulating power is the gravitational force of the work, bestowed by the Creator, which allows the whole to operate in harmony, with life emerging on the planets and excitement created by the passage of comets.[26]

Footnotes stands apart from this analogy and the tradition it represents. There is no single Creator, no sun, no regulating force. Rather than a heliocentric system of bodies, *Footnotes* is more like a galactic cloud, a Horsehead Nebula, largely dark, and visible as a whole only from a vast distance. In the nebula, gases, dust,

26 A similar but far more nuanced construction, based on geology rather than astronomy, can be found in Paulo de Assis, *Logic of Experimentation* (2018); see especially chapter 1, section 6.

and small and greater bodies swirl unpredictably, each mote arising from the acts of an indefinitely large number of Creators. Each mote attracts and repels, and the behaviour of the whole is complex beyond calculation; but over time, materials aggregate, and at a certain moment the aggregation is sufficient to make the body visible: a star is born, identified, and begins to accrue a history, a story that the viewer supplies—perhaps in constellation with other bodies, perhaps as a solitary entity. *Footnotes* comes into being like the Pleiades did, from separate accretions arising from an indefinitely large cloud; each of its six movements is what is left when part of the cloud hangs together while the rest disperses.

Does this make *Footnotes* "postmodern"? By analogy that would suggest that clouds are formed when solar systems disperse, when a mighty cataclysm has shattered the order and the substance of the works that Creators have made. Possibly that is the case; but it seems more plausible to suggest that *Footnotes* is "premodern"—that it results from an early stage of the musical universe, reconstructed from images captured from the very edge of time and space. In the region we occupy, here in the West, in our privileged lives, the cloud of life has indeed formed stars and planets and comets, precessing and passing in an orderly manner. But on a larger scale all is chaotic, a constant process of construction and deconstruction. *Footnotes* asks only that we relish that process, that we take delight in the arbitrary nature of the stories and musics that we create.

Part 2

2.1. Performing authenticity

Following Karen Leistra-Jones (2013), we will in this section discuss authenticity as a performed quality, situated in the practices of musicians as well as in the art world of public performance, concert halls, and the recording industry. Authenticity, in musical performance or composition, "is not inherent in the object or event that is designated authentic but is a socially agreed-upon construct in which the past is to a degree misremembered" (Peterson 1997, 5). The role of misremembering, the discontinuation of tradition, the juxtaposition of incompatible wishes and intentions—all those genuinely human aspects of the composition and performance of music—are at the heart of this discussion, and they are essential in our engagement with the score to *Footnotes* and our recordings of this music.

In our discussion we will be drawing on a ghost from the recent past, a philosophical construction of four types of authenticity proposed by Peter Kivy (1995).[27] Without wanting to return to the original discussion, we find that these four perspectives on authenticity as a socio-cultural construct can be a starting point for unpacking some of the constituting factors. What Kivy calls "authenticity as intention" refers to how a realisation of a composer's intentions for performance is imagined to define its authenticity. "Authenticity as sound" is instead related to the notion of recreating the original sonority of the music, first and foremost through the use of period instruments. "Authenticity as historic practice" is more widely related to the reconstruction and application of the original practice of performers in the context in which the score can be situated. The fourth category is of a different nature, and refers to the personal authenticity of the performer, a contrasting form which Kivy refers to as "the other authenticity." While Kivy aimed to create an opposition between the first three types and the "other" authenticity, we find all four to be relevant for a discussion of *Footnotes* and, in particular, of the process of post-producing the recording of the piece. But before we return to these authenticities and their relation to the emergence of subjectivity in musical creation, a historical backdrop must be considered.

In nineteenth-century European culture, authenticity and theatricality came to serve as polar opposites not only in theatre and music but also in the broader domain of cultural performance, including conceptions of masculinity and femininity (Sennett [1997] 2002; Leistra-Jones 2013). If Liszt can be seen as a manifestation of the theatrical performance ideal, the circle around Johannes Brahms came to represent the emerging ideals of authenticity related to the notion of *Werktreue*, in which "authenticity as intention" is central. The field of tension between authenticity and theatricality can be traced to the notorious

27 Ever since the conflict regarding the early music movement's attempts at reconstructing the historic conditions of performance, launched by the powerful critique from Adorno in 1951, there has been an ongoing debate among scholars and philosophers of music concerning the central issues of authenticity and the relevance of historic performance practices. Until the mid-1990s, with the publication of Richard Taruskin's collection of essays *Text and Act* (1995) and Peter Kivy's *Authenticities* (1995), much of the debate was centred on notions of historical authenticity and authorial intention.

aesthetic war between Wagner and Brahms, with dark expressions of some of its foundations found in Wagner's publication of the anti-Semitic *Das Judentum in der Musik* (1850/1869). Jewishness, for Wagner, represented an inability to authentically experience the true essence of German music and thereby "stood for inauthenticity, deception, and cultural alienation" (Leistra-Jones 2013, 423). Brahms's companion, the violinist Joseph Joachim, was a converted Jew born in Hungary, and his admirers (and Joachim himself) stretched far to provide arguments for his true Germanness. Efforts to create an image of Joachim as the carrier of the spirit of *Werktreue* included an unusual number of publicly disseminated photographs that often depicted Joachim "performing," completely absorbed in his tasks and focusing on his instrument. Leistra-Jones (2013) observes that the exposure time at this stage in the development of photographic technique would not have accommodated the speed of movement required in actual performance. Hence, these photos depicting "performance" are all thoroughly fabricated to create a certain image of the musician, and Leistra-Jones continues by observing how

> in each of these photographs Joachim avoids looking at the camera and its implied spectator. In fact, he is never depicted looking anywhere other than his violin or (occasionally) the musical score. His eyes are cast downward, his face is expressionless, and he seems completely absorbed in the source from which his music emanates, to the exclusion of everything else. These photographs, in other words, are carefully staged so as to leave us with the impression that we are looking in from the outside on a private moment, one in which our observing presence is not only unacknowledged but also fundamentally unnecessary. (Leistra-Jones 2013, 403–4)

Leistra-Jones continues by pointing out how the close affinity between the notion of absolute music and of the ascetic, *werktreue* virtuoso was embodied by Brahms and Joachim. But at the same time, in the moment of performance and the encounter with an audience, a paradoxical situation emerges in which the latter is required to perform an authentic self. Paraphrasing Max Weber, Leistra-Jones notes how the ascetic virtuoso rejects the world but also creates out of it a theatre in which his asceticism can be performed and affirmed by an audience. She concludes that "there is a theatrical dimension to any social identity marked by unusually disciplined levels of restraint and asceticism. The authority to which an 'ascetic virtuoso' aspired, then, was not autonomous but fundamentally relational, existing in an unacknowledged but crucial relationship to an audience" (Leistra-Jones 2013, 418).

Personal authenticity is a key component in the aesthetics of popular music. Tracing its roots back to the early 1930s, Hugh Barker and Yuval Taylor, in their seminal book *Faking It* (2007), identify Jimmie Rodgers's 1931 recording of his *T. B. Blues* as a starting point. They argue that this was the first time that an autobiographical song was recorded by a celebrity singer. From then on, personal authenticity gradually worked itself into the aesthetics of popular music until, in the waves of punk and grunge music, it emerged as either a moral and aesthetic value or, indeed, a requirement. But concurrently with Rodgers's career, other notions of authenticity also emerged in the 1920s, like the "old-timer image of authenticity" (Peterson 1997, 66), with unschooled but skilled performers embodying the rural, uncommercialised, traditional country music. Clearly related to authenticity-as-practice, this also rests on the personal authenticity of these old mountain men or farm hands, supposedly brought straight from the farm into the radio or recording studio. Peterson (1997) takes Fiddlin' John Carson, who lived most of his life in Atlanta working in one of that city's most modern factories, as an example of how this may sometimes be more construction than fact. Similarly, "the singing cowboy and the hillbilly character were deliberately constructed images created selectively out of available symbolic resources and contemporary styles" (Peterson 1997, 68). Personal authenticity is an ambiguous quality in the aesthetic appreciation of music. Certainly, all art is to a certain extent a transformation of lived experience, but not in the sense that a performer should be expected to live through the emotions of a certain character in a play or musical work in the act of performance. Jerrold Levinson (2011, 294) reminds us how "music stands to emotional life not as a literal record or report but more as a general map of the region, some of it unvisited. So even if music reveals emotional life to us, it need not be taken to reveal actual occurrences in any individual's personal history."

Umberto Eco, in his collection of essays entitled *Faith in Fakes* (1986), identifies a strong movement in American popular culture that has a peculiar approach to the notion of authenticity in artworks. In the first chapter, "Travels in Hyperreality," Eco makes a grand tour around the United States, visiting wax museums, amusement parks, and other venues that make the fake more real than reality itself. It should be no surprise to find, for example, a wax figure of Vincent Van Gogh, surrounded by objects such as he once painted them, but also with his face reproduced just as faithfully from his self-portrait, as if he was suffering from some kind of terrible skin disease. At least since the time of the pioneering musicologist and folklorist John Lomax, cultural and personal authenticity has been a strong feature in the aesthetics of popular music. Barker and Taylor (1997) remind us of the pitfalls of the seemingly straightforward notions of authenticity. A brilliant example from their book is the account of how John Lomax constructed the public image of the black singer and guitarist Lead Belly in the 1930s (perhaps modelled on the success of *King Kong* two years earlier). Lead Belly went on tour after he was released from jail in 1934 (after being convicted both for murder in 1918 and for attempted murder in 1930), and Lomax did not allow him to play in the concert suit he himself normally wore. Instead he was marketed as a primitive "negro minstrel" and had to play in prison garb. The headline in the *New York Herald Tribune* went: "Leadbelly, Negro Minstrel: Sweet Singer of the Swamplands Here To Do a Few Tunes Between Homicides" (Barker and Taylor 2007, 11). In Lomax's view, music played by black prisoners represented "authentic" music without "white influence," since they were incarcerated separately from the white convicts. With this in mind, Lomax only allowed Lead Belly to do the more "primitive" tunes in his repertory, thus representing the kind of construction that has been part and parcel of personal authenticity in popular music ever since, faking "authenticity" to produce "the real thing."

What was marketed and appreciated as both culturally and personally authentic was in fact a construction forced on Lead Belly by John Lomax, in turn influenced by a racist view of what was authentic about what Lomax termed "genuine Negro folk songs" (Barker and Taylor 2007, 8–19). In that sense, there is little difference between John Lomax's approach to African American music and the chain of museums that Robert Ripley created, after first presenting odd objects from journeys all over the world in a newspaper cartoon panel in the *New York Globe* that premiered in 1918. In the museums, some objects are originals but many are copies or are said to be authentic duplicates. But this distinction is not of importance in this context: "The authenticity the Ripley's Museums advertise is not historical, but visual. Everything looks real and therefore it is real; in any case the fact that it seems real is real, and the thing is real even if, like Alice in Wonderland, it never existed" (Eco 1986, 16).

The *Footnotes* project encompasses all four authenticities proposed and discussed by Kivy, but they are present in many different manifestations, and perhaps often in ways which were not imagined by the author (as happens every so often in writing). Authenticity-as-intention is most tangible in situations when a performer and a living composer interact in a joint venture towards a reconstruction of the composer's decisions in the act of writing, perhaps thirty years earlier. Similarly, authenticity-as-sound emerges as a central component when trying to establish exactly the sound once imagined and represented in instructions and comments such as "Crump may sound best on a twelve-string instrument," or how to respond to the observation that "Certain of the effects in Cage . . . may be produced more clearly with an instrument with steel strings" (Brooks [1986] 2019). The problem of authenticity certainly informed and sparked much of the composer's engagement with tradition, memory, and transformation, and it was equally central in the reconstructive venture of recording the music of *Footnotes*.

2.2. Tools

In this section, I will unpack some of the choices made before and during the recording sessions regarding the performance of individual movements, with particular attention to the various ways in which these decisions can be related to the authenticities introduced above. Most of the work discussed here was carried out in August and early September 2014, in an intensifying email dialogue with Bill that started at the beginning of September. In section 1.2, above, I have already described how this also involved making test recordings that I would send to Bill as part of that discussion.[28]

An initial challenge in *Footnotes* was to choose an appropriate guitar for each individual movement and for each unit of "Cage, *passim*." The rationale for these choices can and did vary: it could involve convenience (availability of a certain instrument, the possibility of resolving technical challenges) or aesthetic preference—which suggests the entire range of culturally situated notions of

28 These exchanges are reproduced in "SF2.9 A True History of *Footnotes* Perhaps (Part 2)," in the online respository (www.orpheusinstituut.be/en/voices-bodies-practices-media-repository).

authenticity of (historical) sound and of composerly intention—but also it could entail a personal sense of identity with a certain instrument and an association between its sonority and material found in the score. The latter perspective opens up the negotiation of the intentionality of the score and of the instrument. Some instruments were indeed used with reference to historical authenticity: as discussed above, these included the semi-acoustic electric guitar used for unit C of "Cage, *passim*" and the classical concert instrument used in "Cotten, *loc. cit*." Others—the fretless *Glissentar* and the Vietnamese electric guitar used in unit F of "Cage, *passim*"—were chosen for their particular affordances, which I found to resonate with certain characteristics of the score. Instruments afford not merely possibilities but also particular constraints through their inherent resistance.

When I started working on "Cotten," my first choice of instrument was the Line 6 Variax,[29] motivated by convenience: first, the piece demands a lot of barré stops and this would be facilitated by playing an electric guitar, modelling a steel string acoustic, and, second, I did not have a steel string guitar at home that seemed to work with the piece. I decided to make a test recording with a click track, so that I could add in the foot taps ("foot notes," if you will), also notated in the score, at a later time. This followed a model I had previously used successfully for a recording of Per Nørgård's *Papalagi*, a piece that calls for a mechanical clock or a metronome to be playing throughout the piece. For that recording I used a silent timer and click track, adding a beautiful sample of a clock mechanism after recording the guitar part. I imagined creating a similarly "beautiful" foot-tap recording here, to add on to the guitar track. Hence, the choice of instrument in this case was also related to a concept for producing the recording of the piece, including the quality of the foot taps. For this recording, I set the tempo according to the metronome marking in the score (half note equals 132), and I played the piece with the metronome on all the way through. There are some moments of indicated hesitation and rubato in the performance instructions in the score, but I adjusted these in the framework given by the metronome.[30] Clearly, this recording did not concur with authenticity as practice (since that would have demanded the use of a period steel-string guitar); but how did it respond to authenticity as intention? Would the composer now be happy when the piece was represented with the notated pitches at the given tempo (which admittedly gives a rather virtuosic result)? At this stage, when the test recording was made, there was not much to say about "the other authenticity"; I had not even made an attempt to create a version that I could resonate with, and in some ways, I did find this pastiche even harder to embrace than its counterpart, "Cotten, *loc. cit.*" (see above).

29 The Variax series were created by Line 6 starting in 2002. (A photograph of the Variax guitar is available in the online repository, file "SF3.18 Variax guitar.") They were the first electric guitars to successfully model the sound of specific guitars and other instruments. The bridge of a Variax electric guitar has an individual piezo electric pickup for each string. The instrument's electronics converts each of these six signals to a digital signal and digitally processes each to emulate the selected sound. Since the system processes the strings separately, it can model the effects that one string of a target emulation might cause on another. It can also shift individual string pitches to digitally create alternate tunings instead of pitch-shifting all strings at once.

30 Again, the Variax is a very light instrument to play and on this instrument, the piece can easily be played at the indicated speed.

In response to my test recording, on 9 September, Bill replied in another email saying that, while he had never heard the piece played in the given tempo before, this now gave him some "pause . . . in the sense that the virtuosity and dexterity somewhat works against the 'historically informed' 'amateur' field-recording quality that we're after." He went on to say, "I wonder if I set the tempo too high? How would you feel about dropping it back to somewhere around 120? So that you can play a bit more heavy-handedly—with, for instance, the bass notes?" (Email, WB to SÖ, 9 September 2014). But Bill was also not too convinced by the virtual Western guitar in the track, and said he "did always imagine a bigger, heavier sound (Lead Belly, Doc Watson, that sort of thing). Of course, most of those guys were flat-picking, and Elizabeth Cotten herself is more soft and subtle . . ." and he concluded by exclaiming: "Gosh, this really IS an exercise in historical re-creation . . . as in: what WAS I thinking???!!" (ibid.). Hence, so far, our exploration of authenticity as sound and as intention had only led to further questions regarding how to shape the piece in the recording.

Other initial recordings made in Malmö in August 2014 made it all the way onto the final master, as discussed above in section 1.2. Another instance in this series of initial experiments was my work on unit I of "Cage, *passim*." On 6 September, I sent a test recording of this unit to Bill, explaining that I had chosen "to record it with a steel stringed sound" but that "it demands a small fretboard to make some chords possible. Hence I tried it on a Godin electric guitar which also outputs a kind of steel stringed 'acoustic' signal" (Email, SÖ to WB, 5 September 2014).[31] This email, sent in the afternoon, launched a series of conversations that evidence an interpretative process in which authenticity-as-intention sometimes was very present. In these, we find a composer trying to recall the decisions he once took and the rationale behind them, and a performer very obviously seeking to identify the nature of these intentions and make them the grounds for further decisions regarding the recording. My initial question was typical of any initial reading of a score: the choice of tempo. Bill found the tempo to be too fast, suggesting that it be thought of as a "kind of a dignified 'andante,'" and he further suggested that, with a slower tempo, the rests in individual lines could be more clearly articulated: "I can't remember now exactly what the compositional method was, but it had something to do with splices and overlays. (I can't remember the source material either!—but then, it was thirty years ago!) Lines and phrases that have expressive potential (or expressive 'reality') just get chopped off—others crash into the scene" (Email, WB to SÖ, 6 September 2014). In the ensuing conversation, Bill made reference to intentions for performance that at times counter the letter of the score (suggesting, for instance, that the three sections should be experienced as in three tempi, while the modulations actually imply that the basic pulse remains the same through the shifts of metre), also adding that he thought he remembered "that, writing it, I was hoping for a kind of lopsided feel in the last section" (ibid.) But then in the next email he

31 Two small technical corrections followed immediately; the final version can be found in the online repository, file "SF3.19 *Footnotes*, 'Cage, *passim*,' unit I, ver2," together with the full email exchange in "SF3.9 A True History of Footnotes Perhaps (Part 2)." The score for this unit is also included there; see file "SF3.20 *Footnotes*, 'Cage, *passim*,' unit I (score)."

backed away from that reading, having discovered that in other respects there was convincing evidence that he should mistrust his recollections. However, many of his observations were carefully integrated into the new recording that was made some days later, which became the track which was ultimately integrated into the final continuity of “Cage, *passim*.”

But the movement that would most of all drive us towards a search for the composer’s intentions was “Cage.” Furthermore, this search was to launch a series of events that linked the questions raised by this score also to the recordings of “Crump” and “Cotten.”

The score to “Cage” very beautifully incorporates the rationale of the title for the entire cycle, replete as it is with footnotes that explain how the preparation of the guitar should be carried out (figure 3.4).

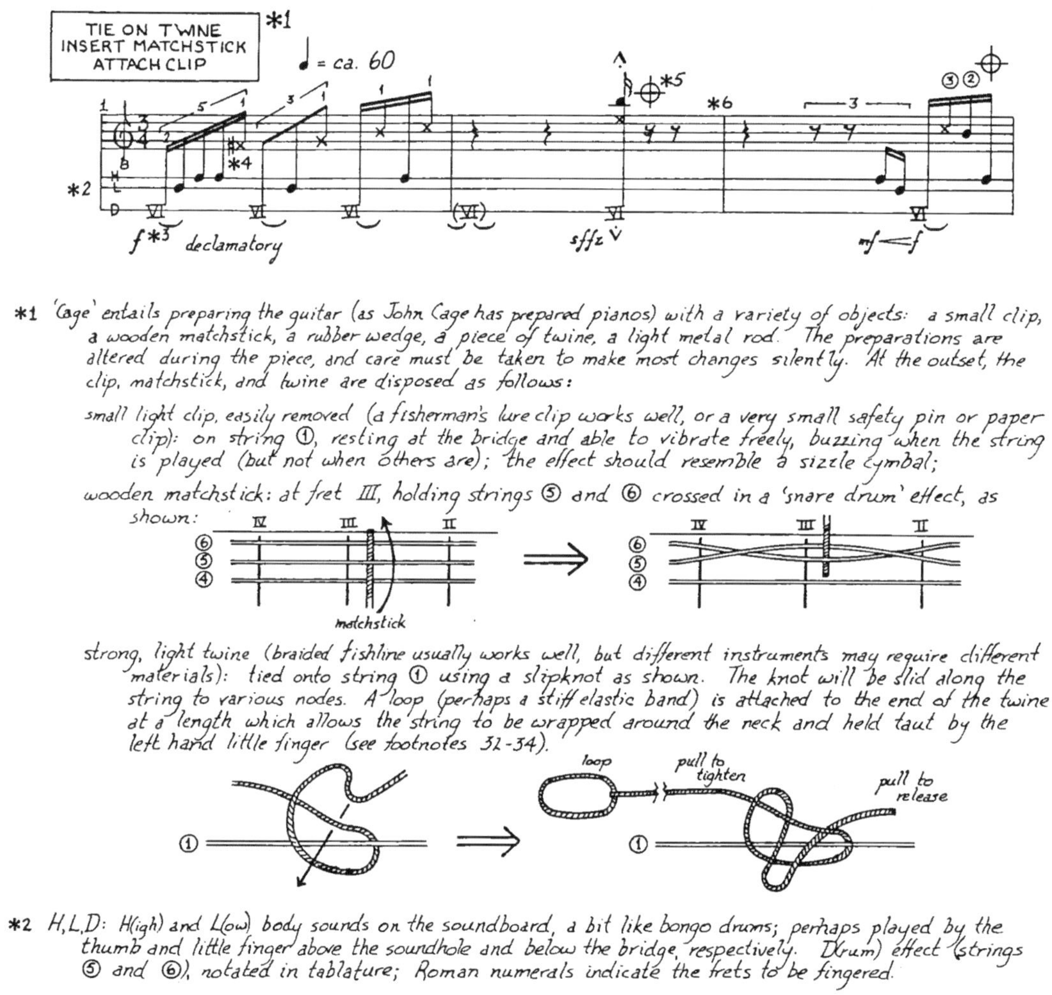

Figure 3.4.

Figure 3.4. “Cage,” bottom of page 1.

While these instructions are clear and even given with some illustrative drawings, the initial problem remained how to create the originally intended sound. Despite the detail, I was struggling to figure out the exact quality of some of the objects used for preparing the guitar. In particular, it was very hard to acquire twine or fishing line that would be suitable for the preparation of the first string, around which twine should be tied in order to bring out certain harmonics. I contacted Bill regarding this, and he struggled to remember the exact nature of these objects, which drove him to excavate file drawers and boxes in search for the original tools, but with little success.

When we met in York to start the recording sessions, we also agreed that it would be interesting to have a look at the guitar that Bill had at the time when he wrote the piece. It was a steel-string acoustic instrument and we were hoping it might be suitable for recording "Cotten," resolving the issues discussed above.[32] At the same time we were well aware that this instrument had been kept in its case for nearly thirty years without being played. We first made sure to have new strings prepared for it, the day when Bill brought it over from his house. We opened the guitar case in Bill's office at the university, and I spent a bit of time shifting strings on the instrument. Thereafter, we were meaning to head off for dinner. But, in a sudden shift of fate, when we were to leave, Bill's keys turned out to be missing. He walked all the way to his house and back searching for the keys on the ground (and of course checking whether they were still in the lock of the front door), but without success. Upon return and in increasing frustration (and hunger, since we had already meant to be having dinner at this point) we sat down in his office to consider what to do next. At this moment, Bill moved over to the guitar case to have another look at his old guitar, and when doing so he also opened the little storage for strings and other tools. A magic discovery happened, which held the key to the questions raised by the instructions for the preparations in "Cage": in the guitar case was not only a complete set of all the preparations for "Cage" but also, and mysteriously so, Bill's house keys![33]

32 Bill's guitar was a Gibson J-45, first introduced under a different name in 1934, renamed in 1942, and still in production today. The serial number for Bill's instrument indicates it dates from the mid-to-late 1960s. (Pictures of the instrument and its serial number can be found in the online repository, files "SN3.21 Bill's Gibson guitar" and "SN3.22 Bill's Gibson serial number.") Photographs confirm that this model was played by Elvis Presley, Bob Dylan, and a host of other folk and traditional musicians, so claiming authenticity for it in playing "Cotten" is not unreasonable. However, Elizabeth Cotten herself played a Martin, now at the Smithsonian (https://americanhistory.si.edu/collections/search/object/nmah_606741), and moreover she inverted it (see https://www.youtube.com/watch?v=N5MTbScgKVE), fingering with the right hand and picking with the left. Authenticity to that degree was clearly unattainable, nor did Bill ever try playing "Cotten" on an inverted instrument. We are indebted to Matt Redman for much of this information (email, Matt Redman to WB, 15 April 2019).

33 Bill found the whole incident so amusing that he insisted that we reconstruct it for video the next morning. That clip is in the online repository, file "SF3.23 Discovering the preparations for 'Cage.'" A photograph of the original preparations, exhumed from their encasement, can also be found there (file "SF3.24 Original preparations for 'Cage'").

Just as we had suspected, using the original metal rod and twine produced results that were different in quality to those produced by the preparations that I had managed to collect; all issues with "Cage" were immediately resolved. We did indeed decide to record "Cotten" on Bill's Gibson, also driven by the knowledge that this was the instrument on which the music had been composed thirty years earlier.[34] But the instrument was to provide still more input in the recording process when our focus moved to the blues pastiche titled "Crump."

For this piece, Bill and I had a number of different initial ideas, including using a semi-acoustic electric guitar,[35] but on 31 August I wrote to Bill saying that I had just "been trying Crump on the 12-string today and I realize that this is how it should be recorded . . . You get a beautifully singing tone on the slide stuff" (email SÖ to WB, 31 August 2014). Also, I could see how the octave doubling, which characterises this instrument, would bring out the rhythmic complexity, created through the layering of materials that results from the left-hand trajectories over the fretboard with the slide. While the choice of a twelve-string guitar for a blues would be typical enough, this decision turned out to challenge several notions of authenticity once we found ourselves in the recording studio.

I was to record on a borrowed instrument, since flying to the UK with something like eight instruments did not seem feasible. Hence, I had not tried the instrument before the day of the recording. To my great discontent, when I started playing the opening bars on this new instrument, I realised that tapping on the fretboard ("hammering-on"), required in the opening, resulted in all the wrong pitches when compared to the letter of the notation. Footnote 4 on the first page of the piece explains this passage as follows: "The right hand damps all strings at the bridge; the left-hand, hammering on with maximum force at the fret indicated, produces a thin but clear pitch from behind the fret. (The tuning of these pitches is eccentric and is only approximated in the notation)" (see figure 3.5).

34 It was a somewhat heavy instrument to play, and it would have been much appreciated to spend a day or two practising, to figure out how to better deal with some of its eccentricities, but the way we had set the project up, this was not possible.

35 This idea was discarded, since knocking on the body, which is required by the performance instructions on the first page, would be very unclear on such an instrument.

Crump

*1 A metal cap is worn on the left hand little finger and used to play strings ① and ② (and occasionally ③) in bottleneck style.

*2 Rhythms can and should be distorted ad libitum when the steady blues pulse weakens, becoming more secure when it is re-established; the bottleneck melodies, in particular, can be inflected in rhythm as well as pitch. Rhythms have been written with precision only to ensure a certain kind of irregularity; in performance all should sound spontaneous rather than practiced. Imagine a drunken bluesman, with oddly mistuned guitar, gradually rousing himself to more and more forceful gestures and ending with a flourish.

*3 H: Body sound, relatively high but resonant; perhaps made with the side of the right hand thumb, just above the soundhole.

*4 [note symbol] or [note symbol]: The right hand damps all strings at the bridge; the left hand, hammering-on with maximum force at the fret indicated, produces a thin but clear pitch from behind the fret. (The tuning of these pitches is eccentric and is only approximated in the notation.)

*5 [note symbol] or [note symbol]: The lower strings (⑤ and ⑥, and ④ briefly) are damped with the heel of the right hand. All such muted pitches are played with the ball of the thumb.

*6 Pitches produced conventionally in measures 4-12 must be played extremely quietly, so that their volume and timbre are consistent with those of the hammered, muted and bottleneck pitches.

*7 All pitches on this staff are played bottleneck style, with the capped little finger, on strings ①, ②, and sometimes ③. In general, the glissandi which will always occur between pitches should be savored; scoops, slow shakes, and other inflections characteristic of blues guitarists may be added ad libitum, at first sparsely but by the end of the piece with exuberance.

Figure 3.5.

Figure 3.5. “Crump,” first page of score.

Because the neck of this twelve-string guitar differed in length from the instrument used by the composer when composing the piece, the pitches produced behind the fret also differed. (The length only affects the pitches that result on the left-hand side of the fingered pitch.) The first question for a performer in this situation is how "eccentric" can the resulting pitch be? Did this phrasing allow for "any" resulting pitches and sets of intervals? I was strongly convinced about the overall musical result of using a twelve-string guitar, but the pitches the instrument produced in the opening page were a major concern. But by now I also had access to the very six-string guitar that the composer had used thirty years earlier. I immediately got this instrument out, and it (of course) produced exactly the pitch structure notated in the score. However, this discovery only proved that I was facing an artistic choice that appeared to have no simple solution. I was facing an immediate conflict between *authenticity as intention* and *authenticity as sound* (referring to the higher intentions of the composer and to the original sound, such as produced with original instruments, respectively).

I was not keen to perform the entire piece on the Gibson, since the twelve-string guitar captured qualities in the composition that I found more essential than the original sonority of the composer's guitar. In addition, moreover, the second footnote on the title page states that "Crump may sound best on a 12-string instrument." Hence, in the choice between authenticity-as-intention and authenticity-as-sound, choosing a twelve-string guitar could be viewed as instantiating the former and seemed additionally to hold several convincing musical opportunities. Still, we needed to find a solution: how were we to make a recording of the piece that did not have all the wrong pitches in the opening page? That is when I got the idea of working with multi-tracking. If the knocking, which opens the piece, were to be performed on the twelve-string guitar in order to retain a continual sonic identity throughout the piece, the initial hammering-on could instead be recorded separately on the six-string guitar. This solution, however, could perhaps be thought to be in conflict with Kivy's category of *authenticity-as-practice*, since it would not have been available in recordings made at the supposed time of creation. However, it seemed not so hard to accept the fraud of overdubbing a supposed solo recording when (a) it was not carried out with the aim of simulating the mastery of technical difficulty and (b) the aim of the overdubbing was, in fact, to truthfully represent the sound structure intended by the composer.

Two guitars were also used—in a very different way—in the recording of "*ibid.*" This piece has a multi-layered structure: the score consists of fully notated polyphonic aggregates and, across the piece, letters specifying certain pitches, with brackets indicating the span in which these should be played (figure 3.6). Footnote 2 provides instructions for how this should be carried out:

> The pitch indicated is played as a natural or artificial harmonic the number of times indicated anywhere between the brackets. (Thus the pitch E is to be sounded as a harmonic five times between the beginning of measure 1 and halfway through measure 5.) The pitch may be sounded in any octave, but the octave must remain the same for all repetitions. The harmonics, while clearly audible, should be slightly

softer than the surrounding texture. The addition of the harmonics should not be improvised, but rather planned and practiced in advance. In some cases some ingenuity may be required to find a solution that is idiomatic and appropriate. (Brooks [1986] 2019)

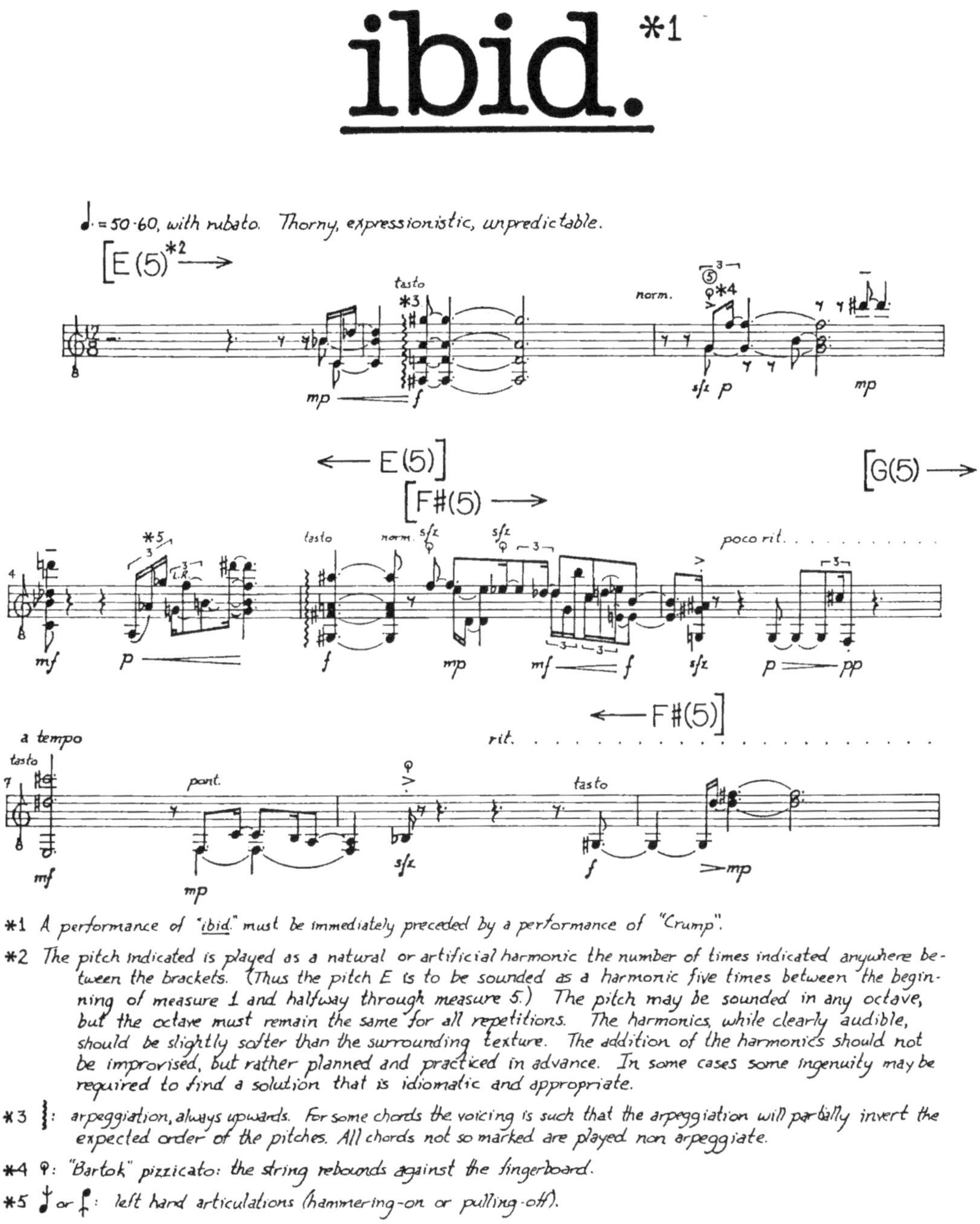

Figure 3.6.

Figure 3.6. "*ibid.*," first page of score.

But it is in fact not quite idiomatically possible to find harmonics that can be allowed to ring in many of these instances. That impossibility gave me the idea of tuning a second guitar to a scordatura that would allow me to play all the eleven tones indicated in the score on natural harmonics. By placing the second guitar in front of me, and a bit to the right, I could conveniently shift between plucking the guitar I was holding normally, and the second guitar, sounding the harmonics. To me, this arrangement appeared to be the most convincing way of realising the intentionality of the score, although the actual intention of the composer may have been different. In this case, then, *authenticity-as-intention* aligns perfectly with *authenticity-as-sound*, though it occupies a more ambiguous position regarding *authenticity-as-practice.*

2.3. Capturing time and place

> Most sound recordings are representations of space, and the spatial perception of sound is a fundamental way in which people make sense of their surroundings. Recordings contain information about the spaces in which they were made, whether or not the represented space is made explicit in, for example, representing the recognizable acoustics of a concert hall. The opposite can occur when spaces are sonically decontextualized, as with exceptionally close microphone placement, inverted or counterintuitive volume relations among elements in a mix, in the fragmentation of sounds through editing, and in any of a multitude of sound-processing effects. (Grubbs 2014, 55)

All the acoustic recordings for these productions were made over a single five-day period in September 2014. They were made using typical recording equipment of the present era: Schoeps, DPA, and Neumann microphones, Focusrite amplifiers and a Macintosh computer running Cockos Reaper. This combination afforded a high signal-to-noise ratio, a broad and uncoloured frequency response (save for the designed characteristics of the microphones), and vanishingly low levels of distortion and inter-channel contamination. The recording location was the Trevor Jones studio in the Department of Music at the University of York. The studio has a variable acoustic configuration that enables the reverberation time to be varied and it can be set so that the reverberation time (RT_{60}) is as low as 0.2 seconds (Myatt, Larkin, and Malham 2010). Additionally, it is a non-uniform shape without parallel walls. These characteristics mean that it behaves as a high-quality "neutral" recording space, typically used in pop production. Thus the actual time and place of the raw materials assembled for the production process are contemporary and neutral; there are no circumstances that necessarily place them at an earlier point in time or in a specific environment. Time and place as heard in the final audio artefacts are suggested by subsequent processing and mixing. The text that follows (immediately and at other points in this and the following sections) describes some of that processing and the reasoning and the technical and technological precedents that underpin it. Time exists across decades of recording practice, but also across milliseconds in the deviated movements of a record stylus. Places can be different geographical regions, the points between which medium radio waves travel, or the places in a record's groove. All these create meaningful context and meaningfully change the materials that we originally captured in those first recording sessions, five years ago.

Two-channel stereo capture techniques consist of one or more of the following: an array of (usually identical) microphones that have a particular positioning and orientation in relation to each other, intended to capture a general soundfield within a recording space, and sets of individual "spot" microphones intended to capture a specific sounding object or some radiating part of it. Arrays exist somewhere on a continuum between coincident, where the microphone capsules occupy the same position in space (as far as is physically possible), and spaced, where they are separated, typically by a distance of more than thirty centimetres. For coincident arrays the microphones must have a non-uniform directional response and be rotated at different angles relative to each other. Without this difference in orientation and response direction, the signal captured at each microphone will be identical and the array will behave as a single microphone with a monophonic output. This constraint does not exist for spaced microphones since they are capturing the soundfield at different points in space and there will be differences in the time-of-arrival of acoustic signal components that are dependent upon the position and size of the sources of those components, relative to each microphone's position, within the recording space. For truly coincident microphones the only difference between the captured signals will be differences in signal level due to the different orientations of the non-uniform directional pick-up patterns.

Microphones with uniform directivity (known as "omnidirectional") directly capture the instantaneous pressure at their diaphragm. Bidirectional microphones, on the other hand, capture the difference in pressure between the front and rear of their diaphragm, resulting in a sensitivity that falls with falling frequency. Mechanical and/or electrical compensation is required to correct this, and this is challenging at the lowest audible frequencies. For this reason, omnidirectional microphones, particularly in terms of low-frequency capture, are sometimes preferred over figure-of-eight microphones or microphones from the cardioid family (with unidirectional directivity arising from a combination of omnidirectional and figure-of-eight patterns). However, omnidirectional microphones constrain the choice of stereo array to spaced microphones, and these do not offer such an accurate translation of source positions and widths from the recording scene to the phantom image that is created between loudspeakers. Just as verisimilitude and definition are not necessarily correlated with each other, the same may also be true for the accuracy of spatial representation of a soundfield. Many have expressed a preference for the less spatially accurate sound of spaced arrays (particularly the three-microphone tree of Decca records), arguing that such spatial presentation is more enveloping and three-dimensional even if is less spatially accurate in terms of positioning and width of sources.

This debate over the relative merits of different approaches to spatial capture has run through commercial stereo recording since the middle of the last century and therefore affects many of the histories we have sought to create. It was Alan Blumlein, working at EMI, who recognised that level differences should be captured to produce between two loudspeakers an accurate "phantom" image of sources in front of a microphone array. The coincident arrangement that he proposed consisted of two figure-of-eight microphones at ninety degrees to each other. Because the original Blumlein pair picks up energy equally from all directions and offers excellent imaging of point sources it has earned a reputation as a (or even "the") purist technique (Lipshitz 1986). Blumlein realised that, when replayed over loudspeakers, the captured level differences would be converted into timing differences between the ears that closely corresponded with those that would have been produced by those actual sources in those actual positions. His patent was published in 1933 (Torick 1998, 29).

Meanwhile, at Decca, the three-microphone tree was devised and employed (Gray 1986). This pragmatic adaptation of their method for recording monophony enabled them to use the same microphones, and it was preferred by some engineers and listeners for the sound quality of the recorded sources and for spatial impression, even though it lacked the image accuracy of the Blumlein pair. Compromises between coincident and spaced configurations included the pairs developed at NOS (Holland Radio, two cardioid microphones at 90 degrees, spaced by 30 cm) and ORTF (French Radio, two cardioids at 110 degrees, 170 mm spacing). Despite the imaging accuracy of Blumlein pairs, many successful recordings were made using near-coincident, spaced, and multi-microphonic methods. In addition, studies of listener perception of multi-channel audio (including that from Blumlein and spaced pairs) have demonstrated that ascribing quality is a more complex process than simply preferring the most accurate and stable imaging between the speakers, a view supported (though often for completely different reasons) by historians of technology such as Sterne (2012).

Given these strands of perceptual and acoustic science, audio engineering, and philosophy that have woven themselves through the era of commercial sound recording, and given the multiple times and places suggested by *Footnotes*, we chose to use a variety of techniques without crowding the performer with an overwhelming number of microphones. Two DPA 4003 omnidirectional microphones were used for spaced capture. With fewer microphones used, more time could be spent attending to the quality of signal that is captured by each. A pair of Schoeps Colette microphones was used for coincident capture: a forward-facing cardioid and sideways-facing figure-of-eight (in what is known as a mid-side configuration). A single Neumann KM-184 functioned as a cardioid spot microphone. But—again consistent with the underlying multiplicity—flexibility was exercised within this over-arching approach. Typically, the spaced DPAs were just at each end of the guitar, the Schoeps pair was pointing towards the body of the guitar, to the right of the sound hole (enabling the cardioid to act as a spot microphone on the guitar body), and the Neumann was placed in front of the fretboard. However, deviations from these standard positions were designed to enhance or focus on particular aspects of the instrumental output that were suited to the demands (as articulated by composer and performer) of particular movements.

The discussions around these variations in microphone positions are the first points during the production process at which ideas about the suitability of particular sonic presentations began to emerge, along with their relation to time and space. For example, the session notes from the recording of unit D of "Cage, *passim*" include "harsh sound: bright, close, maybe a little clipped," "vivid stereo," "all mics were moved much closer for this," and "Stockhausen, 1960s." The notes also contain specific ideas for balancing the multitrack recordings down to stereo, which was the first stage of post-production. For example, from the notes for "Crump": "six-string overdubs: more DPA, less Schoeps & more KM-184 to keep the brightness but maintain distance" (compared with the capture of the twelve-string guitar). However, despite the varying configurations, we retained the possibility of choosing between, or combining, array types at later stages. In the event, however, the rough mixes for each of the pieces that were created at these sessions to provide stereo listening copies for the creation of edit maps were never changed, and they became the final mixes of the acoustic guitar recordings that were made during the September 2014 sessions.

For two movements, contact microphones were attached to the body of the guitar. These were deployed in situations where it was felt that it would be useful to collect vibrational components of signals travelling through the guitar that would not necessarily propagate well through air away from the body and, therefore, would not be captured well by the other microphones. In "*ibid.*," such microphones were used to gain greater flexibility in the presentation of playing methods such as the Bartók pizzicato. However, what had been captured with the acoustic microphones turned out to be sufficient to adequately and satisfyingly represent the sound, so the contact microphones were not used in the final mix. The other movement was unit A from "Cage, *passim*"; here, a small amount of the signal from one of the microphones, an AKG C411 L, was introduced into the mix. It offered a duller, yet more strongly resonant, presentation than the acoustic microphones. Large objects where mass dominates stiffness have lower resonant frequencies, so including these characteristics within the final balance, albeit subtly, influences perception of the guitar, affording it a greater solidity and presence.

These captures, with their acknowledgement of the trajectories of sound recording technique, technology, and aesthetic, but also with a pragmatism that recognised the dangers of delving into rigid historical recording practices (as discussed in Section 1.4), yielded the tangible audio media that were the products of our recording sessions in September 2014. These were the artefactual starting points for the rest of the project: multiple prototype masks with the potential for further shaping, colouring, and dressing, even though, at that stage, it was far from clear exactly what appearances the movements might finally assume.

2.4. Fables and fictions

By October 2016 all of *Footnotes* had been edited, and many of the edited recordings had been processed. Seventeen individuals (five distinct movements and the twelve units of "Cage, *passim*") had been given new identities and new histories. They had new and separate homes, safe and secure, and these could be visited individually; but the seventeen individuals could also be brought together in a shared location that allowed them to be appreciated as a socio-historical totality, a kind of ethnological unit. A new phase of the project began: testing the viability of these new identities. Could they "pass"? Or were their "real" origins, their "true" natures still discernible?

Testing was entangled with marketing: would these new identities be able to make their way in the world? Could they be sold to a public—and if they were in fact "sold," did this constitute fraud or fiction? Were they more like a collection of short stories or more like a series of deliberately deceptive government "white papers"?[36] A new *persona* was required, and so BillyCom and BillyMus were joined by BillyMark: WB reinvented himself as an expert in market research. BillyCom was the ghost of *Footnotes* past, and BillyMus of *Footnotes* present; BillyMark was the spectre of *Footnotes* to come.

Market research commenced on 19 October 2016, when BillyMark presented the then-current state of "Cotten, *loc. cit.*" to a group of postgraduate students at the University of York. Post-production of this movement thus far had entailed applying an overlay of radio static to a subtly altered guitar recording. The processed recording was presented to the students with no preliminaries whatsoever, and the students were asked to comment on any aspects they wished. One group of students seized on the noise but were puzzled by the intention: "I don't know whether it's an electronic track or whether it's trying to reference a sort of older, lo-fi recording—like [a] field recording," one responded. Another focused on the guitar music, independently of the noise, but still heard a kind of distortion in the way the tremolo pattern fades into scrambled notes (see figure 3.7)—whereupon BillyCom whispered in BillyMark's ear that this was indeed part of the composer's intention. But, in the end, the students were receptive but unconvinced: "It sounded a bit like a clean performance on guitar with [a background] track," one summarised. BillyMark decided more market research was needed.

Figure 3.7.

Thus, on 28 October BillyMark offered the track to a class of undergraduates who had been studying the music of Charles Ives under the guidance of BillyMus. Although BillyMark again played the recording with no preliminary explanation,

36 Roughly contemporaneous with the composition of *Footnotes* were, for example, politically sanctioned cover-ups of health hazards, environmental consequences, and economic inequalities; also roughly contemporaneous were Vladimir Nabokov's *Pale Fire* and Jorge Luis Borges's *Ficciones*. These and others blur the boundary between fact and fiction, fiction and fraud; although BillyMus cannot demonstrate a direct influence on the making of *Footnotes*, it is undeniable that BillyCom was very aware of them. In 1972, for example, he had composed an extended music-theatre piece based entirely on Borges's writings.

Figure 3.7. "Cotten, *loc. cit.*," score excerpt.

this group of thirteen subjects had been indirectly prepared by the lecture that had just concluded, in which BillyMus had discussed Ives, quotation, and memory (consistent themes throughout the module) and the nature and extent of Ives's legacy. Perhaps because of that orientation, BillyMark found the reception more gratifying this time: six students offered comments, one of which was "I think of it as a radio being tuned in and out," with another suggesting that "[it's] sort of half-remembered." In this market test, BillyMark had resolved to make a slightly more systematic attempt to gather data; thus, in response to those observations, he asked two specific questions. The first was "how many people thought something about radios or a signal being received?"; in response, seven students' hands were raised, slightly over half the group. In response to the second question, "how many people thought something about memories that weren't quite there?," four hands went up, just under a third of the group.

The next opportunity came two weeks later, on 14 November, at the Orpheus Institute Anniversary Festival. On this occasion each of the research clusters at Orpheus was given an hour to present its work to the festival participants, numbering about thirty-five. The "subjectivity" cluster had four projects (the four large chapters in the present volume), and it briefly summarised three before discussing the details of the fourth—*Footnotes*—more extensively. The *Footnotes* group, in turn, chose to narrow the focus still further by presenting a forty-five-minute account of "Cotten, *loc. cit.*" In the early drafts for this presentation, BillyMark continued as he had been doing: presenting the recording at the outset and without preparation. But in consultation with the entire subjectivity team, he eventually adopted a radically different approach: he introduced BillyCom, who gave a compact description of the original concept, as follows:

> The piece arose from two memories. First, as a ten-year-old boy I used to listen to a big, old analogue radio next to my bed. I had to keep the volume low, since I was supposed to be asleep, and the classical station in New York barely reached my location in New Haven, Connecticut. The signal, then, drifted in and out of focus, sometimes fading completely into static, sometimes quite clear. I too was drifting, and the sound of the static (which even then I thought very beautiful) fused with my fading consciousness: a lovely sense of confusion, loss, and clarity that I still treasure. The second memory is very precise: at the age of eighteen I heard Andrés Segovia play "Recuerdos de la Alhambra," by Francisco Tárrega. It was my first guitar recital, and I'd never heard the piece before. It fascinated me then, and it still fascinates me—the beautiful, chilling precision of Segovia and the magic trick created by the guitar tremolo. (Laws, Östersjö, and Brooks 2016)

Hence, before the track was actually played, the audience had heard: BillyMus give an overview of all six movements; Stefan discuss instruments, agencies, and voices; BillyCom give the description above; Jez discuss the engineering technologies and approaches; and BillyMus, Jez, and Stefan trace the history and decisions required to produce this single track. The audience understood what was intended and what had been done to realise the intention; not surprisingly, by their own report, they heard exactly that, rather than what they might have heard with no preparation. When virtually the same presentation was given again at Orpheus on 22 February 2017, virtually the same result happened. BillyMark duly noted that providing the right orientation prior to playing the recording can substantially clarify the intentions (no surprise there), but he also concluded that far too much information had been provided on these occasions.

Two weeks earlier, on 7 February, BillyMark had presented "Cotten, *loc. cit.*" to a group of about twenty composers at the University of Illinois. This presentation resembled that done for the York undergraduates, in that a purportedly unrelated lecture preceded it, with no other information given before playing the recording. In this case, however, the previous talk concerned time, artefacts, and especially recordings: the disjunction that occurs when the sound-trace arising in a certain place and time is experienced in a different place and time; how one decides *what* is being heard, from *where*, *when*, and *why*. BillyMark's hidden research agenda was to determine what effect that very different prolegomena would have on listeners' reported experiences. And the responses suggested that the effect was to turn the ear towards the background noise; several listeners speculated about the "static"—how and where it was made, and why—but no one commented on the guitar music itself. Moreover, virtually everyone had immediately disassociated the two components: the guitar recording had its own history, and the noise had been subsequently overlaid, for reasons hard to determine.

In five presentations thus far, then, BillyMark had come to feel that certain materials should be provided listeners if the tracks were indeed to "pass" for "authentic." But it also seemed clear that choosing how much and what to say was crucial. With too little information, listeners could be baffled; with too much, they simply marched in step down the road in front of them. Orienting listeners toward technology and the nature of recording created an inclination to fracture the heard material into constituent components; orienting them toward memory and quotation had precisely the opposite effect.

And there the matter rested for over a year. There was work to be done: some recordings had not yet been processed in any way, and others needed adjustments of various kinds. "Cotten, *loc. cit.*" was tweaked again and again, as the team worked to make the integration of noise and guitar more convincing. And the other movements were gradually brought to a conclusion. The compiled six movements were available as early as 13 April 2017, though "Cage, *passim*" was incomplete, and two rounds of critical assessment and adjustments followed. "Cotten, *loc. cit.*" was revisited in three days of post-production in September, when Jez proposed broadcasting the movement so that it could actually be received on vintage radio equipment. That was done in mid-October (see below), when the remaining sections of "Cage, *passim*" were also added; and a new continuity, version four, was distributed on 20 March 2018. Although all were agreed that there was still some fine-tuning to be done, BillyMark arranged for the first test of the complete audio files to take place on 11 April at the Orpheus Institute.

Two questions remained, however: how would the listeners be prepared, if at all; and how would their responses be gathered and assessed? In the two weeks before the audience test, BillyMark wrestled with these; and by 8 April he had reached a decision: he would create "sleeve notes"—fictional accounts that would situate each track in time and place, framing the entirety as the product of archival, musicological research—and he would distribute these on a handout, with substantial blank space provided for listeners to record their thoughts. After playing the full recording, collecting the responses, and soliciting additional conversation, BillyMark would explain the real creative history, and further conversation would follow.

The results were gratifying, though only five listeners elected to respond in writing. One—a historical musicologist and performer—said in conversation that he had been "completely fooled"; several others were taken in at first but gradually became aware of the deception. At least two felt that "Crump" had been the turning point, but only one noticed the clue that BillyMark had infused through the whole: every name mentioned bore the initials JW, WB, or SO. Several made very penetrating, helpful observations about specific movements or about the fictions themselves, and BillyMark and the others resolved to modify both the tracks and the text in response.

Those modifications were made over the next two months; version five of the audio continuity was distributed on 25 May, and slightly rewritten sleeve notes were drafted on 12 June. Both of those were used in a second audience test for York students and staff on 13 June initiated by BillyMark but run primarily by Jez, since many of the listeners were students in music technology degree programmes. Again, five listeners responded in writing, and most were very enthusiastic; because of the attendees' backgrounds, however, the conversation tended to focus on the persuasiveness of the technology, not on the music or the sleeve notes.

One more audience test took place the next autumn, on 9 October, at the University of Illinois, when the same audio and a very slightly modified set of sleeve notes were presented to an audience of about twenty student and staff composers and performers. Only two responded in writing, and those rather minimally; but in conversation it became clear that with a very small handful of exceptions, all there were completely persuaded by the authenticity of the accounts and the tracks. Indeed, when the recording had been played and BillyMark asked for questions and comments, the first several queries had to do with how the purported recordings had been acquired and whether the originals were being stored in archival conditions. Two very experienced staff members confessed that they believed every word; only one, an ethnomusicologist who was very knowledgeable about field recordings, expressed suspicion. Two students who were not taken in singled out one movement as problematic; unexpectedly, this was "Cotten," which had previously raised no alarms. BillyMark noted, however, that the stereo speakers were extremely widely placed, and that possibly this magnified the intrinsic difference between an essentially monophonic guitar and the constructed stereophonic environment.

The series of three tests of the full continuity—each more successful than the last—persuaded BillyMark that an optimal presentation had been reached. Subsequent alterations were made only with LP mastering in mind; version six was distributed on 28 October, and minor adjustments were made thereafter, as pressing approached. The creation of the fictions was complete: the recordings had "passed."

Part 3

3.1. The collaborative self

Much of the foregoing has provided a seemingly objective, "historical" account of the actions undertaken over six years (2013 to 2019) that resulted in the manufacture of an LP that you, the reader, may already have purchased, together with this publication. And, indeed, at the outset, that was the basic intention: "Let's make a recording." But this objective was immediately framed by circumstance: the initial conversations occurred at the Orpheus Institute, which is devoted to artistic research—that is, research in and through musical performance. Was this in fact a research project? It would seem that it might be; and that inclination was furthered when it was additionally framed by the "subjectivity" research cluster, discussed above, in the introduction to this publication. Certainly, the nature of the score and the history of the participants were conducive to a study of subjectivity, seen through the lenses of composition, performance, and recording. And so it was decided: the initial purpose would be placed on a co-equal basis with a second objective: to discover how the various selves and agencies would be constituted and de-constituted in the process of making the recording.

To study that process, it was decided almost immediately, it would be necessary to generate a large quantity of documentation. An email archive was begun, in which all communications pertinent to the project would be assembled. Each stage of the process—each sound file, each edit, each assemblage—would be saved and stored. And, subject to practical constraints, video recordings would be made of actual working sessions. At a later date, then, all this data would be put in order, and a full analysis could be made in order to tease out the construction and deconstruction of the interactive, collaborative selves. That full analysis has yet to be completed, but enough data is available to draw some preliminary conclusions.

3.1.1. Qualitative analysis and stimulated recall

Stimulated recall is a common qualitative research method in education, medicine, and psychotherapy. The term was coined by Benjamin Bloom in 1953, in a study using audio recordings of classroom teaching as stimuli, aiming to allow the student to relive the original experience and give an account of their original thought processes. While Bloom made a selection of clips from the teaching situation, Kagan and colleagues (Kagan and Krathwohl 1967) developed the method further by asking each subject to view the entire documentation and to stop it to identify moments that required comment. Stimulated recall has been used to study collaborative processes in music-making (Bastien and Hostager 1988, 1992, 1996; Bastien and Rose 2014); and in 2009, Stefan Östersjö initiated a collaborative study of interaction between improvising musicians in the Vietnamese/Swedish group The Six Tones as part of an international research project "(Re) Thinking Improvisation" (Frisk and Östersjö 2013). In this research, the design of the stimulated recall studies was especially challenging, due to the intercultural negotiation of the creative process, which was further complicated by the need to translate speech and texts between Vietnamese and English. The study built on repeated coding of the same video documentation of rehearsals and concert performances, during which different constellations of the four members would gradually construct a shared understanding of the interactions within the group and of the collaborative process. In 2010, when David Gorton and Stefan Östersjö began their collaboration (see chapter 1), qualitative analysis of video also became a central method. However, in their first study, which looked at the evolution of *Forlorn Hope* for alto guitar, with a focus on the interaction between the two protagonists in the early working sessions, this analysis was not carried out through stimulated recall but was instead based on joint observation and analysis of verbatim transcriptions as well as of selected video clips. In the second study, however, which is discussed in chapter 1, stimulated recall was used as a central component in a multi-method design (Coorevits et al. 2016). In this case, negotiating a shared understanding between the participating researchers was central to the design of the method; the aim was to identify perceived expressive gestures in Östersjö's performance of Gorton's composition, and the study involved two musicologists who worked together with the two artists. Hence, rather than merely reconstructing an original experience, the repeated exposure to the video documentation in each of these studies had dual objectives: to create a reflexive understanding of the event and, further, to allow the participating researchers to negotiate an intersubjective understanding.

In March 2018 we began applying some of the same techniques—notably, stimulated recall—to the video documentation of *Footnotes*. It is important to note that this analysis, so far limited to "Cotten, *loc. cit.*" and "Crump," was carried out on a selection of samples from the original documentation. The editing prior to the analysis was done by Bill Brooks, who simply compressed the relevant information by deleting all video during which no interaction took place.[37] This material was analysed using Open Coding, an analytical approach drawn from grounded theory.[38] The coding was further defined by drafting detailed annotations that provided a further analysis of each coded instance in the video. These annotations and also the creation and sometimes gradual redefinition of codes were both outcomes of a negotiated, joint understanding between the two researchers.

37 In the type of session documented here, a substantial amount of time is dedicated to waiting—for someone to complete a task at a computer, for a file to render, or for coffee to brew.

38 The aim of the procedure is to let an analytical understanding emerge *from* the data, rather than starting the analysis from a predetermined theoretical grid. In the video analysis, the two researchers would start the playback from the beginning of the selected video material and stop the playback when anything in the recording caught their attention. Using software for organising the video data and the analysis, each such instance can be marked and named, or coded. Through this process, "the researcher discovers, names, defines, and develops as many ideas and concepts as possible without concern for how they will ultimately be used. How the issues and themes within the data relate must be systematically assessed, but such relationships can be discovered only once the multitude of ideas and concepts it holds have been uncovered. Turning data into concepts is the process of taking words or objects and attaching a label to them that represents an interpretation of them" (Benaquisto 2008, 581).

3.1.2. Models and (im)possibilities

In the persona I've called "BillyCom" resides all the baggage associated with composerly authority, authorship, and intention. In that sense the relationship in *Footnotes* between composer and performer (setting aside for now the third component, the sound engineer) would seem to resemble that described in chapter 1, which also concerns the interactions between a composer (David Gorton) and a guitarist (again Stefan Östersjö). Therefore one might expect figure 1.7 (adapted here as figure 3.8) to be a viable representation of the formation of a "discursive voice" in *Footnotes*, just as it is for *Austerity Measures I*.

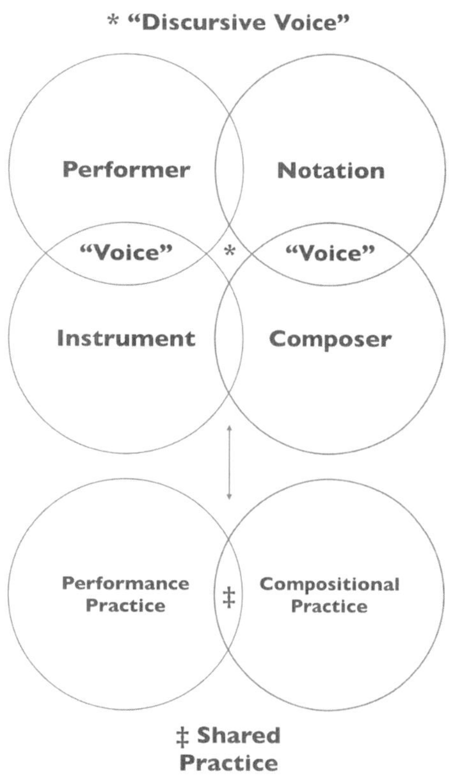

Figure 3.8.

But the two pieces are very different; and hence there are significant differences in the ways in which that diagram can be constituted and function. Crucially, in *Austerity Measures I*, the four agencies at work (performer, notation, instrument, composer) are each uniquely constituted: *one* performer, *one* score, *one* guitar, *one* composer. Furthermore, all are taken as temporally synchronous—that is, assumed to have been created and to operate in a relatively short span of time.

In *Footnotes*, on the other hand, at least two of these agencies are multiple. There are *many* guitars, and there are *many* composers. And the nature of the multiplicity

Figure 3.8. The discursive voice (adapted from chapter 1, figure 1.7).

differs for these two agents: the guitars are synchronous, in the same sense as are all the agents in *Austerity Measures*, while the composers are distributed diachronically, not merely because the composition of the different movements spanned four years but also because the composer is so removed from the present that his composerly authority can only be stipulated after penetrating multiple archival layers. The circles "instrument" and "composer" thus each contain a set of smaller circles (figure 3.9), and each of these interacts with the singular "performer" or "notation" to produce a complex set of "voices," which in turn generate an even more complex set of practices and, ultimately "discursive voices."

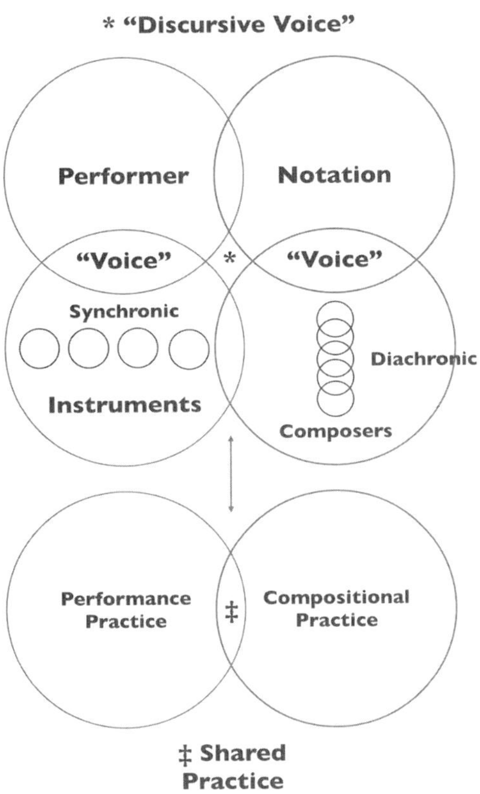

Figure 3.9.

Moreover, part of the intentionality (made explicit in the notation) was that *one* composer would become *many* even in the act of composing. Hence there are not one set of circles contained in "composer"; there are several sets (figure 3.10).

Figure 3.9. Discursive voices: many instruments, many composers.

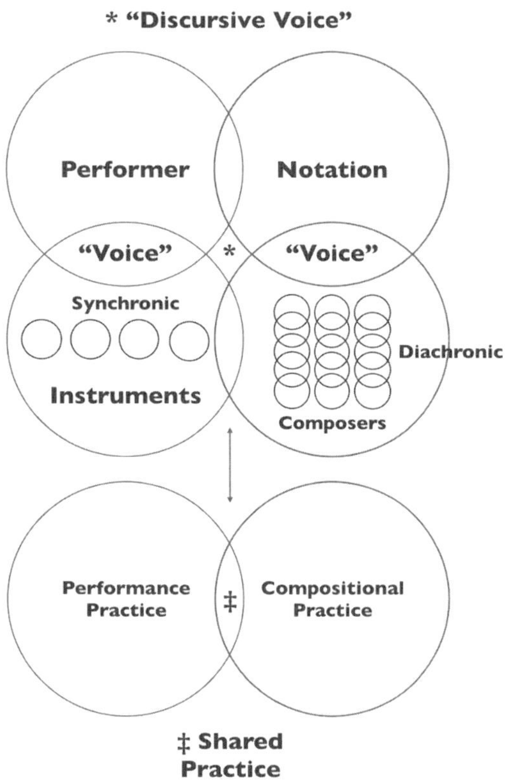

Figure 3.10.

And there is a further complication: access to those sets is, in the present, more complete for some than for others; BillyCom's "authority" is sometimes largely lost and sometimes quite potent (figure 3.11). All these multiplicities and all their interbreedings have a marked effect on the way the "discursive voice" is constituted, as a brief qualitative analysis of two movements makes clear.

Figure 3.10. Discursive voices: many sets of many composers.

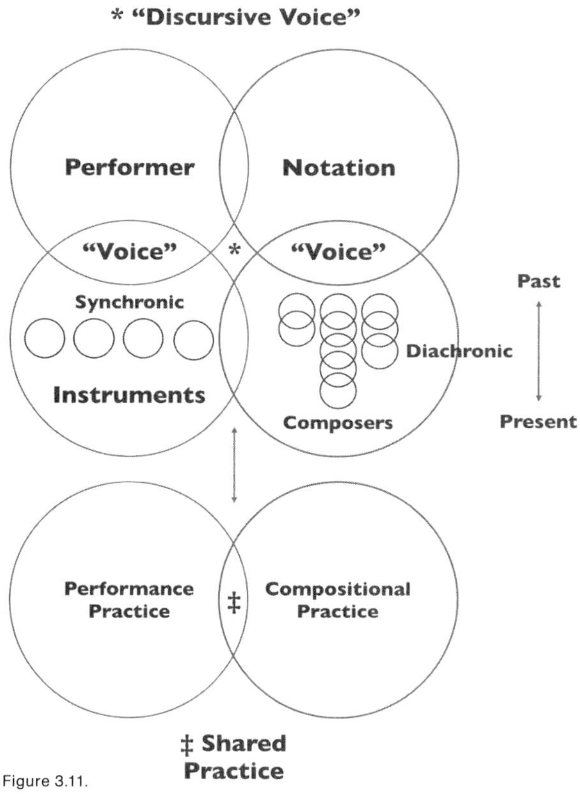

Figure 3.11.

3.1.3. Cycles of collaboration

The qualitative analysis was limited to roughly one and a half hours of compressed video from the working process of mixing "Crump" and thirty minutes of compressed video of "Cotten, *loc. cit.*" Most codes appear in the analysis of both pieces, with two exceptions; of these, the second—"autobiographical account"—appears to be more significant. While the interactions between the three protagonists appear to follow similar patterns in the work on the two pieces, an important difference in "Cotten, *loc. cit.*" is how Bill Brooks (or rather, the composer BillyCom, or is it the actual person, William Brooks?), steps forward to deliver autobiographical reflections in the search for the means to render a sonic representation of this tremolo etude:

> Bill: This is really based on, my image of this is, personal experience. I had a very big clunky old radio next to my bed and I was listening [*interrupted by Jez*]
>
> Jez: Is it one of those with the light on the back and the dial across the . . . [*gestures*]
>
> Bill: Pretty much, it wasn't quite that, but yes, pretty much. It was very good quality and it was an AM and FM radio and I listened to WQXR (is that it?), the classical station in New York, sometimes, in the evening, and the sound would come and go, because we were just on the edge of reception, and it went, and I loved it,

Figure 3.11. Discursive voices: many degrees of loss of many sets of many composers.

> actually, I mean, it is a very positive memory, because I was falling asleep as this was happening, it was beautiful, you'd hear piano music happening or something and then it would go szzzshhhhshhh . . .[39]

Little did we know how much trouble the reconstruction of this memory of radio static would eventually give us. But the authenticity of this composerly experience certainly became a reference point through all the work that followed. In our understanding, these autobiographical references became instrumental in the identification of working methods and informed our work on finding relevant reference recordings, which in turn triggered more autobiographical accounts, closing the loop (figure 3.12, top).

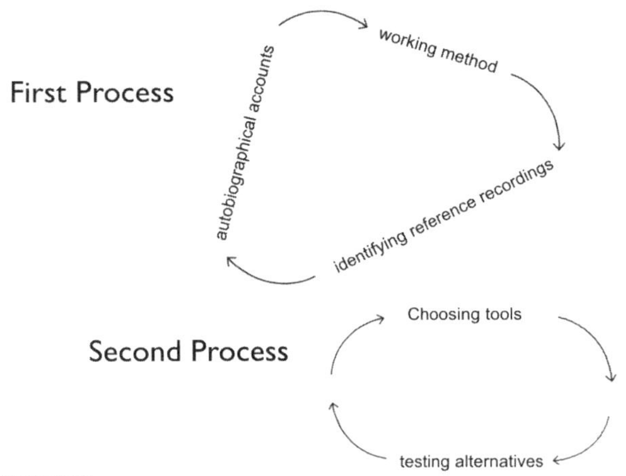

Figure 3.12.

We also observed a second loop (figure 3.12, bottom), in which a choice of tools—a particular reverberation or type of distortion—leads to a series of tests in which different alternatives are jointly evaluated; again, the latter leads to another choice of tools, closing the circle. We marked several instances in which the evaluation component was carried out through what we termed "analytical listening," which we found to be "the fundamental mode in the loop between choosing tools and testing alternatives, a process which Bill suggests is more to be understood as bricolage than experimentation" (annotation by Brooks and Östersjö, 6 March 2018). An overarching observation that can be made is that all these different activities, denoted by the given codes, are shared among all three protagonists. Even if Jez often (but not always) implements the choosing and testing, Stefan and Bill are constantly active in suggesting alternative tools and evaluating those currently in use.

However, as mentioned above, the dynamic is somewhat different in the making of "Crump." Here, the authority of the composer's autobiographical experience is lacking; instead, the working method is more immediately related

39 This clip is available in the online repository (www.orpheusinstituut.be/en/voices-bodies-practices-media-repository); see file "SF3.25 *Footnotes*, "Cotton, *loc. cit.*," discussion.

Figure 3.12. A graphical representation of two fundamental artistic processes identified in the qualitative analysis of the making of "Cotten, *loc. cit.*"

to the choice of tools and their evaluation. Discussions of method refer not to authenticity, drawn from the composer's intentions, but rather to the perceived difficulty in negotiating

> a conflict between the intended mask in the recording and the demands of the specific situation chosen, that is, the space and the audio technology at hand. . . . Jez proposes a method that would entail a transition from the desired space towards a sound that retains more of the qualities in the original recording (is this then to retain the original voice?) and then eventually to return to the situation at the end of the piece. The negotiation between the sound of the instrument and the sound of the space is a recurring problem in the project, and this transitional approach comes up again in *passim*. (Annotation by Brooks and Östersjö, 6 March 2018)

Further, in "Crump," the objective of much searching among reference recordings is to find audience noise that can be used to create a suitable situation within which the performance will be understood to have taken place. This produces a second loop that differs from that in "Cotten, *loc. cit.*"; in "Crump" the loop links "identifying reference recordings" with "composing the continuity" (figure 3.13). Nevertheless, in "Crump" as well as "Cotten, *loc. cit.*" all three participants take turns taking initiatives and making suggestions and alternations.

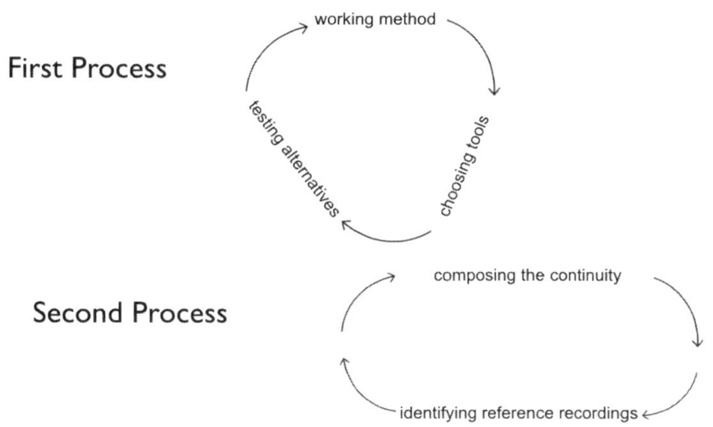

Figure 3.13.

3.1.4. Multiple subjectivities, multiple analyses

Even this preliminary analysis—which uses less than 5 per cent of the total available documentation—confirms that the project of creating *Footnotes* provides a rich research lode that will be mined over the next few years. It is already evident that a "collaborative self" was constituted in very different ways in making each of the six movements (actually seventeen "selves" when the units of "Cage, *passim*" are considered separately). Further, some of these multiple collaborative selves acquired agency themselves as the project proceeded; and some of the components (notably the composer and the technology) carry complex histories that must be deconstructed when considering matters of authority and intention.

Figure 3.13. A graphical representation of two fundamental artistic processes identified in the qualitative analysis of the making of "Crump."

And still further, our analysis does not yet take into account the affordances and resistances of non-human actors; we need to find a way for the agency of a guitar, a reverberation unit, an archival document to "speak" as a part of the unfolding collaborative multilogue. There is, indeed, work to be done.

3.2. The technical self

One may think of each constellation of performer, instrument, score, and technology as a specific assemblage that has come into being in the process of making the recordings that constitute *Footnotes*. But, as in chapter 1, the interactions between performer and technology need to be further unpacked through an analysis of their respective agencies. I have previously discussed the agency of instruments through the poles of resistance and resonance (Östersjö 2013). In *Footnotes*, one form of such resonance between performer, score, and instrument became apparent while recording unit B in "Cage, *passim.*" The composer had expressed no particular intention for this music, but I found that the characteristics of the score, which contains long chords and harmonics interrupted by Bartók pizzicatos, would be most clearly represented on a twelve-string acoustic guitar. I quickly associated this idea with the sound of Joni Mitchell's more experimental recordings in the 1970s, and these reference recordings served as an interpretative filter in my reading of the score. We see here that resonance can function as an analytical concept and is not equivalent to idiomaticity: the music would have been much more easily mastered on a classical six-string guitar or, for that matter, even more so on an electric guitar, because some of the chords and faster figurations are rather tricky on a heavier instrument like many twelve-string guitars. But, once the performer and instrument had been aligned, this unit posed no difficulties in post-production. Jez, who was very familiar with the agreed Joni Mitchell reference, added a bright plate reverberation, and we were happy with the result.

There is no specific point at which the augmentation of Joni Mitchell's compositional, performative, and tonal palette suddenly accelerated, but the stylistic move away from conventional folk and pop idioms is perhaps most marked between *Court and Spark* (1974) and *The Hissing of Summer Lawns* (1975). The latter recording also marks the first time she used a guitar by the luthier Steve Klein. By the time of *Don Juan's Reckless Daughter* (1977) Klein had completed the I Ching guitar that Mitchell had commissioned from him, using his trademark body-shape: "'The roundness of the top makes the instrument a more efficient plate resonator,' Klein says. Coupled with the split, asymmetrical bridge and an advanced bracing system, this makes for a more even frequency response. The result is a louder tone with a richer harmonic content" (Gans 1980, 39).

There is a bleached, albeit not unpleasant, quality to the final mixed and mastered sound of *Don Juan*. Perhaps to accommodate the bass of Jaco Pastorius, whose playing is more prominent than bassists on her earlier recordings, there is a thinness in the sound of the guitar and drums (for example, on "Overture" and "Jericho"), that is seemingly afforded by the interaction of the sound qualities of the I-Ching (the brightness of the upper strings), the microphone techniques and/or equalisation applied to it, and, most saliently, the reverberation. The latter is most likely an EMT plate, given that there were many of these available at A&M studios, where the recording was made and mixed (Lambert 1997). Thus the continuity that arose from the reference recording was eventually implemented in three ways: the brighter sound of the twelve-string, equalisation, and an impulse-response capture of an EMT plate. We used the "EMT 03 Bright Plate 03" impulse response from the Greg Hopkins collection to reverberate our dry studio recordings (Hopkins 2012).

The other sections of "Cage, *passim*" inhabit a variety of times and places, and they are discussed here in the order in which they appear in our production. For many of them, reference recordings fed into and arose from decisions about technologies and processing in the closed loop depicted in figure 3.13. Unit C, discussed in section 1.2, above, depicts a modest jazz club of the type that someone like Wes Montgomery might have played in the latter part of his career, with the same classes of treatment as for "Crump": crowd noise, reverberation (this time the impulse response of a salon, which gave a suitably lively yet short reverberation), analogue tape noise, and distortion applied to the guitar. In addition, a 60-hertz mains hum, along with the brief sound of a lead being plugged into an amplifier just before the playing begins, was added to complete our simulation of a "live at" (or possibly bootleg) recording.

Unit E was also discussed earlier. In this case, no specific recordings were used as references, but the music was created with a 1960s experimental or psychedelic rock music sound in mind, and it entered the compositional continuity much like elements in albums from that time. The score for unit F is to be generated through applying a series of chance operations that eventually determine the specific, numerically defined, nature of musical parameters in a series of events. The performer is asked to first "choose, by chance, a page from an atlas of the world. Choose, by chance, coordinates for a point on that page. Overlaying a transparent sheet of paper, trace the political boundaries that most closely surround the point chosen" (Brooks [1986] 2019). By continuing to create lines on transparent film, a series of coordinates are created which will eventually define the instructions for performing the unit.[40] While this study in Cagean compositional techniques already constitutes a negotiation of the composerly voices of Cage and Brooks, it was never my intention (nor was it my intention in unit C) to re-create a Cagean sound. Rather, I chose to shift between my Vietnamese electric guitar and the fretless Glissentar and also to sometimes multitrack these instruments. The Glissentar, in its mid-register, sounds very similar to a fretless bass; here, as with unit B, I was keen to evoke the playing of Jaco Pastorius—for instance, on *Hejira*, one of my favourite Joni Mitchell albums. However, in building this unit into the compositional continuity, the reference recording was wholly obscured; rather, the dry, studio-bound sound was contrasted with the ambience of a live performance situation (with audience noise from online

40 For an image of the score thus created and performed by Stefan, see the web repository.

videos and an impulse response from a medium-sized hall), all contained within a radio presentation (the spoken word being taken from a broadcast of a piece by Pauline Oliveros in the 1960s).

Unit A revisits the same place and time as "Cage," described previously, and units P, Q, and R (which are always performed as a group) are similarly situated. For unit D a more forensic approach was taken to capturing the guitar. As described earlier in section 2.3, the intention was to create something vivid and bright (even harsh) that somehow evoked Stockhausen's studio work of the 1960s. Our closely placed microphones ensured detail and spatial width (albeit with a profound distortion of the geometry of the instrument's actual acoustic radiation). In post-production we explored the use of cavernous reverberation (specifically the impulse response of a concrete tunnel, again from the Hopkins library), dynamically altering its application throughout, so that the resultant texture is as much "makrofonie" as "mikrofonie."

For unit I we are transported to a very large church in the present day, via the impulse response of York Minster and audio excerpted from an online video recording of a church service. And finally, unit H is framed as a cocktail party in the function room of some hotel, with the impulse response of a large living room, crowd noise from a variety of online sources and samples of glassware. The presentation here is inverted from that which would be typical for a recording of such an event: the people are closest, the glasses and other noise more distant and the guitar is the furthest away. It is there and it is audible, but the relative importance of its surroundings, its context, are exaggerated well beyond what we typically expect in a sound recording.

Still, the most resonant constellation of instrument and score was perhaps the use of my Ramirez six-string classical concert guitar in "Cotten, *loc. cit.*," once my initial resistance to the score had been resolved, as described above. The relation between José Ramirez III and Andrés Segovia is a celebrated example of collaborative technological development in instrument design. The two met in person for the first time in 1952, by which time Segovia had embraced and celebrated guitars made by the German luthier Hermann Hauser.[41] In this initial encounter, Segovia tried a guitar by the then thirty-two-year-old Ramirez and offered some sincere criticism. He then played a short concert to the luthier on his Hauser. Ramirez describes how he then "realized what an authentic classical guitar should be" concluding that "the typical Spanish guitar, with its bombastic basses and rickety trebles, was not adequate for performing an important role in the solo instrument field in the large concert halls where Segovia had introduced it" (Ramirez 1993, 195–96). The challenge to redesign the Spanish guitar had been sparked by Segovia's expansion of the expressive range of the

41 Interestingly, Hauser's success was the result of a long period of experimentation with copies made of a guitar given to Segovia by Ramirez's great-uncle Manuel Ramirez in 1913. Over a period of approximately ten years, Hauser worked to create an instrument that preserved and surpassed the qualities of this instrument. In February 1937 he eventually finished a guitar which Segovia would play in most concerts for the coming twenty-five years (Ramirez 1993).

classical playing technique. Ramirez's methods were based on reconsidering the proportions of the instrument, starting out with an exploration of golden section proportions (an attempt that failed). Over a period of eight years, José Ramirez III repeatedly presented Segovia with new experimental models, and in 1960 he created the first instrument that Segovia decided to use on tour. From that time onwards, Ramirez's guitars were to accompany Segovia to the end of his career. The Ramirez I play was built in 1980 and affords some qualities akin to the models played by the Segovia around the time of his last recordings.

The score implies a late Romantic performance practice in the style of Segovia, and while I was initially hesitant about the idea of recording the piece in this manner, my Ramirez guitar certainly allowed for such an approach. But in producing the recording of this movement, we were depending not merely on the technology of this classical guitar but even more so on technologies that would re-create the experience described by the composer (see above): hearing Segovia's performance of a tremolo étude by Tarrèga on an AM radio through and in the noise produced by a drifting signal. While the technology of the guitar was entirely resonant with our aims, the virtual radio to be created by modifying the original recording became the most resistant object in the entire project.

Indeed, this is the movement in which the evoked recording and, in this case, broadcast media were most carefully controlled and interwoven with composition and performance. This movement took the most time in post-production to reach a point where all—composer, performer, and recordist, informed by playbacks to test audiences, as described above in section 2.4—were satisfied. The intention was to evoke a medium-wave radio broadcast at some point during the 1950s, heard in a modest-sized domestic room.[42] Hence, in this movement noise is woven around the guitar, and different processings of it (variously applying filtering, subtle amplitude modulation, and gentle amplitude distortion) are used to colour and embellish its sound. For example, one or two notes in the lower register at the beginnings of phrases are marked by an increase in the amount of clipping/saturation applied. Noises come and go, representing the channel fading that occurs in analogue radio transmissions, but here this is coordinated with the phrasing of the melodic lines, which themselves deteriorate in ways that represent the signal loss. The noises were originally sourced from a pink noise generator and a modern transistor radio, deliberately tuned between stations and manipulated dynamically to create timbral variation. The hope was that this noise could be combined with the guitar (reverberated twice—once to

42 Such broadcasts were characterised by the usual suspects associated with other analogue media: noise, distortion, and an uneven frequency response. In addition there can be pure tone-like components that appear in the audible part of the spectrum as a result of beating between carrier waves (the sinusoids at transmission frequencies—usually well out of the audible spectrum—that are modulated by and "carry" the audio signals of interest) that are adjacent in frequency and whose difference is less than 20 kHz (the upper limit frequency limit of human hearing) and is therefore present within the audible band. In some rare situations, usually as a result of defective transmission or reception, the modulated audio appears within the audible band with a constant shift in all frequency components which renders harmonic sounds inharmonic (since the frequencies are shifted and not scaled, the ratios between them are not preserved). This gives rise to the alien, clangourous, and bell-like quality that is typical of ring modulation (which is very closely related to amplitude modulation).

represent the original notional recording space, and then again to represent the domestic context of the radio—and with micro-distortions applied, moment by moment) to provide a convincing, yet malleable, set of components with which to dynamically embellish this mediated sound with an impression of mid-century broadcast technology. Yet the results were unconvincing.

We realised that, in this instance, we would have to adopt the actual technology that we were attempting to emulate. Therefore, an Invicta Model 30 radio was sourced from a local repair shop, and a one-hour slot was arranged on a low-power campus-based AM transmitter. And so it was that in October 2017 "Cotten, *loc. cit.*" was broadcast as a medium-wave signal from the University campus and received by the Model 30, which dated from the late 1940s, in the living room of a house built sometime in the 1920s, just over a mile away. The output from the Model 30's built-in speaker was captured by two microphones, as shown in Figure 3.14.

Figure 3.14.

Also captured was the direct line output of a modern AM receiver located in a village approximately five miles from the transmitter. While this lacked some of the authentic characteristics of the Invicta (only one such model was available to us) it offered a signal that was weaker and more distressed because of the greater propagation distance, and therefore it contributed an additional flavour available to us at the final mixing stage. The final post-production sessions included the output from both receivers, dovetailed with each other and blended with the direct sound from the original recording sessions, fed through

Figure 3.14. Capture of Invicta Model 30 radio with Shure SM58 and Schoeps Colette MK4.

simulations of vintage analogue compressors and mild waveshaping distortion. Subtle amplitude modulation was also applied to the direct sound at various points. The result is an impressionistic collage, not entirely "plausible," given the wealth of different treatments that are presented, but somehow "authentic" (authenticity-as-intention and, perhaps, authenticity-as-sound)—and certainly expressive.

> Plausible: seeming reasonable or probable … mid 16th-century (also in the sense "deserving applause or approval").
>
> Authentic: made or done in the traditional or original way, or in a way that faithfully resembles an original. (Lexico 2019)

3.3. The historical self

We like to think that we have agency; that we "make a difference"; that our way of doing things is . . . well, *our* way. But it can equally be asserted that agency rests *upon* us, not *in* us; that we *are made by* differences; that "our way" is actually an amalgam of behaviours foisted upon us by life itself. Philosophers have wrestled with this issue for decades; for me, the most helpful analysis has been provided by American pragmatists, who observe that the very question presupposes a split between self and environment, each exerting some mysterious force on the other. Rather, they propose, the double noun (*self/environment*) should be dissolved into the unitary noun *experience*: environment and self are perpetually and continually *inter*acting, rather than acting *upon*. In his early *Principles of Psychology* (1890), William James writes that "experience is remoulding us every moment, and our mental reaction on every given thing is really a resultant of our experience of the whole world up to that date" (1:234). Our (re)actions, then, are a consequence of what has gone before; and simultaneously and instantaneously they shape what is to come. There is no break between past, present, and future.

In the timelines of recording technology and technique presented in section 1.3 there are developments—changes, additions, etc.—but there is also continuity. The things that are often referred to as "disruptions" by present-day commentators are equally accelerations (because some innovation or other makes "progress" momentarily easier) or sudden changes in direction (because new avenues of possibility open up that are at a tangent to the current direction of travel). But these things remain connected to their precursors. For example, modern digital user-interfaces usually imitate aspects of earlier, more physically tangible tools such as mixing desks and tape machines; and the recording media is often still magnetic.[43] This retains familiarity: old notions and habits are not immediately redundant; rather, they are accommodated alongside new comforts and features.

43 These imitations of older hardware characteristics in current user interfaces are identified as skeuomorphisms: "From the standpoint of pure functionality, skeuomorphism in software design is unnecessary. There was a time when all computer interfaces relied solely on text entered into command lines; in theory, DAWs could still work this way" (Bell, Hein, and Ratcliffe 2015).

The computer on which I type this now was previously dressed as a recording studio, but now it presents itself as a typewriter. Like Abulafia in *Foucault's Pendulum*, it "is merciful, [it] grants you the right to change your mind" (Eco 1989, 26). It is the "undo" key that creates the significant difference between before and after, typewriter and word processor, reel-to-reel and digital storage. The acts of typing words, or of pressing record and stop, do not change much; but the ability to undo what we have already done is relatively new and profoundly changes the risks involved. "Once I know that I can remember whenever I like, I forget" (ibid.). Many of the practices of recording, the ways of imagining the capture, flow, and control of signals, reach back a long way into the past; but the scale, the cost, and the risk of those practices is significantly altered.

But if the stuff of our existence is experience—no matter how much we embrace the "thingness" of our lives—where does history reside? If we are perpetually borne along in a never-ending "stream of consciousness" (James 1892, chap. 11), where is the "thing that happened twenty years ago today"? It has no tangible reality; we cannot handle it, cannot taste it or hear it or set it aside for safe-keeping. If it is a part of experience—and it most certainly is—that is only so because we put it there. I might say that it's "in my head," but that again implies a physical existence. History enters experience only because my consciousness—my *self*, my *subjective* self—is itself a part of experience; what I "think" and what I "am" is merely one component in what is constantly sensed and acted upon. The "subject" in "subjectivity" requires that we ourselves be experienced in the recursive stream of what Dewey ([1934] 1980, chapter 3) calls "doing and undergoing."

We partition that stream for practical ("pragmatic") reasons; at root, we partition it to survive. The infant, James famously wrote, is "assailed by eyes, ears, nose, skin and entrails all at once" and thus feels the world as "one great blooming, buzzing confusion" (1890, 1:488). But the infant *learns*, and it learns above all to separate eyes from ears, skin from entrails—and, crucially, "thinking" from all the rest. Thinking is not different, but we choose to make it so: it is useful for us to separate it. And as experience aggregates, thinking itself is partitioned into components, just as sight is partitioned into colours and shapes and intensities: there is "judging," there is "predicting," and there is "remembering."

The components thus created are constantly re-aggregated into constellations that we call "events" or "experiences" (note the plural). There is, let's say, a "concert"; at some point the concert "ends." There is no change in consciousness, but it is useful to partition the experience: *now* we must find a taxi; *then* we were sitting still. And as soon as we do that, we have created *history*.

History, consciousness, and memory are thus ineluctably entangled, not only with each other but with other "things" that enter our sensoria. We see a photograph, and "it" *reminds* us of something. We hear a sound, and we "think of" a church. The "things" in our lives become tags for memories, and vice versa; and all is constantly recycled and rearranged in the stream of existence.

Footnotes, BillyCom avows, was from the start an attempt to scrutinise that process; to *attend* to the workings of its mechanism. BillyMus—there from the start—was devoted to John Cage and Charles Ives, and *Footnotes* is reverberant with their echoes: a prepared guitar, a borrowed tune, "an old man's memories." And the making of *Footnotes*-the-recording was simultaneously an attempt to recover the traces of that starting point and to give renewed attention to the *present* moments in which a performance is devised, recorded, edited, and processed. To the extent that that attempt and that attention characterises all human existence, as each of us seeks to move beyond "blooming, buzzing confusion," there is only *one* subjectivity at work here, and it belongs to all of us together.

It can be (and often is) argued that infinite undo and limitless storage are not inherently good things. There can be a reluctance to make decisions, to fix things in place. Options are retained and choices deferred. Perhaps this is the most important difference in the technology that we have used, and the way we have used it, compared to that which we have imagined or evoked. We have technologically reserved the right to change our minds at pretty much any stage during the production and post-production process. We have gone back to the things that we thought were fixed and finished, and we have revised them where we were so inclined to do so or when audiences suggested to us that we might. In the case of *Footnotes* this lack of "fixedness" is the only way in which this multitude of layers, or masks, could have been overlaid on these compositions, performances, and captures. The things that we have set out to evoke are clothed in all these things as a result of the agencies of the people and technologies working on them *in that instant*: those agencies that arise from their design and context (for technologies) or from their training and experience (for people, bodily and mentally). The "era of undo" that we now inhabit, but which arrived after those times, has enabled us to audition, ponder, and deliberate. In this way we have become able to browse different pasts, to select that which satisfies us best, that tells the story of itself and ourselves that we most want to hear.

The metaphor—a "stream of consciousness"—implies that we can enter and leave the flow; we can choose to swim, float, drown, or clamber onto the banks. But that is wrong; in clambering out, we carry the stream over the banks and with us. We are not so much *in* the stream as *a part of* it. What we *can* do, however, is to attend to the stream itself, and especially to the flotsam that is thrown by, over, and on us. And we can make our own flotsam, our own ark-i-facts—small boats, small things, that we hope will drift away from us, to be freshly aggregated by a consciousness (perhaps our own) "some other time."

Research consists in large part in making such ark-i-facts. Re-search: to search again. And thus the *Footnotes* project has attempted to make not only a record (an LP), but a record of a record—and a record of a record of a record, and so on ad infinitum. What you read now is one such ark-i-fact; but so are the various films and recordings and documents that have accrued in the web repository, on hard drives and on shelves. We use these much the way we use the score, or BillyCom's memories, or Jez's radios: they become elements in aggregates that we assemble in order to be, we hope, useful. Those aggregates *are*, in a sense, our "historical selves"; and like all the rest, those selves do and they undergo: they change, always in a changing world, and the aggregates change with them.

3.4. Multiple selves

Who is the "I" that performs? That is the question that opens the introduction to this volume, and it is the question that underlies all the chapters and thinking contained therein. In (re)making *Footnotes*, it has been extended to other, notionally separate, domains: Who is the "I" that composes? Who is the "I" that records? That edits? That listens? That writes? That . . .? And further: the *Footnotes* project asks that the pronoun itself be interrogated: Have "I" (re)made *Footnotes*? Ought the underlying question take a pluralist form: *Who is the "we" that performs?*

Even in the most prosaic account, *Footnotes* would be characterised as a "collaboration." Collaborations arise among two or more "individuals"—so from the outset, there are at least multiple "I's," multiple individuals, multiple subjectivities at work. In the least subtle formulation there are three of these, tagged with a name for convenience: William Brooks, Stefan Östersjö, Jez Wells. But as we have seen, each of these is in itself a multiple—indeed, throughout the preceding discussions, "William Brooks" has been split in three: BillyCom, BillyMus, BillyMark. But even that triple persona is wholly inadequate to capture the sense of mutable self that has permeated this entire project: BillyCom shades indiscernibly into BillyMus, who mutates equally into BillyMark. At any given movement all three are rising, falling, or in equilibrium; an infinity of selves are encompassed by the single tag *William Brooks*.

Similarly the Östersjö playing the Ramirez—employing his classical guitar skills in an attempt to recreate an embodied understanding of Segovia's voice—is quite distinctly removed from the other guitarist, curiously also named Östersjö, playing an electric Vietnamese guitar or a fretless Glissentar, looking to create a contemporary reading of voices otherwise typically heard on the pop and jazz scene in the 1980s. But to return to Bill's suggestion in section 3.1 that in *Footnotes* there are "many composers," I would propose that this is only metaphorically true. A model for the emergence of voice presupposes a lived body, a musician's habitus, as well as interactions with actual technical and psychological tools. True, a composer who approaches a compositional project by filtering or intentionally masking one's voice may—as observed by David Gorton in chapter 1 (p. 54)—find new facets of one's "compositional 'voice' through that of another," but this is not the same as the composer actually *being* another.

However, this play with voice may indeed have a lot to say about composerly and performerly identity. It may be argued that any performer of a score-based composition that is already situated in a performance practice will be engaged in a similar process of negotiating voice with multiple other performers. As suggested by Catherine Laws in chapter 2 (p. 116), a pianist performing a Beethoven sonata operates with the score through an embodied archive, and the performance can be seen as an embodiment of "the pianist's physical relationship to the personal archive of piano-related experience—playing, listening, and the handling of scores and recordings—that feeds into a performing life." But in *Footnotes*, such processes are manifested even more clearly than in a conventional performance, and the filtering of one voice through that of another is also applied to the shared agency of a virtual, or absent, record producer,[44] embodied sometimes by all three protagonists and sometimes by one or two at a time.[45]

While I am recording, I am not touching or interacting with anything to do with that recording. I am listening and I am thinking, and occasionally I am writing about what I think of what I am listening to. I begin the recording by pressing a single key or button, and I end the recording by pressing another. But during the recording, I am not doing the recording: the recording is happening, and I am listening to what is being recorded, but I am not doing it. Prior to the time of the recording there is the 'I' that discusses and plans; then there is the 'I' that books equipment and arranges session times: then the 'I' that puts microphones on stands and iteratively listens and adjusts their positions; and alongside and alternating with this is the 'I' that turns on the computer and gives it instructions for how to record. When the recording is actually taking place, these actions of different instances of myself collapse down into *how* this recording is being made, but the 'I' that is present *at that very time* does nothing but listen to, and think on, what the other selves have done, while the performer plays and the composer, perhaps even more dislocated from the actions of "right now" than I am, listens and thinks about the instantaneous audible manifestations of his or her selves and ourselves. In that sense the score and the audio artefact are the singularities into which all things collapse but also from which all things emerge. They are the freeze-dried packets of music and sound (or sounding music) that both nourish and vanish under the agencies of these multiple selves, instruments, and others.

And what of these "others"? Who are "they" that perform, that record, that *act*? Again, in a crude formulation, the designated parties ("humans") that collaborate "use" tools to "make" things. And the tools, like the humans, are given unitary names: *guitar*, *microphone*, *equaliser*. But *Footnotes* makes very evident what is sometimes concealed but is always the case: the tools are using the humans, and the "making" is an interactive, experiential process, circular and unending. There are many guitars, and each *acts*—together with Stefan—to make sound. To some

44 Lefford and Thompson (2018) observe how the record producer has a mediating role "between people, performers and recording technologies" and importantly that the final aesthetic decisions normally lie with the producer: "although the finished recorded artefact cannot be characterized at the start, the producer says when the work suffices, and verifies and validates it" (545).

45 To illustrate how the three protagonists have tended to divide the role of the producer between them, compare the accounts in 3.1 to Lefford and Thompson (2018), who observe how a producer may use a reference recording "to match through technical means the sound currently being recorded to a template provided by a commercially successful recording. The upshot of this would be to make the sound typical of the genre. At the same juncture, the producer might recognize the similarities between the to-be-recorded sound and the reference, and still without using any sort of classical analysis of outcomes, choose to depart from the template. In such situations, metacognitive reflection is one way to explain this decision. Importantly, in both cases, the choice of template pre-supposes some form of meta-analysis" (546).

extent we distinguish them: six-string, twelve-string, Glissentar. . . . And these can be further qualified—there is "Stefan's guitar"; there is "my Gibson"—and these differentiated guitar selves mutate and combine, just as do BillyCom and BillyMus and BillyMark. And so also for the scores: crudely speaking there are six entities, six "movements"; but more subtly, each partakes of the others, shapes and is shaped by them. And the categories of tools interact: in the presence of the score to "Crump," the "twelve-string" becomes, momentarily "my Gibson"; "*ibid.*," working together with Stefan, compels a single instrument to be twinned.

In *Footnotes* (which in itself is characterised by multiplicities: a project unfolded through collaboration,[46] a compilation of recordings, a set of pieces in a score[47]) the *intentionality* of non-human agents,[48] like the guitars or the ubiquitous instruments of the recording and editing studio, and their interaction with the intentionality of each individual score[49] are constantly played with, but also play, the human agents, as they jointly negotiate the shaping of the piece. Again, the intentionality of the score, and of the instruments we chose to work with open up for "an infinite sequence of decisions"[50]; and, thereby, the *Footnotes* project counters "the view of musical works as static, timeless objects and allows us to see them as something much closer to the process of performance itself"[51] (Butt 2002, 85). Ultimately, this chapter aims to provide some (fractional and somewhat arbitrary) examples of how subjectivity in musical performance, be it

46 While composer–performer collaboration is discussed throughout this book, a framework for the analysis of such practice is presented only in chapter four, drawing on the work of Vera John-Steiner. Through the lens of her four modes of interaction, one may conclude that a characteristic feature of the *Footnotes* project is an oscillation between the "distributed" and "integrative" modes.

47 Perhaps the recording project is the strongest manifestation of multiplicities, with its refusal of the dyad One/Many, and its focus on the infinite resonance with other voices, other performances, recordings, and scores within any unit.

48 See Butt (2002) and chapter 1 of this book for further discussions of the intentionality of non-human agents in musical creativity.

49 One of the footnotes in "Cage, *passim*" can be seen as a more overarching instruction, which indeed had a bearing on all the movements; it is clearly expressed in unit E, but even more in "*ibid.*" (which is not part of "Cage, *passim*"), with the solution constituted by the "invention" of the two guitars played simultaneously by one player. It reads: "If certain combinations of notes are unplayable with conventional techniques, invent extraordinary ones" (Brooks [1986] 2019). But when is a solution "extraordinary"? This was surely not the first time two guitars were used simultaneously in this manner. Indeed, double-necked guitar instruments, which allow for similar combinations of performance on two fretboards, date back to the seventeenth century (see http://www.harpguitars.net/history/org/org-multi-neck.htm). Gibson started making double-necked electric guitars in 1958. An instance closer to the present is Steve Goss's *Oxen of the Sun*, composed in 2003 for Jonathan Leathwood, which uses a ten-string and a six-string guitar in a similar manner.

50 As observed in 3.1, decision-making has often been achieved through consensus, as in the loops depicted in figures 3.12 and 3.13; but it also can result when one of the protagonists actively seeks to grasp the wishes and intentions of the others. In the latter case, this entails the protagonists momentarily agreeing to "become" producers—who, as observed by Lefford and Thompson (2018), often are found to be "reflecting on another's thinking, considering their goals, their perceptions and their problem-solving—with the aim of optimizing the producer's own decisions and actions" (551).

51 The process of performance is discussed by Catherine Laws in chapter 2 (p. 155) as a "becoming material," the performer comes to be perceived as something or someone that "in its very disappearance is both formed from remains and continues to remain, but in our bodies, our ears, our touching and feeling, as much as in our minds."

in a recording studio[52] or in a concert hall,[53] emerges through the inter-reaction[54] of many different agencies.

All these agents, human and technological, come before, at, or after the times that we have intended to evoke. I was born five years after "Crump," yet some of the crowds we hear within it are from that time. The Invicta Model 30 had left the Pye factory some years before "Cotten, *loc. cit.*" is supposedly heard in its imaginary bedroom, but the transmitter used to broadcast to it in 2014 is from somewhere between those two times. The convolution process that we have used so extensively to play recordings into spaces, without the signals representing each ever having to leave a computer, can trace its development back to Laplace in the eighteenth century, and the transform which enables it to happen so efficiently is rooted in Fourier's work of the early nineteenth century. Cooley and Tukey, working during the same era in which much of *Footnotes* is set, made ingenious refinements to Fourier's transform that brought its tractability—for the computing hardware that was beginning to emerge in the post-war era—within touching distance.[55] We have used hard drives, reel-to-reel tapes, digital models, a wooden podium, vinyl disks, old microphones, and new microphones. We have worked on the creation of this audio artefact over a span of nearly five years; yet it all collapses into a single signal that lasts for about forty minutes and will not change at all from now on (unless it, itself, is sampled, or remixed, remastered) except in the selves of its listeners.

---

52 Lefford and Thompson (2018) observe how sometimes, in the recording studio, "production decisions are contingent on pragmatic matters such as time and available technology, values for creativity and contributors' biases and preferences, as well as factors external to the production environment" (552), a perspective also suggested by Östersjö above, in his reflection on the "convenience-factor" in the choice of instrument. Of course, section 3.3, above, argues in part that pragmatism, as a philosophy, underpins the entire project.

53 In the post-production of "Cotten, *loc. cit.*," seeking a Segovia-like sound, we discussed the in-between spaces: the large recording studios, created for their concert hall-like reverberations, that were often used at the time. But throughout, the project situates many of its components in spaces other than recording studios and concert halls, with virtual locations and occasions ranging from a Communion service in a church to a cocktail party. It is important, though, to note that these framings were entirely *post hoc*; the simulation was not conceived at the time of recording.

54 In a study of performer–performer interaction in chamber music, Murphy McCaleb (2014, 101). proposes the perspective of inter-reaction, which he describes as a flow-like experience, through which "an ensemble may gain its own collective interpretative momentum—a state that performers refer to as the music 'playing itself.'" The experience of flow is not a typical characteristic of post-production in an editing studio; but over the years, moments of inter-reaction in the construction of the various movements have occurred. Though well removed from performance—which entails a specific experience in a specific time and "ignites itself in the here and now" (Siegmund 2008, 192, see also chapter 4, below)—the moments when the "right" recorded church is found or when a fictive radio show is constructed from various archival broadcasts indeed evidence a state of inter-reaction.

55 Laplace used the continuous convolution operation for finding the distributions of means in 1788 (Dominguez 2015). Fourier, in 1807, stated that *any* function defined over a finite interval (which translates to any finite-duration waveform in the specific context of audio analysis and processing) can be represented by an infinite series of harmonically related sines and cosines (Robinson 1982, 887). Cooley and Tukey introduced the Fast Fourier Transform in 1965 and it had an effect "on scientific and engineering practice [that] cannot be overstated" (ibid., 901).

*1 A performance of Footnotes must include at least two movements. Movements may be played in any order, except for ibid., which must be immediately preceded by a performance of Crump. Footnotes was written in 1981-3 for Michael Cedric Smith, and its composition was supported in part by a grant from the National Endowment for the Arts.

*2 Different instruments, with or without amplification, may be used for different movements. Certain of the effects in Cage, for instance, may be produced more clearly on an instrument with steel strings; similarly, Crump may sound best on a twelve-string instrument, and Cage, passim, might be realized on an electric guitar.

*12 The damping, done sharply and precisely in rhythm, is the final sound.

Chapter 4

Arrival Cities: Hanoi

Nguyễn Thanh Thủy and Stefan Östersjö

ARRIVAL CITIES: HANOI

Concept: Jörgen Dahlqvist, Kent Olofsson, and The Six Tones
Transcribed stories by Lưu Ngọc Nam, Ngô Trà My, Nguyễn Thanh Thủy, Stefan Östersjö, and various street vendors in Hà Nội
Dramaturg: Jörgen Dahlqvist
Music: Kent Olofsson and The Six Tones
Choreography: Miguel Cortés

[Light fades away. Black. A text is projected on the screen in the back of the stage]

The worst part of holding the memories is not the pain. It's the loneliness of it. Memories need to be shared.[1]

[Text fades away. Light appears to the left in the venue. A long transition from early morning to night starts and continues through the performance. Sounds from the city of Hà Nội are being heard at a distance. Ngô Trà My enters the room and walks up towards the audience to one of three microphone stands.]

Trà My: I was born in the countryside in Vietnam in a small village called Ninh Phúc. When I was six years old my parents moved to Hà Nội because they wanted to change their life. Hà Nội is a very big city. I was shocked when my parents brought me to the Hồ Chí Minh mausoleum. The square is huge, and I had never seen that many people in my life. I was dizzy and nearly fainted, and my parents had to bring me back to our flat immediately. I was sick for several days afterwards. The first sound I heard of Hà Nội was the call from the street vendors selling bread and vegetables in the street. My family lived just by the school of music so there were also many sounds of traditional instruments around me, like the đàn bầu, which is the instrument I play today. Many young students lived there. They had moved from the countryside because they wanted to change their lives, like my family.

[A video with an interview with Nam, the costume maker from the Tuồng Theater in Hà Nội, appears on the screen behind Trà My. Sounds from a Vietnamese performance of Tuồng are also being heard in the background. Pictures from the interview with Nam, from Tuồng performances and women living and working in the countryside.]

1 This citation in the libretto is taken from Lois Lowry's *The Giver* (1993, 154).

Nam: I was part of a group with adult artists, and I was just a boy. I became the treasure for the group. A six-year-old boy who could sing Tuồng that well made the group become famous. When I was fourteen, I left my village. I had been accepted to study Tuồng in Hà Nội. It was a big pride for my family, the whole village and the region. All the excitement in the village boosted my own expectations. I was floating on top of this flurry. I moved to Hà Nội at a very difficult time in the country. It was war. There was no food and no soap. You could not even buy clothes. At home in the village I was very well looked after. Now I was alone.

[Video fades away.]

Trà My: When I was ten years old, my family moved to Mai Dịch, an area where many artists live.

[Thủy enters the room. Walks up to the front of the stage.]

Trà My: That's where I met Thủy and from there we went by bike to the Academy of Music with our instruments on the back.

Thủy: Yes, that's a long time ago, and later we worked in the same school. In 2006, our school sent us to Sweden to work on an exchange project between the two countries. That's why we met Stefan and after two months of working together he came to Hà Nội to do a concert with us. I don't remember this very well, but later he told me that I was the one to pick him up in the airport. So I guess that's how it was. Even though it was the first time he came to Hà Nội, I remember he was busy all the time, either working in the hotel room or rehearsing with us. Right after the concert he went to China for another gig. Trà My and I were a little surprised, we thought he came from so far away and should spend some time to see the country, but he didn't.

[Stefan enters the room. Walks up to the front of the stage.]

Thủy: My first impression of Stefan was that of a big, long-haired Western man who spoke English very fast. And actually, Trà My had a big headache after her first meeting with him.

Stefan: It's funny how Asian faces blur in the eyes of a European.

[Trà My leaves and sits by her đàn bầu. She starts to play and continues throughout Stefan's story.]

Stefan: When Thủy met me in the airport, I didn't really recognise her, even though we had been rehearsing together in Sweden some months earlier. She brought a driver and we went by car down to the city centre, stopping by a shed somewhere on the way down town to change my dollars to dong. But it was only when I got to the hotel that I realised how crazy the traffic was. It seemed the only way even to cross the street by the hotel was when Thủy came to pick me up, take me by the hand, and lead me through the traffic.

[Music: solo by Trà My.]

[Thủy leaves and starts doing movements in the back of the stage.]

1. Introduction

This is not the libretto to *Arrival Cities: Hanoi*. It is a transcription of the opening of a performance at the National Tuồng Theatre in Hà Nội on 6 April 2015. *Arrival Cities: Hanoi* is an experimental piece of music theatre, with documentary film. While the piece does not have a script, the dramaturgy is thoroughly composed, in collaboration between the director Jörgen Dahlqvist, the composer Kent Olofsson, and the three members of The Six Tones: Ngô Trà My, Nguyễn Thanh Thủy, and Stefan Östersjö.[2] Much of the music is fully scored, and other parts are based on improvisations, developed in interaction between Olofsson and The Six Tones. The documentary was created by Jörgen Dahlqvist and The Six Tones and consists of interviews with people who have migrated to Hà Nội. The stories told by these people are all very different. Most of the interviewees were women, since the project took special interest in the lives of street vendors, a category of rural–urban migrant worker that almost completely consists of women. These itinerant street vendors normally have their families in villages in the countryside, and they would commonly be "sharing rented rooms in Hanoi with other vendors from the same village and returning home to visit their families monthly" (Eidse, Turner, and Oswin 2016, 344). Other interviewees, like the Tuồng actor and costume maker, Lưu Ngọc Nam, have been resident in Hà Nội for a long time but arrived in their youth from their homeland. Lưu's life story constitutes a central narrative in the piece. His experience of moving from the countryside to Hà Nội, his homesickness, and the tension between traditions within Vietnamese Tuồng theatre together draw a portrait of a city vibrant with memories from the Vietnamese countryside. In an interview with Lê Minh Huệ for the Hanoian newspaper *Nông Nghiệp Việt Nam*, Lưu describes his perception of the piece: "To me, the countryside and Hà Nội are like the two sides of the hand. One side is an overwhelming image of a modern city with offices in skyscrapers. If you turn the hand over you see a rural culture being broken to pieces. *Arrival Cities: Hanoi* expresses exactly what I have experienced, the transition from traditional to modern society" (Lê 2015, our translation).

After the war for independence (first with France and then with the United States) and the reunion of the North and the South in 1976, Vietnam was devastated and one of the poorest countries in the world. In the late 1970s and early 1980s, economic development was "paralysed by high inflation, low productivity, low-quality export standards, energy shortages and inefficient management of the economy" (Vandemoortele and Bird 2011, 4). But the Vietnamese economy has developed rapidly since the country opened up to market-oriented economic systems with the *Đổi Mới* reforms in 1986. This economic growth has led to significant improvement of the living standards in the country, but the development has not been shared equally. Vandemoortele and Bird, in a report looking at eighteen years of economic growth, conclude that these reforms have "enabled significant progress, but this progress has not been equitable—

2 The Six Tones is a Vietnamese/Swedish group started in 2006. For further information, see 2.2, below.

although it started from a relatively equitable point. Poorer groups, ethnic minorities and rural populations have seen their share in economic progress decline. Income growth has been concentrated mainly around the large cities and in areas with export-oriented economic activities. Growth has been slower in the Northwest and Central Highlands regions and among particular ethnic minorities" (Vandemoortele and Bird 2011, 8).

Lucas (1997) has proposed a model for understanding domestic migration in developing countries that includes temporary and circular patterns, a model that seems true of Vietnam. Although the migration streams are diminishing, a strong rural–urban movement is still prominent in the country. According to a recent study, one reason for the statistical decrease is that more itinerant vendors return home, since their trade is getting less profitable. Another trend is that many women venture into street vending with the wish "to provide financial support for younger family members pursuing higher education in cities" (Luong 2018, 603).

It is a hard life to work as a street vendor. With the current legislation, itinerant vendors are working on the margins of the law and have to negotiate their presence by bribing the local police. "Stationary vendors often have an established informal relationship with local law enforcement officers—such as regular unofficial payments—and a degree of social capital from connections that enable them to maintain their trade" (Eidse, Turner, and Oswin 2016, 346). In a video paper, Nguyễn offers the following reflection: "The stories that we collected were shared with us by people in fragile situations, and we felt the need to consider how these images could best be presented, from both an artistic and an ethical perspective. We also became concerned with our own role as individuals and artists in the process of creating this piece" (Nguyễn and Östersjö 2018). It was only while we were collecting the documentary material that we realised how the individual stories of migration to and from Hà Nội, which were part of the lived experience of the performers in the group, also had to be part of the piece. The political nature of the piece emerges from the presence of the three musicians of the group onstage as individuals rather than as musicians or actors. The notion of creating performative situations through which the performers could share individual memories became a central concept for the dramaturgy, similarly to how the script in verbatim theatre is drawn from interviews with people's experience of real-life situations (Forsyth and Megson 2009). The stage is set up so that the three performers either play their instruments or tell stories in a position at the front of the stage, where three microphones on stands are placed. The storytelling was developed from memories of encounters with people in migration zones in Hà Nội, but it draws even more on personal memories from the city.

In 2015, the entire team returned to Hà Nội to continue shooting documentary material and to integrate the new documentation into the Vietnamese premiere. In December the same year, a new version of the music was created, adding a chamber ensemble to the score. This version was premiered in Vienna with Ensemble Reconsil, conducted by Roland Freisitzer.[3]

2. Modes of collaboration

This section outlines the various artistic collaborations that were brought together in the making of *Arrival Cities: Hanoi*. Such a backdrop is essential for creating an understanding of the artistic method development within the project, but also, and more importantly, for the creation of an analytical understanding of the interaction between the participating artists.

2.1. Analytical approaches

For the analysis in this chapter, we find useful Vera John-Steiner's (2000) theoretical work on artistic collaboration. Building on the work of Lev Vygotsky, she challenges the individualistic focus on human endeavour that has been predominant in Western culture. Emphasising instead the amount of ground-breaking research and artistic work that has been performed in different collaborative contexts, she argues that the possibilities for stretching the individual's potential through collaborative work make a strong argument for reconsidering the fundamental conceptions of our practices. In contrast to a maturational theory of the self, this analysis emphasises the potential of stretching one's identity through partnership, through sustained and various actions, and through the interweaving of social and individual processes.[4]

John-Steiner distinguishes between four different patterns in collaborative work: distributed, complementary, family, and integrative collaboration. *Distributed collaboration* is the most informal mode, in which the participants, linked by similar interests, exchange knowledge and explore ideas, typically in conferences or in more ad hoc contexts. *Complementary collaboration* is regarded by John-Steiner as the most typical form, generally speaking. It is especially common in scientific partnership, in which diversity in skills and modes of thinking lead to the creation of new knowledge. Here, differences in training, skill, and temperament support the project through division of labour. The third pattern, *family collaboration* refers to collaboration not only between actual family members but also in artistic collectives and other community-like environments. Aspects of shared lives and group dynamics make family collaboration more typical of long-term collaboration in ensembles than in a collaboration between a composer and a performer, which normally tends to be more temporary in nature. In the context of family collaboration, roles may be flexible and change over time. These collaborations can indeed become dynamic through developed social relationships. According to John-Steiner,

3 While much could be said about this expanded version, the new score will not be explicitly discussed in this chapter, since it does not immediately contribute to an understanding of the central topics discussed.

4 This process is well captured by Vygotsky's concept of the zone of proximal development. In Vygotskian terms, partners create zones of proximal development for each other (John-Steiner 2000, 188–89).

it is the fourth mode that is most typical of artistic collaboration: in *integrative collaboration*, the partners suspend their stylistic differences in order to aim for a common artistic goal. This involves the merging of visions and technical skills in projects that have proven to be typical of transitory periods, "motivated by the desire to *transform* existing knowledge and paradigms into new visions" (John-Steiner 2000, 70). Beginning with the collaboration between Picasso and Braque that gave birth to cubism, John-Steiner gives several examples of how the shared risks and practices in this kind of artistic collaboration have been essential to many crucial moments in experimental artistic practice. She argues that, eventually, integrative collaboration may transform "both the field and the participants" (ibid.), as was the case with Picasso and Braque. In our analysis of the collaborative practices of The Six Tones, all four modalities can be observed. Importantly, there are many examples of integrative and family collaboration in the later work of the group; but an oscillation between different roles or modes of collaboration contributes to an even greater dynamic.

2.2. The Six Tones

The Six Tones comprises two Vietnamese performers—Nguyễn Thanh Thủy (who plays đàn tranh) and Ngô Trà My (who plays đàn bầu)—and the Swedish guitarist Stefan Östersjö (also playing many other stringed instruments). The group was formed while the two Vietnamese performers were visiting Sweden as guest teachers at the Malmö Academy of Music in 2006. Since then, The Six Tones has been developing an artistic practice that wishes to challenge hierarchical constructions of musical experience. The group invites composers, performers, and artists in other fields to join in collaborative projects that cross the boundaries between disciplines and cultures. Initially, The Six Tones aimed to create an amalgamation of art music from Vietnam and Europe. An important component of its thinking has been how the transmission of a tradition always involves an element of transformation. Over the first few years, the group developed artistic strategies for playing traditional Vietnamese music in hybrid settings, using Western stringed instruments and traditional Vietnamese instruments, improvising in traditional and experimental Western idioms, and commissioning new music by composers in Asia as well as in Western countries. The name of the group derives from the nature of the Vietnamese language, which is a tonal language using six tones or intonations. A principal objective has been to create a foundation on which two distinct musical cultures can meet on equal terms. The group's practice implies the need to question what is *centre* and what is *periphery*: is Western art music the norm (*centre*) and traditional Vietnamese music an exotic *other*?[5] Already at the outset, the initial spark for the development of a method for intercultural work was the notion of creating situations of mutual learning.

5 A related question underlies chapter 3, above, which asks (in part) how, with seventeen hugely different components scattered across a universe of possibilities, *Footnotes* can possibly have a stylistic centre or a predominant "voice."

In his thesis, Stefan Östersjö (2008, 197) observes how, when the group was started in 2006, the persons involved "were all intending and expecting it to be a highly integrative collaboration, and always on equal terms." He continues by remarking how this was "ignorant and over-optimistic. In the first two years of our work, the mode in which we have mostly been working has been of the highly hierarchic master and apprentice-kind. . . . This was, I think, a big surprise for all of us" (ibid.). In many respects, the first three years were an intense crash course in intercultural collaboration. It was only in 2009–10 that more mature artistic results and a more articulated analytical understanding of the practice of the group began to emerge. Over the first three years, the learning wasn't always *mutual*; rather, in many situations, the musicians who had the most knowledge of and experience with a certain type of music would typically take the role of *master* and instruct the other players. However, the experience from later collaborative projects suggests that more interactive forms of collaboration are indeed also possible; but they demand careful curatorial attention, a component that was thoroughly lacking in the first three years. We will argue further below that The Six Tones has developed into a platform for intercultural and interdisciplinary collaboration and that the core of this practice is a *family collaboration* that extends from the original members of the group to a number of other artists.

2.3. Kent Olofsson

The collaboration between The Six Tones and composer Kent Olofsson started in 2009, long before the ideas emerged for *Arrival Cities: Hanoi*. In 2009 and 2010 Kent composed two shorter pieces which were released on CD in 2012. The first two scores reveal some specific points of friction in the relation between his mode of composing and the musical backgrounds of the two Vietnamese performers. In particular, the rhythmical structures were difficult to master; and for the composer, the traditional Vietnamese instruments caused other difficulties that were only gradually resolved. However, and thanks to the sustained collaborative process, by the time of the recording sessions in 2012, a more in-depth understanding had begun to emerge, laying the foundation for the music in *Arrival Cities: Hanoi*.

2.3.1. A longitudinal collaboration

First, we need to take a step further back in time, since the collaboration between Stefan Östersjö and Kent Olofsson goes back much further, in fact to the mid-1990s. At that point, Stefan was active on the contemporary music scene, a member of Ensemble Ars Nova (a leading group in Sweden at the time, started in 1986 by its first artistic director, Johannes Johansson), and initiating collaborations with composers in Sweden and abroad. The starting point for their work was when Stefan made a re-notation of the most complex parts of the score to Kent's guitar solo piece *Treccia* (1992), on the assumption that what the composer understood to be unresolvable technical difficulties in the piece were partly due to the notation and not its musical and idiomatic properties.[6] Without reducing the musical content or taking any information (or actual notes) out of the score, the re-notation, which Stefan first thought of as a study-score, enabled him to perform the composed structure as intended. Stefan and Kent met to assess this re-notated score, a meeting that immediately led to performances not only of *Treccia* but also of Kent's *The Garden of Earthly Delights* (1992), a concerto for guitar, chamber ensemble, and tape. Both of these works were recorded on Stefan's first solo CD (Östersjö 1997), an album for which Kent was the producer. The recording and post-production sessions became an important starting point for their collaborative work, centred on the exploration of contemporary guitar techniques and plucked string instruments that have affordances beyond the classical six-string guitar. Their work spanned different forms of exchange, composition, performance, recording (music by Olofsson but also by other composers), editing, mixing, testing live signal processing, and so on, and the collaboration cut very deeply into their practices. In his thesis, Stefan turned to John-Steiner's typology of collaborative modes (discussed above), noting how the collaboration oscillated between three different modalities:

> Even if the integrative aspect has dominated in later years, the "complementary" side to our work is still strong: In many ways, we have been doing a lot of work in the specialised manner typical of classical music of today, keeping with the respective roles of composer and performer. But, looking at the intensity of our work, at least since 1995, and considering the fact that we live in the same city, have worked in the same studios, with the same ensembles, and arranged festivals and concerts together, I would in the last analysis also find patterns of "family collaboration" in our work. True, we do not share lives in the literal sense but the various modes in which we have collaborated during the years and the seemingly endless stream of new projects, makes this a particularly strong musical association that has enriched both of our lives. (Östersjö 2008, 203)

In 2008, Stefan, as artistic director of the Swedish Ensemble Ars Nova, took the initiative in creating a collaboration with Teatr Weimar, an independent group in Malmö, with the aim of creating experimental music theatre building on the aesthetics of the hörspiel and other similar forms in electronic music. Teatr Weimar was created by the director and playwright Jörgen Dahlqvist, who directed the first production in 2008 and subsequently wrote the script for the second production, *Indy 500*, for which the music was composed by Kent Olofsson. This piece became the beginning of an extensive collaboration between Dahlqvist and Olofsson, and a new orientation in Olofsson's compositional practice (see Olofsson 2018).

6 The issues were specifically to do with the middle section, when the density of events increases; the notation, which gave a clear representation of the structure as an abstraction, did not give an immediately readable representation of the required action.

2.3.2. The Six Tones: from resistance to resonance

In March and April 2009, The Six Tones were touring in Scandinavia with a programme consisting almost entirely of new works for the group by Swedish composers. Olofsson was one of these composers, and he contributed one of the shortest pieces on the programme, thought of as a first étude, to be followed by other studies in writing for this particular group. He commented on his initial ideas for the piece in a recent interview:

> In the programme that you were rehearsing for the tour in 2009, I was struck by how many pieces used extended techniques, and I felt that this was too simple a solution, a quick fix compensating for not really knowing how the instruments work. But for me, I wanted to start from the very basic affordances of the instruments, checking out the range and the fundamentals of the playing technique. But I realise now, looking back at the first etude which you played in the tour that my solutions were equally simplistic. (Olofsson 2019a)

Seen from the outside, that score certainly did look much less demanding than most of the other works on the programme, but it is important to note that, when the tour started, the two Vietnamese players worried only about this piece. The reasons were entirely to do with a particular cultural resistance experienced in relation to the musical structure.

> 2008 was a transformative period in my compositional work. At this time I wrote a number of chamber music pieces that in different ways sought out classical music elements and structures, exploring how they might offer possibilities for a new music. In this etude I approached the Vietnamese instruments in a similar way to in these other chamber works. But importantly, when writing for Stefan two things were very different. Like when I integrated the charango into *Il Liuto d'Orfeo*, I knew his playing and also, since he was applying guitar techniques on this instrument, I knew exactly how to do it, because I also know the guitar. Here, with the three Vietnamese instruments and with the two Vietnamese players, when I employed more classical forms and materials, without really knowing neither the instruments nor the musicians more closely, the music that came out was rather simplistic. (Olofsson 2019a)

Figure 4.1.

Figure 4.1. Kent Olofsson, *Mirage* trio, 2009, bars 39–45.

Though the music may have been simplistic from the composer's point of view, passages like that in figure 4.1[7] certainly proved to be great stumbling blocks in the rehearsals of the group. While all the other pieces for the Scandinavian tour seemed to be much more demanding, virtuosic, and bigger in scope, in terms of both duration and playing techniques and sonorities, Kent's little trio continued to worry the two Vietnamese players. As Thủy explained, the difficulties were also culturally grounded:

> Kent's music was a challenge for both Trà My and I. There were some years in between the first trio for the group and the duo for Trà My and I. In the trio, the fast tempo, together with the changing metre, [which] included $\frac{5}{8}$ and $\frac{7}{8}$ in the middle of $\frac{3}{4}$ or $\frac{4}{4}$, were a nightmare for us. When I worked in the Malmö Academy of Music, I had some Swedish folk music students who introduced me to this kind of metre. My student could play the fiddle while his feet were bouncing the rhythm on the floor, changing his weight between the right and the left foot according to the shifting metre in the music. Even without my instrument, I was completely unable to follow the dance. I had never embodied this kind of swing. Vietnamese traditional music for my instrument uses only $\frac{2}{4}$ or $\frac{4}{4}$ metre, and we don't have a tradition of folk dance! Perhaps that was part of the reasons why it took so long for Trà My and me to practise that shifting metre in Kent's first trio. For only one line with five bars we could spend a lot of time, playing the instrument while nodding, singing the notes, swinging our bodies, tapping our feet loudly on the floor at the same time, and very often found that at least one or two parts of the body did not go together. This kind of basic rehearsing went on without much progress, and still, when we went on tour, we kept worrying only about this one piece in the entire programme. (Nguyễn 2019)

The fast, shifting metre in the trio was a kind of music that by no means could have been embodied by the two Vietnamese performers at this time. The struggle to get the music into the body, as described by Thủy above, was obvious and lengthy, and it was only several years later that the musical structures seemed to come more naturally to them.

Looking back at this score, Kent noted that "however simplistic the piece may have been, it still held materials that were eventually used in *Arrival Cities: Hanoi*, but in modified form. Paradoxically, what was eventually used had more to do with the few extended techniques that I used" (Olofsson 2019b). The rhythmic material with extended techniques were expanded and transformed for the opening part of the second trio in *Arrival Cities: Hanoi*. This music seeks to capture some of the complexity of the noise in the streets of Hà Nội, with percussive sounds performed on all three instruments and transformed in a tape part that was initially created for the pre-premiere performance at Manzi. Trà My describes her experience of playing this music, specifically how it connected to the moment "when you told of how you liked the image of street vendors selling flowers in the early morning, and when you told the story of your cousin working as a street vendor—right after that, we play the music with

7 An audio excerpt can be heard in the online repository (www.orpheusinstituut.be/en/voices-bodies-practices-media-repository) see file "SF4.1 *Mirage* trio (bars 39–45)."

a lot of noise from Hà Nội, and you also knock on the instrument; I had a very strong emotional reaction, I was transferred to Hà Nội, as if I were not anymore onstage, living in that scene, with the sound of people talking and of the street vendor calls" (Ngô 2019). The later stages of the collaboration between Kent and The Six Tones are discussed below; but the type of transformation, from the struggle to achieve an embodied understanding of a scored material to a holistic understanding of the music described here, became a characteristic feature of the work on the music for *Arrival Cities: Hanoi*.

2.4. Jörgen Dahlqvist

The Six Tones have a long history of collaborative work with the Swedish director Jörgen Dahlqvist that began with a piece of music theatre called *Idioms*. *Idioms* was created within the frame of "(Re)Thinking Improvisation" (2009–11), a project looking into the nature of musical improvisation in different cultures, in which The Six Tones took part. It brought together artists and researchers from different musical traditions and from different continents. The studies carried out by the members of The Six Tones focused on the interactions in the intercultural collaboration within the group, with specific reference to the forms for improvisation in traditional Vietnamese music, on the one hand, and "free improvisation," on the other. By 2010, The Six Tones had reached an increased awareness of the political implications of its work and wanted to move into more conceptually driven projects. *Idioms* became one of the major artistic outputs of "(Re)Thinking Improvisation" and also the beginning of a method to develop intercultural collaboration, with The Six Tones used as a platform. In 2012, Stefan, as principal investigator, launched a second senior research project that involved The Six Tones and Dahlqvist, "Music in Movement" (2012–15). Within the frame of "Music in Movement," a series of works were created that further developed artistic methods that allow for collaboration not only across cultures but also, importantly, between theatre, choreography, music, and film.

2.4.1. *Idioms* (2010)

The experimental music theatre project *Idioms* was developed in workshops with actors and musicians from the United States, Vietnam, and Sweden over a period of eighteen months. The music was created by the composer Richard Karpen, in close collaboration with The Six Tones, following methods for composer–performer collaboration that allowed for compositional processes that were not represented as scores but in performance. Hence, the aim was to devise a composition that is "not improvised, but that doesn't require notation" (Östersjö 2008, 33).[8]

8 For further discussion see Östersjö (2008, 2018); Östersjö and Nguyễn (2017).

The first working sessions took place at DXARTS in Seattle and involved Karpen, Dahlqvist, and the three musicians of The Six Tones. What emerged was a music that intentionally explored the contrasting formal characteristics of contemporary Western art music and traditional Vietnamese idioms. Dahlqvist was present in these sessions more as an observer, but he also created a series of short prose poems in response to the ongoing compositional process. The final manuscript, in the form of a more formalised script, emerged much later and involved materials drawn from several sources. The spoken, recited, and sung materials are in Vietnamese, Swedish, and English. They are a synthesis of three classic stories of impossible love across cultures and social barriers: Marguerite Duras's *The Lover*, Shakespeare's *Romeo and Juliet*, and the Vietnamese tale of *Mỵ Châu and Trọng Thủy*. The three main narratives were selected because they share similar archetypal structures and content. Hence the aim was to create shared layers in the narrative across three languages, layers that could be grasped by performers and audiences alike. The different traditions that the actors represent provided a range of expression in a span between spoken theatre and traditional music in Asia, Sweden, and the United States.

Just as the making of the music began with the friction between traditions, the entire process of creating the piece can be described as an oscillation between shared and opaque materials and modes of expression. Coessens and Östersjö (2014, 334) argue that in *Idioms*, "a space of intercultural musical experimentation emerges that tends to challenge the habitus, bringing out the resistance of materials, the body, and culture." The resistance of culture was manifest, for instance, in the traditional movement sets and facial expressions of Tuồng theatre, conventions known as *ước lệ*, and also in traditional costumes, which are associated with particular roles in which an actor is schooled as part of studying with a master. But cultural resistance is equally evident in negotiating understanding across European experimental theatre practices and in American conventions in many performing arts.[9] In making *Idioms*, the collaborators brought to bear multiple strategies, which we have analysed as "strategies of coexistence, the gradual establishing of trust between all participating artists, which in turn allowed for an increased openness of listening," with the result that "through the framework of interlocking narratives, the hybridity of the piece emerges exactly through the friction between incompatible entities such as the formal structures of contemporary Western and traditional Vietnamese music. Here, the composer and playwright employ similar compositional strategies, based on collaborative process and cross-cultural dialogue but also on the confrontation of the culturally and stylistically distinct materials brought into the piece by the artists involved" (Östersjö and Nguyễn 2017, 137).

9 The ensuing artistic challenges in the making of *Idioms* are discussed by Coessens and Östersjö (2014).

2.4.2. *Seven Stories* and *Nam Mái*

Two pieces, with immediate relation between their materials, were created in 2013–14. The first project was the dance film *Seven Stories*; this led directly to the second, a triple concerto with choreography and film titled *Nam Mái*, premiered with the Seattle Symphony and The Six Tones in April 2014. *Seven Stories* explored the choreographic elements of Tuồng theatre mentioned above. The artistic method was to collect video recordings of sets of movements associated with particular scenes in seven ancient plays, and to use these as basic material with which choreographer Marie Fahlin would create new movement vocabularies for the members of The Six Tones. These would be filmed to create fundamental gestural material that would then be employed in making the music, a collaboration between Karpen and The Six Tones. Both *Seven Stories* and its continuation in *Nam Mái* demanded intense collaborative work and also entailed staying together for several weeks at a time, since both projects took place in Seattle.[10] All this had a strong impact on the ideas for *Arrival Cities: Hanoi*, since *Seven Stories* was the first bigger film project carried out by Dahlqvist and The Six Tones and since both works suggested further possibilities implicit in the intersection between theatre and documentary.

3. Documentary, empathy, and inter-subjectivity

3.1. Musical interactions: listening, engagement, and voice

This section seeks to create a foundation for understanding the intercultural collaboration that is at the heart of *Arrival Cities: Hanoi*. It also returns to the question of performativity and to the specific forms of knowledge activated in performance (discussed above in chapters 1 and 2). Further, the discussion of the provisionality of the "I," as discussed by Catherine Laws in chapter 2 (p. 88),[11] is here taken further into a discussion of the ethics of musical interactions, broadly speaking. What we seek is an understanding of the ethical relation of the "I" to the other and how this may be expressed through performance in music and theatre. Through a close reading of Emmanuel Levinas, Matthew Rahaim (2017) proposes an ethical perspective on the relation between individuals in music-making through an exploration of what he calls the metaphysics of unity and alterity. This understanding of musical interactions is built on an intention to approach the Other—an acceptance and "absorption of the Other into an overarching unity" (ibid., 179). But this overarching unity is not reached through an act of totalising, of reducing, the other, but rather through an acknowledgment of the poles of alterity and unity. This Levinasian perspective has a strong

10 For a further discussion of this work, see Östersjö (2018).

11 There is a strong kinship between Agamben's discussion of testimony and the argument unfolded here, building on Levinas. In particular, in intercultural artistic collaboration, the suspension of the "I"—which may require a negotiation of a novel shared voice—is closely related to Agamben's notion of "testimony" (2000). For further on this, see chapter 2 in the present volume.

bearing on our understanding of world music and on how we conceive of musical Others. Rahaim further observes:

> the sound that I constitute as "chanting" would not strike me as a different voice, a different subjectivity, were it coming from my furnace; the sound that I constitute as "bell patterns" would not seem to both invite and frustrate dancing were they coming from a melting glacier. Perhaps the sounds would cause me concern or curiosity (about the workings of my machines or the progress of climate change), perhaps I might even imaginatively constitute them as a kind of cosmic *musica universalis*, but unless I constitute them as a (specific) type of (general) music, they would not arise as exotic, as different, as a "quality that would distinguish him from me."
>
> This felt exoticism is a particularly important affective resource in the age of nation-states, in which each person seems to require a nation and each nation seems to require a distinct culture, just as a census form requires each citizen to have unequivocal designations of gender, race and citizenship. (Rahaim 2017, 184)

Ethics, for Levinas, is defined by the relation between the *I* and the *Other*, a relation that emerges from the resistance of the face of the other to be reduced or assimilated to the *Self.* "For the presence before a face, my orientation toward the *Other*, can lose the avidity proper to the gaze only by turning into generosity, incapable of approaching the other with empty hands. This relationship established over the things henceforth possibly common, that is, susceptible of being said, is the relationship of conversation. The way in which the other presents himself, exceeding *the idea of the other in me*, we here name face" (Levinas 1969, 50). The unconditional conversation with the *Other* "is to welcome his expression, in which at each instant he overflows the idea a thought would carry away from it. It is therefore to *receive* from the Other beyond the capacity of the I" (ibid., 51). Derrida discusses in a similar way this relation with the other; he proposes an "absolute hospitality" that gives place not only to the foreigner (who has an accepted status and is able to claim hospitality by right) but also to the anonymous other (Derrida 2000).

3.1.1. Listening and voice

All human engagement with music starts with listening. We listen even before any sound is produced. Listening to the silence before the moment of sounding is part of the way pacing and rhythm is defined. Moreover, all listening is participation. The inter-subjective nature of listening is expressed in the lived experience of the reciprocal relation between subject and object. Salomé Voegelin (2010, 14) observes how, in the act of listening "the sonic object/phenomenon blasts the systemic and rational reality through its insistence on being heard, being experienced rather than abstracted." An ecological understanding of musical creativity also presumes that listening is embodied and situated. As observed by Roger Sessions ([1950] 1971, 11), "since music is created by human beings, we must regard the sources, or raw materials, first of all as human facts. For it is not rhythm and sound as such but their nature as human facts which concerns us. And if we look at them closely we perceive that they are actually human facts of the most intimate kind." Hence, musical experience is grounded in the basic properties of the human condition, the lived experience of breathing, of gravity, of day and night. But even more, it is the human experience of acting upon the world that constitutes the grounds for the musical experience. The fundamentals of such an ecological understanding, based on a theory of embodied music cognition, are articulated by Gorton and Östersjö in chapter one. What we wish to develop in this chapter is a further discussion of the inter-subjective nature of this experience, and even more, how the cultural situatedness can be negotiated in intercultural collaboration.

Östersjö and Nguyễn have previously addressed the intercultural practice of The Six Tones, building from Gadamer's discussion of the conditions for the hermeneutic experience and the necessity of a radical kind of openness, an openness that is the result of listening: "Anyone who listens is fundamentally open. Without this kind of openness to one another there is no genuine human relationship" (Gadamer [1989] 2004, 355). In what follows we will consider the specific challenges confronted by a musician seeking an encounter with the other through listening in intercultural collaboration. In a study carried out in 2009–11 we analysed rehearsals and performances of a specific traditional piece (see Östersjö and Nguyễn 2013), where the artistic aim was to develop strategies to transition from performing a Vietnamese traditional piece to free improvisation (which we at the time considered as a largely "Western" tradition). But rather than moving from one tradition to the other, we increasingly found that we were no longer firmly situated in either one. The difficulties we experienced in making aesthetic judgements in this working process may than be understood as the result of working in a liminal space, where such values are not yet established; that is, in a no-man's land between the aesthetical frameworks of our respective cultures. These observations also suggest why notions of mutual learning, of sharing musical traditions, and creating new music from a gradually deepening mutual understanding, are not sufficient to navigate such encounters. Showing hospitality to the other is the heart of ethics. It also is a prerequisite for a true openness of listening. "Welcoming the other means to be led by curiosity, to adopt an expectant attitude, to spare so much world space that in it each thing—a tree, a mountain, a house, the cry of a bird—loses all indifference and commonplaceness" (Cobussen and Nielsen 2012, 25).

We find the concepts of musical and musicianly listening, developed in the writings of Pierre Schaeffer, to be useful for creating a further understanding of the role of openness in intercultural musical performance. Michel Chion (2009, 39) defines musical listening as referring "back to traditional heritage, to established and accepted structures and values, which it attempts to rediscover or recreate; whilst *musicianly* hearing or invention seeks rather to locate interesting new phenomena or to innovate in the facture of sound objects. The musical attitude rests on old values; the musicianly attitude actively seeks new ones." But these two modes of listening are not to be understood as opposed; rather, they normally complement each other. Chion continues by suggesting that "by going backwards and forwards, by successive approximations between these two approaches, it might be possible to discover and establish values for a new music" (ibid.). In a recent paper, Östersjö (2018, 38) argues that "the pair of musical and musicianly listening cuts deep into the embodiment of the musician, whose tacit knowing is a musical backbone which can be understood as a performer's habitus. If 'musical listening', then, is resonant with tradition, its counterpart, 'musicianly listening' constitutes a resistance to the performer's habitus." The listening demanded in intercultural exchange demands a particular openness to the musical *other* of unfamiliar musical traditions. Such hospitality can develop through *musicianly listening*, activating a search for the unexpected under the surface of a sonic event.

As proposed by Gorton and Östersjö (2016), and as argued in chapter 1 above, the interaction between performer and instrument, also defined by the performer's habitus, can be analysed through the notion of a performer's voice; and when a composer enters the picture, a related idea—the "discursive voice"—enters as well. The present chapter is particularly concerned with a special case: the development of a discursive voice in the negotiation between performers across different cultural boundaries. Listening is essential to this process, and we believe that musicianly listening plays an important role in such negotiations, not only between human and non-human agents but, in the present context, also between cultures.

3.1.2. Empathy

Empathy has been studied in philosophy, aesthetics, and cognitive science since the early twentieth century, but it remains debatable whether empathy should be understood "as a genetic predisposition, a personality trait, an emergent attribute of perception-action coupling, a skill, or a social achievement" (Clarke, DeNora, and Vuoskoski 2015, 83). The theory of innate intersubjectivity that, according to Trevarthen and Aitken (2001, 4) proposes that "the infant is born with awareness specifically receptive to subjective states in other persons," was put forward in the 1970s to account for empirical observations. Indeed, it has been observed that "while the understanding and sharing of intentions emerges ontogenetically in all cultural settings at around 1 year of age—with no known individual differences due to environmental factors—the understanding of beliefs emerges some years later at somewhat different ages in different cultural settings" (Tomasello et al. 2005, 690). Building on such observations, Tomasello and his colleagues have developed the concept of *shared intentionality*. The human capacity for shared intentionality may very well constitute the grounds for the phenomenon of empathy. In the present chapter, we will follow the definition of empathy as either affective (built on sharing someone's mental state through emotional contagion) or cognitive (the ability to imagine being in someone else's shoes) (Ockelford 2017). However, we will first discuss how this definition can be challenged by a consideration of musical empathy.

Chapter 2 noted the work of Deniz Peters with regard to empathic qualities of listening, drawing on his argument that we hear—and empathically "feel in"—the touch of the performer as part of the embodied process of listening. Peters thereby proposes that social and musical empathy are distinct phenomena, but that they may be dialectically entwined, proceeding "through the lived body and [involving] a bodily hermeneutic. It is supported by, and in turn supports, social empathy with those factually or imaginatively involved in the musical event" (Peters 2015, 11).[12] Here, he acknowledges the complexity of this relation and observes that there are many possible situations in which music supports empathy. But he suggests that these are not equivalent to musical empathy; rather, they are better understood as *empathy through music* (ibid., 5).

Ian Cross and colleagues make similar observations, suggesting that music be understood as "a process that requires us to be sensitive to the inner states of others; as an environment that may allow us to experience feelings that are congruent with the feelings of others; and as a manifestation of a state of shared intentionality, a state of which the goal may be simply the maintenance of that state. Music seems to embody the attitudes and emotions of others, which provides us with a basis for engaging both reflexively and reflectively with the music and with the inferred internal states of those with whom we are busy making music" (Cross, Laurence, and Rabinowitch 2012, 340). They further suggest that intersubjectivity in musical interaction becomes possible through "the combined contributions of disinterest, flexibility, and ambiguity that transform shared intentionality from a mere sharing of intentions and attention into a condition in which each individual is completely free to be herself—to the extent that she can openly and unrestrainedly experience others, fully cooperate and merge with them through the music, and feel their affective and cognitive dynamics as if they were her own" (ibid., 342).

But the use of empathy in qualitative research has also been contested. As summarised by Watson (2009, 114), empathy is often referred to as a means in qualitative research to gather more reliable data, and it is assumed to be useful as "an authenticating device that persuades the reader of the validity of the account" when results are presented. However, Watson argues that "the easy assumption of empathy potentially stifles research and can give rise to unethical practices. In the first case, . . . the possibility of entering into another's situation, can give rise to complacency in research terms" (ibid., 114). She continues by discussing a second case, in which an interviewer may exploit the interviewees by assuming commonalities and identification and thereby reproducing structures of oppression. The practice of The Six Tones has been characterised by an awareness of the risk of structural oppression, either through the repetition of historical archetypes or by such assumed "understanding" of the Other; and, hence, its approach to qualitative analysis, developed in the artistic research practices of the group,[13] has also involved the development of an articulated understanding of these matters. Still, in the making of *Arrival Cities: Hanoi*, there are several reasons for particular scrutiny of the working process, taking Watson's plea for caution seriously. She argues for a considered understanding

12 The concept of bodily hermeneutics is closely related to Becker's notion of a habitus of listening, and refers to how our listening is culturally acquired; but, as also discussed by Gorton and Östersjö in chapter 1, Peters (2015) observes how such bodily interpretation is on the one hand an active and partly voluntary process, while on the other hand it is also subconscious, a differentiation which can be related to the levels of the body image and body schema. Peters's assertion about social empathy is further supported by a study of musical empathy in autistic children carried out by Ockelford (2017).

13 For a further discussion of the use of video-stimulated recall see chapter 3 of this volume; that method has been developed in the work of The Six Tones through a series of projects that began in 2009.

of the relational complexity "in which we have to confront not only difference between ourselves and those we seek to engage with, but also . . . our own internal multiplicities and differences" (Watson 2009, 114). We will discuss below how a performative approach to the research process, applied in particular in the final staging of the findings, has been a method for addressing these issues related to the role of empathy in the interaction between people in the making of *Arrival Cities: Hanoi.*

3.1.3. Interaction

Cobussen and Nielsen (2012) emphasise the ethical dimension of the interaction between improvising musicians, which they identify by observing how an improviser operates in a space between the individual and the collective. Building on a reading of Jean-Luc Nancy, they argue that "being does not precede the possibility of being-with-others: our ontological condition is fundamentally social. Existence is always already coexistence" (ibid., 81). But this is not communitarianism. Nancy (1991a, 15) observes how community "assumes the impossibility of its own immanence, the impossibility of a communitarian being in the form of a subject." It is not a project of collectivity or fusion; rather, through Nancy's emphasis on *being-with-others*, it signals "the possibility of connection but simultaneously exposes distance, difference and space" (Cobussen and Nielsen 2012, 81).[14] Such *being-with-others* is expressed through listening; and, as observed by Cobussen and Nielsen, through the possibility of a non-listening, agonistic mode of hospitality, acts of resistance are carried out that still serve the community. They conclude that "only through contest can existing values be questioned, tested and, when necessary, reformed or created anew" (ibid., 88). We believe that the ethics of improvisation is expressed through the emergence of a discursive voice by means of such interactions. In free improvisation, this process can be immediate or gradually emerging, with spontaneous and intuitively successful adaptations, or it can be a more searching negotiation between distinctly articulated voices. The formation of a discursive voice can certainly also be a matter of modifying or restricting one's individual characteristic voice in order to bring out a specific shared voice. Such blending is one basic feature of the discursive voice in improvisation. However, a contrasting principle is equally important. In many forms of music, and in much free improvisation, attention centres on difference and a sonic ideal based on heterogeneity.[15] Here, the core principle is co-existence—not through sameness but rather through what Glissant (1997) discusses as an acknowledgement of the right to opacity. We must not understand

14 As pointed out by Catherine Laws in chapter 2 (p. 159), drawing on a similar discussion of Nancy, the complexity of the relation between self and other has a strong bearing on the formation of discursive voice in composer–performer collaboration.

15 Such heterogeneity is a typical feature of several forms of traditional Vietnamese music. One example is Tài Tử, a form of chamber music in the south of Vietnam, with which The Six Tones are currently engaging in the research project "Musical Transformation." Here, improvisational skills are central, but musicians seek out other players whose voice is distinct from their own. The ensembles normally include not more than six instruments, but, more importantly, "no two of the same instrument are found in performance; this also is related to the heterophonic texture, as audience members should be able to discern the tone color of each instrument" (Cannon 2016, 143).

the unknowable. The individual character of each performer must be highlighted to create a discursive heterogeneous voice.

We find these two contrasting approaches to be equally strong expressions of an ethical approach to the musical other. Hospitality expressed through the principle of blending may be understood as attentive listening based on adaptation. Blending emerges from a search for sameness. The discursive heterogeneous voice instead builds on the creation of a space for co-existence and a celebration of difference.

3.2. Performative ethnography

It is only in the last decade that the critique of Western research methodologies from a postcolonial perspective has begun to receive proper attention in the field of music (Agawu 2003; Smith 2012; Solomon 2012; McCollum and Hebert 2014). A considered understanding of the issues raised by postcolonial theory and its critique of the emic/etic perspective on method also demands the development of new research methodologies as well as a reconsideration of formats for effective presentation of results to diverse audiences. A globalised society with the increasing speed of modern communication technologies and the current streams of migration not only places new demands on Western societies at the political level but also permeates every aspect of contemporary culture; transmission of cultural traditions and values and the function of artistic creativity are some key elements in this scenario. A decolonised ethics of ethnology entails a "participatory mode of knowing" which "privileges subjectivity, personal knowledge, and the specialized knowledges of oppressed groups. It uses concrete experience as a criterion of meaning and truth" (Denzin 2003, 243).

In the early 1970s, anthropologists began to approach performance through ethnographic methods by developing a wider perspective on cultural performance, building on Goffman's sociological frameworks, which "encapsulate all interactive moments as the negotiated performances of individual selves in the politics of social life" (Haanstad 2014, 94). As argued by Victor Turner, by approaching anthropology through performance "the actors' 'inside view,' engendered in and through performance, becomes a powerful critique of how ritual and ceremonial structures are cognitively represented" (Turner and Turner 1982, 34). Turner's practice takes Goffman's notion of performance-as-mimesis as a point of departure and turns it into poesis, a process through which performative methods for anthropology were established (Haanstad 2014). Denzin (2003, 8) claims that performative ethnography may "contribute to an epistemological and political pluralism that challenges existing ways of knowing and representing the world. Such formations are more inclusionary and better suited than existing ways for thinking about postcolonial or 'subaltern' cultural practices. Performance approaches to knowing insist on immediacy and involvement. They consist of partial, plural, incomplete, and contingent understandings, not analytic distance or detachment, the hallmarks of the textual and positivist paradigms."

The artistic method that emerged out of the collaboration between The Six Tones, Dahlqvist, and Olofsson was built on collaboration across disciplines and cultural boundaries. It began with aiming to create working conditions built on trust and mutual learning (Östersjö and Nguyễn 2013). While we have problematised the concept of mutual learning in previous publications (Östersjö and Nguyễn 2017), we still find this approach essential in order to arrive at collaborative forms that allow the participating artists to transcend the regulative framework of each discipline through the activation and further challenging of one's habitus (Coessens and Östersjö 2014; Gorton and Östersjö 2016). The ethics of interdisciplinary and intercultural collaboration is a central focus of attention. Sara Ahmed (2002, 570) suggests that every meeting with someone else is "bound up with responsibility—with recognizing how relationships of power mediate and frame the encounter itself." Further, she observes that "a dialogue must take place, precisely *because* we do not speak the same language" (ibid.). Performative ethnography creates a liminal space, both between artistic disciplines and between cultural processes, building on "a collaborative social science research model that makes the researcher responsible not to a removed discipline (or institution), but to those he or she studies. This model stresses personal accountability, caring, the value of individual expressiveness, the capacity for empathy, and the sharing of emotionality" (Denzin 2003, 258). This liminal space is also characterised by aesthetic challenges, which Rachel Swain suggests may give rise to "a dramaturgy of incompleteness; an incomplete experience" (2014, 161). "It is compelling, it evokes a curiosity in the spectator, a need to listen for meaning as it emerges between what is seen and what is unseen" (ibid.). Some of these challenges are discussed in section 3.1.1, above, in relation to the act of listening, in particular with regard to the development of openness and with reference to the notion of *musicianly listening*.

Art historian Grant H. Kester (2011) argues that social and collaborative work in itself carries potential and points at the direct political and social agency of art. It follows that art "is no longer merely a semantic reflection of social and political situations, rather it has the potential to change and intervene in the social through temporal processes and collaborative practices" (Groth and Samson 2017, 104). This implies that collaborative explorations of interdisciplinarity can only be carried out through a conceptually driven understanding of artistic practice.

Ethnomusicology has long made use of recorded audiovisual materials as a way of accessing the music of other cultures; this has primarily taken the form of observational documentation (e.g., Baily 2009; Zemp 1988). This practice has led to the emergence of interactive, reflexive, and performative modes of ethnographic film-making, which are being explored in visual anthropology and in other areas of the arts, humanities, and social sciences (Schneider and Pasqualino 2014; Schneider and Wright 2010, 2013; Ingold 2011). With the emergence of digital materiality, Pink et al. (2017) argue that technology affords widened possibilities for creating participatory formats for video ethnography. Empathy is a central component in their research process, which they see as the opposite of objectifying the other. Rather, they argue for a reflexive understanding of empathy, which evades the notion of achieving perfect empathy. This reflexive form of empathy they define

> not as a capacity of the researcher as beholder of the experience of others, but as a form of imagination only ever emergent from specific and intentional encounters. If we consider that in a processual and contingent world our feelings of empathy are emergent, then it is possible to align the environment/context and the feelings that are generated through and are also constitutive elements of it. This removes the tendency for knowledge to be "closed down" . . . and by offering a different analytical path invites us to understand what we learn through our contact with the experiences of others in research as open and fluctuating. (Pink et al. 2017, 374)

But the possibilities inherent in digital video technologies and internet-based interactions also entail combinations of methods. We are specifically interested in how "the link between performative engagement, auto-ethnography and ethnographic desire can be articulated in order to overcome the subordinating gaze of ethnography that, despite anthropology's reflexive turn, often excises the ethnographer's role as an active participant" (Haanstad 2014, 99).

Contemporary European theatre has experienced a similar development over the past decades, looking for "ways to articulate reality without contributing to making private, daily life a theatrical spectacle" (Dreysse and Malzacher 2008, 10). In a study of the German performing arts collective Rimini Protokoll, Dreysse and Malzacher note how, by inviting *everyday experts* onstage—a term coined by the collective—they make *real* people stand in the centre of the production as experts, and "create the performances through their stories, their professional or private knowledge and lack of knowledge, through their experiences and personalities" (ibid., 9)., Thus, regardless of what theme is addressed, theatre can "stake a claim for the particular, concrete person against the politically generalised, in the way that documentary material is confronted with subjective experiences, the social and the individual are combined, and information about subjective perception is expanded" (ibid.). Hence individual and collective—or cultural—memory become central perspectives.

In a study of two theatre projects engaging with the memorial culture in Flanders concerning the First World War, Karel Vanhaesebrouck (2017, 46) observes that "artists use documentary material not to get at the truth, but to question power and truth, to show how truth is fabricated. Rather than a positivist documentary theatre, the theatre-makers offer a metahistorical perspective laying bare the ideological bloodlines of historiography, interpreting history ideologically and therefore politically." Vanhaesebrouck reminds us that forgetting is also an essential part of individual and cultural memory, and that our understanding of the past is always constructed from a particular perspective. "Our relation to the past is invariably multiperspectival. The historian, therefore, should not gloss over that variance, the fact that the past is fundamentally unknowable. On the contrary, it is precisely this variety the historian should reveal—not *the* historical reality, but the range of historical realities. Rather than bring order to events, the historian accepts the disorder of history as a starting point" (ibid., 42).[16] Gerard Siegmund (2008, 209) similarly observes how the practice of Rimini Protokoll holds the possibility of radicalising "the concept of the enactment of the imaginary in that they use the supplementary character of the imaginary for the creation of reality. Although they play with fictive elements, they do not present an exclusively imaginary image representing the world as a possible other." Theatre, as a site for the mediation between individual and collective memory through performance, can allow for a negotiation between the passing on of information and the sharing of experience and emotion:

> Memory becomes important as a process of finding something again after its loss, after the moment of disorientation that comes through the destructive (since physicality entails destruction) and temporal process of moving away from a place even as memory recreates it. Memory, by reopening a situation, stands, in the first instance, no longer in a semiotic context, but rather in one of performative processes. . . . It ignites itself in the here and now with specific materials that it organises as a constellation in space to create logic through their use. Simultaneously memory marks the point at which individual loss writes itself into collective remembrance. (Siegmund 2008, 192)

In discussing *The House with the Ocean View*, a piece of performance art by Marina Abramović, Peggy Phelan (2004, 574) explores how "live performance might illuminate the mutual and repeated attempt to grasp, if not fully apprehend, consciousness as simultaneously intensely personal and immensely vast and impersonal." In her reading she returns to Levinas and to the notion that ethics is essentially expressed in the face-to-face relation to the other. Here, the role of the body in performance, understood as layered in social, cultural, and biological strata, is underlined, as part of this conversation with the other:

> The condition of witnessing what one did not (and perhaps cannot) see is the condition of whatever age we are now entering. Whether we call this period "the post-postmodern age" or "the age of terrorism," it is characterized both by an intimate reawakening to the fragility of life and a more general sense of connection to one another that exceeds simple geophysical, ideological, or cultural proximity. If Levinas is right, and the face-to-face encounter is the most crucial arena in which the ethical bond we share becomes manifest, then live theatre and performance might speak to philosophy with renewed vigor. So far the language of this conversation has been largely nonverbal. Becoming fluent will require practice, patience, humility, and the recognition that the social body, like our own all-too-human body, is both stronger than we guessed and unbearably tender. The connection between the social body and the mortal body is defiantly metaphorical. The metaphorical link, however, is fused by the literal physical body—whether the body of a suicide bomber or of an earnest artist—as its actions and inactions make vivid the drama we face every moment of this, our dismaying young century. (Phelan 2004, 577)

16 This understanding, differently inflected, underlies much of the historical "reality" fabricated in the course of creating *Footnotes*; see chapter 2, above.

Such face-to-face conversations are to a great extent non-verbal and situated in embodied and artistic domains. Thomas Fuchs discusses bodily memory through a phenomenological inquiry into habit and claims that the lived body can only be understood through other bodies: "each body forms an extract of its past history of experiences with others that are stored in intercorporeal memory. In the structures of the lived body, the others are always implied: They are meant in expression and intended in desire. Thus, a person's typical patterns of posture, movement, and expression are only comprehensible when they refer to actually present or imaginary others" (Fuchs 2012, 15).[17] We believe that the body can hold multiple archival functions that can be engaged with in performance, as implied by Catherine Laws in chapter 2 (p. 155), above, when she referred to her embodied knowledge of piano playing as "the archives of the performing body." The choreographer André Lepecki cites Foucault's depiction of an archive as a "*general system of* formation and transformation of statements" (Foucault 1972, 130) and then argues that, similarly, "choreography is also a dynamic system of transmission and of transformation, an archival-corporeal system that also turns *statements* ... into corporeal events and kinetic things" (Lepecki 2010, 37). To Lepecki, "these zones, or regions, or dimensions form and transform not only our notions but our very *experiences* of time, presence, identity, alterity, body, memory, past, future, subjectivity. The archive as border becomes the vertiginous skin where all sorts of onto-political 're-writings' (Foucault 1972, 140) take place, including the re-writing of movement, including the re-writing of the archive itself" (Lepecki 2010, 38).

4. The making of Arrival Cities: Hanoi

In the following sections we will outline the collaborative process through which *Arrival Cities: Hanoi* was created. We draw on several layers of data collection and analysis: qualitative interviews with the key participants; stimulated recall sessions carried out while the project was underway, and further, on a comparative analysis of musical scores produced at different stages in the longitudinal collaborative processes that led to the making of *Arrival Cities: Hanoi.*

4.1. Creating the documentary

We (the two authors) went to Vietnam in early May 2014 to shoot materials for the film, mainly in the Highlands. Our objective was to capture there the life of people who had not made the journey into the city. We were particularly interested in hand gestures, and we wanted to capture everyday examples of gesture in handicraft and other daily chores in the countryside. The idea of working with hand gestures had its origins in the previous work we had done with actors

17 But the body can also have the opposite function: it can create a detached sense of estrangement, as described by Catherine Laws with reference to the film with close-ups of her hands in *Player Piano*, through which her hands appear as "strange, dismembered, almost abstract forms, positioned this way and that; objects with, often, no apparent function" (see chapter 2, p. 118, above).

from the National Tuồng Theatre in Hà Nội, first with *Idioms*, but even more in the making of the film *Seven Stories* and the concerto *Nam Mái*, which had just been premiered in Seattle. We had also tested some hand gestures in a working session with Kent Olofsson earlier that spring, and we now hoped that gestures from traditional theatre and also from daily life could become choreographic material, from which we could also create some of the music. Much of the travel was done by bicycle, stopping in little villages, and conducting short interviews here and there. When we set out to collect these video materials, we did not yet have a clear plan for how the project was to be carried out or what would be the actual focus.

When we returned to Hà Nội, some days before the arrival of Jörgen Dahlqvist, we were getting increasingly engaged in the question of how to go about making the piece. Thanh Xuân, Thủy's mother, was a professional Tuồng actress. In discussions with her about the ideas for an inquiry into migration from the countryside to Hà Nội, she first gave an account of her own journey from her homeland in Bắc Ninh to Hà Nội, when she was twelve, in order to study Tuồng at the National Tuồng Theatre. But when she finished her own story, she continued with another, about a boy named Lưu Ngọc Nam, who came from a little village in the north but decided to study southern-style Tuồng. He became a professional actor but, when the war ended in 1975, the southern-style theatre was sent south. Since he now had family in Hà Nội, he decided to stay, a decision that meant he would have to bring his skills into a different type of theatre. This turned out to be an aesthetic conflict that he could not resolve and, after some years struggle, he gave up his career and decided to become a costume-maker.

We were immediately struck by some of the qualities in this story and called Lưu to arrange a meeting. Later the same day we went to his apartment, in the area around the theatre where he still works. He was very open to us—of course he had known Thủy since she was a child—and was immediately interested in the project we described. We agreed to meet again after Jörgen Dahlqvist had arrived, when we would discuss how to go about the interview.

Some days later, we again met up with Lưu to introduce him to Jörgen. We agreed to film him while he performed one or more scenes from Tuồng, and we told him that we wanted material that had choreographic qualities and made use of hand gestures. But the main focus was to record his life story, and this we agreed to do in an interview carried out by Thủy. The filming took two days: the first day for the interview and the second for the performance and other outdoor shots. As the first day proceeded, it became very obvious that we had found the central story of the piece. Lưu was a great storyteller, and his life story had all the components of a Greek tragedy. Furthermore, his experience—not being able to use his individual voice as an actor and his tragic defeat when he had to give up the dream of his life, to be an actor, and instead become a costume-maker—captured so many perspectives of what to us seemed to characterise the fate of a migrant.

But the day when we recorded his performance was also very touching. We were clearly witnessing the performance of an aging man's memories of this particular scene. The passage of time has its impact on memory, and the decay of the aging body imparts a certain character to movement. But, in the performance, his conviction and strong presence still expressed his passion for this art form and reflected the qualities his performance once must have had. This performance became another central focus, and we decided more or less immediately to incorporate the video of Nam's performance into the piece. The project thereby had a flying start, but we were still not clear how to continue the work. We knew we wanted to interview people who had migrated to Hà Nội from the countryside, but we had no clear idea how to go about it. Nor did we know what groups of people this would include. Jörgen later reflected on his own starting point for the work:

> At the time when I went to Hà Nội to start up the project, there were many migrants coming to Sweden, and a heated discussion of migration was in the media. There were rumours spread that migrants would force young people and women to beg in the street and that this was organized by criminal organisations. Also, the police tried to evict people from the camps and politicians proposed to criminalize begging. So this was a backdrop for me when we set out to explore migration and the life of street vendors in Hà Nội. (Dahlqvist and Nguyễn 2018)

Even at the outset we were convinced that we wanted to explore the situation of street vendors in Hà Nội. In 2008, the city of Hà Nội "banned street vending along sixty-two streets in the city center and in forty-eight public spaces around hospitals, schools, and bus and train stations" (Eidse, Turner, and Oswin 2016, 343). This had a much stronger impact on itinerant vendors, who do not have the social network to allow them to bribe the local police, as resident vendors do. Hence, the position of migrant vendors is much more fragile, as noted by Turner and Schoenberger (2012, 1038): "In Hanoi, street vendors differentiate sharply by residential status: long-term city residents operating fixed stalls, or migrant itinerant traders. While groups of itinerant migrant workers do share accommodation and support each other, there is currently little space in Hanoi for democratic participation and we have found no evidence of vendors organising beyond immediate bonding and bridging social capital ties and networks among neighbours and friends; albeit these remain crucial." We wanted to interview migrant vendors, and we knew that many were staying more or less temporarily in the Long Biên and the Phúc Tân areas, both near the Red River. At this point we heard about a couple who rented out the first floor of their house to street vendors in Phúc Tân. We called the couple and agreed to interview them, after which they would let us talk to the vendors in their house.

> We had this assumption that the landlords would be corrupt and cheating, or making benefits from hosting the street vendors. Therefore we carefully hid the zoom recorder and agreed to Wallraff[18] the owners of the house. We started the audio recording before entering the house, but when we met them they were really nice. When Thủy asked them if they were ok that we filmed them they were

18 Günter Wallraff is a German writer and undercover journalist. His investigative methods have led to the creation of the Swedish verb *wallraffa*, referring to undercover action with the aim of exposing misconduct, a word currently included in the dictionary *Svenska Akademiens Ordlista*.

> very positive. To our surprise, they appeared to be very happy and even proud to share their experience of hosting the women in their house. Since Thủy made the interview in Vietnamese, translating only central bits along the way, my understanding of the situation was fractional. But still I realized that their role was very different to what we had expected, and that they expressed that their aim was to take care of the women and help them to manage in the city. So rather suddenly it was decided that this first interview was over and that we would go down to meet with the women. (Dahlqvist and Nguyễn 2018)

When we went downstairs to meet the street vendors, they were initially very shy and tired after a long working day, and not so keen to share their stories. Jörgen wondered whether we were intruding and disturbing their privacy. At first we didn't film them—just the interiors of the house where they stayed. But Thủy started up conversations with some of the women, and more and more of them became curious and joined in.

> I had seen images on television of migrant camps, where people stay in very poor conditions, with just an empty room and a carpet to sleep on. When we walked down to the cellar of the house, I was shocked to find that these street vendors were living under similar circumstances. While the house where we interviewed the landlord was nice, the basement afforded only a naked concrete floor on which the women slept on bamboo carpets. It was very dark, with a naked light bulb in the middle of the room, and the women kept their bikes inside the bedroom as well. I was very hesitant about filming this scene, since their situation seemed so vulnerable. What happened then was that Thủy started to talk to the women, and it seemed to me that they started to share their stories with her, and that they did so on their own initiative, as if they wanted to tell their stories. Then I started filming more and more and in the end I was seated next to Thủy and Stefan, trying to capture their stories. (Dahlqvist and Nguyễn 2018)

Thủy played a central role here, first explaining the aims of the project to the women, and then trying to build trust so that they might feel comfortable in sharing their experiences. She made it clear that they were of course free to pull out of the interview at any time and that the recorded material would only be used with their agreement. This is how she described her role in making the documentary:

> When we approached street vendors in Hà Nội, it was initially not easy to convince them to participate in the interviews. Many were shy or unwilling to talk to us. We were aware of the fragility of their situation, and careful to ask for the consent from each individual. Often I had to approach them on my own to start a conversation, and if they agreed to make an interview, I would introduce the director and the other members of the group. Eventually we managed to record a good number of interviews with street vendors, several of them made in the sheds and other locations where they stayed (often upon invitation from them), but also in the streets. Once the conversations got started, many generously shared their life stories, while others gave only sparse accounts, and we of course did not want to urge anyone to share more than what they wanted. (Nguyễn and Östersjö, unpublished text)

At the same time, Trà My, the đàn bầu player of The Six Tones, was in tears in the back of the room, and so she did not participate at all in the interviews. When Jörgen started to film the interviews, he tried to be very discrete and film only from a distance.

As mentioned by Turner and Schoenberger (2011), migrant vendors commonly support each other, and such cooperation was very evident here. The women we interviewed were all from the same village, which gave them a social network—a fragile one, but one that was strengthened by the support they were given from their little community and the landlord. Jörgen described his impression of this visit:

> What I realized through this situation, and the interviews with the landlord and the women, was that my prejudices regarding migration and the existential situations it creates were completely Eurocentric. I realized that the landlords were truly aiming to help the women by offering them a place to stay. The women were not stigmatized by their poverty, nor by their profession. Rather, they were proud that they were able to help their family and their children through their profession. Also, the context, which I first experienced as threatening, was in actual fact completely harmless, and the people I met this evening made me see how empathy is central to how people can manage in vulnerable situations like here in one of the poorest parts of Hà Nội. (Dahlqvist and Nguyễn 2018)

A similar experience is articulated by Östersjö as part of *Arrival Cities: Hanoi*. But even for the two Vietnamese members of the group, this experience was transformative, although in different ways. As mentioned, Trà My was crying all the way through the interviews, and the next day, we had a conversation about her experience and why she cried (and really could not participate at all). She said she had been reminded of her life situation some years back, when she stayed in an area not far from where we made the interview, and where many of her neighbours were street vendors: "I was not a street vendor myself, but my situation was similar to theirs. It was so hard to make ends meet" (Ngô 2019). She continued by describing how she had lived in a single room with her son while her mother lived in the pigsty next to it, on the concrete floor and with only three walls and no way to keep out the rain and the cold.

> For me, or perhaps for all of us, but I speak for myself here, this kind of meeting shifted the project in a new direction. First of all, we all had a first-hand experience of the reality of migration to Hà Nội. Second, the project became a personal challenge to all of us. I realized that this project had to change my prejudices regarding migration. I also discovered my European gaze through the interviews made this evening. The poverty and the poor circumstances in this site, combined with the tenderness expressed by the landlords in relation to the street vendors and also the care that the street vendors expressed for one another, shifted my view both of myself and of each of the individuals that I met on this evening. (Dahlqvist and Nguyễn 2018)

The first interviews with street vendors shifted the project towards addressing these social perspectives as clearly as possible. The more abstract approach to hand gesture faded out, and the use of choreography would only find its way back into the structure of the piece a little later. We now knew that the piece would have to focus on how stories are shared and on the empathy that was expressed between the women in this house. But we still had not decided how to use these interviews and structure a performance from the video. Moreover, we were soon to start working on the music with Kent Olofsson, who was also arriving in Hà Nội. The aim now was to produce and rehearse enough music and create enough video for a performance of a work-in-progress at the Manzi gallery in Hà Nội.

4.2. Creating the music

When Kent arrived, he brought with him a draft of the first trio, which used the Vietnamese electric guitar. He also had some sketches and ideas for trios, one of them also using the tỳ bà (a four-stringed Vietnamese lute), but these were incomplete and meant to be tested and negotiated with the group. However, the immediate plans were not only to work on instrumental music, but also to record soundscapes from the city. These recordings were largely produced by Stefan and Kent, with some assistance from Thủy. Recording was also used to document various materials that were improvised in sessions in Hà Nội to develop material for the piece. Hence, the work began with a much more integrated mode of collaboration than had been evident previously. But how, when, and why did this shift in the working modality take place? In an interview in February 2019, Olofsson situates this shift at the later end of 2009, the year when he composed the first trio for the group:

> Olofsson: At around this time there was a change in my relation to scores, which has changed so much for me. In 2009, the work was still very much in the score, and it's not anymore. Over the past ten years, this has really changed for me.
>
> Dahlqvist: I am thinking of *Hamlet: Exit Ghost*, isn't that where it really changed? This process was so much about emotion.
>
> Olofsson: I think the shift was with *Indy 500*; it is a mental thing, how you feel about the work. Before this piece, it was so much connected to the score, but from here on, it became more and more related to the situation, the emotion, and the interaction with the performers. (Dahlqvist and Olofsson 2019)

The different approach to composition that Kent identifies as a mental shift in relation to the musical work is thoroughly discussed in his thesis (Olofsson 2018). It entails working with musical composition as part of a dramaturgical strategy:

> As such, [composition] operates in relation to all the other elements of a performance and the way the overall creative process is shaped is decisive for how the concept can be implemented. It has been essential to find general methods that embrace all art forms and that the artists involved can use in their part of the

> creation. In this way these methods become common tools that work both for each art form as well as for the overall dramaturgical work. A fundamental precondition for the methods, as discussed above, is the concepts of shared space and shared time. The works analysed show that the elements of the performances are largely created in intertwined parallel processes, in an oscillating movement between the conceptual level, the large-scale forms (macroform) and the moment of performance (mesostructures). (Olofsson 2018, 246–47)

After this change, Kent's compositional practice was increasingly related to its qualities as a staged production, and thereby to the situation and a direct interaction with the performers, shaping materials on the floor, in a studio, or in rehearsals onstage. This implies an integration of composition and improvisation and certainly also a move towards more integrative forms of creative collaboration. The first trio was written before the work on *Indy 500* had started (the premiere of this music theatre production took place in November 2009), but this observation from Olofsson also seems consistent with the experience of the members of the trio. When the trio was created, the interaction between composer and the performers was more limited than had been usual in the work of The Six Tones. Although Olofsson was given an introductory presentation of the instruments, there was never time for a more in-depth exchange about the traditions of traditional Vietnamese music and Olofsson's compositional universe. Perhaps this can partly be attributed to the fact that Stefan and Kent had had such a long history of close collaboration that a collaborative mode of working was simply presumed. The resistance of the intercultural collaboration also put constraints on the compositional process: "With The Six Tones, there is a distance from the beginning. I really found the cultural difference very difficult. I had so much experience of collaborating with classical musicians, and especially with soloists playing contemporary music. In such collaborative work, like with Stefan, I was very much at home. But this felt distance of course changed over time" (Dahlqvist and Olofsson 2019).

The process by which this distance was overcome is central to our discussion. But the shift happened only gradually and laboriously. In 2009, the collaboration was very distributed, like a conventional commission from a chamber music group to a composer; but a substantial change took place in the period between the premiere of the trio and the creation of the next piece, the duo for đàn tranh and đàn bầu. The change lies not in the nature of the collaboration; rather, the interactions underlying the different, and much more idiomatic, nature of the second score are situated in the composer's listening. We would suggest that the more elaborate way in which the traditional instruments are operated with here results from the composer's musicianly listening. Traditional playing techniques, in particular the bending of a plucked pitch, which in traditional Vietnamese music is essential to the ornamentation, is here used to structure the harmony. The musical *other*, here represented by traditional Vietnamese ornamentation, is present in the score, but it is transformed through attentive listening.

Figure 4.2.

The difference between the two études can be illustrated by the organisation of the pitch material in the two pieces. With the đàn bầu and the đàn tranh, the most immediate connection lies in the bending technique in the đàn tranh, since the đàn bầu is entirely operated by bending. In the first piece, pitch is thought of as discrete steps, and the entire pitch range is used without a clear understanding of how the instrument responds in different registers and, even less, of how the choice of pitch material affects the playing technique. In the second piece, in contrast, pitch structure and harmony is drawn out of the idiomatic playing technique of bending (see figure 4.2).[19] The same technique is used in the first trio in *Arrival Cities: Hanoi*, here with a third instrument on which bending is the central idiomatic feature, the Vietnamese electric guitar (figure 4.3),[20] which is carried through in the score for the later version with chamber ensemble (see 4.2.5 below).[21]

Figure 4.3.

Something radical has happened with the composer's voice in the duo. As suggested above, there appears to be an element of musicianly listening involved in his different engagement with the Vietnamese instruments. But the felt resistance of this second score was still very strong. As expressed by Thủy:

19 An audio excerpt can be heard in the online repository (www.orpheusinstituut.be/en/voices-bodies-practices-media-repository) see file "SF4.2 *Mirage* duo (bars 9–14)."

20 For an audio excerpt see file "SF4.3 *Arrival Cities Hanoi* trio I (bars 37–40)" in the online repository.

21 In the instrumentation for the ensemble, some instruments, like the harp, do not afford such glissandi, but then, compound sound objects are created where the pluck may be found in the harp, and the glissandi distributed to the strings and to the sampler part.

Figure 4.2. Kent Olofsson, *Mirage*, 2009, duo for đàn tranh and đàn bầu, bars 9–14.

Figure 4.3. Kent Olofsson, *Arrival Cities: Hanoi*, 2015, trio I, bars 37–40.

> The duo presented different difficulties. When I received the score in 2010, it was the most complex music I had been presented. The basic pulse was slow, but the rhythmical structure was much more complex than in the trio. In Vietnamese traditional music for đàn tranh, bending is a very common technique, but I would only bend one string at a time. We don't use harmony as in Western music. In Kent's score for the duo there were many instances where the đàn tranh should have two strings bending at the same time, and then the bending slowly changed into different directions, or just one string changing while the other pitch would remain. On the đàn tranh, you can bend up to a third or a fourth, and the control of such extensive bending relies completely on muscle memory and listening. The complex instructions in the score, regarding dynamics, rhythm, and unconventional playing techniques, and the shifting metre demanded a lot of rehearsal time, both individually and together. Although we started looking at the score in 2010, we were not too keen to rehearse it, and it was only in 2012, when it was scheduled to be recorded on CD, that we finally gathered the motivation to learn it. Also, we would never have learnt this music had Stefan not very patiently rehearsed it with us, conducting, singing our parts, and treating us like a very kind schoolteacher would treat young pupils. (Nguyễn 2019)

The first two pieces, the trio and the duo, together with a trio by Nguyễn Thiện Đạo, were recorded for CD release on three days in 2012, between 31 August and 2 September. The duo had not yet been played in performance, due to the resistance that the two performers experienced. As put by Trà My in an email to Thủy in June 2012: "His music is really a tough nut to crack. If I do not practice I will never be able to play it." But when the recording was made, something changed in their relation to this music: "Learning this piece was hard work. Something happened when I shifted from the role of a performer to a listener. The struggle of keeping the music together was now replaced by more relaxed listening. It was only when the piece was recorded and we were working on the mix, that I realised that I found the music both fascinating and beautiful" (Nguyễn 2019). But the shift was not only on the side of the performers. Kent similarly cites these recording sessions as indeed an important turning point in the collaboration: "The recordings we made were important, first the ones for the CD, because there I also learnt a lot about the instruments. We pushed the limits of what was possible. But, when we made recordings in Hà Nội, it was much more of a joint testing situation. What happened I think is that, here, we recorded to see what more can be done. In a sense, the recording technologies became an alternative score in this collaborative mode of working" (Olofsson 2019a).

The recordings laid the grounds for a more integrative collaboration, which became evident in the years to follow. In the rest of this part we will look at how the three solos in *Arrival Cities: Hanoi* were created, and how a discursive voice was negotiated with each of the performers of the group. But first we will return to Kent's first visit to Hà Nội in June 2014 and to the recordings of street vendors and environmental sounds in the city.

4.2.1. The sounds of Hà Nội

The soundscape of Hà Nội has shifted radically since the economic reforms of *Đổi Mới* in 1986. When bicycles were supplanted by motorbikes, Hà Nội turned into one of the noisiest cities in South East Asia. Vietnam is among the countries with the highest number of motorbikes per capita (Phan et al. 2010). Hà Nội has developed into a typically *lo-fi* soundscape (Schafer 1977), mainly because of the "traffic noise in Hà Nội and Hồ Chí Minh City" that "has an impulsive, percussive character that is mainly due to frequent horn sounds" (Phan et al. 2010, 484). When Kent and Stefan set out to record the sound of the city, much of what was captured was street noise and car horns.[22]

Hà Nội is a city full of paradoxes. While the sound of the street vendors' calls are often featured in tourist agencies' depictions of the city, the government has actively banned street vendors from many streets. The tradition of street vendors goes far back in time, and the calls are a fascinating sonic signature of urban life in Vietnam. There are calls concerning almost any kind of service—not just the obvious offers of various kinds of bread and fruit but also for many other chores: to sharpen your knives and scissors, to sell your broken machines, to exchange your old pots and pans for new ones, and so on. It would be more correct to divide these activities into two branches: the actual street vendors, who walk the main streets and market their items to passers-by, and the various services offered to people in their own houses and advertised with calls from a bicycle or motorbike. The latter category are the ones you hear the most, and today, most of them are pre-recorded and played back from little horn speakers. The particular sound of this amplification situates the sound of the street vendors of today at the threshold between ancient and modern Vietnam. The women selling fruit in the streets now rarely use any calls; instead, they walk up to people and address them individually. Sometimes they also bribe policemen to be allowed to set up their bikes with their goods in a certain spot and stay there throughout the day. This is the work situation that street vendors today prefer. As concluded by Östersjö and Nguyễn (2016): "In this respect, the fruit vendors [walking the streets] with their bicycles are some of the most silent of all inhabitants in Hanoi, surrounded by the clamor of car horns and the many machines that fill the air from morning to night. The ability to contribute to the noise in the city is partly related to one's income."

We (Kent and Stefan) intended to record not only the pre-recorded, louder calls of street vendors but also the original acoustic calls, which are more rarely heard these days. But when we headed out in the heat to spend an afternoon trying to capture vendors' calls, we heard the official news announcement from the public speakers announcing the details of the ban on street vendors and confirming that the police will be out in the streets that day. Of course, when

22 While cars in general are a poor fit for the narrow streets, already crowded with motorbikes and people, automobiles are becoming increasingly present in Hà Nội traffic. This phenomenon caught the interest of the Norwegian sociologist Arve Hansen (2014), who was the first to point out that cars are in fact unusually expensive to purchase in Vietnam, due to high taxes, and that this makes the car an even more "powerful expression of the inequalities embedded in the new economic system." Since cars function as status symbols, the number of large luxury cars is striking, and Hansen continues with the observation that this constitutes a "sharp break with the country's socialist past, when displays of personal wealth were frowned upon and could lead to serious trouble. In post-*Doi Moi* Vietnam, the automobile is one of the more obvious symbols of the new reality, in which getting rich is considered glorious and displaying personal wealth has become normal. In contemporary Hanoi, expensive cars are used actively to display wealth—sometimes strategically to show business partners that you are successful" (ibid.).

we walked off with our zoom recorder, there wasn't a single call from a street vendor anywhere. We got increasingly desperate, since our time in Hà Nội was running out, and we needed these sounds for the piece. When walking the narrow lanes in Mai Dịch later in the day, we were joined by Thủy, who spotted one woman who would normally be buying junk (plastic, paper, metal, and glass) in the neighbourhood. We asked her to perform her call on a secluded lane, where there were apparently no police, and we offered her a fee for her performance. She agreed, and we got an excellent recording of the call emerging and disappearing through the blocks in the immediate area. This recording, which Kent post-produced into a little composition, eventually became one of the core materials in the collection of street vending calls in *Arrival Cities: Hanoi*.

4.2.2. The solo for tỳ bà

Kent's score for the first trio was also actually the first piece that Stefan learned to play on the tỳ bà, although he worked in parallel on a few traditional pieces, some of which were played on the tour. Several idiomatic compositional approaches found in the tỳ bà part of the trio were reflected and developed in the solo written for *Arrival Cities: Hanoi*, which can also be traced back to earlier works developed in the collaboration between Kent and Stefan, as the composer explained:

> Writing for the tỳ bà I experienced as somewhat similar to when I first wrote for the charango in *Il Liuto d'Orfeo*. This was almost exactly ten years earlier. The situation then was a little different, since I had already heard Stefan play another piece for charango and electronics,[23] which therefore suggested some possibilities, but here, the tỳ bà was a new instrument for both of us. Still, just like with the charango, when confronted with this Vietnamese lute, I could rather immediately identify possibilities and limitations that were related also to how I imagined that Stefan would play the instrument. (Olofsson 2019a)

The comparison with the earlier composition for the charango is useful in several ways, because the instruments afford some similar playing techniques but are also very different sounding results. While the charango is a very sharp and distinct instrument that projects very well in a concert space, the tỳ bà does none of this. On the other hand, while it is almost impossible to bend notes on the charango due to the very small fretboard and the high string tension, the tỳ bà is created for a music built on ornamentation with pitch-bends. On the tỳ bà, the only way to keep a note alive, at least for a moment, is through bending or vibrato. The use of arpeggio is also part of Stefan's individual playing technique; he is a classically trained guitarist who has brought the associated playing techniques to other instruments, first the charango and here the Vietnamese lute. Kent later observed:

---

23 Agustín Fernandez's *Wounded Angel* (1989), first performed and recorded by the composer, is arguably the first serious composition for charango and electronics. After hearing Fernandez perform the piece at an electronic music festival, *Wounded Angel* became the impetus for Stefan to buy a charango and learn to play it. In fact, when Stefan first played the piece in the UK, he actually borrowed Fernandez's newly purchased concert instrument. After the concert, the composer gave the instrument to Stefan, who used it on his CD recording of the piece some years later (Östersjö 2004).

> I never only write for an instrument but always also for a specific performer. When writing for the guitar, and for Stefan, I know the possibilities, through the instrument and his playing. But when I was to write for the đàn tranh, both of those forms of pre-understanding were lacking. When you really know an instrument, it is like an embodied experience to write the score; in my imagination I feel what it would be like to play, on a violin or a guitar. Something like that happened, like "now I can start thinking through the instrument," when we were in Hà Nội working on the music in 2014. But when I wrote the tỳ bà solo (in the later end of the working process in 2014), I remember I felt particularly confident, because now, when writing for Stefan, even if for him playing a Vietnamese instrument, I even more felt I knew exactly what was possible to do, I can write exactly this kind of right-hand figurations, and so on. (Olofsson 2019a)

Bars 36–39 of *Mirage I* (2009) (figure 4.4)[24] also reflect the shared voice developed by Stefan and Kent in the making of *Il Liuto d'Orfeo* (1999). Here, the arpeggio figuration in the tỳ bà over a chord that is gradually shifted by bending recalls the second movement of *Il Liuto d'Orfeo*, composed for a retuned six-string guitar. In addition, the figuration that follows in bars 40–42 has a certain affinity with the melodic lines in the same movement of *Il Liuto d'Orfeo*, although in the earlier piece, such figurations were played with natural harmonics. Although it doesn't approach the radical scordatura of the earlier guitar piece, the tỳ bà is also retuned in the trio, and Olofsson uses the same scordatura for the solo piece: the top strings adhere to a typical tuning (1 is A, 2 is E, 3 is D) but the fourth string is lowered to an A♭.[25]

Figure 4.4.

The tỳ bà solo was written in November, in parallel with the final rehearsals before the premiere. Time was short, and the mode of collaboration was similar to that used when we worked out the music to be played in the pre-premiere in Hà Nội; but now the music was also made in response to the emerging dramaturgy. Hence, the compositional work was negotiated in working sessions, new ideas were discussed, and then Kent would go home and compose new materials to bring in the next day. "It's a pain to work in this way, although I also realize it is the only way, and also it is perfectly enjoyable at the same time. Only when you can integrate the compositional work with testing materials with the per-

24 An audio excerpt can be heard in the online repository (www.orpheusinstituut.be/en/voices-bodies-practices-media-repository); see file "SF4.4 *Mirage* trio (bars 36–39)."

25 Also, in traditional music, the top string on the instrument is more commonly tuned to C, not A. The lower tuning allows for more extensive bending.

Figure 4.4. Kent Olofsson, *Mirage I*, 2009, for trio, bars 36–39.

formers, just as the staging of the work is emerging, this integration of music and theatrical action can be achieved" (Olofsson 2019a).

Such immediate interaction between staging and writing music can be seen in the first duo in *Arrival Cities: Hanoi*, for đàn tranh and tỳ bà. This emerges from the choreographed movement, in which the three musicians perform elements from Lưu's final inventory of gestures; during this choreographed section, Trà My sits down to play a solo for đàn bầu (the first music performed in the piece). When her solo ends, Stefan takes over with a new music, first as if accompanying Thủy's solo movements. But then Thủy sits down by the đàn tranh and the duo starts to unfold from the initial material. This little piece was composed in one night, between rehearsals, and the actions described above were developed in immediate dialogue with the making of the music. This plasticity in relation to the choreographic elements and the dramaturgy was partly created by retaining some improvised elements in the opening, but it also depended on allowing all agents to have input on the creation of the music. Hence, the final shape of the music was negotiated by Kent, the choreographer Miguel Cortés, the three musicians, and Jörgen. Moreover, the opening music—the solo for đàn bầu and the trio that follows—was also composed into the dramaturgical structure through its recurrence towards the end of the piece, with an added đàn bầu solo (see below). Thus the opening music also becomes part of the ending, leading up to the coda.

Figure 4.5.

Returning to the tỳ bà solo: just as its part in *Mirage*, the first trio, is notably similar to the instrumental writing in *Il Liuto d'Orfeo*, so also the tỳ bà solo resembles the charango part in *Il Liuto d'Orfeo*, in particular in its exploration of *campanella*-style playing.[26] But perhaps there is an even stronger parallel to another piece by Kent that features the charango: *Fascia* (2002), the first part of *Corde* (2006), his concerto for guitarist and orchestra. The arpeggiated chords and, in particular, the use of grace notes within figurations are strikingly similar, as can be seen by comparing the first bars of figures 4.5 and 4.6.[27]

26 *Campanella* is Italian for "little bell," and it denotes a particular style of arpeggiated performance in melodic lines that is typical of the Baroque guitar. Because of similarities in the tuning of the Baroque guitar and the charango (which developed from the Baroque guitar as a result of colonisation), campanella playing is an idiomatic right-hand technique on the charango. When Stefan and Kent started exploring the charango in the late 1990s, campanella-style figurations were central. This technique gives the charango a more intimate and resonant sonority, which is characteristic of the first movement of *Il Liuto d'Orfeo* (1999).

27 For audio excerpts, see files "SF4.5 *Arrival Cities Hanoi* solo for tỳ bà (bars 64–66)" and "SF4.6 *Fascia* (bars 46–49)" in the online repository.

Figure 4.5. Kent Olofsson, *Arrival Cities: Hanoi*, 2015, solo for tỳ bà, bars 64–66.

Figure 4.6.

However, the tỳ bà does not really afford a lot of resonance, despite the *campanella*-style playing. Hence, although the gestural qualities are similar (and typical of the shared voice of composer and performer), the sounding outcome is less immediately reminiscent of the earlier piece than is the notated structure and the idiomatic qualities—that is, the "feel" on the instrument.

It may be argued that the arpeggio figurations were drawn from a discursive voice. But there are other features in the solo that can be understood as expressive of a close—or attentive—listening to the instrument, drawing out much more fine-tuned material than that found in the first trio. An example is the repeated, and varied, figurations around a single pitch, as found in bars 44–47 (figure 4.7).[28] These always start with a sharp attack, with a Bartók pizzicato, followed by typically Vietnamese vibrato and bisbigliando between two or three strings. Hence, such new material also has origins in traditional playing techniques and therefore reflects the parallel learning curves of performer and composer in their increasing knowledge of these traditions.

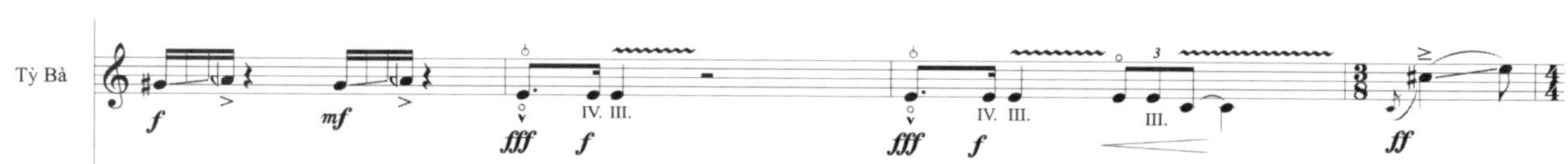

Figure 4.7.

4.2.3. The solo for đàn tranh

The solo for đàn tranh was also composed in November 2014, in the final weeks before the premiere. It marks a shift in the interaction between Kent and Thủy and can be analysed as an expression of a discursive voice using the model set out in chapter 1, above. While the harmonic material may be said to be even more typically Western than even the first Étude, the use of bending in the left hand situates the piece right between two musical idioms. Immediately striking in this solo is the simplicity of the musical structure and the juxtaposition of Western and Vietnamese elements. Here, the composer arrives at a resolution of the negotiation of voice that is much more restrained, organic, and constrained when compared with the examples given above or with the experimentation initiated in the first Étude.

Thủy's intonation in the solo is shaped by a Vietnamese mode, so the đàn tranh does not sound well tempered in the Western sense. For instance, although the B♭ is notated without instructions for any microtonal inflection, it is performed notably flattened, as in the Ai mode (see figure 4.8).[29]

28 For an audio excerpt, see file "SF4.7 *Arrival Cities Hanoi* solo for tỳ bà (bars 44–47)" in the online repository.

29 For further reading about intonation in traditional Vietnamese music, see Östersjö and Nguyễn (2013);

Figure 4.6. Kent Olofsson. *Fascia*, 2002, for charango and orchestra, bars 46–49.

Figure 4.7. Kent Olofsson, *Arrival Cities: Hanoi*, 2015, solo for tỳ bà, bars 44–47.

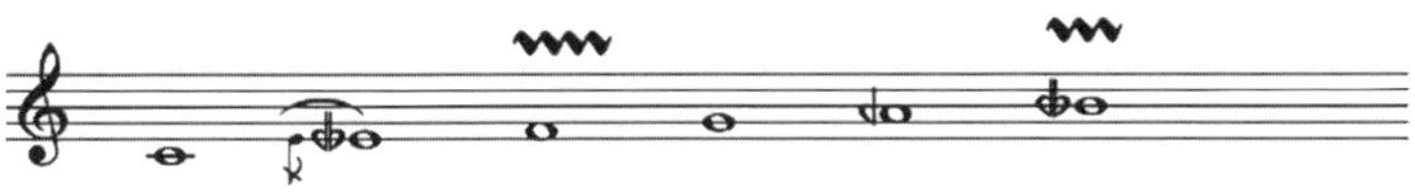

Figure 4.8.

Figure 4.9.

The use of left-hand bending also recalls traditional playing technique; and with the characteristic intonation, the recurring bending in minor thirds, sometimes followed by vibrato, gives the music a distinctly Vietnamese quality (figure 4.9).[30] The treatment of vibrato is different in this piece compared with the duo for đàn bầu and đàn tranh, in which the score indicates the type of vibrato, shape, and length of the vibrato in great detail. Here, the performer shapes the vibrato more freely.

> With this music I never experienced any resistance. Even though it uses a tuning system that is very non-Vietnamese and also has a very tonal, and thereby Western, material, I immediately could relate to this music. For me, it has a strongly emotional function in *Arrival Cities: Hanoi*. It constitutes a bridge from the story that Stefan is telling over to Nam's final video, where he gives an account of the moment when he decided to give up acting and become a costume-maker. The moment when he starts crying is the emotional core of the piece. I always felt that this solo was like an aria, which expresses the emotional direction of the dramaturgy. When I listen back to my playing I can hear the Vietnamese intonation but, also, the non-Vietnamese vibrato, which I employ, to situate the piece both inside and outside tradition. (Nguyễn 2019)

---

for a quantitative study also see Keefe, Burns, and Nguyen (1991).

30 For an audio excerpt, see file "SF4.8 *Arrival Cities Hanoi* solo for đàn tranh (bars 1–6)" in the online repository.

Figure 4.8. The Ai mode with its characteristic articulation types.

Figure 4.9. Kent Olofsson. *Arrival Cities: Hanoi*, 2015, solo for đàn tranh, bars 1–6.

Clearly, any score, irrespective of musical style and content, affords some resistance for a performer. Still, Thủy's account suggests that the gap between composer and performer is being bridged. The music is experienced as an integrated element of the theatrical performance, a quality that we will discuss further in the next section. And from the composer's perspective, when creating the music as part of the staging process and in direct interaction with performers and the director, new perspectives on musical composition also emerge:

> Here, the classical writing situation, a composer working alone on a score, recordings made in a studio, and the work onstage are intertwined, as I also discuss in my thesis. Through such processes you can make more complex things. I see this as a way of going deeper into the compositional process. When you bring the score to the performers, it doesn't have to be seen as the finished work; instead, you can continue to discover new things that are possible to do with instruments, with performers. The possibilities lie in how you can go back and forth between these different ways of working. (Olofsson 2019a)

In making the solo for đàn tranh, the creative process was largely carried out in a distributed manner, and the material in the score was entirely created without direct input from the soloist. However, in performance we find that the voices of composer and soloist merge, since the composed structures in the score allow a Vietnamese performance practice to dominate the piece as performed. Or, phrased differently, the way the score is composed leaves space for the voice of the performer to come through. Perhaps this strategy of leaving space can be understood as one of many possible ways of creating a discursive voice in composer–performer collaborations.[31]

4.2.4. The solo for đàn bầu

Arrival Cities: Hanoi starts with the voice of Ngô Trà My, telling the story of how she arrived in Hà Nội as a child, when her parents moved to the city from the countryside, looking for a better life. Also, the first music that is played in the piece is Trà My playing a solo for đàn bầu. This is a slowly emerging melody, built around a rising minor third, a slow glissando gesture, with an explosive, expressive energy that bursts out in the third bar with the leap from the low B up to B♭ (figure 4.10).[32] "Writing for the đàn bầu was, I believe, even more difficult than the đàn tranh. It is in some ways such a simple instrument and limited to the one string and its harmonics. With the đàn tranh there are so many possibilities to work with harmony and extended playing techniques. The đàn bầu demanded finding a way of melodic writing, literally finding a voice" (Olofsson 2019b).

31 This informal conclusion supplements but does not contradict the conclusions from the more formal research discussed in chapter 1.

32 For an audio excerpt, see file "SF4.9 *Arrival Cities Hanoi* solo for đàn bầu (bars 1–6)" in the online repository.

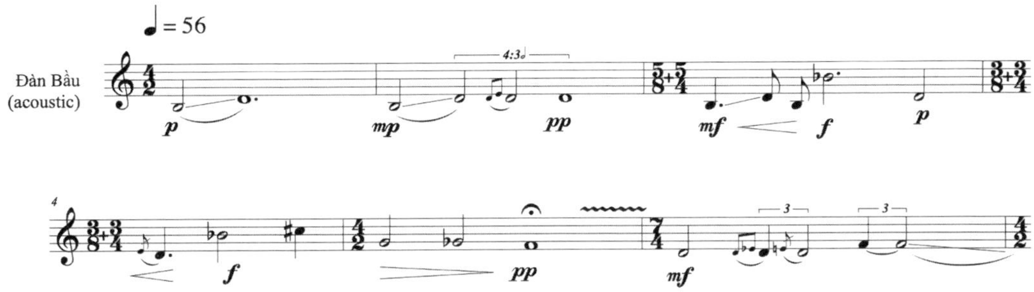

Figure 4.10.

When The Six Tones worked with Kent in Hà Nội, we experimented with bowing all three instruments, as part of creating the third and last trio for the piece. The resonance in the đàn tranh and the electric guitar creates a space within which a different writing for the đàn bầu emerged: "I cannot explain for myself exactly how it happened. But when I think of the music I wrote for the đàn bầu—and for the trio—since I arrived in Hà Nội and experienced the soundscape, hanging out with the group in rooftop cafes, the immersive experience of tropical rain, and the heat, composing for the đàn bầu suddenly became an integrated part of that experience" (Olofsson 2019b).

The solo for đàn bầu rested firmly on the experience of writing for and performing with the group. Kent describes how writing this melodic piece emerged naturally from the entire experience:

> Not only was my composing somehow situated in the experience of being in Hà Nội with the group, but I also had a tangible sense of the very detail of Trà My's playing. The sessions when we were improvising, creating material for the pre-premiere at *Manzi*, getting sleepy (often taking a real Vietnamese nap), going for coffee, and returning again to the playing: perhaps simply that we could spend this much time together, somehow it gave me a very immediate sense of what Trà My would make with a certain little melodic phrase, a glissando, and so on. (Olofsson 2019b)

The solo for đàn bầu and Kent's collaboration with Trà My both capture a different aspect of the process of developing a shared voice. They seem to suggest that the emergence of a discursive voice depends on the development of social empathy and on shared experiences in everyday situations.

> I think the longtime collaboration between Kent and us is important. We needed that time. It has been more than ten years up to now. I think it took time for Kent to understand not just the instrument but also the musician who plays that instrument—in this case, to understand me, in person. I think he not only composed for my instrument, but he composed the piece specifically for me. He knew how I could play his piece my way. In *Arrival Cities: Hanoi*, those music parts for the đàn bầu, as I said, I feel so much connected since during the time Kent worked on it, we often had conversations in which Kent wanted to know my emotional reaction to the music. The conversations were not only about playing techniques or the structure in the score, but very much about my emotion, and this I have found very uncommon in my work with composers. (Ngô 2019)

Figure 4.10. Kent Olofsson, *Arrival Cities: Hanoi*, 2015, solo for đàn bầu, bars 1–6.

It can be argued, then, that the production of this score can be understood as a process of negotiating an understanding of the other. Rather than an exploration of the musical possibilities of the đàn bầu, this solo is the outcome of a dialogue between composer and performer that builds on empathic engagement.

4.2.5. Summary

The music for *Arrival Cities: Hanoi* currently exists in two versions. The first version, premiered in November 2014, is scored for three performers, electronics, and surround soundscape.[33] When the second version of *Arrival Cities: Hanoi* was created in 2015, some of the musical ideas in the first version were further elaborated and expanded. For instance, in the first trio, the basic idea—to create a slowly shifting harmony by means of slow glissandi—was expanded in the resonant body of the chamber ensemble, amplifying the composed structure. In this sense, the orchestration functions similarly to Kent's earlier concertos, in which the orchestral writing has been drawn from the solo parts; in *Corde*, for example, the concerto for guitarist and orchestra mentioned above (figure 4.6), the orchestra takes its material from the first twenty-three bars of the charango part. In the second version of *Arrival Cities: Hanoi*, a new movement for the chamber ensemble alone was created using the materials that became the ending of the piece: the duo for đàn tranh and tỳ bà, the đàn bầu solo, and the combination of these two in the ending of the third trio.

It is evident that the long history of the collaboration between The Six Tones and Kent Olofsson has been a central factor in the creation of this music. The modes of collaboration have shifted over the years, and early developments occurred during the long-term collaboration between Kent and Stefan, which started in the mid-1990s. Although distributed collaboration and a relatively clear division of labour were initially typical of their early interactions, a shift towards more integrative forms was traced by Stefan in his thesis (2008). A similar pattern can be observed in the interactions between Kent and the two Vietnamese performers of the group, although all three make it clear that intercultural differences initially contributed quite substantial resistances. Still, we propose that the three solo pieces created for *Arrival Cities: Hanoi* exemplify the process by which collaboration results in the development of discursive voices.

4.3. Staging the piece and composing the performance

The next phase of creating *Arrival Cities: Hanoi* took place in Sweden, in November 2014. We worked on many levels simultaneously at Teatr Weimar's Wlabs, editing video, rehearsing and workshopping music, and creating and rehearsing the choreography, now in collaboration with Miguel Cortés. But above all, we developed the dramaturgy, and thereby also the compositional structure, of the entire piece. And this is when the elements of memory and storytelling came to the fore.

33 A video from the premiere, taken by Maria Norrman, can be found in the online repository; see file "SF4.10 *Arrival Cities Hanoi* premiere."

While working in Hà Nội, we gradually came to see ourselves as participants in rather than makers of a documentary. Now, when the experience of creating the documentary was beginning to sink in and we had started creating the staged performance, this became even clearer. The artistic concept expanded to include in the piece our individual experiences of migration to and from Hà Nội. Through these personal narratives we wanted to create a situation built on sharing and empathy within which the stories from the street vendors could be presented. Our decision can also be seen as a response to the call for engagement phrased by Doug Saunders (2012, 3): "These transitional spaces—arrival cities—are the places where the next great economic and cultural boom will be born or where the next great explosion of violence will occur. The difference depends on our ability to notice and our willingness to engage."

4.3.1. Methods for structuring the performance

Our first idea was to present the three musicians onstage, performing gestures drawn from the video in which Lưu showed a scene from Tuồng theatre, but somehow the form of the piece did not seem to work. Jörgen Dahlqvist recalled the situation this way:

> Stefan was very concerned, and the three musicians went home after the rehearsals. Kent and I stayed in the rehearsal space and continued to discuss how to resolve the issues we experienced. Then the idea of working with each individual's memories, widely speaking, as related to the project, and the theme of migration, came up. The idea came from how Nam gradually would remember and tell his life story. The concept for the staged performance then, was drawn from how the interview with Nam had unfolded. I presented an idea the day after, which also included the light design, the role of the music in the creation of a sense of space, and finally how a series of citations dealing with memory could frame the entire performance. I was worried that the three musicians might be unable to learn a script by heart, and also, I wanted them to feel comfortable with being onstage, and therefore I proposed that we would create an audio track with questions, played back over headphones, to which they would spontaneously respond in the performance. Built into this idea was the notion that, just like when we made the interviews with the street vendors, the performers should also be free not to respond to the questions, if they seemed too personal or otherwise uncomfortable. The idea of using headphones was also part of creating situations onstage, to which the performer could respond. By creating situations in which they would merely have to respond to questions, I wanted them to feel more safe. (Dahlqvist 2019)

After our first attempt, even before Jörgen had made any audio tracks, we decided not to use the headphones and not to structure the participation of the performers onstage around the questions. Rather, it seemed that the questions could be implicit in dialogues (and sometimes monologues) with and between the performers. Hence, the questions intended for the audio track were used only in rehearsal, as a way of structuring and directing the storytelling. Kent and Jörgen started developing an event score for the piece, a format for composing the dramaturgy, through which this storytelling, the videos, the choreography, and the music could be structured (see figure 4.11).

Arrival Cities: Hanoi
Composition/dramaturgy
Event Score
Draft

Part 1. The past / Morning in the city / first encounters

1. The door opens and the audience take their seats.
2. Light fades away. Black.
3. Video: *The worst part of holding the memories is not the pain. It's the loneliness of it. Memories need to be shared.*
4. Trà My enters the room.
5. Light appears to the left in the venue. A long transition starts.
6. Question to Trà My: Do you remember the first sound you heard? Can you describe how it sounded?
7. Question to Trà My: Do you remember the first time you heard the đàn bầu?
8. Nam's voice appears in the room, sounds from the city: "I became the star of the group..."
9. Thủy enters during Trà My´s story.
10. Question to Trà My: Can you show us how it looks when you play?
11. Question to Thủy: Do you remember the first time you met Stefan. How did he look?
12. Stefan enters and stops in the middle of the room so we can all see him.

Figure 4.11.

The event score above can be compared to the transcript of the performance from Hà Nội that opens the chapter. We find it striking that the overall structure remains the same. The main difference is that explicit questions are posed to Trà My in the event score; but the story that she tells in the performance does in fact respond to these questions, more or less, even though they were never used in performance. In a dialogue with Thủy, Jörgen offered a series of reflections on this initial stage of the rehearsal process:

> Dahlqvist: It's interesting, now when I look back at the process, these questions were very clearly posed by a playwright.
>
> Nguyễn: Asking the questions . . .
>
> Dahlqvist: . . . was a way of writing. (Dahlqvist and Nguyễn 2018)

Figure 4.11. *Arrival Cities: Hanoi*, 2015, the beginning of the first event score.

The conversation continued on the topics of method and of personal engagement. But the line of thought began with Thủy's observation that "at the outset I was really nervous to be acting in a theatre piece. I had never done this before, and we had no script or idea of what we were to do in the piece" (Dahlqvist and Nguyễn 2018).

> Dahlqvist: I think the method is that you never have any pressure to do anything. Instead one has to take obstacles away.
>
> Nguyễn: Yes, you have to create a situation where the person wants to open up.
>
> Dahlqvist: It goes both ways. When you've worked for a long time, it might be necessary to ask more difficult questions. I remember when I was working with Linda and Rafael, it became necessary for me to write more difficult texts.[34] It was the two actors who demanded texts that would create specific challenges. So it goes both ways.
>
> Nguyễn: That's what I was saying before, all participants need to be active and take responsibility for the process.
>
> Dahlqvist: Yes, you need everyone to engage, to engage in the other.
>
> Nguyễn: That is like in the citation of the opening of the piece, about the loneliness of keeping memories for yourself: "Memories need to be shared." And that's how you also start to getting to know each other better. (Dahlqvist and Nguyễn 2018)

This conversation recalls the collaboration between Trà My and Kent: the way forward may be found in very ordinary interactions, or even in just spending time together. Jörgen notes how "in theatre, sometimes you do work that is personally engaging and difficult, and when this happens, in Teatr Weimar, and in my work with Linda and Rafael, we spend two thirds of the time just drinking coffee and small-talking, just in order to process the situations emotionally" (Dahlqvist and Nguyễn 2018).

Even though Jörgen did not produce a script for the piece, during the first few weeks the three performers would sit down and write possible responses to the questions he had posed, and they would also prepare possible dialogues. These responses would be rehearsed not just with Jörgen, but also with the choreographer Miguel Cortés, who would then direct the body language of the performers, rather than the stories told. Later in the process it became clear that the structure of a piece like *Arrival Cities: Hanoi* is remarkably malleable, since the script will naturally change with time as the lived experience of the performers changes. Thus the piece has incorporated new stories during its existence, sometimes because of new understandings or developments. For instance, when the group returned to Hà Nội in 2015 to give the Vietnamese premiere, one of our objectives was to again interview the women in the house in Phúc Tân. To our surprise, this was not possible, since times had got harder

34 Linda Ritzén and Rafael Pettersson were central to the early work of Teatr Weimar, and played the roles of Romeo and Juliet in *Hamlet: Exit Ghost*. For further information, see Olofsson (2018).

for street vendors and they had all given up on their trade and returned to their homelands. This political perspective was then immediately integrated into the new version.

> For me this is really the most exciting and interesting part of it. It's a question of what the boundaries are [between truth and fiction]. And especially since I did not write the text myself; I just pose the questions and then structure the text. And then, instead of rewriting it you can just adjust it a little bit, just by asking whether you can tell a little bit more about a certain aspect. So it is kind of the same process [as when creating a fully scripted piece] but it happens in a different way. But the method of rehearsing is entirely different. It affects your playing and also telling the stories. (Dahlqvist and Nguyễn 2018)

The process of creating the piece was transformational for all participants, due to forces in several different dimensions simultaneously. Already, in conducting the interviews in Hà Nội, we not only had been confronted with unknown aspects of life there but also had come to see ourselves in a different light. But these experiences were shared during the artistic collaboration in which we created the staged version and developed the storytelling. Jörgen reflected on this connection between the process of responding to questions and the shared experience of visiting sites in Hà Nội:

> As an actor you are presented with a situation in the text that you do not know. The rehearsal process is an embodied processing of understanding your impulses or actions in this context. That's why it worked so well to use memories as the structuring component in the piece, because when I ask, "do you remember the first sound you heard in Hà Nội?" you must imagine a situation you know. What we did in the second round, when we were back in Hà Nội a year later, was to visit the house where Trà My stayed with her family in 2010. When we went there, not only could we witness the extreme conditions under which she was living, but she also added more individual experiences to the stories she had told in the first version of the piece. (Dahlqvist and Nguyễn 2018)

In 2015, when we returned to Hà Nội to play the Vietnamese premiere of the piece, we decided to take some additional time to record more video. As Jörgen explained, we also went to the house where Trà My had lived in 2010, a difficult part of her life, as related above. This was in an area where many street vendors stay, so when we went to make the interview with street vendors in Phúc Tân and she was beside herself in tears, she had been brought back to the memories of this time in her life. Everyone found that it was a very strong experience to go with Trà My to see the place where she had stayed; and this experience, as well as many others across 2014 and 2015, were central in building trust and empathy within the group.

But the working process also brought to the fore topics that were more politically oriented, and the novel perspectives that the process provided were certainly eye-opening for each artist in the project:

> During the rehearsals, I had conversations with all three musicians, and one theme that emerged was the relation between the majority population, the *Kinh* people, and the many minorities in the country. I learned that actually there was a somewhat colonial process going on also on a national level in Vietnam, so that for instance musicians from the majority population would visit a minority village and learn (and thus appropriate) some of their music and bring it back to the concert halls in the city. It made me see that the complexity of the power relations was greater than I had expected, and that the very individuals that I was very careful not to exploit in the creation of the project themselves could face similar issues when working in their home country. Such conversations became central in the creation of a shared understanding within the group of the central issues of migration and colonisation addressed by the project, but also for the development of the story-telling in the piece. It became a building block in the method for how to create the piece. (Dahlqvist and Nguyễn 2018)

The method and the role of empathy in the collaboration was discussed in a conversation between The Six Tones, Kent, and Jörgen at the Inter Arts Center in 2018:

> Nguyễn: We all bring ourselves out of our position as director or musician but we are now in the same room talking with street vendors and Nam, here's Trà My, here's me, here's Stefan, here's Jörgen, we talk, we share our stories together. I think that's what makes the piece work well, to me, as a way of presenting a character or presenting topics.
>
> Dahlqvist: And that's why it takes time, also, to make it. Because of the labour. . . .
>
> Olofsson: You could not have done that in a year or half a year. It would not have been possible.
>
> Nguyễn: It is a sensitive topic. It is not easy to just share our personal story onstage, in this . . . with some other people, the street vendors already shared their stories, and we also of course dare to share our stories in that context, to share with them.

In an interview in Hà Nội in January 2019, Trà My described a similar experience, but she also highlighted its performative dimensions, noting that the music and the choreography was an integrated part of the storytelling:

> It is not easy to tell personal stories onstage. I think I should give credit to Jörgen, who knew how to evoke these stories and memories, so that I can tell my own stories, and do it even in English and still feel natural. The questions that he posed to me at first made me want to open up. Later on, the way the piece was shaped created a space for me to tell these stories, through music, through movement, and through the interaction with the other performers of the group. That inspired me and encouraged me to share my experiences. It is a special experience to be sharing something that personal onstage like this, with all the music, and the choreography, and the documentary. (Ngô 2019)

The choreography developed by The Six Tones, Dahlqvist, and the choreographer Miguel Cortés was all related to the performances by Lưu, recorded in Hà Nội in 2014. Here, a central idea was to use the embodied memory as a way of bringing elements from these choreographies onstage, a process that also became a tool for empathising with Lưu and engaging in his life story. In the final scene, the video of Lưu performing a scene from Tuồng is screened in parallel with the performance of each musician's remembered movements from this video. When this choreography was created, each musician experienced a process of "rewriting" the movement that Lưu had performed (Lepecki 2010). But other movements from Tuồng theatre were also used in the piece, all taken from videos with Lưu. In the same interview, Ngô talks about one of the instances when the choreography was drawn into the actual playing of her instrument and explains how this embodied experience affected her playing: "When we played the second trio and I integrated movement from Tuồng, which represents horse riding into the music, that part, combining the musical performance with the struggle of controlling a horse was so intense, and I often felt like I could cry any second even when we had performed the piece many times. The movement became so personal to me" (Ngô 2019).

As discussed earlier, in section 4.2, the long-term collaboration with Kent had a strong impact on the development of the music. But during the weeks at Wlabs in 2014, some of the specific experiences from the work in Hà Nội were channelled into the design of the surrounding soundscape and the use of the field recordings.

> I can see now that there was an unbalance in the interaction between us when we started working, which only changed when I visited Hà Nội the first time. Only when I experienced the city, and the friendship with the two of you, which emerged from this change of perspective, my artistic practice could change along with our relations. When I composed the first two études, my role as a Western composer was not changed. It was all about delivering a score. While, of course, in 2014 when I came to Hà Nội, the way we worked was changing (and it also comes from the collaboration with Jörgen and Teatr Weimar). I remember that I sent sketches on beforehand; they were perhaps also difficult to play, and sometimes also relatively unidiomatic, but they were only suggestions and points of departure. It was now more about expressing shared experience rather than delivering a score. . . . This new sensitivity is so much about the detail, like when recording the soundscapes of Hà Nội. It's in the moment, in the strong experience. The rain, and the little things inside the field recording I made, and how you can focus these details. But it's also the sensations, the experience of being in the heat, ordering coffee out in the street, that creates this connectedness. It's not about a naive idea of "understanding the culture" by coming here, visiting the place. The lived experience of place shifted my experience of being a composer in collaboration with two Vietnamese performers. A different balance emerged through the shared experience of the life of the two of you: I now had a lived experience of Thủy and Trà My, but the detail of this experience was only mine. Suddenly I was situated in your environment, as an individual and not anymore just as a Western composer with a commission for an intercultural project. (Olofsson 2019a)

Perhaps the many layers of sonic, theatrical, and choreographic material reflect an immersion into many such details, a manifestation of this transformative experience that is framed in the moment. In this sense, the field recordings are less a way of drawing the audience into an *authentic* representation of the soundscape of Hà Nội than they are an after-image of a composer's experience of the city.

4.3.2. On memory, truth, and fiction

Arrival Cities: Hanoi is essentially an exploration of memory and authenticity.[35] One could perhaps say that in the storytelling, it has been essential to remain in what each performer perceives as an authentic experience, while the form of the piece of course integrates the documentary material into a multi-layered narrative, without presenting the footage as "documentation." Thủy observed that "when we played the piece in Vienna in December 2015, I was asked whether the stories we told were true or fiction. I was happy with the question, since that play with reality and fiction certainly was part of the concept of the piece, and it is also one of the things I enjoy the most about playing the piece—the way in which you alternate between different 'roles': sometimes I am 'just' a musician on stage, sometimes I am telling my own private memories, and sometimes I do feel more like an actor or a dancer" (Östersjö and Nguyễn 2016).

While the narrative in *Idioms* (2009–10; see 2.4 above) was built using archetypes in Vietnamese and Western literature, mimetic elements are almost completely absent in *Arrival Cities: Hanoi*. The three performers represent their lived experience and present their memories in the situations created onstage; the process by which the documentary was made became a working method for embodying these stories. The form of the piece, with its performance of memories onstage, reflects the understanding that history is always situated and constructed, always articulated from a singular perspective, and yet, as a collaborative creation, intrinsically multiperspectival (Vanhaesebrouck 2017).

When Jörgen was in Hà Nội in 2010, auditioning Vietnamese actors for the *Idioms* production, he was led back to his childhood memories of staying in Vietnam:

> The way memory works is interesting. As you know, I lived for a few years in Vietnam when I was a child. When I returned to Hà Nội in 2010, to work on *Idioms*, I recognised many of the smells, and the taste of fish sauce. . . . I remember how, on the first days in Hà Nội I would think that I recall a certain street, but I realised it was more because I wanted there to be memories. I wanted to have memories of Hà Nội from my childhood there, but I gradually realised that my memories were drawn from photos my parents took, rather than recollections of my own experience. But at the same time, constructed memory is also true in a certain way. That's how memory works. (Dahlqvist and Nguyễn 2018)

35 In this sense, *Arrival Cities: Hanoi* operates in the same conceptual universe as *Footnotes*, discussed in chapter 3, above. The two pieces are very different, but they share similar preoccupations.

The problem of authenticity and its role in contemporary Western culture is discussed in more detail in chapter 3. *Arrival Cities: Hanoi* is more concerned with notions of personal authenticity and of the processes that underlie the construction of memory. One element here is the felt connection between the individual, lived experience and the expression of music and choreography in the piece. Trà My explains: "I often put personal emotions into my playing. But *Arrival Cities: Hanoi* is special, since it also includes our own life stories. It builds on my own experience, and on the work we did collecting the video in the piece, so here there is an emotional engagement in each step of the work. When we play the music, it contains all this experience, and all the emotions that come with it" (Ngô 2019). Similar experiences were discussed in conversation between Thủy and Jörgen:

> Nguyễn: Yes, but it says something outside the text, and in that kind of theatre, I think in a project like *Arrival Cities: Hanoi*, what is important is what is outside theatre, it is lived experience which we share, with all the small talk and meetings with street vendors, which is outside theatre, like, outside the text.
>
> Dahlqvist: Exactly, I think we can see it like when Stefan says, "I am so upset it affects my playing." And I think you said something similar, like, "for me there is no difference between telling the stories and playing the music." And that's what is "outside the text," I think because you see it in the performance. It affects everything that happens onstage. It's the lived experience projected through the first note on the tỳ bà. That's when you can see, and hear, the difference. And thereby you also blur the boundaries between music and text. In those two statements you can see the method, or what it made happen. And this can be experienced by the audience, it feels like real people, because it is real experience. (Dahlqvist and Nguyễn 2018)

It was very different for the group to perform the piece in the National Tuồng Theatre in Hà Nội, compared with the performances in Europe in 2014. A European audience may find the fate of migrants engaging and even moving, but it is very different to face an audience containing many people who have actually lived through similar experiences. Trà My observed that "when we tell 'our' stories onstage in Hà Nội, it is no more just our personal experiences but we are also telling the stories of everyone's lives. Many people came up to me after the performance to share exactly that experience, of hearing the story of their own lives" (Ngô 2019).

But however true the storytelling may appear, the performative situation always invites an element of construction.[36] As described by Dahlqvist, "I remember very well several instances when all three of you [The Six Tones] were negotiating your memories, as it were, between trying to recall an *actual*

36 As discussed in chapters 2 and 3, personal authenticity is best understood as a construct, just as all forms of authenticity are performed. In those chapters, as in the present one, authenticity is understood to be a "socially agreed-upon construct in which the past is to a degree misremembered" (Peterson 1997, 20–21) or, as put by Rebecca Schneider, remembered differently through performance (for further discussion, see chapter 2).

memory, and then in another moment, shaping the storytelling in order to make them fit better with the overall structure" (Dahlqvist and Nguyễn 2018). The performative framework in *Arrival Cities: Hanoi* is intended to create a multi-layered narrative, in which the documentary, music, choreography, and storytelling encourage a multiperspective engagement with the material. A fundamental requirement is the face-to-face encounter with an audience, so that the live performance situation may allow for a conversation that is at the same time "intensely personal and immensely vast and impersonal" (Phelan 2004, 574). This engagement is, in turn, grounded in the body, as argued by Jörgen:

> For me, theatre is true in the same way, not the text, but what Linda [Ritzén] calls "the fiction of reality": it's kind of putting the true impulses onstage, that's what it aims for. It is the same thing with the Tuồng choreography; if you rehearse it long enough it will become embodied, and when you perform it onstage, it is true. For an actor, when you play, the impulse of getting angry . . . is always true, it is not a fiction. The bodily impulse in the situation. Like with Linda and Rafael [Pettersson] in *Hamlet*—it was just like Linda described her experience in *Hamlet*: I just had to open up, I didn't have to do anything, I was just so pissed of him (Rafael). It's *true*, because every system in the body is responding to his verbal attack. (Dahlqvist and Nguyễn 2018)

5. The discursive voice in intercultural collaboration

[Stefan leaves and joins Thủy doing movements at the other end of the stage. Trà My plays her solo to the end. Stefan stops doing the movements, leaves, picks up the tỳ bà, and starts playing. Trà My sits quietly and listens. After a short while Thủy also stops doing the movements and sits down by her đàn tranh. Stefan and Thủy start playing a duet on the instruments.]

[Music: Duet with Stefan and Thủy]

[After they have played their piece, the interview with Nam appears on the screen again]

Nam: I was homesick. I missed my parents. I was hungry in the night. My studies were hard, learning a new style. I have already embodied the southern style working in the group in my village. Now I had to learn a formalised structure, imitating my masters. The two traditions are so different. It was a very hard beginning for me. The many things taken together, the hunger, the homesickness and the difficulties in my studies made me think of giving up. I wanted to go home and leave Hà Nội.

[Video fades away]

[Music: Trio with Stefan, Trà My, and Thủy]

[The music ends with the sound of traffic overwhelming the playing. The light is bright and sharp, like the high noon of a summer's day in Hà Nội. Thủy walks up to the front of the stage. Sound from the city of Hà Nội is heard in the distance.]

5.1. Politics and the discursive voice

The notion of voice in musical creativity carries ethical and political implications. Cobussen and Nielsen (2012, 23) argue that "in and through music . . . ethics sets itself to work." Music, through listening and the interactions that it affords, is not merely a medium able to represent ethical dimensions; rather, "through music . . . ethics, hospitality and alterity come into existence and receive (specific) meaning" (ibid.). In our understanding, the ethical implications of music can only be fully accessed in the performative domain. They are articulated in the face-to-face relation between human bodies in a particular space, and they receive their strongest manifestation in the formation of discursive voice, articulated either through blending or through heterogeneous co-existence.

Rebecca Adami (2014, 168) proposes an understanding of human rights articulated beyond the common juridical definitions, "beyond the dichotomy in legal terms between universal rights and national jurisdiction." The fundamental challenge arises, for her, when the rights of the other are not covered by the legislation of the nation-state. She seeks to articulate a relation to the other not as something which can be "reduced to the application of laws, but as something that is acted, in political community" (ibid., 165). Building on Cavarero's notion of a relational understanding of a political space, constructed through the individuality of *voice*, Adami proposes an understanding of human rights through which the political is articulated as "the reciprocal communication of voices who raise their uniqueness in relations that can take place anywhere" (ibid., 176). Cavarero argues for an ontology of political space articulated beyond logos, through the unique sonic engagement by means of which any humans can interact: "In the voice both uniqueness and relation—indeed, uniqueness as relation—manifest themselves acoustically without even taking account of what is Said. The voice, which is embodied in the plurality of voices, always puts forward first of all the *who* of saying" (Cavarero 2005, 30). Such a relational understanding of human rights has an immediate affinity with an ethics based on hospitality. In particular, it resonates with Derrida's insistence that "the law of absolute hospitality commands a break with hospitality by right, with law or justice as rights" (2000, 25). Adopting Adami's language, we believe that the performative ethnographies in *Arrival Cities: Hà Nội* can be seen as an attempt to embody a "politics that concern identity, where the agonistic self gets a glimpse of herself in voicing her uniqueness in relation to different others, and where this identity is relational, complex, and dependent on the reciprocity of speech and action" (Adami 2014, 173).

> Thủy: When I was a child, sometimes I thought that, if I could not become a musician, I could be a street vendor. But there was only one thing I wanted to sell, and that's flowers. I liked that image, a woman with a bike surrounded by flowers. I had no idea how hard the life of a street vendor could be. Only in 2013, when I worked on a project in my homeland, I had time to talk to my relatives. And then I learnt that one of my cousins actually used to work as a street vendor in Hà Nội. She had to wake up very early in the morning, around 3 a.m. She would bike to Hà Nội with seventy kilos of rice and sell it in the street. She would return only in the late afternoon, and

start working on the raw rice right away, preparing for the business the next morning. For many years, I had no idea how hard she had been working.

[The sound of a street vendor chanting.]

Stefan: So, actually, when we went to Long Biên Market, looking to make interviews with street vendors, had we done this a few years earlier we could have met your cousin there?

Thủy: Yeah, we could have met her. And can you imagine how heavy it must have been to ride the bike with seventy kilos of rice?

Stefan: Indeed, and I remember that bike. It's a historic family bike. Your father bought it in Russia and brought it to Vietnam in the late seventies. But when we met your cousin last time in spring she described how she would get back after selling all the rice, and then, what she earned was only just enough for her to buy the raw rice, and the only gain from all this work, was the leftovers she got from the new rice, that she could use to feed the pigs.

Thủy: Yes, and sometimes the money she got in return was even less. If the quality of the raw rice was too low, even after working the rice, she would earn less than she had paid for it herself. So how did you find the situation of the street vendors in Hà Nội?

Stefan: One of my strongest impressions was when we visited a house near the Red River, where we met ten women, who slept on the concrete floor in a single room in the basement of a house, on bamboo carpets. And of course, as a Westerner, I was at first struck by the poverty and the poor conditions they were living under. But then, when we talked to them, we realised that there are many stories behind. First of all, these women all came from the same village. So, a reason for them to stay together was that they could take care of each other and also create more contact to the village and their families there. They also had quite a close relation to the couple who owned the house. Every day, when they returned from the streets, they would hand the money they earned to them. Once every month or every second month, they would collect the money they had earned and bring it to their families.

5.2. Ethics and musical interactions

Arrival Cities: Hanoi wishes to create a space for a conversation, in the Levinasian sense, with the *absolute foreigner*. The presence of the three musicians onstage, and the stories that they share, is essential to this creation of a political space in the moment of performance. As observed by an audience member in a performance at Radialsystem in Berlin in December 2017, "the performers are there as people, who only happen to be musicians" (Nguyễn 2019). Through performance, the music—without aiming to represent any ethical argument or claim—embodies a dialogical relation between culturally distinct others. Thus it manifests the ethical dimension in music as described by Cobussen and Nielsen (2012, 165): "Music takes us to an ethics of affinity and engagement evoked through aesthetic sensibility. And this aesthetic sensibility is first of all corporeal. Rather than falling back on a metaphysics of morals, music's call for an affective ethicality, resulting from a premediated contact with sounds, is dependent on bodily experiences and perception. Perception is triggered by the affectivity of its object on the listener." They go on to conclude that music becomes ethical neither through extra-musical references to the discursive domain nor from the contexts in which it is presented. But they also claim that ethics cannot be ascribed to specific, intrinsic qualities of a certain music. "Instead, a musical ethics can only come into existence on the basis of a contact with a perceiver—that is, through the act of listening. Thus, ethical moments can only be understood as strategies of engagement, through receptive interpretation, affected and formed by both doubt and astonishment" (Cobussen and Nielsen 2012, 166).

Such engagement has informed the making of the music in *Arrival Cities: Hanoi*. We have traced moments of attentive listening back to the early experiments when Kent Olofsson was composing the duo for đàn bầu and đàn tranh in 2010. This music was certainly not originally created for the context of an ethnography of migration to Hà Nội. It instead reflects the search for a different music at the cross-section between traditions, and the score embodies a composer's musicianly listening, as well as an intentionality that became a resistant material in the work of the group in the period between its composition in 2010 and the time of the studio recording in August–September 2012. It puts virtuosic demands on the performers, not only in the command it requires of specific materials but also, and perhaps even more, through intricate chamber music playing. Without the long-term engagement of the artists involved, this music could never have existed. When it is performed, as part of the staged production of *Arrival Cities: Hanoi*, it invites the audience to a similar engagement with a music that is created in a liminal space between traditions.

Thủy: We always asked the street vendors whether they felt like Hanoians . . .

Stefan: And the answer was very consistent, they always said no. But there was this one woman who had been working as a street vendor for twenty years and her children were now in university in Hà Nội. So of course, for her children, the situation would be different, and they probably already now felt like Hanoians. But My, when we went to their house you didn't take part in the interviews, since you were seated in a corner, crying . . .

Trà My: Yes, when I met those women, I was reminded of a hard part of my life when I stayed near the Red River, and many of my neighbours were street vendors, just like the women we met.

[Trà My continues in Vietnamese]

Thủy *[translating]*: She cried because she felt sorry for the women, for their poor living conditions, and she remembered the time when she was struggling for her family and working very hard for their survival.

Trà My: I rented a house very cheap from a friend. Actually, it was just a kitchen, by a house near the Red River. This was several years ago. The kitchen was in a very bad condition, and Stefan, you were there?

Stefan: Yes, we went there together, to see what it looked like. And I guess, well, it wasn't really a kitchen either, it was a shed outside a house, and it had been used as a kitchen, and then there was a pigsty next to it, where your mother stayed. So it had only three walls and a concrete floor. In Hà Nội it actually does get like ten degrees in winter time so here it would be hard to stay warm. And then there are of course the tropical storms and the hard rain.

Trà My: And you know, my friend had to come and help me repair the roof, but the rain and the wind would still come through.

Stefan: Yes, you showed us where you used to put the bucket in the bed, between you and your son, the two of you staying in the kitchen, and then you had this big barrel by the door to collect water from bigger holes.

5.3. Empathy and Trust

A performer's habitus is built on investments in both cultural and social capital. It is a basic foundation in any group of musicians that the co-performers are regarded as trustworthy. This in turn is a way of co-regulating socio-emotional factors, such as stress, for instance, related to performance anxiety.[37] Anthony Gritten (2017, 253) argues that trust is "found in all kinds of interactions between performers, and underpins their activities as both an assumption and a goal. Trust enables and facilitates interaction, collaboration, risk taking, experimentation, interpretative leaps." In a paper discussing chamber music performance in Western art music, Mina Doğantan-Dack (2012, 43) observes that "the social dynamics among the co-performers in an ensemble are as important as the musical dynamics for a successful performance, and each live performance is in fact an opportunity to further develop and strengthen the social bonds between the co-performers. Psychological research provides abundant evidence that for any collaborating group of people to work well, there needs to be a sense of trust and support between them, as well as a sense of belonging in the group." While this is certainly true of any context in which musicians get together to perform, we would argue that in intercultural collaboration the social dynamic in the group becomes even more important. Deniz Peters (2015) proposes that acts of social empathy and the experience of musical empathy may be dialectically entwined. In the making of *Arrival Cities: Hanoi*, such inter-relations have at times had a central role. We have observed, for instance, in the collaboration between Trà My and Kent, how the musical empathy that was central to the formation of a discursive voice in the making of the solo for đàn bầu emerged from oscillations between social and musical empathy. Kent described in an interview how, in the initial phase of the collaboration with the group, he experienced "a distance from the beginning," and he continued by observing how he "really found the cultural difference very difficult. I had so much experience of collaborating with classical musicians, and especially with soloists playing contemporary music" (Olofsson 2019a). He contrasts this experience with the process of creating the solo for đàn bầu, which he describes as "situated in the experience of being in Hà Nội with the group," about which Trà My comments, "I think it took time for Kent to not just understand the instrument, but also the musician who plays that instrument, in this case, to understand me" (Ngô 2019).

37 Anthony Gritten suggests that interaction in chamber music performance, which builds trust and trustworthiness, can (sometimes) be understood as an investment in social, rather than cultural, capital (2017, 250–53).

Trà My: Thủy nhớ cái nhà mà Thủy đến thăm chị . . .

Thủy: Cái nhà gần bờ sông trong ngõ mà ô tô không vào được phải không?

Trà My: ừ đúng rồi. Hôm đấy Thủy đến cùng ông Đại ý.

Thủy: Vâng. Em nhớ trước nhà có con chó.

Trà My: . . .

[Music: Solo with Stefan]

[When Stefan starts playing, Thủy and Trà My slowly turn and start doing movements. On the screen a video with images from the hectic traffic in Hà Nội *is projected. When the music stops the light fades. A text is projected on the screen.]*

I construct my memories with my present. I'm lost, abandoned in the present. I try in vain to rejoin the past: I cannot escape.

[The text fades away. Nam appears on the screen.]

5.4. Modes of collaboration

The solo for tỳ bà constitutes one manifestation of shared voice in *Arrival Cities: Hanoi*. The account given in section 4.2.2 above, discussing collaboration between Stefan and Kent, suggests that a long-term collaboration may result in a practice that makes it almost second nature to access a discursive voice. As Kent remarked, "when confronted with this Vietnamese lute, I could rather immediately identify possibilities and limitations that were related also to how I imagined that Stefan would play the instrument" (Olofsson 2019a). In 2008, Stefan had summarised the modes of collaboration between composer and performer:

> Collective work that would fit into the frame of "family" collaboration is found with performers working in chamber music, for instance in long-term projects such as string quartets tend to be. But collaborative work between a composer and performer(s) that approach the "family" kind are, I would say, sadly rare. The same goes for "integrative" patterns: it is hard to determine how a performer and a composer could venture into collaborative work of a kind similar to that of Picasso and Braque, simply because in the case of performers and composer, their practices are so strictly divided. (Östersjö 2008, 377–78)

However, that same year Stefan identified integrative and family modes of interaction in his work with Kent:

> looking at the intensity of our work, at least since 1995, and considering the fact that we live in the same city, have worked in the same studios, with the same ensembles, and arranged festivals and concerts together, I would in the last analysis also find patterns of "family" collaboration in our work. True, we do not share lives in the literal sense but the various modes in which we have collaborated during the years and the seemingly endless stream of new projects, makes this a particularly strong musical association that has enriched both of our lives. (Östersjö 2008, 203)

When Kent embarked on creating *Indy 500*, a journey towards a new identity as a composer was launched. Over the past ten years, Kent has developed an interdisciplinary compositional practice in constant and very close collaboration with Jörgen Dahlqvist. This integrative collaboration, "motivated by the desire to *transform* existing knowledge and paradigms into new visions" (John-Steiner 2000, 70), is discussed extensively in Kent's thesis (Olofsson 2018).[38] At the same time, The Six Tones embarked on a series of projects with Jörgen and began a collaboration with Kent that is now ten years old. We would argue that *Arrival Cities: Hanoi* could not have been created without the *family collaboration* that emerged out of the process of its making. We also argue that the solo pieces for đàn bầu and đàn tranh also express a discursive voice, although they emerge out of collaborations that are much more distributed than the one between Kent and Stefan. We must again point out that the solo for đàn tranh exemplifies how a negotiation between culturally distinct voices can be carried out without any felt resistance. The collaboration between Trà My and Kent followed a different path and was much more centred around an empathic engagement with voice.

> Nam: If a person becomes an artist the family and the whole village will be proud. Still it is difficult. But these were the golden days of Tuồng theatre. Anywhere we would go people were so welcoming. We had no time to go to the countryside and play because we were fully booked in the cities. In the winter time the audience had to keep their seats from 3 p.m. until the performance in the evening. In 1975 the country was united so the southern Tuồng theatre moved back to the south while I stayed. I decided to stay in Hà Nội while the other artists returned to their homeland in Bình Định. The future of the country was so unclear after the American war. Now the war time started in my life. I was a trained Tuồng actor but I couldn't work.
>
> *[The voice of Thủy]*: Why could you not perform?
>
> Nam: There was a strong tension between the northern and the southern traditions.
>
> *[The voice of Thủy]*: What kind of conflict?
>
> Nam: It was like a war. A conflict in art, life, and between people.
>
> *[The video fades away. Thủy and Trà My start playing]*
>
> *[Music: Duo with Thủy and Trà My]*
>
> *[On the screen quotations from two different street vendors are projected.]*

---

38 In his thesis, Olofsson describes how the change in his individual practice as a composer in the period between 2009 and 2018, instigated by the collaboration with Dahlqvist, also changed the roles of all participating artists: "The text and music were here created more in parallel in an ongoing dialogue with extensive exchanges of ideas for shaping the dramaturgical structures. The work on the stage design and visuals started much earlier in the process. The early rehearsal sessions with the performers became much more of creative and improvisatory processes, which provided ideas and materials that became integral parts of the overall work. This changed the working process from a linear order to a more parallel. It also expanded and changed the roles of the participants, as everybody became involved in all parts and processes of a production. However, this did not mean that we all were doing a little bit of everything. Everyone worked with their respective areas of expertise, but was influenced by, and likewise influenced the others' work. This helped connecting the different artistic ideas into one coherent artwork: the overall dramaturgical work became a collaborative effort. The hierarchical working structure usually found in theatres and operas, with a leading director, has thus been absent in our productions. Instead, the artistic ideas, visions and responsibilities for a performance have been shared among the participants" (Olofsson 2018, 196–97).

[A street vendor (unnamed)]: It's hard to sell anything, because the days are too hot. I go home every ten days to rest and to wait for the weather to get better. I prefer to sell in the streets rather than in the market, then I'm free to go home when I want to. I work around Hàng Ngang, Hàng Đào, and Tràng Thi in the old town. Very often I am stopped by the police because it's illegal to sell in the streets. We're allowed to walk in the street but not stop to sell anything. If we see the police, we just have to keep walking.

[A street vendor preparing a pineapple is shown on the screen]

[The second quotation on the screen]: I start work at 3.30 in the morning. I sell bananas near the Hanoi Academy of Music. My mother-in-law has a banana field. I started this job when I had my first daughter. I was nineteen years old. Now she's twenty. She's already graduated from the gymnasium. It cost me six million đồng a month to have children in school. I take care of everything in the family. We have sold our rice field so my husband at home doesn't do anything.

[A street vendor walking away with her bicycle in one of the alleys near Hà Nội Academy of Music. Trà My and Thủy stops playing. The music has now transformed into a percussive sound.]

Thủy: Mỗi khi tôi nghe thấy những âm thanh này . . . Những âm thanh này . . . lại gợi cho tôi nhớ về Hà Nội. Tôi cảm thấy . . . Tôi cảm thấy như mình đang ở nhà vậy . . .

[Music: Trio 2]

[The video is showing snippets from the Tuồng performance we saw in the first video clip with Nam. After a while the imagery suddenly transforms into the Long Biên Market where we see small children playing outside, lorries driving, and women selling fruit. The film ends up in a shed where three sisters who work as street vendors live.]

[Music: Duo with Stefan and Trà My]

[The soundscape becomes a thunderstorm and rain; and after they have stopped playing the piece, we start hearing the voices from Thủy and Trà My talking to each other in Vietnamese. Stefan walks up front.]

5.5. Performativity

The methods used in the making of *Arrival Cities: Hanoi* are related to the work of groups like Rimini Protokoll, in that it wishes to "stake a claim for the particular, concrete person against the politically generalised" and also "in the way that documentary material is confronted with subjective experiences" (Dreysse and Malzacher 2008, 9). At the same time, the extensive collaborative work on the making of the documentary means that the project partakes of the nature of a piece of performative ethnography. As the staged version has developed, the meaning of the video and audio recordings has shifted, with differing interpretations expressed in the storytelling and shifting perspectives of the participating artists. The activation of memory has been the central concern, and the creation of a foundation of empathy and trust has been a prerequisite for the sharing of personal experience. As observed in the practice of Rimini Protokoll: "Memory, by reopening a situation, stands, in the first instance, no longer in a semiotic context, but rather in one of performative processes. . . . It ignites itself in the here and now with specific materials that it organises as a constellation in space to create logic through their use. Simultaneously memory marks the point at which individual loss writes itself into collective remembrance" (Siegmund 2008, 192). Clearly, what a piece like *Arrival Cities: Hanoi* offers are "partial, plural, incomplete, and contingent understandings, not analytic distance or detachment, the hallmarks of the textual and positivist paradigms" (Denzin 2003, 8). But, as argued by Gorton and Östersjö in the first chapter, performative knowledge can be combined with discursive forms of knowledge, such as the present chapter is attempting to provide, through the interviews carried out with the participating artists. It is our hope that these accounts and reflections can contribute to a better understanding of how knowledge situated in the performative, artistic, and discursive domains can be articulated and communicated (see also Östersjö 2017).

> Stefan: When we came to Hà Nội in spring 2014, to start making the piece, we knew we wanted to record documentary with people who were in different states of migration, but we weren't really clear exactly what to do. We were having breakfast with Thủy's mother, who has been an actress in the Tuồng theatre, and she told of this actor who had come to Hà Nội when he was fourteen to study southern style Tuồng theatre, although he was in the north. After the war, the southern theatre moved south, but for family reasons, he decided to stay. And then he struggled for ten years to make his skills work in the northern style theatre instead. But the gesture, there's a lot of choreography in this kind of theatre, the gesture you learn is very different in the two traditions, and the forms of recitation are also different. This conflict between traditions also had a political dimension and reflected the division of the country. You could say he lived the archetypal experience of a migrant, where his body movement, his gesture, his voice, were all wrong and not understood, and after ten years he gave up and decided to become a costume-maker. So we got interested in this story and decided to call him, and we met him in the afternoon the same day. He agreed to do the interview, and that's how the documentary with Nam happened. But then, as we continued working, and made interviews with street vendors and other people, we realized that the piece could not only be about the people we met, but also had to incorporate our own histories of migration to and from Hà Nội.

5.6. Embodiment

The role of embodiment in *Arrival Cities: Hanoi* is perhaps most clearly evident in the choreography, just as the choreography also constitutes one of the central sources for expressing empathy. Moreover, to return to the discussion of presence in musical performance in chapter 2, the choreography and the story-telling both contribute to a stronger presence for each of the performers, in the sense suggested by Fischer-Lichte (2012).

We have described above how a scene from Tuồng theatre, first performed by Nam, became the material for choreography drawn from each musician's memory of this performance. These different choreographies are performed twice, first in the opening and then again at the very end. Only at the end are they explicity connected with the documentation of Nam's performance. If we think of performing bodies as archives, Nam, to a certain extent, performs a transmission of a Vietnamese theatre tradition, but the three musicians rather engage in an act of remembrance, not of this particular piece of Tuồng theatre but of Nam's individual fate: a re-writing of movement which is also a transformation, shifting, perhaps, for a moment, our sense of time, opening a door to a much earlier time when the same choreography was studied by a fourteen-year-old boy in Hà Nội, who had just arrived, alone, from the countryside.

This interpretation is supported by Trà My's description of her experience in drawing choreography from Tuồng theatre into actual playing on her instrument: "When we played the second trio and I integrated movement from Tuồng, which represents horse riding, into the music, that part, combining the musical performance with the struggle of controlling a horse, was so intense, and I often felt like I could cry any second even when we had performed the piece many times. The movement became so personal to me" (Ngô 2019). We believe that several layers of embodied memory underlie this account. First, the choreographies of Tuồng theatre are part and parcel of the traditional music with which Trà My grew up. Second, even though there is no shared gestural content between theatre performance and musical training in Vietnam, the close connection between music and theatre in traditional culture in Vietnam suggests that a relation between stylised horse-riding choreography (which is ubiquitous in this form of theatre) and the music she studied since childhood may be a source for the strong, embodied experience.[39] Third, and very importantly, we have seen several examples of the resistance of the body in the earlier stages of the collaboration between The Six Tones and Kent Olofsson. Hence, the embodied experience of emotional engagement also evidences an embodied listening, which is the outcome of a long-term challenge to her musical habitus.

[Music: Solo with Thủy]

[After Thủy's solo the interview with Nam appears on the screen]

Nam: Tuồng had become my blood and body. It really hurt when I decided to leave the stage and become a costume-maker.

[Music: Trio 3]

Nam: Many sleepless nights. I cried many times. Then I started my new work in the theatre. I got lower salary as a costume-maker. I have experienced many times in my life how, in the desperate situations, a new path opens up.

39 It should also be noted that, in 2012, Ngô Trà My was active in creating the installation and performance piece *Inside/Outside*. The making of the piece, with choreography by Marie Fahlin, included an analytical process drawing on gender analysis and a collaborative working out of each performer's individual movements that effectively became a way for the two participating Vietnamese performers to address the gendered gestures (not at all drawn from traditional theatre, but instead created as part of the emergence of television shows about traditional Vietnamese music) which they had been socialised into performing as professional female musicians. Hence, she had already developed an awareness of bodily gesture in performance, and how it can enhance the sense that, as put by Catherine Laws in chapter 2 (p. 95), "the event is performative of selfhood."

[Footage from when Nam draws a costume. His voice resonances as a memory in the room. After a few minutes the video and his voice fade away, and the lights are low and almost glowing as if it were night in the city of Hà Nội. The music continues.]

[Thủy walks up front.]

Thủy: Five years ago I moved to Sweden. Since then, each time I have a chance to go back to Vietnam I bring my daughter with me, because I want her to have her own memories of Hà Nội, and to know the sound of the city, the life of Hà Nội, just as the memories that I have with me now.

[Thủy goes to the back of the stage, again performing movements. Stefan comes downstage.]

5.7. Listening

To be engaged in intercultural collaboration is to challenge one's habitus of listening (Becker 2010). We propose above that a musician's listening can shift between different modalities, arguably both voluntarily and sub-consciously, and that a mode of listening which can bend a musician's ear toward the unexpected in a sonic event is what Schaeffer describes as musicianly listening. We have identified a number of such instances in the making of the music for *Arrival Cities: Hanoi*. Our initial example is when Kent composes the duo for đàn bầu and đàn tranh, finding ways to construct the harmonic vocabulary from the idiomatic technique of bending. But attentive listening can also take forms other than the resistance to habit intrinsic to musicianly listening. Kent describes finding a voice for the solo for đàn bầu, commenting that it emerged from a resonance with the idiomatic qualities of the instrument, first observed while workshopping music for the very ending of the piece, during which all three musicians improvised with bowing the electric guitar, đàn tranh, and đàn bầu. Such oscillation between resonance and resistance are, we would argue, typical of all forms of musical creativity, but they tend, again, to come to the fore in intercultural collaboration. But ultimately, resonance—or, rather, the resonant subject, connected to other vibrating bodies—constitutes the foundation for musical empathy and for subjectivity and intersubjectivity in musical performance. While we have, above and elsewhere in this book, discussed a musician's relation to habitus as characterised by either resonance or critique, here we might stipulate a level of resonance that is much more fundamental. However, in view of the longitudinal processes traced above, which eventually lead to an embodied listening to a certain music, we would rather suggest that there is a possibility for resonance or resistance in attentive listening and, further, that a critical engagement with a musical Other—the agonistic hospitality proposed by Cobussen and Nielsen (2012)—can also constitute the foundation for shared listening.

Stefan: When we returned to Hà Nội to continue the filming we had meant to meet again the street vendors in the house by the Red River. But when we called the owner, it turned out that no one was staying there anymore. The women had all left Hà Nội and gone back to their homeland. The times are harder for street vendors nowadays; it's actually hard to earn enough for it to make sense. And one reason is that the fruit that the street vendors buy at Long Biên market and then sell in the streets, is imported from China, and now with the increasing conflict between the two countries, people boycott

Chinese fruit, and we can see how sometimes global politics can affect the lives of poor women in the countryside outside Hà Nội.

[Stefan goes to the back of the stage. He also starts doing movements. Trà My comes up onstage. The music has now faded out. Silence.]

Trà My: If you come back again to Hà Nội, I might invite you to visit my new house. *[She continues in Vietnamese.]* Đấy là tổ ấm bé nhỏ của tôi mà mỗi khi đi xa tôi luôn muốn trở về. You might wake very early in the morning from the call of the street vendor, or to the sound of the sewing machine. The costume-maker next door might be Nam.

[Trà My goes to the back of the stage. All three musicians are now performing movements. On the screen Nam appears again, now outside, on a small bridge. He starts showing the movements he learnt as a young actor, and we now understand that the movements Stefan, Thủy, and Trà My have been doing are the same as Nam is now performing. The three fade out their movements and just stand still onstage. Nam also stops. He fades away. A last text is projected on the screen.]

Nothing is ever really lost to us as long as we remember it.

[The text slowly fades away. Black.]

[Curtain]

Conclusion

Catherine Laws

We started this book by asking "who is the 'I' that performs?" There is no clear and simple answer, but that was never really the intention. Instead, the question offered an opportunity: to open up certain key matters of subjectivity, agency, and identity—matters that underpin the more often discussed questions of musical expression, communication, and meaning—and from there to explore the complexities of their actions and interactions. The four projects are in many respects diverse, not merely in artistic content but also in their methodologies and framing. This, too, was intentional. What seemed to us most important was to explore where and how the various projects exposed, in and through practice, similar manifestations of agency and comparable processes by which a sense of a self is produced, and to find the most appropriate theoretical levers with which to prise open these issues in each context. As noted in the introduction, we shared certain core questions from the start, along with a commitment to practice as a key component of the research, and we have shared the ideas (both artistic and theoretical) along the way without defining a singular theoretical position or framework.

The result is a series of parallel projects with clear intersections and crossovers but significant differences. While the construction (but also the deconstruction and reconstruction) of selfhood, and related matters of intentionality, agency, and identity lie at the heart of each project, the nature of the discussions and the emphases within are as different as the artistic work itself. Something mentioned briefly in one chapter is taken up more substantially in another, or is reiterated in different terms or with different emphasis, or branches off in a different direction.

There are certain broad commonalities between the projects. All are explicitly collaborative, though the nature of those collaborations—their processes and artistic relationships—varies considerably. All operate in the field of contemporary musical practice, and this facilitated our fundamental, shared desire to research primarily through "doing"—to explore the key research questions through artistic processes of making and performing, designed to probe the core concerns. This was a matter of research experimentation in and through practice.

However, while some projects involve extensive intermedial collaboration, others are more purely musical, and while composition is significant in every project, improvisation features more in some than in others. All the projects are to an extent concerned with materiality, but to different degrees and with different emphasis: the agency of instruments is a recurrent theme, while questions of mediation, particularly through recording, are so fundamental to chapter 3, with the *Footnotes* project, that its significance is dealt with only lightly elsewhere. Likewise, the materiality of scores and the ways in which notation both mediates agency and constitutes composing and performing subjects is an important topic in chapter 1, then briefly revisited in the very different contexts of subsequent chapters. The role of the body is also a crucial topic. However, we were concerned to explore not only the different manifestations of the performing body-subject, in both "purely" musical performance and more overtly theatrical contexts, but also different theoretical approaches; hence, for example, the empirical methods of gesture analysis in chapter 1 are complemented with the more critical-theoretic approach to the "layered" body in chapter 2. Questions of time—the temporal processes of artistic creation and the emergence and transformation of subjectivities in and through time—are embedded in each chapter, but these become most apparent in chapter 3. Ethical issues of self and other, of identity and testimony, are introduced early in the book but emerge most substantially in the last chapter, with its cross-cultural context.

Perhaps most importantly, central to all this work was a commitment to iterative and reflexive processes of artistic research: cycles of making and reflection that feed one another, allowing questions to be explored and articulated in both verbal and nonverbal forms, through sounds and bodies as well as words. In this way, the textual discourse was formed through understandings exposed in and through practice, even as the practices formed objects of reflection. Mareli Stolp's observations sum this up: "Self-reflexivity [in artistic research] not only allows for reflection on the knowledge inherent in artistic experience, it also facilitates a 'feedback' of the articulated insights into ensuing artistic events. . . . It enables repeated accessibility to subjective knowledge generated within the constellation of practical aspects related to music-making, and thus allows for this knowledge to be articulated in some discursive way that is shareable beyond the realm of the personal" (Stolp 2017, 5).

Ultimately, the projects all, in different ways, reveal the composite or multiple constitution of any apparently singular "I" in the creative process. The model proposed in chapter 1 posits the seemingly discrete "voice" as constituted through the interaction of artists, instruments, and tools (in the widest sense), musical and wider cultural practices, and the specific contexts in which all these operate. Quite how that happens—which agents are most influential at different stages of a process, how they interact and transform—is then mapped out; and it is here, in the understanding of the dynamics of interaction within a particular context, that we start to understand how a "voice" might form. That the composer is somehow manifested "in" the performer's voice in playing Western classical music is perhaps self-evident, but the analysis is striking in its exposure of quite how this is constituted, in and through materials and socio-musical practices, and reciprocally: performer subjectivity is, also, partially constitutive of a composer's "voice," but equally within a discursive process fed by cultural practices and through negotiations of tools and materials. This theme is taken up, albeit in different terms and in an intermedial context, in chapter 2, and it persists throughout the book. The notions of subjectivity as multiple rather than singular, as a process rather than a stable entity, as embodied and contextual: none of these are remotely new, nor, in most fields, at all contentious. Nevertheless, as we argue, the tendency of discourses of musical practice is to proceed as if the entities of composers, performers, and listeners are separate, discrete, and identifiable. The projects in this book each reveal the interdependencies of self and other that operate in musical practices: the constitution of the other in the self.

It is this, perhaps, that nags away at us most, as it underlies the fundamental question of who speaks and how: the ethics of subjectification. This involves examining the need to find a voice, to say "I"—to experience a sense of agency and to be heard—set alongside the fundamental recognition of the other in that "I," the impossibility of pure subjectification, and hence the responsibility to that other: to the "not I" that is always, already part of us. This is explicit in chapter 4: here, the question of the artistic mediation of a range of voices and cross-cultural identities becomes crucial and is thematised in the production of *Arrival Cities: Hanoi*. Listening and empathy were explicit, critical components in the processes of making this piece, but also become significant in the production of identity in performance and, for audiences, in reception. However, this draws into the foreground the key underlying significance of our topic, since these same issues of agency and identity are embedded and exposed in each of the projects. From the practical, creative negotiations of subjectivity in each project there emerges an understanding of the possibilities and limits of individuation within the constraints of embedded cultural practices and their various modes of reception. To strive towards a better understanding of how the subject takes it place in musical performance—how discursive, distributed, embodied, subjects emerge, but continue to transform through time and memory, through repetitions and deviation, and through the dynamics of presence and absence—each of the chapters in different ways speaks to this aim.

This is, of course, only a start. One of the points of the book is that these are common questions for which there are no common answers. We can respond only through specifics, through acknowledgement of difference—different practices, different embodied identities, and different contexts. The same issues surely emerge out of all musical practices, historical and contemporary, and through the practices of different musical cultures. In this respect, this volume is a call to other researchers, especially artistic researchers, to explore this topic more fully in their own contexts, in and through their own practices. Arguably, these matters have been more thoroughly explored with respect to writing and textuality (in terms of who is the "I" that writes or speaks) and, consequently, to an extent in theatre-making. That said, we might suggest that these questions about the very existence of definable selves are illuminated from a helpful angle in work that deals with fields—like performance—that are socially constructed in the liminal space between personal agency and received constraints. In other words, artistic research of the type we have conducted has implications well beyond personal "voices," the agency of "bodies," and performance "practices": it is, perhaps, a way of life.

References

Abbate, Carolyn. 1991. *Unsung Voices: Opera and Musical Narrative in the Nineteenth Century*. Princeton, NJ: Princeton University Press.

Adami, Rebecca. 2014. "Human Rights for More Than One Voice: Rethinking Political Space beyond the Global/Local Divide." *Ethics & Global Politics* 7 (4): 163–80.

Adorno, Theodor W. 2006. *Towards a Theory of Musical Reproduction: Notes, a Draft and Two Schemata*. Edited by Henri Lonitz. Translated by Wieland Hoban. Cambridge: Polity Press. First published 2001 as *Zu einer Theorie der musikalischen Reproduktion: Aufzeichnungen, ein Entwurf und zwei Schemata* (Frankfurt am Main: Suhrkamp).

Agamben, Giorgio. 2000. *Remnants of Auschwitz: The Witness and the Archive*. Translated by Daniel Heller-Roazen. New York: Zone Books. First published 1998 as *Quel che resta di Auschwitz: L'archivio e il testimone* (Turin: Bollati Boringhieri).

———. 2006. *Language and Death: The Place of Negativity*. Translated by Karen E. Pinkus with Michael Hardt. Minneapolis: University of Minnesota Press. First published 1982 as *Il linguaggio e la morte: Un seminario sul luogo della negatività* (Turin: Einaudi).

Agawu, Kofi. 2003. *Representing African Music: Postcolonial Notes, Queries, Positions*. New York: Routledge.

Ahmed, Sara. 2002. "This Other and Other Others." *Economy and Society* 31 (4): 558–72.

Alperson, Philip. 2008. "The Instrumentality of Music." *Journal of Aesthetics and Art Criticism* 66 (1): 37–51.

Appiah, Kwame Anthony. 2018. *The Lies That Bind: Rethinking Identity: Creed, Country, Colour, Class, Culture*. London: Profile Books.

Assis, Paulo de. 2018. *Logic of Experimentation: Rethinking Music Performance through Artistic Research*. Orpheus Institute Series. Leuven: Leuven University Press.

Association Européenne des Conservatoires, Académies de Musique et Musikhochschulen. 2015. "Artistic Research: An AEC Council White Paper." Brussels: AEC. https://www.aec-music.eu/work--policies/artistic-research.

Auslander, Philip. 1999. *Liveness: Performance in a Mediatized Culture*. New York: Routledge.

———. 2006. "Musical Personae." *TDR: The Drama Review* 50 (1): 100–19.

Baily, John. 2009. "The Art of the 'Fieldwork Movie': 35 Years of Making Ethnomusicological Films." *Ethnomusicology Forum* 18 (1): 55–64.

Bakhtin, Mikhail. 1981. *The Dialogic Imagination: Four Essays*. Edited by Michael Holquist. Translated by Caryl Emerson and Michael Holquist. Austin: University of Texas Press. First published 1975 as *Voprosy literatury i èstetiki* (Moscow: Hudožestvennaâ literatura).

Barad, Karen. 2003. "Posthumanist Performativity: Toward an Understanding of How Matter Comes to Matter." *Signs: Journal of Women in Culture and Society* 28 (3): 801–31.

Barker, Hugh, and Yuval Taylor. 2007. *Faking It: The Quest for Authenticity in Popular Music*. New York: W. W. Norton.

Barrett, Estelle. 2014. "Introduction: Extending the Field: Invention, Application and Innovation in Creative Arts Enquiry." In *Material Inventions: Applying Creative Arts Research*, edited by Estelle Barrett and Barbara Bolt, 1–21. London: I. B. Tauris.

Barsalou, Lawrence W. 2008. "Grounded Cognition." *Annual Review of Psychology* 59: 617–45.

Barthes, Roland. 1985. "Cy Twombly: Works on Paper." In *The Responsibility of Forms: Critical Essays on Music, Art, and Representation*, translated by Richard Howard, 157–76. Berkeley: University of California Press. Book first published 1982 as *L'obvie et l'obtus: Essais critiques III* (Paris: Seuil).

Bastien, David T., and Todd J. Hostager. 1988. "Jazz as a Process of Organizational Innovation." *Communication Research* 15 (5): 582–602.

———. 1992. “Cooperation as Communicative Accomplishment: A Symbolic Interaction Analysis of an Improvised Jazz Concert.” *Communication Studies* 43 (2): 92–104.

———. 1996. “On Cooperation: A Replication of an Experiment in Jazz and Cooperation.” *Comportamento Organizacional e Gestao* 2 (1): 33–46.

Bastien, David T., and Jeremy Rose. 2014. “Cooperative Activity: The Importance of Audiences.” In *Revisiting Symbolic Interaction in Music Studies and New Interpretive Works*, edited by Norman K. Denzin, 21–36. Studies in Symbolic Interaction 42. Bingley, UK: Emerald Group.

Baxandall, Michael. 1985. *Patterns of Intention: On the Historical Explanation of Pictures.* New Haven, CT: Yale University Press.

Becker, Judith. 2010. “Exploring the Habitus of Listening: Anthropological Perspectives.” In *Handbook of Music and Emotion: Theory, Research, Applications,* edited by Patrick N. Juslin and John Sloboda, 127–57. Oxford: Oxford University Press.

Beckett, Samuel. 1980. *Company*. New York: Grove.

———. 2012. *The Collected Poems of Samuel Beckett*. Edited by Seán Lawlor and John Pilling. London: Faber and Faber.

Bell, Adam, Ethan Hein, and Jarrod Ratcliffe. 2015. “Beyond Skeuomorphism: The Evolution of Music Production Software User Interface Metaphors.” *Journal on the Art of Record Production* 9. https://www.arpjournal.com/asarpwp/beyond-skeuomorphism-the-evolution-of-music-production-software-user-interface-metaphors-2/.

Bell, Elizabeth. 2008. *Theories of Performance.* Thousand Oaks, CA: Sage.

Bellow, Saul. [1964] 1976. *Herzog*. New York: Viking Press. First published 1961 (New York: Viking Press).

Benaquisto, Lucia. 2008. “Open Coding.” In *The Sage Encyclopedia of Qualitative Research Methods*, edited by Lisa M. Given, 2 vols., 2:581–82. Thousand Oaks, CA: Sage.

Bennett, Jane. 2010. *Vibrant Matter: A Political Ecology of Things*. Durham, NC: Duke University Press.

Berliner, Paul. 1994. *Thinking in Jazz: The Infinite Art of Improvisation*. Chicago: University of Chicago Press.

Berman, Boris. 2000. *Notes from the Pianist’s Bench*. New Haven, CT: Yale University Press.

Blau, Herbert. 1982. *Take Up the Bodies: Theater at the Vanishing Point*. Urbana: University of Illinois Press.

Bloom, Benjamin S. 1953. “Thought-Processes in Lectures and Discussions.” *Journal of General Education* 7 (3): 160–69.

Bolt, Barbara. 2016. “Artistic Research: a Performative Paradigm?” *Parse* 3: 129–42. http://parsejournal.com/article/artistic-research-a-performative-paradigm/.

Bonds, Mark Evan. 1997. “Idealism and the Aesthetics of Instrumental Music at the Turn of the Nineteenth Century.” *Journal of the American Musicological Society* 50 (2–3): 387–420.

Borgdorff, Henk. 2011. “The Production of Knowledge in Artistic Research.” In *The Routledge Companion to Research in the Arts*, edited by Michael Biggs and Henrik Karlsson, 44–63. Abingdon, UK: Routledge.

Born, Georgina. 2009. “Afterword; Recording: From Reproduction to Representation to Remediation.” In *The Cambridge Companion to Recorded Music*, edited by Nicholas Cook, Eric Clarke, Daniel Leech-Wilkinson, and John Rink, 286–304. Cambridge: Cambridge University Press.

———. 2012. “Digital Music, Relational Ontologies and Social Forms.” In *Bodily Expression in Electronic Music: Perspectives on Reclaiming Performativity*, edited by Deniz Peters, Gerhard Eckel, and Andreas Dorschel, 163–80. New York: Routledge.

Braidotti, Rosi. 2018. “A Theoretical Framework for the Critical Posthumanities.” In “Transversal Posthumanities,” edited by Matthew Fuller and Rosi Braidotti, special issue, *Theory, Culture and Society*: 1–31. https://journals.sagepub.com/doi/10.1177/0263276418771486.

Brooks, William. (1986) 2019. *Footnotes.* Lebanon, NH: Frog Peak Music. First published 1986 (Baltimore: Smith Publications).

———. 2002. “Music II: From the Late 1960s.” In *The Cambridge Companion to John Cage*, edited by David Nicholls, 128–47. Cambridge: Cambridge University Press.

———, ed. 2009a. *MetaCage: Essays On and around* Freeman Etudes / Fontana Mix / Aria. Collected Writings of the Orpheus Institute 2. Leuven: Leuven University Press.

———. 2009b. "Sounds, Gamuts, Actions: Cage's Pluralist Universe." In *MetaCage: Essays On and around* Freeman Etudes / Fontana Mix / Aria, edited by William Brooks, 61–95. Collected Writings of the Orpheus Institute 2. Leuven: Leuven University Press.

———. 2012. "In re: 'Experimental Music.'" *Contemporary Music Review* 31 (1): 37–62.

Brown, John Seely, Allan Collins, and Paul Duguid. 1989. "Situated Cognition and the Culture of Learning." *Educational Researcher* 18 (1): 32–42.

Brubaker, Bruce. 2016. "Over and Over and Over . . . : Performing Scripted Music." *Parse* 3. http://parsejournal.com/article/over-and-over-and-over-performing-scripted-music/.

Butler, Judith. 1988. "Performative Acts and Gender Constitution: An Essay in Phenomenology and Feminist Theory." *Theatre Journal* 40 (4): 519–31.

———. 1993. *Bodies That Matter*. London: Routledge.

———. 2005. *Giving an Account of Oneself*. New York: Fordham University Press.

———. 2012. "Can One Lead a Good Life in a Bad Life? Adorno Prize Lecture." *Radical Philosophy* 176 (9): 9–18.

———. 2015. *Senses of the Subject*. New York: Fordham University Press.

Butt, John. 2002. *Playing with History: The Historical Approach to Musical Performance*. Cambridge: Cambridge University Press.

Cage, John. 1993. *Composition in Retrospect*. Cambridge, MA: Exact Change.

Cannon, Alexander M. 2016. "From Nameless to Nomenclature: Creating Music Genre in Southern Vietnam." *Asian Music* 47 (2): 138–71.

Cassidy, Aaron. 2004. "Performative Physicality and Choreography as Morphological Determinants." In *Musical Morphology: New Music and Aesthetics in the 21st Century, Volume 2*, edited by Claus-Steffen Mahnkopf, Frank Cox, and Wolfram Schurig, 34–51. Hofheim: Wolke Verlag.

Cavarero, Adriana. 2005. *For More Than One Voice: Toward a Philosophy of Vocal Expression*. Translated by Paul A. Kottman. Stanford, CA: Stanford University Press. First published 2003 as *A più voci: Per una filosofia dell'espressione vocale* (Milan: Feltrinelli).

Chion, Michel. 2009. "Guide to Sound Objects." Translated by John Dack and Christine North. EARS: ElectroAcoustic Resource Site. http://ears.pierrecouprie.fr/spip.php?article3597.

Clarke, Eric F. 2011. *Ways of Listening: An Ecological Approach to the Perception of Musical Meaning*. New York: Oxford University Press.

Clarke, Eric F., Nicholas Cook, Bryn Harrison, and Philip Thomas. 2005. "Interpretation and Performance in Bryn Harrison's *Être-temps*." *Musicae Scientiae* 9 (1): 31–74.

Clarke, Eric F., Tia DeNora, and Jonna Vuoskoski. 2015. "Music, Empathy and Cultural Understanding." *Physics of Life Reviews* 15: 61–88.

Clarke, Eric F., and Mark Doffman, eds. 2017. *Distributed Creativity: Collaboration and Improvisation in Contemporary Music*. New York: Oxford University Press.

Clarke, Eric F., Mark Doffman, David Gorton, and Stefan Östersjö. 2017. "Fluid Practices, Solid Roles? The Evolution of *Forlorn Hope*." In *Distributed Creativity: Collaboration and Improvisation in Contemporary Music*, edited by Eric F. Clarke and Mark Doffman, 116–35. New York: Oxford University Press.

Cobussen, Marcel, and Nanette Nielsen. 2012. *Music and Ethics*. Abingdon, UK: Ashgate.

Coessens, Kathleen, and Stefan Östersjö. 2014. "Habitus and the Resistance of Culture." In *Artistic Experimentation in Music: An Anthology*, edited by Darla Crispin and Bob Gilmore, 333–47. Orpheus Institute Series. Leuven: Leuven University Press.

Cone, Edward T. 1974. *The Composer's Voice*. Berkeley: University of California Press.

Cook, Nicholas. 2001. "Between Process and Product: Music and/as Performance." *Music Theory Online* 7 (2). http://www.mtosmt.org/issues/mto.01.7.2/mto.01.7.2.cook.html.

———. 2013. *Beyond the Score: Music as Performance*. New York: Oxford University Press.

———. 2018. *Music as Creative Practice*. New York: Oxford University Press.

Coorevits, Esther, Dirk Moelants, Stefan Östersjö, and David Gorton. 2016. "Decomposing a Composition: On the Multi-layered Analysis of Expressive Music Performance." In *Music, Mind, and Embodiment: 11th International Symposium, CMMR 2015*, edited by Richard Kronland-Martinet, Mitsuko Aramaic, and Sølvi Ystad, 167–89. Cham: Springer.

Cross, Ian, Felicity Laurence, and Tal-Chen Rabinowitch. 2012. "Empathy and Creativity in Group Musical Practices: Towards a Concept of Empathic Creativity." In *The Oxford Handbook of Music Education, Volume 2*, edited by Gary E. McPherson and Graham F. Welch, 337–53. New York: Oxford University Press.

Cumming, Naomi. 2000. *The Sonic Self: Musical Subjectivity and Signification*. Bloomington: Indiana University Press.

Dahlqvist, Jörgen. 2019. Interview, 1 February.

Dahlqvist, Jörgen, and Nguyễn Thanh Thủy. 2018. Interview, 17 November.

Dahlqvist, Jörgen, and Kent Olofsson. 2019. Interviewed by Stefan Östersjö, 1 February.

Dalla Bella, Simone, and Caroline Palmer. 2011. "Rate Effects on Timing, Key Velocity, and Finger Kinematics in Piano Performance." *PLoS One* 6 (6). https://www.ncbi.nlm.nih.gov/pmc/articles/PMC3121738/.

Davidson, Jane. 1994. "What Type of Information Is Conveyed In the Body Movements of Solo Musician Performers?" *Journal of Human Movement Studies* 6: 279–301.

———. 2007. "Qualitative Insights Into the Use of Expressive Bodily Movement in Solo Piano Performance: A Case Study Approach." *Psychology of Music* 35 (3): 381–401.

Dawe, Kevin. 2003. "The Cultural Study of Musical Instruments." In *The Cultural Study of Music: A Critical Introduction*, edited by Martin Clayton, Trevor Herbert, and Richard Middleton, 274–83. New York: Routledge.

Deleuze, Gilles, and Claire Parnet. 1987. *Dialogues*. Translated by Hugh Tomlinson and Barbara Habberjam. New York: Columbia University Press. First published 1977 as *Dialogues* (Paris: Flammarion).

Dennis, Amanda. 2018. "Compulsive Bodies, Creative Bodies: Beckett's *Quad* and Agency in the 21st Century." *Journal of Beckett Studies* 27 (1): 5–21.

DeNora, Tia. 1995. "The Musical Composition of Social Reality? Music, Action and Reflexivity." *Sociological Review* 43 (2): 295–315.

———. 1999. "Music as a Technology of Self." *Poetics* 27: 31–56.

———. 2000. *Music in Everyday Life*. Cambridge: Cambridge University Press.

Denzin, Norman K. 2003. "Performance Ethics." In *Performance Ethnography: Critical Pedagogy and the Politics of Culture*, 243–62. Thousand Oaks, CA: Sage.

De Preester, Helena. 2007. "To Perform the Layered Body: A Short Exploration of the Body in Performance." *Janus Head* 9 (2): 349–83.

De Preester, Helena, and Manos Tsakiris. 2009. "Body-Extension versus Body-Incorporation: Is There a Need for a Body-Model? *Phenomenology and the Cognitive Sciences* 8 (3): 307–19.

D'Errico, Lucia. 2018. *Powers of Divergence: An Experimental Approach to Music Performance*. Orpheus Institute Series. Leuven: Leuven University Press.

Derrida, Jacques. 2000. *Of Hospitality*. Translated by Rachel Bowlby. Stanford, CA: Stanford University Press. First published 1997 as *De l'hospitalité* (Paris: Calmann-Lévy).

Desmet, Frank, Luc Nijs, Michiel Demey, Micheline Lesaffre, Jean-Pierre Martens, and Marc Leman. 2012. "Assessing a Clarinet Player's Performer Gestures in Relation to Locally Intended Musical Targets." *Journal of New Music Research* 41 (1): 31–48.

De Souza, Jonathan. 2017. *Music at Hand: Instruments, Bodies, and Cognition*. New York: Oxford University Press.

Dewey, John. (1934) 1980. *Art as Experience*. New York: G. P. Putnam's Sons. First published 1934 (New York: Minton, Balch & Co.).

Di Donato, Balandino, Jamie Bullock, and Atau Tanaka. 2018. “Myo Mapper: A Myo Armband to OSC Mapper.” *Proceedings of the International Conference on New Interfaces for Musical Expression*. Blacksburg, Virginia. http://www.nime.org/proceedings/2018/nime2018_paper0030.pdf.

Doğantan-Dack, Mine. 2011. “In the Beginning Was Gesture: Piano Touch and the Phenomenology of the Performing Body.” In *New Perspectives on Music and Gesture*, edited by Anthony Gritten and Elaine King, 243–66. Abingdon, UK: Ashgate.

———. 2012. “The Art of Research in Live Music Performance.” *Music Performance Research* 5: 34–48.

———. 2015a. “Artistic Research in Classical Music Performance: Truth and Politics.” *PARSE—Journal of Art and Research* 1. http://parsejournal.com/article/artistic-research-in-classical-music-performance/.

———. 2015b. “The Role of the Musical Instrument in Performance as Research: The Piano as a Research Tool.” In *Artistic Practice as Research in Music: Theory, Criticism, Practice*, edited by Mine Doğantan-Dack, 169–203. Abingdon, UK: Ashgate.

———. 2017. “Expressive Freedom in Classical Performance: Insights from a Pianist-Researcher.” In *Musicians in the Making: Pathways to Creative Performance*, edited by John Rink, Helena Gaunt, and Aaron Williamon, 131–35. New York: Oxford University Press.

Dolby, Ray. 1998. “Sound Recording—Will There Be Progress Forever?” *Proceedings of the IEEE* 86 (12): 2469–72.

Dominguez, Alejandro. 2015. “A History of the Convolution Operation.” *IEEE Pulse*, January–February. https://pulse.embs.org/january-2015/history-convolution-operation/.

Dreysse, Miriam, and Florian Malzacher. 2008. Foreword to *Experts of the Everyday: The Theatre of Rimini Protokoll*, edited by Miriam Dreysee and Florian Malzacher, 8–11. Berlin: Alexander Verlag.

Driver, Tom. 1961. “Beckett by the Madeleine.” *Columbia University Forum* 4 (3): 21–25.

Eco, Umberto. 1986. *Faith in Fakes: Essays*. Translated by William Weaver. London: Secker & Warburg. First published 1973 as *Il costume di casa* (Milan: Bompiani).

———. 1989. *Foucault's Pendulum*. Translated by William Weaver. London: Secker & Warburg. First published 1988 as *Il pendolo di Foucault* (Milan: Bompiani).

Edgerton, Michael Edward 2008. “Zappa Speaks Again: The *Tempo Mental Rap* Variations, for Solo Guitar.” In *Facets of the Second Modernity: New Music and Aesthetics in the 21st Century, Volume 6*, edited by Claus-Steffen Mahnkopf, Frank Cox, and Wolfram Schurig, 135–56. Hofheim: Wolke.

Eidse, Noelani, Sarah Turner, and Natalie Oswin. 2016. “Contesting Street Spaces in a Socialist City: Itinerant Vending-scapes and the Everyday Politics of Mobility in Hanoi, Vietnam.” *Annals of the American Association of Geographers* 106 (2): 340–49.

Ericsson, K. Anders, and Neil Charness. 1994. “Expert Performance: Its Structure and Acquisition.” *American Psychologist* 49 (8): 725–47.

Ericsson, K. Anders, Ralf Th. Krampe, and Clemens Tesch-Römer. 1993. “The Role of Deliberate Practice in the Acquisition of Expert Performance.” *Psychological Review* 100 (3): 363–406.

Evens, Aden. 2005. *Sound Ideas: Music, Machines, and Experience*. Minneapolis: University of Minnesota Press.

Fagenblat, Michael. 2002. Review of *Being Singular Plural*, by Jean-Luc Nancy. *Common Knowledge* 8 (1): 210.

Ferneyhough, Brian. 1995. “Aspects of Notational and Compositional Practice.” In *Collected Writings*, edited by James Boros and Richard Toop, 2–13. New York: Routledge.

Fischer-Lichte, Erika. 2012. “Appearing as Embodied Mind: Defining a Weak, a Strong and a Radical Concept of Presence.” In *Archaeologies of Presence: Art, Performance and the Persistence of Being*, edited by Gabriella Giannachi, Nick Kaye, and Michael Shanks, 103–18. Abingdon, UK: Routledge.

Fitch, Fabrice, and Neil Heyde. 2007. “‘Recercar’: The Collaborative Process as Invention.” *Twentieth-Century Music* 4 (1): 71–95.

Forsyth, Alison, and Chris Megson, eds. 2009. *Get Real: Documentary Theatre, Past and Present*. London: Palgrave Macmillan.

Foucault. Michel. 1972. *The Archaeology of Knowledge*. Translated by A. M. Sheridan Smith. New York: Tavistock. First published 1969 as *L'archéologie du savoir* (Paris: Gallimard).

———. (1973) 1989. *The Birth of the Clinic*. Translated by A. M. Sheridan. London: Routledge. First published 1963 as *Naissance de la clinique* (Paris: Presses universitaires de France). Translation first published 1973 (London: Tavistock).

———. 1977. "What is an Author?" In *Language, Counter-Memory, Practice: Selected Essays and Interviews*, edited by Donald F. Bouchard, translated by Donald T. Bouchard and Sherry Simon, 113–38. Ithaca, New York: Cornell University Press. First published 1969 as "Qu'est-ce qu'un auteur" (*Bulletin de la Sociéte française de Philosophie* 63 [3]: 73–104).

Fraser, Julius Thomas. 1982. *The Genesis and Evolution of Time: A Critique of Interpretations in Physics*. Amherst: University of Massachusetts Press.

———. 1990. *Of Time, Passion, and Knowledge: Reflections on the Strategy of Existence*. 2nd ed. Princeton, NJ: Princeton University Press.

Frisk, Henrik, and Stefan Östersjö, eds. 2013. *(Re)Thinking Improvisation: Artistic Explorations and Conceptual Writing*. Malmö: Malmö Academy of Music.

Frith, Simon. 1996a. "Music and Identity." In *Questions of Cultural Identity*, edited by Stuart Hall and Paul du Gay, 108–27. London: Sage.

———. 1996b. *Performing Rites: On the Value of Popular Music*. Cambridge, MA: Harvard University Press.

Fuchs, Thomas. 2012. "The Phenomenology of Body Memory." In *Body Memory, Metaphor and Movement*, edited by Sabine C. Koch, Thomas Fuchs, Michela Summa, and Cornelia Müller, 9–22. Amsterdam: John Benjamins Publishing.

Furuya, Shinichi, and Eckart Altenmüller. 2013. "Flexibility of Movement Organization in Piano Performance." *Frontiers in Human Neuroscience* 7. https://www.frontiersin.org/articles/10.3389/fnhum.2013.00173/full.

Gadamer, Hans-Georg. (1989) 2004. *Truth and Method*. 2nd ed. Translation revised by Joel Weinsheimer and Donald G. Marshall. London: Continuum. First published 1960 as *Wahrheit und Methode: Grundzüge einer philosophischen Hermeneutik* (Tübingen: Mohr). 2nd ed. of translation first published 1989 (London: Sheed and Ward).

Gallagher, Shaun. 2007. "The Natural Philosophy of Agency." *Philosophy Compass* 2 (2): 347–57.

———. 2012. "Multiple Aspects in the Sense of Agency." *New Ideas in Psychology* 30 (1): 15–31.

Gallagher, Shaun, and Jonathan Cole. 1995. "Body Image and Body Schema in a Deafferented Subject." *Journal of Mind and Behavior* 16 (4): 369–90.

Gans, David. 1980. "Steve Klein: Radical Luthier?" *BAM: The California Music Magazine* 74 (March 7): 38–39.

Gardner, Howard. 1994. "The Creators' Patterns." In *Dimensions of Creativity*, edited by Margaret A. Boden, 143–58. Cambridge, MA: MIT Press.

Garfinkel, Harold. 1967. *Studies in Ethnomethodology*. Englewood Cliffs, NJ: Prentice Hall.

Gaunt, Helena. 2017. "Apprenticeship and Empowerment: The Role of One-to-One Lessons." In *Musicians in the Making: Pathways to Creative Performance*, edited by John Rink, Helena Gaunt, and Aaron Williamon, 28–56. New York: Oxford University Press.

Gibson, James J. 1986. *The Ecological Approach to Visual Perception*. Hillsdale, NJ: Erlbaum.

Giddens, Anthony. 1991. *Modernity and Self-Identity: Self and Society in the Late Modern Age*. Cambridge: Polity Press.

Gilroy, Paul. 1993. *The Black Atlantic: Modernity and Double Consciousness*. Cambridge, MA: Harvard University Press.

Glissant, Édouard. 1997. *Poetics of Relation*. Translated by Betsy Wing. Ann Arbor: University of Michigan Press. First published 1990 as *Poétique de la relation* (Paris: Gallimard).

Godlovitch, Stan. 1998. *Musical Performance: A Philosophical Study*. Abingdon, UK: Routledge.

Godøy, Rolf Inge. 2006. "Gestural-Sonorous Objects: Embodied Extensions of Schaeffer's Conceptual Apparatus." *Organised Sound* 11 (2): 149–57.

Godøy, Rolf Inge, and Marc Leman. 2010. Editor's preface to *Musical Gestures: Sound, Movement and Meaning*, edited by Rolf Inge Godøy and Marc Leman, ix–xi. New York: Routledge.
Goebl, Werner. 2017. "Movement and Touch in Piano Performance." In *Handbook of Human Motion*, edited by Bertram Müller and Sebastian I. Wolf, 1–18. Cham, Switzerland: Springer.
Goehr, Lydia. 1989. "Being True to the Work." *Journal of Aesthetics and Art Criticism* 47 (1): 55–67.
———. 1992. *The Imaginary Museum of Musical Works*. Oxford: Clarendon Press.
Gorton, David. 2017. "Variations on Variations." Liner note for *David Gorton: Variations on John Dowland*, performed by Longbow, Peter Sheppard Skærved, and Stefan Östersjö. Toccata Classics, TOCC0396, compact disc.
———. 2018a. *Austerity Measures I* for ten-string guitar (2012). Berlin: Verlag Neue Musik.
———. 2018b. *Forlorn Hope* for eleven-string alto guitar and optional electronics (2011). Berlin: Verlag Neue Musik.
Gorton, David, and Stefan Östersjö. 2016. "Choose Your Own Adventure Music: On the Emergence of Voice in Musical Collaboration." In "'Collaboration' in Contemporary Music," edited by Alan Taylor, special issue, *Contemporary Music Review* 35 (6): 579–98.
Gorton, David, Simon Shaw-Miller, and Neil Heyde. 2013. "Instrumental Choreography: Gesture and Performance in Gorton's *Capriccio* for Solo Cello." In *La musique et ses instruents /Music and Its Instruments*, edited by Michèle Castellengo and Hugues Genevois, 485–93. Paris: Delatour.
Gottschalk, Jennie. 2016. *Experimental Music Since 1970*. London: Bloomsbury.
Gray, Michael B. 1986. "The Birth of Decca Stereo." *Journal of the Association of Recorded Sound Collections* 18 (1–3): 4–19.
Greenhalgh, Trisha, and Sietse Wieringa. 2011. "Is It Time to Drop the 'Knowledge Translation' Metaphor? A Critical Literature Review." *Journal of the Royal Society of Medicine* 104 (12): 501–9.
Gritten, Anthony. 2017. "Developing Trust in Others: Or, How to Empathise Like a Performer." In *Music and Empathy*, edited by Elaine King and Caroline Waddington, 248–66. Abingdon, UK: Routledge.
Grosz, Elizabeth. 1995. *Space, Time, and Perversion: The Politics of Bodies*. New York: Routledge.
Groth, Sanne Krogh, and Kristine Samson. 2017. "Sound Art Situations." *Organised Sound* 22 (1): 101–11.
Grubbs, David. 2014. *Records Ruin the Landscape: John Cage, the Sixties, and Sound Recording*. Durham, NC: Duke University Press.
Haanstad, Eric. 2014. "Performative Ethnography: Observant Participation in Southeast Asia." In *Methodology and Research Practice in Southeast Asian Studies*, edited by Mikko Huotari, Jürgen Rüland, and Judith Schlehe, 91–106. Basingstoke, UK: Palgrave Macmillan.
Habermas, Jürgen. 1984. *The Theory of Communicative Action: Reason and the Rationalization of Society*, vol. 1. Translated by Thomas A. McCarthy. London: Heinemann. First published 1981 as *Theorie des Kommunikativen Handelns, Band 1: Handlungsrationalitat und gesellschaftliche Rationalisierung* (Frankfurt am Main: Suhrkamp).
———. 1989. *The Structural Transformation of the Public Sphere: An Inquiry into a Category of Bourgeois Society*. Translated by Thomas Burger with Frederick Lawrence. Cambridge: Polity Press. First published 1962 as *Strukturwandel der Öffenlichkeit: Untersuchungen zu einer Kategorie der bürgerlichen Gesekkschaft* (Neuwied am Rhein: Hermann Luchterhand).
Haddon, Elizabeth. 2006. *Making Music in Britain: Interviews with Those Behind the Notes*. Aldershot, UK: Ashgate.
———. 2013. "The Development of the Individual Voice within the Institutional Community." Unpublished paper given at the conference *Rhythm Changes II: Rethinking Jazz Cultures*, University of Salford, UK.
Haenisch, Matthias. 2013. "Materiality and Agency in Improvisation: Andrea Neumann's 'Inside Piano.'" In *Noise In and As Music*, edited by Aaron Cassidy and Aaron Einbond, 147–70. Huddersfield: University of Huddersfield Press.

Hagberg, Garry L. 2017. "The Ensemble as Plural Subject: Jazz Improvisation, Collective Intention and Group Agency." In *Distributed Creativity: Collaboration and Improvisation in Contemporary Music*, edited by Eric F. Clarke and Mark Doffman, 300–313. New York: Oxford University Press.

Hansen, Arve. 2014. "Cars and Capitalism in Contemporary Hanoi." *Voices from the Sylff Community*. https://www.sylff.org/news_voices/13623/.

Haraway, Donna. 1988. "Situated Knowledges: The Science Question in Feminism and the Privilege of Partial Perspective." *Feminist Studies* 14 (3): 575–99.

Hardjowirogo, Sarah-Indriyati. 2017. "Instrumentality: On the Construction of Musical Identity." In *Musical Instruments in the 21st Century: Identities, Configurations, Practices*, edited by Till Bovermann, Alberto de Campo, Hauke Egermann, Sarah-Indriyati Hardjowirogo, and Stefan Weinzierl, 9–24. Singapore: Springer.

Haseman, Brad. 2006. "A Manifesto for Performative Research." *Media International Australia Incorporating Culture and Policy* 118 (1): 98–106.

Hayden, Sam, and Luke Windsor. 2007. "Collaboration and the Composer: Case Studies from the End of the 20th Century." *Tempo* 61 (240): 28–39.

Henbing, Li, and Marc Leman. 2007. "A Gesture-Based Typology of Sliding-Tones in Guqin Music." *Journal of New Music Research* 36 (2): 61–82.

Herbert, Ruth. 2017. "Sonic Subjectivities." In *The Routledge Companion to Sounding Art*, edited by Marcel Cobussen, Vincent Meelberg, and Barry Truax, 223–34. New York: Routledge.

Hodkinson, Juliana. 2017. "Just Spoke: Composing with Objects, Performing with Subjects." *Seismograf, 31 May*. http://seismograf.org/en/artikel/just-spoke-composing-with-objects-performing-with-subjects.

Hogg, Bennett, and Sally Jane Norman. 2013. "Editorial Introduction: Resistant Materials in Musical Creativity." *Contemporary Music Review* 32 (2–3): 115–18.

Hopkins, Greg. 2012. "MTSU Impulse Response Library." YouTube video, 5:31, posted by "recordinghopkins," 6 December. https://www.youtube.com/watch?v=cQYpZQXiLNo.

Horn, Rebecca. 1998. *The Glance of Infinity*. Edited by Carl Haenlein. Zurich: Scalo Verlag.

Hunter, Mary. 2005. "'To Play as If from the Soul of the Composer': The Idea of the Performer in Early Romantic Aesthetics." *Journal of the American Musicological Society* 58 (2): 357–98.

Hunter, Mary, and Stephen Broad. 2017. "Reflection and the Classical Musician: Practice in Cultural Context." In *Musicians in the Making: Pathways to Creative Performance*, edited by John Rink, Helena Gaunt, and Aaron Williamon, 253–70. New York: Oxford University Press.

Hymer, Jennifer. 2007. "Annea Lockwood: *Ceci n'est pas un piano*." On *Jennifer Hymer (piano, toy piano and kalimba): Ceci n'est pas un piano: works by Godfield, Hajdu, Lemke, Lockwood, Milliken, Stahnke, Tan Dun*. Ambitus Musikproduktion, none96925, compact disc.

Iddon, Martin. 2013. *John Cage and David Tudor: Correspondence on Interpretation and Performance*. Cambridge: Cambridge University Press.

Ingold, Tim., ed. 2011. *Redrawing Anthropology: Materials, Movements, Lines*. New York: Ashgate.

Jackson, Travis A. 2002. "Jazz as Musical Practice." In *The Cambridge Companion to Jazz*, edited by Mervyn Cooke and David Horn, 83–95. Cambridge: Cambridge University Press.

James, William. 1890. *The Principles of Psychology*. 2 vols. New York: Henry Holt & Co.

———. 1892. *Psychology*. New York: Henry Holt & Co.

———. 1909. *A Pluralistic Universe*. London: Longmans, Green, and Co.

———. 1912. *Essays in Radical Empiricism*. New York: Longmans, Green, and Co.

Jensenius, Alexander Refsum, Marcelo Wanderley, Rolf Inge Godøy, and Marc Leman. 2010. "Musical Gestures: Concepts and Methods in Research." In *Musical Gestures: Sound, Movement, and Meaning*, edited by Rolf Inge Godøy and Marc Leman, 12–35. Abingdon, UK: Routledge.

Jessen, Edward. 2015. *Ten Bellows, for Theatrical Pianist, Assistant Performer and Auxiliary Audio*. Greenwich: Decipherer Arts Press.

John-Steiner, Vera. 2000. *Creative Collaboration*. New York: Oxford University Press.

Jordà, Sergi. 2004. "Instruments and Players: Some Thoughts on Digital Lutherie." *Journal of New Music Research* 33 (3): 321–41.

Kagan, Norman, and David Krathwohl. 1967. *Studies in Human Interaction: Interpersonal Process Recall Stimulated by Videotape*. East Lansing: Michigan State University, College of Education, Educational Publication Services.

Kassabian, Anahid. 2013. *Ubiquitous Listening: Affect, Attention, and Distributed Subjectivity*. Berkeley: University of California Press.

Keefe, Douglas H., Edward M. Burns, and Phong Nguyen. 1991. "Vietnamese Modal Scales of the Dan Tranh." *Music Perception: An Interdisciplinary Journal* 8 (4): 449–68.

Kester, Grant H. 2011. *The One and the Many: Contemporary Collaborative Art in a Global Context*. Durham, NC: Duke University Press.

Kivy, Peter. 1995. *Authenticities: Philosophical Reflections on Musical Performance*. Ithaca, NY: Cornell University Press.

Komorowski, Matthew. 2009. "A History of Storage Cost." http://www.mkomo.com/cost-per-gigabyte.

Kramer, Lawrence. 2002. "Signs Taken for Wonders: Words, Music, and Performativity." In *Word and Music Studies: Essays in Honor of Steven Paul Scher and on Cultural Identity and the Musical Stage*, edited by Suzanne M. Lodato, Suzanne Aspden, and Walter Bernhart, 35–47. Amsterdam: Rodopi.

Lachenmann, Helmut. 1996. *Musik als existentielle Erfahrung: Schriften 1966–1995*. Edited by Joseph Häusler. Wiesbaden: Breitkopf & Härtel / Insel.

Lambert, Mel. 1997. "A West Coast Phenomenon—The Studio That Charlie Built." http://www.mediaandmarketing.com/13Writer/Profiles/AM.AandM_Studios.html.

Latour, Bruno. 1999. *Pandora's Hope: Essays on the Reality of Science Studies*. Cambridge, MA: Harvard University Press.

———. 2005. *Reassembling the Social: An Introduction to Actor-Network Theory*. Oxford: Oxford University Press.

———. 2013. *An Inquiry into Modes of Existence: An Anthropology of the Moderns*. Translated by Catherine Porter. Cambridge, MA: Harvard University Press. First published 2012 as *Enquête sur les modes d'existence: Une anthropologie des modernes* (Paris: La Découverte)

Laws, Catherine. 2018. "Moving Bodies, Piano Body." *Performance Research* 23 (4–5): 351–54.

Laws, Catherine, Damien Harron, and William Brooks. 2013. "Disjointed." Vimeo video, 9:37, posted by "Catherine Laws," 16 July. https://vimeo.com/70437876?utm_source=email&utm_medium=clip-transcode_complete-finished-20120100&utm_campaign=7701&email_id=Y2xpcF9ocmFuc2NvZGVkfGZiZTY4ZmIoMmViMzliMGI4YTlhMGEzZGExZDFiNGY5NTc2fDQoNjM5ODF8MTM3NDAwOTY3Mw%3D%3D.

Laws, Catherine, Stefan Östersjö, and William Brooks. 2016. "Subjectivity." Paper given at *Rethinking the Practices of Music*, Orpheus Institute, Ghent, Belgium, 14 November.

Leech-Wilkinson, Daniel. 1984. "'What We Are Doing with Early Music Is Genuinely Authentic to Such a Small Degree That the Word Loses Most of Its Intended Meaning.'" *Early Music* 12 (1): 13–16.

———. 2012. "Compositions, Scores, Performances, Meanings." *Music Theory Online* 18 (1). http://mtosmt.org/issues/mto.12.18.1/mto.12.18.1.leech-wilkinson.php.

———. 2017. "What's Wrong with Classical Music?" *Challenging Performance*. https://challengingperformance.com/dido-belinda/#1511203354013-d73eecc6-d3dc.

Lefford, M. Nyssim, and Paul Thompson. 2018. "Naturalistic Artistic Decision-Making and Metacognition in the Music Studio." *Cognition, Technology and Work* 20 (4): 543–54.

Le Guin, Elisabeth. 2005. *Boccherini's Body: An Essay in Carnal Musicology*. Berkeley: University of California Press.

Lehmann, Andreas C., John A. Sloboda, and Robert H. Woody. 2007. "Expression and Interpretation." In *Psychology for Musicians: Understanding and Acquiring the Skills*, edited by Andreas C. Lehmann, John A. Sloboda and Robert H. Woody, 85–106. New York: Oxford University Press.

Leistra-Jones, Karen. 2013. "Staging Authenticity: Joachim, Brahms, and the Politics of Werktreue Performance." *Journal of the American Musicological Society* 66 (2): 397–436.

Lely, John. 2012. "On the Use of Grammar in Verbal Notation." In *Word Events: Perspectives on Verbal Notation*, edited by John Lely and James Saunders, 3–74. London: Continuum.

Leman, Marc. 2008. *Embodied Music Cognition and Mediation Technology*. Cambridge, MA: MIT Press.

Leman, Marc, and Rolf Inge Godøy. 2010. "Why Study Musical Gestures?" In *Musical Gestures: Sound, Movement, Meaning*, edited by Rolf Inge Godøy and Marc Leman, 3–11. New York: Routledge.

Lê Minh Huệ. 2015. "Đô Thị hóa Nông Thôn Dưới Góc Nhìn Âm Nhạc." *Nông Nghiệp Việt Nam*, April 7. https://nongnghiep.vn/do-thi-hoa-nong-thon-duoi-goc-nhin-am-nhac-post141094.html.

Lepecki, André. 2010. "The Body as Archive: Will to Re-enact and the Afterlives of Dances." *Dance Research Journal* 42 (2): 28–48.

Levinas, Emmanuel. 1969. *Totality and Infinity: An Essay on Exteriority*. Translated by Alphonso Lingis. The Hague: Martinus Nijhoff. First published 1961 as *Totalité et infini: Essai dur l'extériorité* (The Hague: Martinus Nijhoff).

Levinson, Jerrold. 1996. "Musical Expressiveness." In *The Pleasures of Aesthetics: Philosophical Essays*, 90–125. Ithaca, NY: Cornell University Press.

———. 2006. "Musical Chills." In *Contemplating Art: Essays in Aesthetics*, 220–36. Oxford: Oxford University Press.

———. 2009. "The Aesthetic Appreciation of Music." *British Journal of Aesthetics* 49 (4): 415–25.

———. 2011. *Music, Art, and Metaphysics: Essays in Philosophical Aesthetics*. Oxford: Oxford University Press.

Lexico. 2019. Dictionary.com and Oxford University Press website. https://en.oxforddictionaries.com.

Linden, David J. 2016. *Touch: The Science of the Sense That Makes Us Human*. New York: Viking.

Linson, Adam, and Eric F. Clarke. 2017. "Distributed Cognition, Ecological Theory and Group Improvisation." In *Distributed Creativity: Collaboration and Improvisation in Contemporary Music*, edited by Eric F. Clarke and Mark Doffman, 52–69. New York: Oxford University Press.

Lipshitz, Stanley P. 1986. "Stereo Microphone Techniques: Are the Purists Wrong?" *Journal of the Audio Engineering Society* 34 (9): 716–44.

Livingstone, Steven Robert, and William Forde Thompson. 2006. "Multimodal Affective Interaction: A Comment on Musical Origins." *Music Perception* 24 (1): 89–94.

Lixenberg, Loré. 2017. "Song." In *Distributed Creativity: Collaboration and Improvisation in Contemporary Music*, edited by Eric F. Clarke and Mark Doffman, 295–99. New York: Oxford University Press.

Lockwood, Annea. 2002. *Ceci n'est pas un piano*, for piano, video and electronics. http://www.annealockwood.com/compositions/.

———. 2007. *Gone*, for music box piano and helium balloons. http://www.annealockwood.com/compositions/gone/

Longbow, Peter Sheppard-Skærved, director, and Stefan Östersjö, guitar. 2017. *David Gorton: Variations on John Dowland*. Toccata Classics, TOCC0396, compact disc.

Lopez-Real, Carlos. 2017. "Musical Artistry and Identity in Balance." In *Musicians in the Making: Pathways to Creative Performance*, edited by John Rink, Helena Gaunt, and Aaron Williamon, 241–44. New York: Oxford University Press.

Losseff, Nicky. 2011. "Projective Identification, Musical Interpretation and the Self." *Music Performance Research* 4: 49–59.

Lowry, Lois. 1993. *The Giver*. New York: Houghton Mifflin.

Lucas, Robert E. B. 1997. "Internal Migration in Developing Countries." In *Handbook of Population and Family Economics, Volume 1B*, edited by Mark Richard Rosenzweig and Oded Stark, 721–98. Oxford: Gulf Professional Publishing.

Luong, Hy V. 2018. "The Changing Configuration of Rural–Urban Migration and Remittance Flows in Vietnam." *SOJOURN: Journal of Social Issues in Southeast Asia* 33 (3): 602–46.

MacRitchie, Jennifer, Bryony Buck, and Nicholas J. Bailey. 2013. "Inferring Musical Structure through Bodily Gestures." *Musicae Scientiae* 17 (1): 86–108.

Manning, Erin. 2007. *Politics of Touch: Sense, Movement, Sovereignty*. Minneapolis: University of Minnesota Press.

Manning, Jane. 2017. "The Creative Voice in Artistic Performance." In *Musicians in the Making: Pathways to Creative Performance*, edited by John Rink, Helena Gaunt, and Aaron Williamon, 126–30. New York: Oxford University Press.

Marsh, Roger. 2014. *Touch and Go*, for solo piano. Greenwich: Decipherer Arts Press.

———. 2019. Interview with Catherine Laws, 15 March, York.

Masing, Elo. 2014. "Mapping or Choreographing? Redefining Musical Notation." *Opticon 1826* 16: 1–8.

McCaleb, J. Murphy. 2014. *Embodied Knowledge in Ensemble Performance*. Abingdon, UK: Ashgate.

McCollum, Jonathan, and David G. Hebert. 2014. *Theory and Method in Historical Ethnomusicology*. London: Lexington Books.

McMullen, Tracey. 2016. "Improvisation within a Scene of Constraint: An Interview with Judith Butler." 2016. In *Negotiated Moments: Improvisation, Sound, and Subjectivity*, edited by Gillian Siddall and Ellen Waterman, 21–36. Durham, NC: Duke University Press.

Merleau-Ponty, Maurice (1962) 2002. *Phenomenology of Perception*. Translated by Colin Smith. New York: Routledge. First published 1945 as *Phénoménologie de la perception* (Paris: Gallimard). Translation first published 1962 (London: Routledge & Kegan Paul).

———. 1964. "Eye and Mind." Translated by Carleton Dallery. In *The Primacy of Perception and Other Essays on Phenomoenological Psychology, The Philosophy of Art, Philosophy and Politics*, edited by James M. Edie, 159–90. Evanston, IL: Northwestern University Press. Essay first published 1960 as "L'oeuil et l'esprit" (Paris: Gallimard).

Millington, Barry. 1980. "Smooth Sounds from Japan." *London Times*, December 10.

Mills, Janet, and Jan Smith. 2003. "Teachers' Beliefs about Effective Instrumental Teaching in Schools and Higher Education." *British Journal of Music Education* 20 (1): 5–27.

Monteiro, Francisco. 2007. "Virtuosity: Some (Quasi Phenomenological) Thoughts." In *Proceedings of the International Symposium on Performance Science*, edited by Aaron Williamon and Daniela Coimbra, 315–20. Utrecht: Association Européenne de Conservatoires.

Myatt, Tony, Oliver Larkin, and Dave Malham. 2010. "Studio Report: Music Research Centre, Department of Music, University of York." *Proceedings of the 2010 International Computer Music Conference*. https://quod.lib.umich.edu/i/icmc/bbp2372.2010.053/1.

Nancy, Jean-Luc. 1991a. *The Inoperative Community*. Edited by Peter Connor. Translated by Peter Connor, Lisa Garbus, Michael Holland, and Simona Sawhney. Minneapolis: University of Minnesota Press.

———. 1991b. Introduction to *Who Comes After the Subject?*, edited by Eduardo Cadava, Peter Connor, and Jean-Luc Nancy, 1–8. London: Routledge.

———. 2000. *Being Singular Plural*. Translated by Robert D. Richardson and Anne E. O'Byrne. Stanford, CA: Stanford University Press. First published 1996 as *Être singulier pluriel* (Paris: Galilée).

Nettl, Bruno. 1983. *The Study of Ethnomusicology: Twenty-Nine Issues and Concepts*. Urbana: University of Illinois Press.

Neumann, Andrea. 2011. "Playing Inside Piano." SARMA: Laboratory for Discursive Practices and Expanded Publication. http://sarma.be/docs/2915.

Ngô Trà My. 2019. Ngô Trà My interviewed by Nguyễn Thanh Thủy, 6 January.

Nguyễn Thanh Thủy. 2019. Personal communication to Stefan Östersjö, 28 March.

Nguyễn Thanh Thủy and Stefan Östersjö. 2018. "Soundscaping Hanoi: Intercultural Collaboration as Politically Informed Theatre." Video paper presented at "Performance and Culture: Cities, Embodiments, Technologies," SPA 5th

Annual Conference hosted by School of Performing Arts, University of Malta, 9 March.

Nijs, Luc. 2017. "The Merging of Musician and Musical Instrument: Incorporation, Presence, and levels of Embodiment." In *The Routledge Companion to Embodied Musical Interaction*, edited by Micheline Lesaffre, Pieter-Jan Maes, and Marc Leman, 49–57. London: Routledge.

Nijs, Luc, Micheline Lesaffre, and Marc Leman. 2013. "The Musical Instrument as a Natural Extension of the Musician." In *La musique et ses instruments / Music and Its Instruments*, edited by Michèle Castellengo, Hugues Genevois, and Jean-Michel Bardez, 467–84. Sampzon, France: Editions Delatour.

Noland, Carrie. 2009. *Agency and Embodiment: Performing Gestures/Producing Culture*. Cambridge, MA: Harvard University Press.

Norman, Sally Jane. 2013. "Contexts of/as Resistance." *Contemporary Music Review* 32 (2–3): 275–88.

Nyman, Michael. 1999. *Experimental Music: Cage and Beyond*. 2nd ed. Cambridge: Cambridge University Press.

Ockelford, Adam. 2017. "Towards a Developmental Model of Musical Empathy Using Insights from Children Who Are on the Autism Spectrum or Who Have Learning Difficulties." In *Music and Empathy*, edited by Elaine King and Caroline Waddington, 39–88. Abingdon, UK: Routledge.

Olofsson, Kent. 2018. "Composing the Performance: An Exploration of Musical Composition as a Dramaturgical Strategy in Contemporary Intermedial Theatre." PhD thesis, Lund University.

———. 2019a. Kent Olofsson interviewed by Stefan Östersjö, 1 February.

———. 2019b. Personal communication to Stefan Östersjö, 28 March.

Orning, Tanja. 2014. "The Polyphonic Performer: A Study of Performance Practice in Music for Solo Cello by Morton Feldman, Helmut Lachenmann, Klaus K. Hübler and Simon Steen-Andersen." PhD thesis, Norwegian Academy of Music, Oslo.

Östersjö, Stefan, guitar. 1997. *Stefan Östersjö*. dB Productions, dbcd31, compact disc.

———, guitar. 2004. *Playtime*. dB Productions, dbcd87, compact disc.

———. 2008. "Shut Up 'n' Play! Negotiating the Musical Work." PhD Thesis, Malmö Academy of Music, Lund University.

———. 2013. "The Resistance of the Turkish Makam and the Habitus of a Performer: Reflections on a Collaborative CD-Project with Erdem Helvacioğlu." *Contemporary Music Review* 32 (2–3): 201–13.

———. 2017. "Thinking-through-Music: On Knowledge Production, Materiality, Embodiment, and Subjectivity in Artistic Research." In *Artistic Research in Music: Discipline and Resistance*, edited by Jonathan Impett, 88–107. Orpheus Institute Series. Leuven: Leuven University Press.

———. 2018. "Musical and Musicianly Listening in Intercultural Practice." *Circuits: Musiques Contemporaines* 28 (1): 35–44.

Östersjö, Stefan, and Nguyễn Thanh Thủy. 2013. "Traditions in Transformation: the Function of Openness in the Interaction between Musicians." In *(Re)Thinking Improvisation: Artistic Explorations and Conceptual Writing*, edited by Henrik Frisk and Stefan Östersjö, 184–201. Malmö: Malmö Academy of Music.

———. 2016. "The Sounds of Hanoi and the After-Image of the Homeland." *Journal of Sonic Studies* 12. https://www.researchcatalogue.net/view/246523/246546.

———. 2017. "The Politics of Listening in Intercultural Artistic Practice." *Studies in Musical Theatre* 11 (2): 131–45.

Peters, Deniz. 2012. "Touch: Real, Apparent, and Absent—On Bodily Expression in Electronic Music." In *Bodily Expression in Electronic Music: Perspectives on Reclaiming Performativity*, edited by Deniz Peters, Gerhard Eckel, and Andreas Dorschel, 17–34. New York: Routledge.

———. 2015. "Musical Empathy, Emotional Co-Constitution, and the 'Musical Other.'" *Empirical Musicology Review* 10 (1–2): 2–15.

Peterson, Richard A. 1997. *Creating Country Music: Fabricating Authenticity*. Chicago: University of Chicago Press.

Phan, Hai Yen Thi, Takashi Yano, Tetsumi Sato, and Tsuyoshi Nishimura. 2010. "Characteristics of Road Traffic Noise in Hanoi and Ho Chi Minh City, Vietnam." *Applied Acoustics* 71 (5): 479–85.

Phelan, Peggy. 1993. *Unmarked: The Politics of Performance.* Abingdon, UK: Routledge.

———. 2004. "Marina Abramović: Witnessing Shadows." *Theatre Journal* 56 (4): 569–77.

Pienaar, Daniel-Ben. 2015. "Canonical Games: Playing Beethoven's Piano Sonatas." Liner note for *Beethoven: The 32 Piano Sonatas*, performed by Daniel-Ben Pienaar. Avie, AV2320, 10 compact discs.

Pink, Sarah, Shanti Sumartojo, Deborah Lupton, and Christine Heyes LaBond. 2017. "Empathetic Technologies: Digital Materiality and Video Ethnography." *Visual Studies* 32 (4), 371–81.

Polanyi, Michael. 1967. *The Tacit Dimension.* New York: Anchor Books.

Rahaim, Mathew. 2017. "Otherwise Than Participation: Unity and Alterity in Musical Encounters." In *Music and Empathy*, edited by Elaine King and Caroline Waddington, 157–93. Abingdon, UK: Routledge.

Ramirez, José. 1993. *Things about the Guitar.* Madrid: Soneto.

Ramirez Ladrón de Guevara, Victor. 2011. "Any Body? The Multiple Bodies of the Performer." In *Performance Perspectives: A Critical Introduction*, edited by Jonathan Pitches and Sita Popat, 21–32. Basingstoke, UK: Palgrave Macmillan.

Redhead, Lauren, and Richard Glover, eds. 2018. *Collaborative and Distributed Processes in Contemporary Music-Making.* Newcastle upon Tyne: Cambridge Scholars.

Ricœur, Paul. 1991. *From Text to Action.* Translated by Kathleen Blamey and John B. Thompson. Evanston, IL: Northwestern University Press. First published 1986 as *Du texte à l'action* (Paris: Seuil).

Rink, John. 2004. "The State of Play in Performance Studies." In *The Music Practitioner: Research for the Music Performer, Teacher and Listener*, edited by Jane W. Davidson, 37–51. Aldershot, UK: Ashgate.

Rink, John, Helena Gaunt, and Aaron Williamon. 2017. Preface to *Musicians in the Making: Pathways to Creative Performance*, edited by John Rink, Helena Gaunt, and Aaron Williamon, xxi–xxx. New York: Oxford University Press.

Robinson, Enders A. 1982. "A Historical Perspective of Spectrum Estimation." *Proceedings of the IEEE* 70 (9): 885–907.

Rosch, Eleanor, Carolyn B. Mervis, Wayne D. Gray, David M. Johnson, and Penny Kaye Boyes-Braem. 1976. "Basic Objects in Natural Categories." *Cognitive Psychology* 8 (3): 382–439.

Rosen, Charles. (2002) 2004. *Piano Notes: The Hidden World of the Pianist.* London: Penguin. First published 2002 (New York: Free Press).

RubyCell Entertainment. 2017. "Top 10 Facial Expressions of Famous Piano Artists." YouTube video, 1:51, posted by "RubyCell Entertainment," 9 August. https://www.youtube.com/watch?v=7uXsNPK9BDY.

Sammler, Daniela, Giacomo Novembre, Stefan Koelsch, and Peter E. Keller. 2013. "Syntax in a Pianist's Hand: ERP Signatures of 'Embodied' Syntax Processing in Music.' *Cortex* 49: 1325–39.

Sandweiss, Martha A. 2009. *Passing Strange: A Gilded Age Tale of Love and Deception across the Color Line.* New York: Penguin Press.

Saunders, Doug. 2010. *Arrival City: How the Largest Migration in History Is Reshaping Our World.* New York: Vintage.

Sawyer, Keith R. 2008. *Group Genius: The Creative Power of Collaboration.* New York: Basic Books.

Sawyer, Keith R., and Stacy DeZutter. 2009. "Distributed Creativity: How Collective Creations Emerge from Collaboration." *Psychology of Aesthetics, Creativity and the Arts* 3 (2): 81–92.

Schafer, R. Murray. 1977. *The Tuning of the World.* Toronto: McClelland and Stewart; New York: Knopf.

Schechner, Richard. 1985. *Between Theater and Anthropology.* Philadelphia: University of Pennsylvania Press.

Schneider, Arnd, and Caterina Pasqualino. 2014. *Experimental Film and Anthropology.* New York: Bloomsbury Academic.

Schneider, Arnd, and Christopher Wright, eds. 2010. *Between Art and Anthropology: Contemporary Ethnographic Practice.* London: Bloomsbury Academic.

———, eds. 2013. *Anthropology and Art Practice.* New York: Bloomsbury Academic.

Schneider, Rebecca. 2012. "Performance Remains Again." In *Archaeologies of Presence: Art, Performance and the Persistence of Being*, edited by Gabriella Giannachi, Nick Kaye, and Michael Shanks, 64–81. Abingdon, UK: Routledge.

Sennett, Richard. (1977) 2002. *The Fall of Public Man.* London: Penguin Books. First published 1977 (New York: Knopf).

Sergeant, Matthew. 2017. "Queered Orientation(s): Re-imagining the Taxonomy and Interrelation of Musical Materials in *The Velvet Rage.*" Paper presented at the *Eighth International Symposium on Music and Sonic Art: Practices and Theories*, Karlsruhe, Germany. https://static1.squarespace.com/static/56238aa4e4b059c47b4ad818/t/5970b305e6f2e1822b67cb91/1500558141689/sergeant_queered_orientations.pdf.

Sessions, Roger. (1950) 1971. *The Musical Experience of Composer, Performer, Listener.* Princeton, NJ: Princeton University Press.

Shusterman, Richard. 2000. *Performing Live: Aesthetic Alternatives for the Ends of Art.* Ithaca, NY: Cornell University Press.

———. 2002. "Regarding Oneself and Seeing Double: Fragments of Autobiography." In *The Philosophical I: Personal Reflections on Life in Philosophy*, edited by George Yancy, 1–21. Lanham, MD: Rowman and Littlefield.

———. 2008. *Body Consciousness: A Philosophy of Mindfulness and Somaesthetics.* New York: Cambridge University Press.

Siddall, Gillian, and Ellen Waterman, eds. 2016. *Negotiated Moments: Improvisation, Sound, and Subjectivity.* Durham, NC: Duke University Press.

Siegmund, Gerald. 2008. "The Art of Memory: Fiction as Seduction into Reality." In *Experts of the Everyday: The Theatre of Rimini Protokoll*, edited by Miriam Dreysse and Florian Malzacher, translated by Daniel Belasco Rogers, Ehren Fordyce, Geoffrey Garrison, Mat Hand, Sophia New, and Walter Suttcliffe, 188–211. Berlin: Alexander Verlag.

Simoens, Veerle L., and Mari Tervaniemi. 2013. "Musician–Instrument Relationship as a Candidate Index for Professional Well-Being in Musicians." *Psychology of Aesthetics, Creativity, and the Arts* 7 (2): 171–80.

Small, Christopher. 1998. *Musicking: The Meanings of Performing and Listening.* Middletown, CT: Wesleyan University Press.

Smith, Linda Tuhiwai. 2012. *Decolonizing Methodologies: Research and Indigenous Peoples*, 2nd ed. London: Zed Books.

Solomon, Thomas. 2012. "Where Is the Postcolonial in Ethnomusicology?" In *Ethnomusicology in East Africa: Perspectives from Uganda and Beyond*, edited by Sylvia Nannyonga-Tamusuza and Thomas Solomon, 216–51. Kampala: Fountain Publishers.

Spatz, Ben. 2015. *What a Body Can Do: Technique As Knowledge, Practice As Research.* Abingdon, UK: Routledge.

Stapleton, Paul. 2013. "Autobiography and Invention: Towards a Critical Understanding of Identity, Dialogue and Resistance in Improvised Musics." *Contemporary Music Review* 32 (2–3): 165–74.

Steen-Andersen, Simon. 2007. *Study for String Instrument #1.* Copenhagen: Edition S.

Sterne, Jonathan. 2012. *MP3: The Meaning of a Format.* Durham, NC: Duke University Press.

Stolp, Mareli. 2015. "Artistic Research Reports: Subjectivity and Reflexivity in Artistic Research." *Artistic Research Reports* (blog), October 16. http://artisticresearchreports.blogspot.com/2015/10/mareli-stolp-on-reflexivity.html.

———. 2017. "Self-Reflexivity and Subjective Artistic Experience." Unpublished paper given at the Society for Artistic Research Conference, Helsinki. Available at https://www.academia.edu/s/bdd02a792e/self-reflexivity-and-subjective-artistic-experience.

Stover, Chris. 2016. "Musical Bodies: Corporeality, Emergent Subjectivity, and Improvisational Spaces." *M/C Journal* 19 (1). http://journal.media-culture.org.au/index.php/mcjournal/article/viewArticle/1066.

Straus, Erwin W. 1966. *Phenomenological Psychology: The Selected Papers of Erwin W. Straus*. Tavistock, NY: Basic Books.

Sudnow, David. 2001. *Ways of the Hand: A Rewritten Account*. Cambridge, MA: MIT Press.

Swain, Rachel. 2014. "Time and a Mirror: Towards a Hybrid Dramaturgy for Intercultural-Indigenous Performance." In *New Dramaturgy: International Perspectives on Theory and Practice*, edited by Katalin Trencsényi and Bernadette Cochrane, 145–63. London: Bloomsbury.

Szendy, Peter. 2008. *Listen: A History of Our Ears*. Translated by Charlotte Mandell. New York: Fordham University Press. First published 2001 as *Écoute: Une histoire de nos oreilles* (Paris: Minuit).

Tanaka, Atau. 2019. "Embodied Musical Interaction." In *New Directions in Music and Human-Computer Interaction*, edited by Simon Holland, Tom Mudd, Katie Wilkie-McKenna, Andrew McPherson, and Marcelo M. Wanderley, 135–54. Cham, Switzerland: Springer.

Taruskin, Richard. 1996. *Text and Act: Essays on Music and Performance*. New York: Oxford University Press.

Taylor, Alan, ed. 2016. "'Collaboration' in Contemporary Music." Special issue, *Contemporary Music Review* 35 (6).

Taylor, Diana. 2003. *The Archive and the Repertoire: Performing Cultural Memory in the Americas*. Durham, NC: Duke University Press.

———. 2016. *Performance*. Durham, NC: Duke University Press.

Thompson, John B. 1995. *The Media and Modernity: A Social Theory of the Media*. Stanford, CA: Stanford University Press.

Thompson, William Forde, Phil Graham, and Frank A. Russo. 2005. "Seeing Music Performance: Visual Influences on Perception and Experience." *Semiotica* 156 (1): 203–27.

Tilbury, John. 1993. "On Playing Feldman." https://www.cnvill.net/mftilb.htm.

Tomasello, Michael, Malinda Carpenter, Josep Call, Tanya Behne, and Henricke Moll. 2005. "Understanding and Sharing Intentions: The Origins of Cultural Cognition." *Behavioral and Brain Sciences* 28 (5): 675–735.

Tomes, Susan. 2010. *Out of Silence: A Pianist's Yearbook*. Woodbridge, UK: Boydell and Brewer.

Torick, Emil. 1998. "Highlights in the History of Multichannel Sound." *Journal of the Audio Engineering Society* 46 (1–2): 27–31.

Torrence, Jennifer. 2019. "Percussion Theatre: A Body in Between." https://www.researchcatalogue.net/view/533313/534335.

Trevarthen, Colwyn, and Kenneth J. Aitken. 2001. "Infant Intersubjectivity: Research, Theory, and Clinical Applications." *Journal of Child Psychology and Psychiatry, and Allied Disciplines* 42 (1): 3–48.

Turner, Sarah, and Laura Schoenberger. 2012. "Street Vendor Livelihoods and Everyday Politics in Hanoi, Vietnam: The Seeds of a Diverse Economy?" *Urban Studies* 49 (5): 1027–44.

Turner, Victor, and Edith Turner. 1982. "Performing Ethnography." *TDR: The Drama Review:* 26 (2): 33–50.

Uitti, Frances-Marie. 2017. "Beyond Convention: Listening to One's Inner Voice." In *Musicians in the Making: Pathways to Creative Performance*, edited by John Rink, Helena Gaunt, and Aaron Williamon, 344–46. New York: Oxford University Press.

Vandemoortele, Milo, and Kate Bird. 2011. "Viet Nam's Progress on Economic Growth and Poverty Reduction: Impressive Improvements." Overseas Development Institute. https://www.odi.org/publications/5057-vietnam-viet-nam-economic-growth-poverty-development-progress.

Vanhaesebrouck, Karel. 2017. "Theatre of War: Commemorating World War I in Belgium." *TDR: The Drama Review* 61 (4): 40–58.

van Maas, Sander, ed. 2015. *Thresholds of Listening: Sound, Technics, Space*. New York: Fordham University Press.

Varela, Francisco J., Evan Thompson, and Eleanor Rosch. 1991. *The Embodied Mind: Cognitive Science and Human Experience*. Cambridge, MA: MIT Press.

Voegelin, Salomé. 2010. *Listening to Noise and Silence: Towards a Philosophy of Sound Art*. New York: Continuum.

Vygotsky, Lev S. 1978. *Mind in Society: Interaction between Learning and Society: The Development of Higher Psychological Processes*. Edited by Michael Cole, Vera John-Steiner, Sylvia Scribner, and Ellen Souberman. Cambridge, MA: Harvard University Press.

Walshe, Jennifer. 2016. "The New Discipline." http://www.borealisfestival.no/2016/the-new-discipline-4/.
Watson, Cate. 2009. "The 'Impossible Vanity': Uses and Abuses of Empathy in Qualitative Inquiry." *Qualitative Research* 9 (1): 105–117.
Weeks, Jeffery. 1990. "The Value of Difference." In *Identity: Community, Culture, Difference*, edited by Jonathan Rutherford, 88–100. London: Lawrence & Wishart.
Whitty, Paul. 2012. "Auditory Archaeology: Object, Text and Place as Sonic Time Capsule." https://soundcloud.com/pittriversound-1/d-paul-whitty.
Williams, Kathryn. 2017. "Performance PhD Research Proposal: Restriction as a Means to Go On." University of Huddersfield. http://www.kathryngwilliams.com/uploads/9/9/7/5/997508/kathrynwilliamsfinalproposal.pdf.
Windsor, W. Luke, and Christophe de Bézenac. 2012. "Music and Affordances." *Musicae Scientiae* 16 (1): 102–20.
Wishart, Trevor. 1985. *On Sonic Art*. York: Imagineering Press.
Wöllner, Clemens. 2013. "How to Quantify Individuality in Music Performance? Studying Artistic Expression with Averaging Procedures." *Frontiers in Psychology* 4: article 361. https://www.frontiersin.org/articles/10.3389/fpsyg.2013.00361/full.
Wong, Mandy-Suzanne, and Nina Sun Eidsheim. 2016. "*Corregidora*: Corporeal Archaeology, Embodied Memory, Improvisation." In *Negotiated Moments: Improvisation, Sound, and Subjectivity*, edited by Gillian Siddall and Ellen Waterman, 217–32. Durham, NC: Duke University Press.
Zahavi, Dan. 2006. *Subjectivity and Selfhood: Investigating the First-Person Perspective*. Cambridge, MA: MIT Press.
Zarrilli, Phillip B. 2009. *Psychophysical Acting: An Intercultural Approach after Stanislavski*. Abingdon, UK: Routledge.
Zemp, Hugo. 1988. "Filming Music and Looking At Music Films." *Ethnomusicology* 32 (3): 393–427.

William Brooks is Professor of Music at the University of York, Emeritus Professor at the University of Illinois, and a Research Fellow at the Orpheus Institute. A composer as well as a scholar, his previous writings range from studies of American experimentalists to popular music before 1920; his most recent compositional project has been a series of works based on the theories of declamation put forth by William Butler Yeats, to be published online with a set of essays in 2020.

David Gorton is a composer based in London. A winner of the Royal Philharmonic Society Composition Prize, his large-scale works include *The Fall of Babel* for the BBC Symphony Orchestra, *Oblique Prayers* for Claire Booth and the London Sinfonietta, and *Schmetterlingsspiel* for Christopher Redgate and Ensemble Exposé. Since 2010 three portrait albums have been released of his music on the Métier and Toccata Classics labels. The most recent, *Variations on John Dowland*, was featured on BBC Radio 3's Record Review, and contains two substantial pieces based on original material by Dowland: *Lachrymae Variations* for Longbow and violinist Peter Sheppard Skærved, and *Forlorn Hope* for guitarist Stefan Östersjö. David Gorton was a student at Durham University, King's College London, and the Royal Academy of Music, studying composition with Harrison Birtwistle and Simon Bainbridge. He has taught at the Royal Academy of Music since 2006, where he is Associate Professor of the University of London. His music is published by Verlag Neue Musik, Berlin.

Catherine Laws is Reader in Music at the University of York, UK, and a Senior Artistic Research Fellow at the Orpheus Institute, Ghent. As a pianist Catherine specialises in contemporary music, working collaboratively with composers and often drawing other artists, especially theatre- and film-makers, into her projects. Her artistic research is focused variously on processes of embodiment, subjectivity, and collaboration in contemporary performance practices. She currently leads the research cluster "Performance, Subjectivity, and Experimentation" at the Orpheus Institute, in collaboration with the University of York, and her solo multimedia performance piece, *Player Piano*, is one outcome of that work. Recent recording projects include music by Annea Lockwood, Morton Feldman, and Martin Iddon, plus a series of "piano films": filmic versions of theatrical pieces for piano developed in collaboration with a number of composers, including Damien Harron, Juliana Hodkinson, Edward Jessen, Roger Marsh, and Paul Whitty. Catherine's research in the field of word-and-music studies examines the relationship between music, language, and meaning, focusing especially on Samuel Beckett and composers' responses to his work. Her book *Headaches Among the Overtones: Music in Beckett/ Beckett in Music* came out in 2013.

Nguyễn Thanh Thủy is a leading đàn tranh player / improviser in both traditional and experimental music. She was born into a theatre family and was raised with traditional Vietnamese music from an early age in Hà Nội. She later studied at the Hanoi Conservatory of Music and at the Institute of Cultural Studies. Since 2000 she has held a teaching position at the Vietnam National Academy of Music. She has toured in Asia, Europe, and the United States, received many distinctions, recorded several CDs, and has collaborated extensively with choreographers, composers, and theatre directors on many interdisciplinary projects. Between 2009 and 2011, she was involved as an artistic researcher in the international research project "(Re)Thinking Improvisation," a collaboration between the Vietnam National Academy of Music and the Malmö Academy of Music. Since 2012 she has been carrying out an artistic doctoral project at the Malmö Academy of Music concerned with gesture in traditional Vietnamese music.

Stefan Östersjö is a leading classical guitarist specialising in the performance of contemporary music. Since his debut CD (Swedish Grammy, 1997) he has released twenty CDs and toured Europe, the USA, and Asia. He has collaborated extensively with composers and in the creation of works involving choreography, film, video, performance art, and music theatre. Since 2006 he has been developing inter-cultural artistic practices with the Vietnamese–Swedish group the Six Tones as a platform. As a soloist he has worked with conductors such as Lothar Zagrosek, Peter Eötvös, Pierre-André Valade, Mario Venzago, and Andrew Manze.

Jez Wells is a graduate of the Tonmeister course in music and sound recording. Subsequently he worked for Digital Audio Research and Fairlight before continuing his studies at the University of York, graduating with an MSc in music technology in 2001 and a PhD in "Spectral Analysis and Resynthesis for Creative Sound Transformation." He now teaches in the Department of Music at York, having previously been based in the Department of Electronics. His research is focused on music signal processing and analysis, as well as studio techniques and sound capture. In 2011 he held a public engagement fellowship with the Royal Academy of Engineering, investigating the nature of modern sound recording practice and its relationship to the discipline of engineering. He is active as a sound recordist and editor and has worked for a variety of labels including Touch Music, Naxos, NMC, Sabres of Paradise, Cadenza, Herald AV, and Emissions Audio Output.

Index

A

Abbate, Carolyn, 36n7, 299
Abramović, Marina, 256
actor-network theory, 143
Adami, Rebecca, 284, 299
Adorno, Theodor W., 143–44, 192, 299
affordance, 18, 25, 40, 42, 44, 49, 51, 109n35, 138, 154, 183, 196, 220, 242, 243
Agamben, Giorgio, 17, 87–89, 100, 247n11, 299
Agawu, Kofi, 253, 299
agency, 14, 16–25, 38n11, 40, 42, 43, 45, 46, 76, 83–84, 86, 89–90, 93–95, 99–106, 108n30, 121, 132, 134–36, 138–39, 142–44, 146, 148, 150–54, 156–58, 166, 175, 182, 188–89, 209, 212, 214–15, 219–20, 225, 227, 229–31, 250, 254, 269, 295–97
Ahmed, Sara, 254, 299
Aitken, Kenneth J., 250, 313
Ajemian, Maro, 173
Alperson, Philip, 40, 41, 108, 109, 129, 299
Altenmüller, Eckart, 110n36, 304
analogue technology, 37n8, 176, 178, 180, 183–86, 209, 221, 223, 225
Appiah, Kwame Anthony, 14, 24, 299
Archer, Mary, 83n2
archiving, 116, 134, 150, 151, 154, 155, 158, 185, 211–12, 215, 220, 228–29, 257, 292
Aristotle, 138
Asimov, Isaac, 189n25
assemblage, 14n4, 44, 75–77, 212, 220
Assis, Paulo de, 45n17, 190n26, 299
Auslander, Philip, 15, 93n14, 94, 98, 99, 155n73, 299
authenticity, 13, 16, 47, 88, 91–92, 97–99, 101, 115n40, 144, 171, 173, 176–77, 180, 182, 185, 192–97, 199n32, 200, 202, 204, 210–11, 218, 219, 222, 224–25, 251, 281–82
authority, 16, 20, 47, 86, 101, 105, 121, 132, 148, 155, 163, 164, 193, 214–16, 218, 219

B

Bach, Johann Sebastian, 185
Bailey, Nicholas J., 78, 299, 309
Baily, John, 254
Baker, Chet, 41
Bakhtin, Mikhail, 18n11, 299
bandwidth, 184, 186
Barad, Karen, 144, 151n69, 299
Barker, Hugh, 193–95, 299
Barrett, Estelle, 85, 299
Barsalou, Lawrence W., 40, 299
Barthes, Roland, 78, 299
Bastien, David T., 212, 299–300
Bataille, Georges, 87n5
Baxandall, Michael, 46, 300
Becker, Judith, 251n12, 293, 300
Beckett, Samuel, 165, 300
Beethoven, Ludwig van, 47–48, 78n34, 97, 165, 228
Behne, Tanya, 250, 313
Behrman, David, 173
being-with-others, 252
Bell, Adam, 225n43, 300
Bell, Elizabeth, 15, 300
Bellow, Saul, 164, 300
Benaquisto, Lucia, 213n38, 300
Bennett, Jane, 14n4, 22, 143–44, 174, 300
Berliner, Paul, 91, 300
Berliner Ensemble, 156
Berman, Boris, 91, 300
Beuys, Joseph, 140
Biggelaar, Johann den, 108
Bird, Kate, 237–38, 313
Black Hair, 127, 166n78
Blau, Herbert, 155, 300
Bloom, Benjamin S., 62, 212, 300
blues, 160, 176, 200
Blumlein, Alan, 205–6
body, 15, 17, 18, 22, 24, 36n7, 37–38, 40–42, 56, 67, 69, 72, 79, 83–85, 88–89, 95n18, 96, 98, 99n22, 100–115, 117–18, 120–21, 123–25, 127–29, 131–38, 143, 144, 151n69, 153–58, 165, 191, 228, 230n51, 244, 246, 250, 256–57, 259, 277, 283, 284, 291–93, 296, 297
body image, 38, 56, 76, 79, 113, 125, 132, 134–37, 251n12
body schema, 24, 38, 56, 76, 79, 107, 109n35, 110, 113–14, 125, 134–36, 137, 251n12
Bolt, Barbara, 37, 133, 300
Bonds, Mark Evan, 96n20, 300
Bongers, Bert, 108
Borgdorff, Henk, 17, 300
Borges, Jorge Luis, 208n36
Born, Georgina, 117, 183, 186, 300
Boulez, Pierre, 37
Bourdieu, Pierre, 43, 138
Boyes-Braem, Penny Kaye, 40, 311
Brahms, Johannes, 47, 192–93
Braidotti, Rosi, 144, 300
Braque, Georges, 240, 288
Braxton, Anthony, 174
Brayshaw, Teresa, 83, 86, 116, 133, 158
Bream, Julian, 98
Brecht, Bertolt, 156
Broad, Stephen, 93n13, 97, 100, 101n24, 306
Brooks, William, 21, 22, 54n25, 104n26, 171–232, 300–301, 307
Brown, John Seely, 40, 301
Brubaker, Bruce, 96, 132, 301
Buck, Bryony, 78, 309
Bullock, Jamie, 108n34, 303
Burns, Edward M., 271n29, 307
Busoni, Ferruccio, 82
Butler, Judith, 22, 23, 87–88n5, 99–101, 136, 139, 155, 157, 301
Butt, John, 46, 77, 143n62, 174n8, 230, 301
Butterfield, Hannah, 117, 163
Byrd, William, 53

C

Cage, John, 128–29n48, 173, 174, 175, 188, 195, 221, 301
Call, Josep, 250, 313
Cannon, Alexander M., 182n24, 252n15, 301
Cardew, Cornelius, 110
Carpenter, Malinda, 250, 313
Carson, Fiddlin' John, 194
Cassidy, Aaron, 104, 105, 301
Cavarero, Adriana, 284, 301
Charness, Neil, 42n14, 303
Chion, Michel, 249, 301
choreography, 93, 99, 104–5, 123, 124, 133, 245, 247, 257–58, 262, 269, 274, 275, 277, 279–83, 291–92

Clarke, Eric F., 14n6, 18n12, 31n3, 36, 44, 51, 77, 86n3, 96n19, 107n29, 250, 301, 308
Cobussen, Marcel, 249, 252, 284–86, 293, 301
co-creativity, 93, 97
Coessens, Kathleen, 43, 138, 178n16, 246, 254, 301
Cole, Jonathan, 24n17, 38, 113, 125, 304
collaboration, 14n4, 18–19, 21–23, 31, 36–37, 44, 48, 51, 54–55, 77–78, 83, 85–86, 91, 95, 96, 127, 133, 136, 141, 159, 174, 180, 184, 186, 212–13, 217, 219–20, 222, 228–30, 237, 239–42, 245–47, 249, 252n14, 254, 257, 262, 263, 265, 267, 268, 272–74, 277–81, 283, 287–90, 292–93, 295
Collins, Allan, 40, 301
composition, 16, 18–19, 21–22, 31, 33–34, 36–39, 45–46, 50–55, 76–79, 94, 96–97, 103, 104n26, 106, 115n40, 124, 127, 150, 158, 174, 182, 189, 192, 197, 212, 215, 220, 221, 223, 228, 242, 245, 246, 262–63, 267, 268, 272, 274, 288, 295
Cone, Edward T., 36n7, 43, 301
convolution, 183, 231
Cook, Nicholas, 15, 44, 75, 77, 93–94, 301–2
Cooley, J. W., 231
Cooper, Imogen, 91n8
Coorevits, Esther, 56, 61n27, 67, 68n32, 72n33, 213, 302
Cortés, Miguel, 235, 269, 274, 277, 280
Cotten, Elizabeth, 173, 174, 197, 199n32
Cross, Ian, 251, 302
cultural memory, 162, 255
Cumming, Naomi, 15, 39, 43–44, 48, 75, 90, 100, 302

D

Dahlqvist, Jörgen, 235, 237, 242, 245, 246, 247, 254, 258–61, 269, 275–83, 288–89, 302
Dalla Belle, Simone, 110n36, 302
Davidson, Jane, 110n36, 302
Dawe, Kevin, 41, 302
de Bézenac, Christophe, 42, 314
Deleuze, Gilles, 14n4, 45n17, 302
Demey, Michiel, 39, 302
Dennis, Amanda, 90, 302
DeNora, Tia, 13, 15n7, 95, 102, 149, 151, 152n70, 250, 301, 302
Denzin, Norman K., 253, 254, 291, 302
De Preester, Helena, 38, 104, 106, 107, 109, 111, 113–14, 115n41, 120, 124, 125, 134, 136n53, 302
D'Errico, Lucia, 45n17, 160, 302
Derrida, Jacques, 248, 284, 302
Desmet, Frank, 39, 302
De Souza, Jonathan, 42, 51, 302
Dewey, John, 13n2, 226, 302
DeZutter, Stacy, 18, 91n9, 311
Di Donato, Balandino, 108n34, 303
digital technology, 13, 35, 41, 176–77, 183–84, 186, 189, 196n29, 225, 226, 231, 254, 255
distributed creativity, 18, 91n9
distributed subjectivity, 20, 91
documentary, 23, 182, 237–38, 247, 255, 257, 260, 275, 279, 281, 283, 290–91
Doffman, Mark, 18n12, 31n3, 36, 44, 51, 77, 86n3, 107n29, 301
Doğantan-Dack, Mine, 16, 92, 95–96, 107, 287, 303
Dolby, Ray, 184, 303
Dominguez, Alejandro, 231n55, 303
Dowland, John, 53
Dreysse, Miriam, 255, 290, 303
Driver, Tom, 165, 303
Duguid, Paul, 40, 301
Duras, Marguerite, 246
Dylan, Bob, 199n32

E

Eco, Umberto, 194, 195, 226, 303
ecology, 21, 40, 42, 84, 101, 108n30, 145, 146, 157, 158, 248, 249
Edgerton, Michael Edward, 173–74, 176n9, 303
Eidse, Noelani, 237, 238, 259, 303
Eidsheim, Nina Sun, 127, 314
Electric Phoenix, 172
embodied cognition, 37n9, 92, 105, 111
embodiment, 14, 16–23, 37–38, 41, 42n13, 46, 48, 56, 76, 79, 84–85, 88–89, 92, 93, 95–96, 98, 100–103, 105–8, 111–13, 115, 117, 118, 121, 123, 124, 127–28, 130, 134–36, 138, 139, 143, 149, 153–58, 193, 228–29, 244–45, 248–50, 257, 268, 278, 280, 283–86, 291–93, 296–97
empathy, 23, 111, 112n38, 114, 128, 247, 250–52, 254–55, 261, 262, 273, 274, 275, 278, 279, 280, 287, 289, 290, 291, 293, 297
Ensemble Ars Nova, 241, 242
Ensemble Reconsil, 239
ephemerality of performance, 16, 88, 139, 155
Ericsson, K. Anders, 42n14, 303
ethics, 87, 100, 101, 247–49, 251–54, 256, 284–86, 296, 297
ethnography, 17, 41, 85, 101n24, 253–55, 284, 286, 290
Evens, Aden, 41, 129, 303
experimental music, 23, 98, 104n25, 242, 245
experimentation, 15, 17, 19, 34, 40, 45n17, 51, 54n25, 79, 90, 91, 110, 127, 146, 154, 180, 188, 189, 190n26, 197, 218, 220, 221, 222n41, 223, 237, 240, 242, 245, 246, 270, 273, 286, 287, 295

F

facial expression, 30, 98, 99n22, 246
Fagenblat, Michael, 90, 303
Fahlin, Marie, 247, 292n39
Farnaby, Giles, 53
Feinberg, Samuil, 48
Feldman, Morton, 110
Fernandez, Agustín, 267n23
Ferneyhough, Brian, 50, 174, 303
fiction, 13, 22, 23, 171, 182, 183, 189n25, 190, 207–8, 210–11, 278, 281, 283
fidelity, 50, 184, 190
film, 23, 31, 67, 83, 86, 94, 95, 99n22, 104n26, 113, 115, 118–21, 126n44, 133, 140n58, 143, 144, 151, 155, 159n75, 160n76, 166, 183, 221, 227, 237, 245, 247, 254, 257–61, 290, 293
Finnissy, Michael, 53
Fischer, Annie, 48
Fischer-Lichte, Erika, 22, 88, 104, 136, 156–57, 291, 303
Fitch, Fabrice, 18n12, 51, 303
Fluxus, 140
folk music, 174, 177n13, 189, 194, 195, 199n32, 220, 244
Forsyth, Alison, 238, 303
Foucault, Michel, 89n6, 90, 257, 304
Foulkes, Olwen, 53n24

Fourier, Jean-Baptiste Joseph, 231
Fraser, J. T., 79, 304
Freisitzer, Roland, 239
Freud, Sigmund, 87n5
Frisk, Henrik, 212, 304
Frith, Simon, 92n11, 99n23, 100, 304
Fuchs, Thomas, 257, 304
Furuya, Shinichi, 110n36, 304

G
Gadamer, Hans-Georg, 249, 304
Gallagher, Shaun, 24–25, 38, 113, 125, 304
Gans, David, 220, 304
Gardner, Howard, 18, 304
Garfinkel, Harold, 13n3, 304
Gaunt, Helena, 91n8, 93, 304, 311
gender, 15, 18, 19, 24, 99–100, 248, 292n39
gesture, 30, 36, 38n11, 48, 54, 56, 67–79, 93, 96, 98–99, 104–5, 109, 116, 123, 125, 126, 128, 132–36, 139, 156, 157, 164, 166, 213, 257–58, 262, 269, 272, 275, 291, 292n39, 296
Gibson, James, 40, 42, 304
Giddens, Anthony, 13, 304
Giels, Emil, 48
Gilroy, Paul, 14, 304
Glissant, Édouard, 252, 304
Glover, Richard, 18n12, 311
Godlovitch, Stan, 98, 304
Godin, Robert, 177n13
Godøy, Rolf Inge, 39, 67, 72, 98n21, 105, 109n35, 304, 308
Goebl, Werner, 110n36, 305
Goehr, Lydia, 44, 46, 190, 305
Goffman, Erving, 253
Gorton, David, 21–22, 29–79, 86, 90, 93, 107n29, 115n52, 133, 158, 174, 213, 214, 228, 249, 250, 251n12, 254, 291, 301, 302, 305
Goss, Steve, 230n49
Gottschalk, Jennie, 104n25, 150, 305
Graham, Phil, 39, 313
Graver, David, 94
Gray, Michael B., 206, 305
Gray, Wayne D., 40, 311
Greenhalgh, Trisha, 37n8, 305
Grieg, Edvard, 53
Gritten, Anthony, 287, 305
Grosz, Elizabeth, 137, 305
Groth, Sanne Krogh, 254, 305
grounded theory, 213
Grubbs, David, 204, 305
Guzman, Isaac, 98

H
Haanstad, Eric, 253, 255, 305
Habermas, Jürgen, 13n1, 89n6, 305
habitus, 42, 43, 48, 56, 76, 77, 138, 228, 246, 250, 251n12, 254, 287, 292, 293
Haddon, Elizabeth, 91, 305
Haenisch, Matthias, 153, 154, 305
Hagberg, Garry L., 159n74, 306
Hansen, Arve, 266n22, 306
Haraway, Donna, 18, 106, 118, 306
Hardjowirogo, Sarah-Indriyati, 40–41, 109n35, 306
Harrison, Bryn, 77, 301
Harron, Damien, 104n26, 307
Haseman, Brad, 37, 306
Hauser, Hermann, 222
Hayden, Sam, 18n12, 306
Heap, Imogen, 108
Heidegger, Martin, 87n5
Hein, Ethan, 225n43, 300
Henbing, Li, 39, 306
Herbert, David G., 253, 309
Herbert, Ruth, 15n7, 306
Heyde, Neil, 18n12, 51, 303, 305
Hodkinson, Juliana, 16, 306
Hoffmann, E. T. A., 44
Hogg, Bennett, 25, 306
Hooker, John Lee, 174
Hopkins, Greg, 221, 306
Horn, Rebecca, 140, 144, 306
Horowitz, Vladimir, 48
hospitality, 248–50, 252–53, 284, 293
Hostager, Todd J., 212, 299–300
human rights, 284
Hunter, Mary, 15n8, 43, 93n13, 96–97, 100, 101n24, 158, 166, 306
Husserl, Edmund, 87n5
Hymer, Jennifer, 85, 112, 114, 138, 306

I
Iddon, Martin, 128n48, 306
identity, 13–17, 19–24, 33, 36, 40, 53, 78–79, 88, 90, 91, 94–95, 99–101, 103, 106, 114n39, 115n40, 117, 123, 138, 143, 148, 150–51, 154, 155, 158, 171, 175, 177, 182, 189n25, 193, 196, 202, 207–8, 228, 239, 257, 284, 288, 295–97
Im, Minyung, 133
improvisation, 18–19, 35, 48, 54, 84, 93, 95, 100, 101, 117, 151, 153, 182n24, 212, 237, 245, 249, 252, 263, 289n38, 295
incorporation, 107–8, 109n35, 110, 111, 151
indeterminacy, 85, 150, 154
Ingold, Tim, 254, 306
instrumentality, 41, 45n17, 108, 109, 129, 139, 178n16
instrumental teaching, 38, 42, 47, 85, 91, 96, 113, 120, 128, 138
intentionality, 14, 24–25, 46, 77, 125, 143n62, 175n8, 196, 204, 215, 230, 250, 251, 286, 295
interaction, 13–14, 18, 20–22, 25, 38, 40–42, 44, 46, 47, 49–51, 55, 56, 77, 83–84, 86, 87, 89, 93–95, 101, 103, 106, 107, 108n30, 109, 128, 129, 132, 136, 139, 143–46, 150–54, 157, 159, 166–67, 171, 212–14, 217, 220, 228, 230, 231n54, 237, 239, 245, 247, 250–52, 255, 262–63, 269, 270, 272, 274, 277, 279, 280, 284, 285, 287–88, 295, 296
intersubjectivity, 18n11, 21, 22, 25, 159, 213, 250, 251, 293
Ives, Charles, 208, 209

J
Jackson, Travis A., 91, 306
James, William, 14n5, 175n7, 225, 226, 306
Jarrett, Keith, 156
jazz, 91, 93, 98, 110n37, 118n42, 156, 180, 182, 221, 228
Jensenius, Alexander Refsum, 67, 98n21, 306
Jessen, Edward, 85, 117, 159–63, 165–66, 307
Jewishness, 193

Joachim, Joseph, 193
Johansson, Johannes, 241
Johnson, David M., 40, 311
John-Steiner, Vera, 91n9, 230n46, 239–40, 242, 289, 307
Jordà, Sergi, 41, 307

K

Kagan, Norman, 212, 307
Karpen, Richard, 245–46, 247
Kassabian, Anahid, 14n6, 91, 158, 307
Keefe, Douglas H., 271n29, 307
Keller, Peter E., 127, 311
Kempff, Wilhelm, 48
Kester, Grant H., 254, 307
Kirkup, Wendy, 83, 86, 118, 119
Kivy, Peter, 46, 176n11, 192, 195, 202, 307
Klein, Steve, 220
Koelsch, Stefan, 127, 311
Komorowski, Matthew, 183, 307
Kramer, Lawrence, 15n8, 88, 115, 307
Krampe, Ralf Th., 42n14, 303
Krathwohl, David, 212, 307

L

LaBond, Christine Heyes, 254–55, 311
Lachenmann, Helmut, 51, 307
Lambert, Mel, 221, 307
language, 14, 38n11, 45n18, 48, 71, 86–89, 114, 115n40, 120, 127n47, 129, 159, 160, 163, 240, 246, 254, 256, 277, 284
Laplace, Pierre-Simon, 231
Larkin, Oliver, 204, 309
Latour, Bruno, 25, 37n8, 143, 153, 307
Laurence, Felicity, 251, 302
Laws, Catherine, 13–25, 83–167, 175, 209, 295–97, 228, 230n51, 247, 252n14, 257, 292n39, 307
Lead Belly (Huddie Ledbetter), 194–95, 197
Leathwood, Jonathan, 230n49
Leech-Wilkinson, Daniel, 47, 185, 307
Lefford, M. Nyssim, 229nn, 230n50, 231n52, 307
Le Guin, Elisabeth, 19n13, 307
Lehman, Andreas C., 90, 308
Leistra-Jones, Karen, 192, 193, 308
Lely, John, 146, 308
Leman, Marc, 39, 40, 67, 98n21, 105, 107–8, 109n35, 302, 305, 306, 308, 310
Lê Minh Huệ, 237, 308
Lepecki, André, 257, 280, 308
Lesaffre, Micheline, 39, 107–8, 302, 310
Levinas, Emmanuel, 87n4, 247–48, 256, 285, 308
Levinson, Jerrold, 15, 308
Linden, David J., 110, 111, 308
Linson, Adam, 96n19, 308
Lipshitz, Stanley P., 206, 308
listening, 20, 39, 45, 73, 91, 92, 93, 95–96, 103, 105, 110, 112, 116, 123, 128, 152n70, 165, 174, 180, 217, 218, 229, 246, 247–50, 251n12, 252–54, 263–65, 270, 284, 286, 292, 293, 297
Liszt, Franz, 98, 192
Livingstone, Steven Robert, 39, 40, 308
Lixenberg, Loré, 127, 308
Lockwood, Annea, 85, 107n28, 112, 114n39, 120, 122, 123, 124, 140–41, 145, 308
Lomax, John, 194–95
Longbow, 31n2, 53n24, 308
Lopez-Real, Carlos, 91, 308
Losseff, Nicky, 90n7, 308
Lowry, Lois, 235n1, 308
Lucas, Robert E. B., 238, 309
Luong, Hy V., 238, 309
Lupton, Deborah, 254–55, 311
Lưu Ngọc Nam, 235, 236, 237, 258–59, 269, 271, 275, 280, 283, 288–94

M

Maciunas, George, 140
MacRitchie, Jennifer, 78, 309
Malham, Dave, 204, 309
Malzacher, Florian, 255, 290, 303
Manning, Erin, 111, 128, 309
Manning, Jane, 91, 309
Marron, James, 173
Marsh, Roger, 85, 99, 102, 111, 116, 126–32, 135, 309
Martens, Jean-Pierre, 39, 302
Marx, Karl, 87n5
Masing, Elo, 105, 309
materiality, 37, 38, 78, 117, 143, 144, 146, 150, 151n69, 153, 186, 254, 295
Mauss, Marcel, 138
McCaleb, J. Murphy, 41, 145n64, 231n54, 309
McCollum, Jonathan, 253, 309
McMullen, Tracey, 100, 309
mediation, 16, 21, 22, 114–15, 121, 132, 256, 295, 297
Megson, Chris, 238, 303
Melrose, Susan, 155
memory, 23, 43, 85, 95, 104, 115n40, 117, 127, 129, 148–51, 154, 155, 162, 165, 171, 173–74, 177, 184, 187, 189, 195, 209, 210, 218, 226–27, 235, 237–38, 255–58, 265, 274–75, 277–83, 288, 290–93, 297
Merleau-Ponty, Maurice, 37, 43, 109, 124, 309
Mervis, Carolyn B., 40, 311
microphones, 56, 57, 152, 160, 163, 183–84, 204–7, 221, 222, 224, 229, 231, 235, 238
migration, 23, 237–38, 253, 258–61, 275, 279, 282, 286, 291
Millington, Barry, 173, 309
Mills, Janet, 91, 309
Mitchell, Joni, 220, 221
Mitchell, W. J. T., 143
Moelants, Dirk, 56, 61n27, 67, 68n32, 72n33, 213, 302
Moll, Henricke, 250, 313
Monteiro, Francisco, 41, 309
Montgomery, Wes, 180, 221
Moreno Torroba, Federico, 178
Morley, Thomas, 53
Mozart, Wolfgang Amadeus, 93
Müller, Heiner, 156
Myatt, Tony, 204, 309

N

Nabokov, Vladimir, 208n36
Nancy, Jean-Luc, 87n5, 90, 159, 252, 309
National Tuồng Theatre, 258, 282
Nettl, Bruno, 50, 309
Neumann, Andrea, 153, 309
Ngô Trà My, 235–36, 237, 240, 244–45, 261, 265, 269, 272–73, 276–80, 282–83, 286–90, 292, 294, 309

Nguyễn Đức Mạnh, 178n16
Nguyen, Phong, 271n29, 307
Nguyễn Thanh Thủy, 21, 22–23, 235–94, 302, 309–10
Nguyễn Thanh Xuân, 258, 291
Nguyễn Thiện Đạo, 265
Nielsen, Nanette, 249, 252, 284–86, 293, 301
Nietzsche, Friedrich, 87n5
Nijs, Luc, 39, 107–8, 109, 302, 310
Nishimura, Tsuyoshi, 266, 311
Noland, Carrie, 136, 310
non-human, 20, 22, 46, 83, 84, 88, 106, 143n62, 144, 152, 154, 175n8, 182, 220, 230, 250
Nørgård, Per, 48n19, 196
Norman, Sally Jane, 24, 25, 141, 154, 306, 310
Norrman, Maria, 274n33
notation, 34, 36, 38, 44–46, 49–50, 54, 57, 74, 78, 93, 94, 104, 105, 126, 128, 134, 173, 179, 182, 187, 188, 200, 214, 215, 241–42, 245, 296
Novembre, Giacomo, 127, 311
Nyman, Michael, 146n65, 310

O

Ockelford, Adam, 250, 251n12, 310
O'Hora, Ronan, 91n8
Oliveros, Pauline, 222
Olofsson, Kent, 12, 177, 235, 237, 241–45, 254, 258, 262–63, 265–75, 277n34, 279–80, 286–89, 292, 293, 302, 310
Orning, Tanya, 19n13, 107n29, 310
Östersjö, Stefan, 18n12, 21–23, 29–79, 86, 90, 93, 107n29, 108n30, 115n41, 129, 132, 133, 138, 158, 171–232, 235–94, 301, 302, 304, 305, 307, 308, 309, 310
Oswin, Natalie, 237, 238, 259, 303
Other, 15, 18, 21, 136, 143, 158, 167, 247–57, 263, 284, 285, 293, 296–97

P

Paik, Nam June, 140
Palmer, Caroline, 110n36, 302
Parnet, Claire, 14n4, 302
Parra Cancino, Juan, 31n2
Pasqualino, Caterina, 254, 311
passing, 189n25
pastiche, 180, 196, 200
Pastorius, Jaco, 220, 221
Pavarotti, Luciano, 98
performativity, 16, 22, 23, 34, 36–40, 44, 56, 76–79, 89, 95, 99–101, 115n40, 123, 138, 141, 153–54, 167, 188, 220, 238, 247, 252, 253–56, 279, 282–84, 290–91, 292n39
persona, 22, 36n7, 54n25, 83, 90, 93–95, 99, 152, 174–75, 182, 208, 214, 228
Peters, Deniz, 95n18, 111, 112n38, 114, 128, 250–51, 287, 310
Peterson, Richard A., 192, 194, 282, 311
Pettersson, Rafael, 277, 283
Phan, Hai Yen Thi, 266, 311
Phelan, Peggy, 38, 88, 101, 136, 154–55, 157, 256, 283, 311
Picasso, Pablo, 240, 288
Pienaar, Daniel-Ben, 47–48, 78n34, 311
Pink, Sarah, 254–55, 311
Polanyi, Michael, 37, 311
politics, 13n1, 16, 18, 89, 92, 100, 155, 208n36, 221, 245, 253–55, 257, 259, 278, 284–85, 290, 291, 294
Ponce, Manuel, 178
pop music, 15, 91, 92n11, 94n15, 99n23, 100, 173, 183, 193–94, 204, 220, 228
pragmatism, 13n2, 14n5, 24n16, 87n5, 207, 225–26, 231n52,
presence, 22, 88, 94, 97, 104, 111, 134, 136–37, 148, 154, 156–57, 162, 164–66, 175, 193, 207, 238, 248, 257, 259, 285, 291, 297
Presley, Elvis, 199n32
Preston, Katherine, 172

Q

qualitative analysis, 37, 212–13, 216, 217–19, 251

R

Rabinowitch, Tal-Chen, 251, 302
radio, 165, 173–75, 178, 182, 185, 194, 205–6, 208–10, 217–18, 222–24, 227, 231n54
Rahaim, Matthew, 247–48, 311
Ramirez Ladrón de Guevara, Victor, 104n27, 115, 134, 311
Ramirez, Manuel, 222n41
Ramirez III, José, 222–23, 228, 311
Randall, William, 53
Ratcliffe, Jarrod, 225n43, 300
realism, 183, 186
recording, 13, 20–22, 36, 42n13, 47, 56, 62, 67, 91n10, 92n11, 112, 115–16, 121–23, 127, 146, 148, 150–53, 160, 162, 171n1, 173–80, 182–86, 188–90, 192–200, 202, 204–12, 213n38, 218–27, 229–31, 241–42, 247, 259, 262, 265, 267, 272, 280–81, 286, 290, 295
Redhead, Lauren, 18n12, 311
Redman, Matt, 199n32
resistance, 18, 25, 37, 38, 41–42, 44, 49, 51, 77, 101, 108n30, 109n35, 129, 132, 134, 136, 138, 143, 153–54, 178n16, 196, 220, 222, 243, 246, 248, 250, 252, 263–65, 271–72, 274, 289, 292, 293
resonance, 34, 41, 50, 51, 58, 66, 69–71, 73, 76, 86, 92, 96, 111, 114, 123, 152, 162, 220, 230n47, 243, 270, 273, 293
Ricœur, Paul, 45, 93, 311
Rimini Protokoll, 255–56, 290
Rink, John, 17, 93, 311
Ripley, Robert, 195
Ritzén, Linda, 277, 283
Robinson, Enders A., 231n55, 311
Rodgers, Jimmy, 193
Rosch, Eleanor, 40, 311, 313
Rose, Jeremy, 212, 300
Rosen, Charles, 108n31, 110, 311
Russo, Frank A., 39, 313

S

Sachsenmaier, Stefanie, 155
Sammler, Daniela, 127, 311
Samson, Kristine, 254, 305
Sandweiss, Martha A., 189, 311
Sato, Tetsumi, 266, 311
Saunders, Doug, 275, 311
Sawyer, Keith R., 18, 91n9, 311
Schaeffer, Pierre, 249, 293

Schafer, R. Murray, 266, 311
Schechner, Richard, 101, 311
Scheidemann, Heinrich, 53
Schnabel, Artur, 48, 150
Schneider, Arnd, 254, 311–12
Schneider, Rebecca, 155, 157, 282, 312
Schoenberger, Laura, 259, 261, 313
Schopenhauer, Arthur, 98
Schubert, Franz, 150, 165
scores, 21, 22, 31–32, 33n5, 34, 35, 36n7, 37, 38, 40, 44–48, 50, 54, 55, 56, 62, 64, 75–76, 78–79, 93, 96, 97, 104, 115–16, 122–23, 126–28, 128–29n48, 132, 145, 146–51, 153, 155, 159, 160, 163, 171–81, 187–89, 190, 192, 193, 196–98, 202, 204, 212, 220–23, 227–30, 237, 239, 241–45, 257, 262–65, 267, 268, 271–76, 280, 286, 295
Scott, Ridley, 189n25
Seattle Symphony, 247
Seeger, Charles, 50
Segovia, Andrés, 177, 178, 209, 222–23, 228, 231n53
Sennett, Richard, 192, 312
Sergeant, Matthew, 143, 312
Sessions, Roger, 45, 248, 312
Sewell, Stacey, 144
Shakespeare, William, 246
Shaw-Miller, Simon, 51, 305
Sheppard, Andy, 91
Sheppard-Skærved, Peter, 31n2, 53n24, 308
Shusterman, Richard, 14n5, 24nn, 312
Siddall, Gillian, 19, 312
Siegmund, Gerald, 231n54, 256, 291, 312
Simoens, Veerle L., 108, 312
situated knowledge, 106
Six Tones, The, 22, 36n6, 182n24, 212, 235, 237, 240–41, 243–47, 249, 251, 252n15, 254, 261, 263, 273–74, 279–80, 282, 289, 292
Sloboda, John A., 90, 308
Small, Christopher, 93–94, 312
Smith, Jan, 91, 309
Smith, Linda Tuhiwai, 253, 312
Smith, Michael Cedric, 172, 173, 188
Solomon, Thomas, 253, 312
Sonami, Laetitia, 108
space, 20, 22, 34, 51, 56, 59, 62, 64, 76, 83, 87–89, 95, 102, 106, 117, 121, 123–24, 130, 134, 135, 138, 146, 153, 154, 156, 157, 160, 185, 187, 191, 204–7, 211, 219, 224, 231, 246, 249, 252–54, 256, 259, 263, 267, 272, 273, 275, 279, 284–86, 290, 297
Spatz, Ben, 155, 312
Stapleton, Paul, 151, 312
Steen-Andersen, Simon, 104, 312
Sterne, Jonathan, 184, 206, 312
Stevenson, Robert Louis, 189n25
stimulated recall, 62, 67, 212–13, 251n13, 257
Stockhausen, Karlheinz, 207, 222
Stolp, Mareli, 17, 83–84n2, 95n17, 296, 312
storytelling, 23, 175, 238, 274, 275, 278–79, 281–83, 290
Stover, Chris, 40, 92, 100, 138, 312
Straus, Erwin, 78, 313
Stravinsky, Igor, 37
street vendors, 235, 237–38, 244–45, 259–62, 265–67, 275, 278–79, 282, 284–86, 289–91, 293–94
Sudnow, David, 110n37, 118n42, 313
Sumartojo, Shanti, 254–55, 311
Swain, Rachel, 254, 313
Sweelinck, Jan Pieterszoon, 53
Székely, Zoltán, 97
Szendy, Peter, 14n6, 313

T

Tanaka, Atau, 108, 303, 313
Tárrega, Francisco, 174, 209, 223
Taruskin, Richard, 46, 93, 192n27, 313
Taylor, Alan, 18n12, 313
Taylor, Diana, 101, 155n73, 313
Taylor, Yuval, 193–95
Teatr Weimar, 242, 277n34, 280
Tervaniemi, Mari, 108, 312
Tesch-Römer, Clemens, 42n14, 303
testimony, 87, 274n11, 296
thing power, 14n4, 22, 143, 175n8
Thomas, Philip, 77, 301
Thompson, Evan, 40, 313
Thompson, John B., 13n1, 313
Thompson, Paul, 229nn, 230n50, 231n52, 307
Thompson, William Forde, 39, 40, 308, 313
Tilbury, John, 110, 313
Tomasello, Michael, 250, 313
Tomes, Susan, 91n10, 97, 110, 118n42, 150n67, 313
Torelli, Giuseppe, 53, 54
Torick, Emil, 206, 313
Torrence, Jennifer, 107n29, 313
touch, 48, 96, 110–12, 114, 128, 155, 229, 230n51, 250
tradition, 155, 178n16, 182n24, 194, 199n32, 225, 235, 237, 240, 241, 244–46, 249, 252n15, 258, 263, 265, 267, 268n25, 270, 271, 292
Trevarthen, Colwyn, 250, 313
trust, 31, 246, 254, 260, 278, 287, 290
truth, 13, 23, 37, 86, 98, 171, 202, 253, 255, 278, 281
Tsakiris, Manos, 107, 109, 111, 302
Tudor, David, 110, 128–29n48
Tukey, John, 231
Tuồng theatre, 178n16, 237, 246–47, 258, 275, 280, 282, 289, 291–92
Turner, Edith, 253, 313
Turner, Sarah, 237, 238, 259, 261, 303, 313
Turner, Victor, 253, 313

U

Utti, Frances-Marie, 91, 313

V

Vandemoortele, Milo, 237–38, 313
Van Gogh, Vincent, 194
Vanhaesebrouck, Karel, 255–56, 281, 313
van Maas, Sander, 14n6, 313
Varela, Francisco J., 40, 313
verisimilitude, 184, 205
Vietnamese music, 182n24, 235–36, 240, 244–46, 252n15, 262–65, 268n25, 270n29, 271, 292
virtuosity, 41, 86, 98, 129, 131–32, 139, 142, 174, 193, 196–97, 244, 286
Voegelin, Salomé, 248, 313
voice, 14, 20–23, 36–39, 42n13, 43–44, 47, 49–51, 53–56, 76–79, 85–86, 89–92, 93n13, 94–97, 99, 113, 114, 136, 146, 148, 152, 158, 159, 163–64, 166n78, 171, 177–78, 188, 209, 214–16, 219, 221, 228–29,

230n47, 240n5, 247–48, 250, 252–53, 258, 264, 265, 268, 270, 272–74, 283–84, 287–91, 293, 296–97
Vuoskoski, Jonna, 250, 301
Vygotsky, Lev, 18n11, 38n11, 239, 313

W

Wagner, Richard, 193
Waisvisz, Michel, 108
Wallraff, Günter, 259n18
Walshe, Jennifer, 103, 105, 314
Wanderley, Marcelo, 67, 98n21
Waterman, Ellen, 19, 312
Watson, Cate, 251–52, 314
Watson, Doc, 197
Weber, Max, 193
Weeks, Jeffery, 24, 314
Wells, Jeremy J., 21, 22, 171–232
Werktreue, 44, 98, 192–93
Whitty, Paul, 85, 115, 121, 123–24, 146–48, 150, 154, 314
Wieringa, Sietse, 37n8
Williamon, Aaron, 93, 311
Williams, Kathryn, 107n29, 314
Windsor, W. Luke, 18n12, 42, 306, 314
Wishart, Trevor, 45, 46, 314
Wittgenstein, Ludwig, 87n5
Wong, Mandy-Suzanne, 127, 314
Woody, Robert H., 90, 308
Wöllner, Clemens, 92, 314
Wright, Christopher, 254, 312
Wuttke, Martin, 156

X

Xenakis, Iannis, 174

Y

Yano, Takashi, 266, 311
Young, La Monte, 140

Z

Zahavi, Dan, 23, 314
Zappa, Frank, 174
Zarrilli, Phillip, 104n27, 314
Zemp, Hugo, 254, 314

Authors
William Brooks
David Gorton
Catherine Laws
Nguyễn Thanh Thủy
Stefan Östersjö
Jeremy J. Wells

Production manager
Heike Vermeire

Managing editor
Edward Crooks

Series editor
William Brooks

Lay-out
Studio Luc Derycke

Cover design
Lucia D'Errico

Cover image
© bpk-Bildagentur / Staatsgalerie Stuttgart / Heilige Cäcilie—*Das unsichtbare Klavier (Sainte Cécile—Le piano invisible),* Max Ernst, 1923.

Typesetting
Friedemann bvba

Press
Wilco BV, The Netherlands

Minderbroedersstraat 4
B-3000 Leuven (Belgium)

ISBN 978 94 6270 205 9
eISBN 978 94 6166 306 1

D/2019/1869/42
NUR: 663
https://doi.org/10.11116/9789461663061

This book is published in the Orpheus Institute Series